In its aim to stimulate policy dialogue and help p
lenges that hinder Caribbean economies from ful
and development, this book is a timely success.
research on the challenges of weak macroeconomic
structural impediments, it provides insights and p
coherent answers to these pressing policy concei
point the way toward opportunities for welfare gains from determined but balanced
policy actions targeted at the region's high energy costs, financial exclusion, high
crime rates, and the persistent loss of skilled workers to richer countries.
Consideration of the vulnerabilities and opportunities that arise from financial
interconnectedness across the Caribbean also informs the book's reminder to policymakers of the benefits that remain to be exploited by greater regional cooperation
in a number of areas. With its relevance and range of evidence-based policy recommendations, this volume earns its place on the bookshelves of practitioners and other
students of Caribbean economic development.

—**Brian Wynter**
**Governor, Bank of Jamaica**

This book provides a comprehensive assessment of three major Caribbean contemporary economic challenges—slow growth, macroeconomic imbalances, and structural impediments. The chapters are skillfully written by Fund economists, who are
versed in the various aspects of Caribbean economic issues, to relate the challenges
to the vicious cycle. Policy recommendation is an important aspect of the book and
addressed at both the individual country and regional levels. This book is a must-
read for public policymakers and anyone interested in contemporary Caribbean and
small states economic and financial issues.

—**Dr. Gobind Ganga**
**Governor, Bank of Guyana**

Economic growth in the Caribbean over the last two decades has been slow, both
relative to growth in the region over the previous 20 years and in comparison to other
small, non-Caribbean countries. *Unleashing Growth and Strengthening Resilience in the
Caribbean* provides a thorough analysis of the region's subpar economic performance
and lays out a practical approach for improvement. The authors highlight key policy
changes that merit serious consideration: building greater resilience to increasingly
frequent hurricanes; reducing the cost of energy; greater investment in infrastructure; more regional cooperation and integration; microeconomic reforms to reduce
the cost of doing business; and countercyclical fiscal policy. But the path to faster
sustainable and inclusive growth is different for each of the 13 countries examined
in this book, and it's refreshing to see the IMF embark upon a more collaborative,
tailored approach to its recommendations for developing countries. This country-specific approach is part of a broader—and greatly welcomed—philosophical
change at the Fund, which recognizes that the best kind of economic discipline does
not push extreme measures such as fiscal austerity in a one-size-fits-all manner, but
rather commits to a pragmatic, longer-term growth strategy that is both vigilant and
flexible. This important publication is a must-read for anyone who cares about the

creation of policies that encourage greater economic prosperity for all segments of Caribbean society, and anyone interested in the development of deeper understanding between these island nations and the global economic institutions that exist to help them achieve stability.

—**Peter Blair Henry**
**Dean, NYU Stern School of Business, and author of**
***Turnaround: Third World Lessons for First World Growth***

This book takes a refreshing new look at contemporary problems of Caribbean economies and makes a substantive contribution to the existing dialogue on both analysis and policymaking related to the region. It merits serious attention and careful study by policymakers, researchers, and the general public.

The analysis is focused on identifying sources of the region's long-term weakness in economic performance relative to other "small" states and regions in the world economy. It adopts a multi-faceted approach that integrates a range of social, institutional, and environmental factors (brain drain, violent crime, natural disasters) with issues of chronic debt accumulation, provision of public infrastructure and social services, tax incentives, supply of and access to finance, energy costs, and the trade regime, correctly placing emphasis on the interaction and feedback effects among them. It skirts around some important issues, such as competitive structure and operation of business enterprise, and the problem of governance at the national level, but it recognizes weaknesses in regional cooperation among states on economic matters. Problems in the tourism and financial sectors are given special attention.

What emerges from this diagnosis is a complex picture of factors that have operated to retard the region's progress in catching up with living standards in other relevant nations that have moved ahead. As to what needs to be done about this, there is no simple linear formula here, or magic bullet, that leads from macroeconomic stabilization to sustained improvements in economic efficiency, broad-based growth of income, and social inclusion. By implication, "unleashing growth" requires a multi-pronged, systematic, and sustained effort focused on addressing a wide range of factors arising at both macro and micro levels of the economy. Broad policy recommendations are offered, while choice of policy priorities and details of a specific strategy or plan are implicitly left to be determined by action on the ground.

As the product of a group of technical experts in the IMF, this book represents a significant advance in reporting on the Caribbean region by the IMF. It provides clues into observed weakness in the expected "pass-through effect" from IMF structural adjustment programs pursued in the past; and it offers useful insights for guiding development of the policy framework adopted by the IMF for management of economic programs operated under its purview in this region.

—**Donald J. Harris**
**Professor Emeritus of Economics, Stanford University**

# Unleashing Growth and Strengthening Resilience in the Caribbean

**TREVOR ALLEYNE**
**İNCI ÖTKER**
**UMA RAMAKRISHNAN**
**KRISHNA SRINIVASAN**

INTERNATIONAL MONETARY FUND

**Cataloging-in-Publication Data**
**Joint Bank-Fund Library**

Names: Alleyne, Trevor Serge Coleridge, editor. | Ötker, İnci, editor. |
    Ramakrishnan, Uma, editor. | Srinivasan, Krishna, editor | International
    Monetary Fund, publisher.
Title: Unleashing growth and strengthening resilience in the Caribbean / edited
    by Trevor Alleyne, İnci Ötker, Uma Ramakrishnan, and Krishna Srinivasan.
Description: [Washington, DC] : International Monetary Fund, 2017.
Identifiers: ISBN 9781484315194 (paper)
Subjects: LCSH: Economic development—Caribbean Area. | Caribbean Area—
    Commerce. | Economic indicators—Caribbean Area.
Classification: LCC HC151.U543 2017

ISBN 978-1-48431-519-4 (paper)
    978-1-48431-891-1 (ePub)
    978-1-48431-924-6 (mobipocket)
    978-1-48431-925-3 (PDF)

Please send orders to:

International Monetary Fund, Publication Services
P.O. Box 92780, Washington, DC 20090, U.S.A.
Tel.: (202) 623-7430  Fax: (202) 623-7201
E-mail: publications@imf.org
Internet: www.imfbookstore.org

# Contents

# Foreword

The Caribbean countries—endowed with some of the greatest beauty on this planet—sustained several decades of strong growth following their independence in the 1960s and 1970s. Their success was underpinned by the development of strong democratic traditions, sound institutions, and an active debate of public policies reflecting the aspirations of the Caribbean people. More recently, however, many of the countries in the region have fallen into a trap of low growth and high debt. In addition to the costs posed by frequent natural disasters, which have contributed to low growth, the region has also endured deep macroeconomic, financial, and structural challenges. A large public debt overhang, combined with high energy costs, violent crime, constrained access to credit, a high cost of doing business, and brain drain—to name just a few—have undermined regional growth prospects.

The IMF's focus on small states, in general, and the Caribbean, in particular, has been growing over the years, notably through dialogue and collaboration with key stakeholders. I personally have had the pleasure of engaging through the years with policymakers from the Caribbean during the Annual Meetings of the IMF and the World Bank. In addition, the IMF, with strong support from the donor community, has made significant strides in enhancing technical assistance to build capacity in the region. In some countries, our engagement through IMF-supported programs could even be considered game-changing.

It is my distinct pleasure to be part of this effort to disseminate the analytical work on the Caribbean that has been conducted largely in the IMF's Western Hemisphere Department. This book is timely and important in many respects. With a primary focus on how to raise the region's growth potential while balancing it with stability, it provides rich analyses of key macroeconomic, financial, and structural impediments to growth, and recommends feasible solutions for the Caribbean. The chapters draw on the vast academic literature, and synthesize a substantial amount of analytical work on highly topical issues for the region. The book also broadens the reach of our policy advice to a wider audience across the region and globe.

This book serves as a fresh platform to further our close engagement and policy dialogue with the region. I hope that it will spark a healthy debate on the economic challenges of the region and further research on the path to unleashing sustained higher growth and job creation.

Christine Lagarde
*Managing Director*
*International Monetary Fund*

# Contributors

**Sebastian Acevedo** is an economist in the IMF's Western Hemisphere Department and works on the Ecuador desk. At the IMF, he worked for six years on the Caribbean, covering topics related to natural disasters, economic growth, productivity, tourism, debt, and exchange rate regimes. He holds a B.A. in economics from Universidad EAFIT in Colombia, an M.A. in international trade and economic cooperation from Kyung Hee University in the Republic of Korea, an M.A. in economics from Georgetown University, and a Ph.D. in economics from the George Washington University.

**Trevor Alleyne** took on his current position as an assistant director/division chief of the Caribbean I Division at the IMF's Western Hemisphere Department in September 2013. He is responsible for the economies of the Organisation of Eastern Caribbean States. His previous Caribbean experience at the IMF was as division chief of the Caribbean II Division during 2008–12, serving also as mission chief for Jamaica, Barbados, The Bahamas, and Suriname. Mr. Alleyne has been at the IMF since 1992, with assignments mainly in the African and Western Hemisphere Departments. Most recently, he served as mission chief for Nigeria and Zambia (2012–13). Prior to joining the IMF, he was a principal analyst at the US Congressional Budget Office from 1986 to 1992. He is a professional economist with over 25 years of experience and was educated at the University of the West Indies (B.Sc.), University of Pennsylvania (M.A.), and University of Maryland (Ph.D.).

**Kimberly Beaton** is an economist in the IMF's Western Hemisphere Department, currently covering Panama. Previously, she was a senior advisor to the Executive Director for Canada, Ireland, and the Caribbean. Prior to joining the IMF, she was an economist at the Bank of Canada. She is a graduate of Queen's University in Canada.

**Jacques Bouhga-Hagbe** is currently a senior economist at the IMF and has worked on many countries since joining the IMF in 2002. He holds a Ph.D. in economics from Cornell University, New York, and an engineering degree from the Ecole Centrale de Paris.

**Elie Canetti** has worked for 25 years at the IMF, where he is an advisor in the Western Hemisphere Department. He has also worked on Asia and on financial stability issues. His Caribbean experience includes heading the Financial Sector Assessment Program for The Bahamas and serving as mission chief for Trinidad and Tobago and St. Vincent and the Grenadines. He was adjunct finance professor at Johns Hopkins School of Advanced International Studies and worked at PIMCO with Mohamed el Erian. He holds degrees from the University of California, Berkeley; London School of Economics; and Princeton University.

**Marcos Chamon**, a national of Brazil, is deputy division chief in the Caribbean III Division of the IMF's Western Hemisphere Department and mission chief for Guyana. He holds a Ph.D. in economics from Harvard University. He has published on a wide range of topics, including sovereign debt restructuring, currency mismatches, economic growth, consumption and savings, early-warning models for balance of payments crises, the design of capital controls and macroprudential policies, monetary policy, and foreign exchange intervention in emerging markets.

**Joshua Charap**, a national of the United States, is IMF resident representative in Suriname. He holds a B.S. in physics and an M.S. in economics from the Massachusetts Institute of Technology and a Ph.D. in economics from the University of Pennsylvania. For most of his career, Mr. Charap has worked on countries supported by IMF programs, including as resident representative in Afghanistan, Cambodia, and Yugoslavia. Prior to joining the IMF, he was an economist in the Chief Economist's Office at the European Bank for Reconstruction and Development.

**Qiaoe Chen**, a national of China, is an economist in the Caribbean II Division of the IMF's Western Hemisphere Department. She holds an M.S. in economics from the Tsinghua University of China. Prior to joining the IMF, she worked for many years in the Central Bank of China, covering international financial cooperation and banking supervision issues. Her research focuses on economic growth, financial supervision, and monetary policy.

**Joel Chiedu Okwuokei** is an economist in the Caribbean II Division of the IMF's Western Hemisphere Department. He holds a Ph.D. in economics from the University of Benin, Nigeria, which he attended as an African Economic Research Consortium scholar. Before joining the IMF, he worked with the federal government of Nigeria for several years. His research interests include economic growth, fiscal policy, monetary policy, and financial sector reform.

**Fabio Di Vittorio**, a national of Italy, is an economist in the IMF's Western Hemisphere Department, where he has worked extensively on Eastern Caribbean Currency Union economies. He holds a Ph.D. in economics from New York University. His research covers financial economics, banking, financial regulation, and macroeconomics.

**Thomas Dowling** is an economist in the IMF's Western Hemisphere Department and works on the Barbados and Trinidad and Tobago desks. He has worked at the IMF for eight years on the United States, Canada, and the Nordic countries prior to joining the Caribbean Division. His research interests include international trade, financial intermediation, fintech, and nowcasting.

**Judith Gold**, a national of Canada, has served as advisor to the Canadian Executive Director to the IMF, representative to the Paris Club, and mission chief to Guyana, Panama, Trinidad and Tobago, St. Kitts and Nevis, and, presently, Barbados. She holds an M.A. in economics from the University of York in Toronto. She has contributed to and published several economic articles and, more recently, co-authored an IMF Working Paper titled "Too Much of a Good Thing? Prudent Management of Inflows under Economic Citizenship Programs."

**Laura Jaitman** is an economist at the Research Department of the Inter-American Development Bank (IDB). She joined the IDB in 2014, where she previously coordinated the research agenda for the Citizen Security and Justice sector. Her principal areas of research are the economics of crime, development economics, and political economy. Before joining the IDB, she worked for a decade as a consultant to the World Bank, the IDB, and J-PAL in the evaluation of public policies in various Latin American countries. Ms. Jaitman holds a Ph.D. in economics from University College London. Her work was published in international peer-reviewed journals, such as *The Economic Journal* and *Journal of Economic Behavior and Organization*, among others.

**Jeetendra Khadan** is an economist consultant at the Inter-American Development Bank (IDB). He currently holds the position of country economist for Suriname and researcher in the Caribbean Economics Team. He has written and published books as well as academic papers in peer-reviewed journals and the IDB's working paper series on issues ranging from international trade, regional integration, private sector development, macroeconomics, and applied economics, to other contemporary policy issues. Mr. Khadan holds a Ph.D. in economics from the University of the West Indies.

**Dmitriy Kovtun**, a national of Kazakhstan, is a senior economist in the IMF's Western Hemisphere Department. He also worked in the African, Strategy and Policy Review, and European Departments of the IMF. He holds a Ph.D. in economics from the University of Kentucky (Lexington). His research has focused on macro-financial linkages, nonperforming loans, and monetary sector issues.

**Nicole LaFramboise** attended the University of Western Ontario in Canada and the London School of Economics, receiving an M.A. in economics in 1987. She worked in the research department at the Bank of Montreal, the United Nations Development Programme in Mali, and then at the federal Department of Finance in Canada. She was seconded to the Office of the Executive Director for Canada at the IMF and joined the staff of the IMF in late 1996. Nicole has held various positions at the IMF, including in the areas of policy development and review, as a desk economist on country teams in North Africa and Central Asia, and as a speechwriter for the Managing Director in the Communications Department. As deputy division chief in the Western Hemisphere Department, she has served as mission chief for Barbados, Grenada, and now Bolivia. Recent projects include research on the macroeconomic impact of natural disasters, the determinants of tourism flows to the Caribbean, income and price elasticities of tourism arrivals, and a tourism sector price index.

**Daniel Leigh**, a national of the Czech Republic and the United Kingdom, is deputy division chief in the Caribbean III Division of the IMF's Western Hemisphere Department. He holds an M.Sc. in economics from the London School of Economics and a Ph.D. in economics from Johns Hopkins University. Prior to joining the Western Hemisphere Department, Mr. Leigh worked for several years in the IMF's Research Department on the *World Economic Outlook*. His research focuses on economic growth and monetary and fiscal policy.

**Franz Loyola** is currently a consultant for the World Bank Group's Independent Evaluation Group. Previously, he was a research analyst in the IMF's Caribbean III Division of the IMF's Western Hemisphere Department. He is a

Ph.D. candidate in economics at George Mason University and holds an M.A. in economics from the University of the Philippines.

**Meredith Arnold McIntyre**, a Grenadian national, is a deputy division chief in the IMF's Western Hemisphere Department. Prior to his current assignment, he was coordinator of the IMF Caribbean Regional Technical Assistance Center. Mr. McIntyre holds a B.Sc. (Econ) honors degree from the University of the West Indies (Cave Hill campus, Barbados), an M.A. in economics from Yale University, and a Ph.D. in economics from the University of Toronto. Prior to joining the Western Hemisphere Department, Mr. McIntyre worked for several years in the African Department, including serving as the IMF's resident representative in Ghana for three years.

**Alla Myrvoda** is an economist in the Caribbean I Division of the IMF's Western Hemisphere Department (WHD), where she covers the Eastern Caribbean Currency Union economies. Before joining WHD in 2014, her previous assignment was in the Asia Pacific Department, working on Lao People's Democratic Republic, China, Hong Kong Special Administrative Region, and Macao Special Administrative Region.

**İnci Ötker**, a Turkish national, is the IMF's mission chief for St. Kitts and Nevis and division chief of Caribbean III of the Western Hemisphere Department (WHD), which covers Aruba, Curaçao, Sint Maarten, Guyana, Suriname, and Trinidad and Tobago. She holds a Ph.D. in economics from Carnegie Mellon University, Pittsburgh, and a B.A./M.S. from the Middle East Technical University, Turkey. Before joining WHD, she was an advisor in the Monetary and Capital Markets Department, and senior advisor/deputy director at the World Bank. Her research covers financial stability, systemically important financial institutions, capital controls, exchange regimes, inflation targeting, financial crises, and global risks, including climate change, natural disasters, and pandemics. She has co-edited books on credit growth and financial sector resilience and has worked at the Central Bank of Turkey.

**Uma Ramakrishnan** is an assistant director in the IMF and Division Chief of the Caribbean II Division in the Western Hemisphere Department. She has been mission chief for Jamaica since May 2015. She previously held the position of mission chief for El Salvador and has worked on several countries in Asia and Europe. She has also worked extensively on IMF lending policies. She holds a Ph.D. in economics from Georgetown University.

**Udi Rosenhand** is a research analyst in the IMF's Western Hemisphere Department. A graduate of Tulane University, Mr. Rosenhand's interests include game theory and monetary policy.

**Krishna Srinivasan** has been with the IMF since 1994 and has served in several departments across the institution. In his current capacity as a deputy director in the IMF's Western Hemisphere Department (WHD), he oversees the institution's work on several countries as well as WHD's research activities and flagship publication *Regional Economic Outlook: Western Hemisphere*. He previously served in the European Department as the IMF's mission chief for the United Kingdom and Israel and, before that, in the Research Department, where he led the IMF's work on the Group of Twenty. He obtained his Ph.D. in international finance from Indiana University and an M.A. from the Delhi School of Economics and has published several papers at the IMF and in leading academic journals. He is co-editor of *Challenges for Central Banking: Perspectives from Latin America* and the lead editor of *Global Rebalancing: A Roadmap for Economic Recovery*, published by the IMF.

**Lulu Shui** is a research assistant in the IMF Western Hemisphere Department. She holds a M.A. of International Economics from Johns Hopkins School of Advanced International Studies. Before joining the Fund, Ms. Shui worked for several years at the World Bank on international trade issues.

**Heather Sutton** is a research consultant for the Inter-American Development Bank (IDB) on issues of citizen security. Her work has involved designing, implementing, and analyzing surveys of victimization and violence against women. She has published a book and academic papers in peer-reviewed journals and the IDB's working paper series, focusing on issues of crime and violence, with special attention to prevention. Prior to joining the IDB, she worked for over a decade as a consultant for the International Center for the Prevention of Crime, the United Nations Office of Disarmament Affairs, and Brazil's Instituto Sou da Paz.

**Kalin Tintchev**, a national of Bulgaria, is an economist in the Caribbean III Division of the IMF's Western Hemisphere Department (WHD). Prior to joining WHD, he worked for more than 10 years in the IMF's Monetary and Capital Markets Department, where he participated in Financial Sector Assessment Programs and technical assistance missions on stress testing. He holds a Ph.D. in economics from the George Washington University and an M.B.A. with a concentration in finance from Vanderbilt University. His research focuses on financial stability, contagion, and macro-financial linkages.

**Jarkko Turunen** is deputy division chief in the IMF's Asia and Pacific Department. Previously, Mr. Turunen worked in the IMF's Western Hemisphere Department as mission chief to The Bahamas. Before joining the IMF, he was principal economist at the European Central Bank and visiting scholar at the Economics Department of the Massachusetts Institute of Technology. He holds a Ph.D. in economics from the European University Institute. His main research interests are in macroeconomics, monetary policy, and labor economics, with publications in the *Journal of the European Economic Association, Journal of Economic Perspectives, IMF Economic Review, Journal of Economic Dynamics and Control, Empirical Economics,* and *Economics Letters.*

**Bert van Selm** is a deputy division chief in the Caribbean II Division of the IMF's Western Hemisphere Department. He was the IMF's resident representative in Jamaica from 2013 to 2016. He holds a Ph.D. in economics from the University of Groningen in the Netherlands. He has published several articles on international economic issues and one book, *The Economics of Soviet Break-Up* (Routledge, 1997).

**Alejandro Werner**, a Mexican citizen, has had distinguished careers in the public and private sectors as well as in academia. Most recently, he served as undersecretary of finance and public credit of Mexico (December 2006 to August 2010), professor of economics at the Instituto de Empresa in Madrid (August

2010 to July 2011), and head of corporate and investment banking at BBVA-Bancomer (August 2011 to December 2012). Previously, he held the position of director of economic studies at the Bank of Mexico and professor at Instituto Tecnológico Autónomo de México. He has published widely and was named Young Global Leader by the World Economic Forum in 2007. Mr. Werner received his Ph.D. from the Massachusetts Institute of Technology in 1994.

**Joyce Wong**, a national of Portugal, is an economist in the IMF's Western Hemisphere Department. She holds a Ph.D. in economics from New York University. Her research has focused on drivers of female labor participation, financial inclusion and development, and immigration.

# CHAPTER 1

# Unleashing Strong, Sustainable, and Inclusive Growth in the Caribbean

DANIEL LEIGH, KRISHNA SRINIVASAN, AND ALEJANDRO WERNER

Since attaining independence in the 1960s and 1970s, Caribbean countries have registered strong economic and social outcomes. Per capita incomes have risen, with most Caribbean countries now in the top 25 percent of all emerging market and developing economies (EMDEs).[1] Median life expectancy is 73 years, compared with 70 years for other EMDEs; infant mortality is relatively low; and female labor force participation relatively high (Figure 1.1). Poverty rates are comparable to other EMDEs. Beyond these achievements, Caribbean countries have developed strong democratic traditions, with public policies actively debated and influenced by the aspirations of their people.

In recent decades, however, progress on converging with the living standards of advanced economies has slowed and, in some cases, reversed. Since 2000, real GDP growth of Caribbean economies has been half that of other EMDEs and two-thirds that of non-Caribbean small states (Figure 1.2). The growth weakness is concentrated among tourism-intensive Caribbean economies, which, on average, grew by only 1.6 percent per year, and only 0.8 percent in per capita terms. The per capita incomes of these countries, converted at purchasing-power-parity exchange rates, have stopped converging toward those of advanced economies. Commodity exporters in the Caribbean have grown faster, reflecting the international commodity price boom. More recently, growth across these countries has also slowed or turned negative.

---

The authors thank Lulu Shui for excellent research assistance.

[1] This book focuses on 13 Caribbean economies, divided into two analytical groups: nine tourism-intensive economies (Antigua and Barbuda, The Bahamas, Barbados, Dominica, Grenada, Jamaica, St. Kitts and Nevis, St. Lucia, St. Vincent and the Grenadines) and four commodity exporters (Belize, Guyana, Suriname, Trinidad and Tobago). Income per capita for Caribbean countries is typically lower when measured using gross national product (GNP) rather than GDP, as GNP does not include income earned by foreigners, including, for example, profits of foreign-owned hotels in the region's large tourism sector. Even when measured using GNP, however, income per capita of Caribbean countries is well above that of other EMDEs.

**Figure 1.1. Demographic, Economic, and Social Indicators**

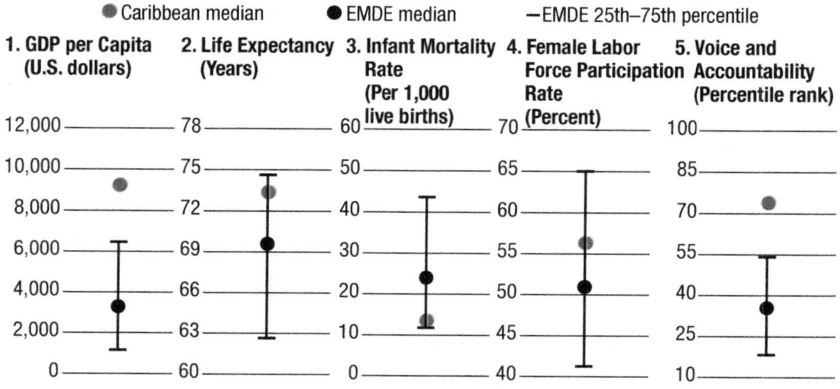

Caribbean median
EMDE median
EMDE 25th–75th percentile
1. GDP per Capita (U.S. dollars)
12,000
10,000
8,000
6,000
4,000
2,000
0
2. Life Expectancy (Years)
78
75
72
69
66
63
60
3. Infant Mortality Rate (Per 1,000 live births)
60
50
40
30
20
10
0
4. Female Labor Force Participation Rate (Percent)
70
65
60
55
50
45
40
5. Voice and Accountability (Percentile rank)
100
85
70
55
40
25
10


Sources: World Bank, *Governance Indicators*; World Bank, *World Development Indicators*; and IMF staff estimates.
Note: EMDE = emerging market and developing economy. Figure reports data for 2015 or most recent year available. The World Bank's "Voice and Accountability" indicator captures perceptions of the extent to which a country's citizens are able to participate in selecting their government, as well as the freedom of expression, association, and media.

No single reason can explain the Caribbean growth slowdown. Drivers include both large adverse external developments and, more important, persistent domestic macroeconomic imbalances and structural impediments. Adverse external shocks include the erosion of preferential trade access to European markets, the decline of official development assistance, and increasingly frequent natural disasters. Caribbean economies have not been able to fully insulate themselves from such shocks because of their large macroeconomic imbalances, notably pertaining to their fiscal position and strains in the financial sector, along with serious structural weaknesses. Elevated government debt burdens have constrained the ability of these economies to pursue a countercyclical fiscal policy response to shocks and to finance priority spending, including on infrastructure, while problems in the financial sector have disrupted credit supply and impeded private sector activity. Meanwhile, structural factors, including the region's high costs of electricity and constrained access to credit for households and small and medium-sized enterprises (SMEs), high rates of violent crime, and a persistent outflow of highly skilled workers to richer countries, have undermined growth prospects. Feedback loops between weak macroeconomic fundamentals and structural impediments have hurt growth and sustainability prospects, preventing these economies from benefiting fully from globalization and technological progress (Figure 1.3).

How can Caribbean economies overcome these challenges and resume their convergence toward the living standards of advanced economies? To shed light on these questions, this book brings together the latest research on the Caribbean economies conducted at the IMF, including on new developments such as

## Figure 1.2. Real GDP Performance

### Caribbean versus Other Regions

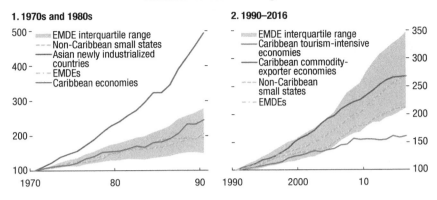

**1. 1970s and 1980s**

EMDE interquartile range
Non-Caribbean small states
Asian newly industrialized countries
EMDEs
Caribbean economies

**2. 1990–2016**

EMDE interquartile range
Caribbean tourism-intensive economies
Caribbean commodity-exporter economies
Non-Caribbean small states
EMDEs

### Tourism-Intensive Caribbean Economies

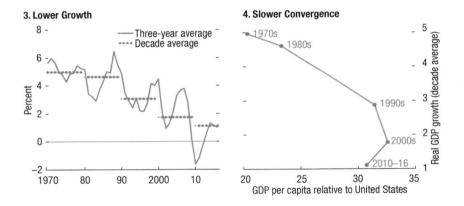

**3. Lower Growth**

Three-year average
Decade average

**4. Slower Convergence**

GDP per capita relative to United States

Sources: World Bank, *World Development Indicators*; and IMF staff estimates.
Note: EMDEs = emerging market and developing economies. Figure reports country-group medians.

potential U.S.-Cuba rapprochement and the interconnected financial sector, where banks are grappling with the consequences of the global financial crisis and the withdrawal of correspondent banking relationships. Following a discussion of growth performance in the Caribbean, various chapters in the book analyze the region's macroeconomic imbalances along with recent initiatives to address them. Other chapters then examine structural impediments affecting competitiveness and growth in the tourism-intensive economies of the Caribbean, which account for about 60 percent of the region's population. The book aims to stimulate policy dialogue and contribute to policymakers' efforts to address these unique challenges.

**Figure 1.3. Self-Reinforcing Structural and Macroeconomic Impediments to Growth**

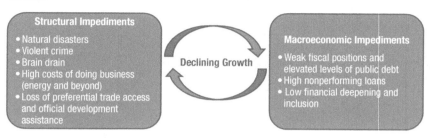

## GROWTH IN THE CARIBBEAN

Economic growth in the Caribbean, particularly across the tourism-intensive economies, has been disappointing in recent years (Figure 1.4). How do growth rates in the Caribbean compare with outcomes elsewhere, including in non-Caribbean small states? Have these upper-middle-income to high-income economies already reached their potential, with little scope for boosting their productive capacity, or could they, by tackling macroeconomic imbalances and structural distortions, grow faster again? To what extent have Caribbean economies leveraged their comparative advantage to secure a preeminent position as tourist destinations?

Chamon and others find, in Chapter 2, that per capita real GDP growth in tourism-intensive Caribbean economies since 2000 has been significantly below that of countries at similar income levels, including non-Caribbean small states. Their analysis establishes a strong association between this puzzlingly weak performance and country characteristics, including elevated levels of government debt, strains in the financial sector arising from high levels of nonperforming loans, emigration of skilled people, vulnerability to natural disasters, high rates of violent crime, an unfavorable business environment, and limited trade integration. The authors conclude that there is ample scope for raising growth in the Caribbean by tackling these macroeconomic and structural challenges, but that policy priorities need to be tailored to individual country circumstances.

The tourism industry is the dominant driver of economic activity in most Caribbean countries, but, as Acevedo and LaFramboise document in Chapter 3, the Caribbean share of the global tourism market has been falling since the 1990s. The authors conclude that this shrinking market share reflects a lack of diversification across tourism source markets, the impact of the global financial crisis, the region's unique vulnerability to natural disasters, and high pricing, which partly reflects weak competitiveness in, especially, labor and electricity costs and a lack of adequate infrastructure. Since global demand for tourism is likely to continue rising, and new tourist destinations are emerging, the authors argue that addressing Caribbean competitiveness challenges is vital for reinforcing the role of tourism as a driver for robust growth in incomes and jobs.

**Figure 1.4. Real GDP Growth**
*(Percent per year; three-year moving average)*

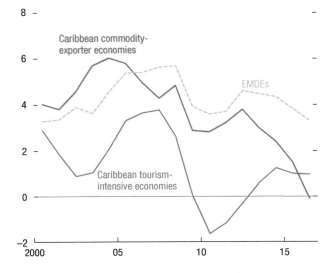

Sources: World Bank, *World Development Indicators*; and IMF staff estimates.
Note: EMDEs = emerging market and developing economies.

The emergence of new tourist destinations could, at least in principle, pose a challenge to the Caribbean tourism industry. To illustrate this issue, Acevedo and Wong investigate, in Chapter 4, the impact on the Caribbean of a potential U.S. rapprochement with Cuba, through a diversion of U.S. tourists. The authors find that, in the short term, a U.S.-Cuba rapprochement could reduce the number of U.S. tourists going to non-Cuban Caribbean destinations, although this reduction would likely be offset by larger inflows of Canadian and European tourists displaced from Cuba by the larger number of U.S. visitors. They also argue that, over time, the whole region is likely to see tourism flows increase.

## FISCAL MALAISE IN THE CARIBBEAN: A VICIOUS CYCLE OF HIGH DEBT AND LOW GROWTH

Caribbean economies face high and rising sovereign debt levels that weigh on their prospects for strong and sustainable growth. The rapid increase in public debt over the past five decades reflects a tendency in these economies to run large budget deficits in bad times, and to not offset these by saving enough in good times. Bad times include natural disaster events that Caribbean economies experience frequently and the attendant reconstruction costs that they need to absorb. But high levels of public debt also reflect a conscious decision by many of these countries to compete for foreign investment by providing large tax

### Figure 1.5. Government Debt
*(Percent of GDP)*

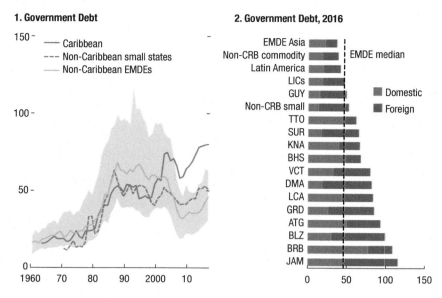

**1. Government Debt**

- —— Caribbean
- --- Non-Caribbean small states
- —— Non-Caribbean EMDEs

**2. Government Debt, 2016**

EMDE Asia
Non-CRB commodity — EMDE median
Latin America
LICs
GUY
Non-CRB small — ■ Domestic
TTO — ■ Foreign
SUR
KNA
BHS
VCT
DMA
LCA
GRD
ATG
BLZ
BRB
JAM

Sources: IMF, *World Economic Outlook*; and IMF staff calculations.
Note: CRB = Caribbean; EMDEs = emerging market and developing economies; LICs = low-income countries. Figure reports country-group medians. Data labels in figure use International Organization for Standardization (ISO) country codes.

incentives, which has led to significant revenue losses and, in turn, to larger budget deficits and debt. Elevated levels of indebtedness have made it difficult for these economies both to insulate themselves from external shocks and to alleviate their impact, through countercyclical fiscal policy responses, when they materialize. In effect, these economies suffer from a vicious cycle of high debt and low growth.

In 2016, Caribbean government debt reached a median level of 81 percent of GDP, its highest in half a century and more than 30 percentage points of GDP above the non-Caribbean EMDE median (Figure 1.5). Only one Caribbean economy—Guyana—has a debt-to-GDP ratio of less than 60 percent, and even that is greater than the EMDE median of 46 percent. The highest debt-to-GDP ratios in the Caribbean, those of Jamaica, at 115 percent, and Barbados, at 108 percent, are in the top 5 percent of all EMDEs.

While government debt is high in all Caribbean economies, budget deficits span a wide range (Figure 1.6). Some countries have large budget deficits, as in Trinidad and Tobago, while others, such as Grenada, are running budget surpluses. Accordingly, the need for additional fiscal consolidation—cuts in government spending or tax hikes—to reduce government debt to less than 60 percent of

### Figure 1.6. Fiscal Balances and Adjustment Needs
*(Percent of GDP)*

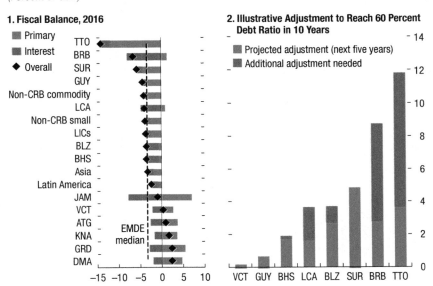

Sources: IMF, *World Economic Outlook*; and IMF staff estimates.
Note: CRB = Caribbean; EMDE = emerging market and developing economy; LICs = low-income countries. Planned adjustment based on April 2017 IMF *World Economic Outlook* projection for the primary fiscal surplus. Figure omits countries with no planned or estimated need for increases in the primary fiscal surplus. Data labels in figure use International Organization for Standardization (ISO) country codes.

GDP over the next 10 years differs greatly across the region, with the greatest need concentrated in high-deficit economies.[2]

To shed light on why Caribbean government debt remains so high, and to assess ways in which policymakers can reduce fiscal vulnerabilities, the book addresses the following questions:

- How have the global financial crisis and the international commodity price cycle affected Caribbean fiscal performance?

- To what extent do elevated levels of debt reflect the costs associated with frequent natural disasters?

- How has tax competition in the Caribbean aimed at attracting foreign direct investment contributed to the fiscal malaise?

---

[2]The adjustment need is the difference between the 2016 primary balance and the primary balance that, if held constant, would result in the debt-to-GDP ratio reaching 60 percent in 10 years. The calculation assumes a constant real exchange rate, and that the real interest rate, growth rate, and share of foreign debt in total debt are as in the April 2017 IMF *World Economic Outlook* through 2022, on average, with no change thereafter.

- What has been the role of two important public policy initiatives—citizenship by investment programs and debt restructuring—in improving Caribbean fiscal health?

The global financial crisis and international commodity price cycle have affected tourism-intensive and commodity-exporter Caribbean economies very differently. To illustrate this point, Figure 1.7 decomposes the change in government debt during the crisis and its immediate aftermath (2006–11) and the years since (2011–16) into four main drivers: the primary deficit, interest payments, inflation, and real GDP growth. It also decomposes shifts in the overall fiscal balance into changes in interest spending, primary (non-interest) spending, commodity revenue, and other government revenue. The following insights emerge:

- *Tourism-intensive economies.* During 2006–11, tourism-intensive economies saw government debt rise by 9.3 percent of GDP. The largest drivers of the increase were high interest payments (reflecting already-high debt levels), negative growth associated with the crisis, and increased (countercyclical) government spending that reduced these countries' primary budget surpluses. Since 2011, however, tourism-intensive economies have seen a partial recovery in fiscal health. The return of growth, combined with government spending restraint, has unwound about one-third (3.6 percentage points of GDP) of the crisis-induced debt increase.

- *Commodity-exporter economies.* Commodity exporters were largely insulated from the crisis, owing to the high international commodity prices that prevailed at the time. During 2006–11, they enjoyed, on average, an 11 percent of GDP *drop* in their government debt, driven by strong growth and primary fiscal surpluses. Since 2011, however, as the commodity boom turned to bust, these economies saw sharp declines in their commodity-related government revenues and an increase in government spending as a share of GDP (Figure 1.7). The resulting rise in budget deficits propelled their debt by an average of nearly 20 percent of GDP.

This analysis clarifies the role of recent global shocks in driving up Caribbean government debt. It also shows how a recovery in growth, combined with fiscal discipline, has helped some economies turn the corner. But the long-term success of debt-reduction efforts will require addressing underlying challenges that are specific to the Caribbean.

Otker and Loyola analyze, in Chapter 5, how frequent natural disasters, such as cyclones, hurricanes, and earthquakes, have contributed to a ratcheting up of public debt in the Caribbean. The authors find that natural disasters have affected Caribbean economies more than other small states, causing physical damage averaging 2.4 percent of GDP per year and depressing tourism arrivals and economic activity. The resulting drops in tax revenues, along with extra government spending on social assistance and rebuilding, have raised budget deficits and debt. Otker and Loyola discuss policies to strengthen countries' resilience to disasters through better preparation and risk management. They recommend explicitly building disaster and climate change risks into policy frameworks, including in

### Figure 1.7. Commodity-Exporter versus Tourism-Intensive Caribbean Economies, 2006–16
*(Percentage points of GDP)*

**1. Debt Accumulation Decomposition**

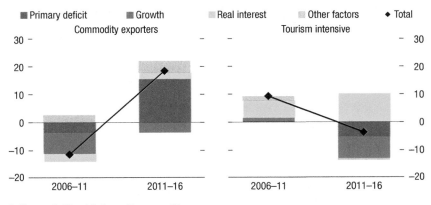

**2. Change in Fiscal Balance Decomposition**

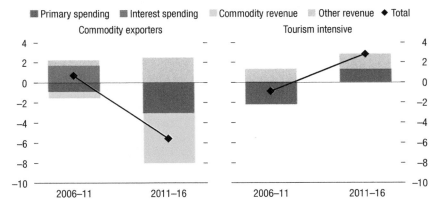

Sources: IMF, *World Economic Outlook*; and IMF staff estimates.
Note: A positive contribution of spending to the change in fiscal balance reflects a reduction in spending.

the design of budgets, fiscal rules, and public investment plans. They also discuss insurance and financial hedging tools that can protect governments from the burden of disasters and increase their capacity to respond appropriately. Finally, the authors underscore the benefits of regional and global efforts, such as the pooling of insurance cover at the Caribbean level, to support countries through capacity building, tools for risk management, and financing.

In Chapter 6, McIntyre examines the role of tax incentives in affecting Caribbean fiscal performance. Tax incentives motivated by a desire to boost private investment, notably foreign direct investment, are an important part of the policy framework in several Caribbean countries. McIntyre finds that tax incentives have supported private investment in the region, but have also imposed significant costs in forgone revenue, which has, in turn, weakened countries' fiscal positions. He argues that a more cost-effective way to encourage companies to invest in the Caribbean is to reinforce structural reform efforts aimed at strengthening competitiveness and improving the business environment. To reduce the fiscal cost of tax incentives and to make them more transparent, he recommends streamlining them and moving to rules-based administrative arrangements. McIntyre also warns that, if left unchecked, tax competition to attract investment could cause a "race to the bottom," and that coordination across the region's countries is needed to avert this risk.

Turning to factors that have helped improve fiscal positions in Caribbean countries, Gold and Myrvoda investigate, in Chapter 7, the role of economic citizenship programs (ECPs), which offer citizenship or residency in exchange for a substantial financial contribution to the domestic economy. The authors find that ECP inflows in the Caribbean have surged in recent years as a result of global demand for secondary citizenships and their increasing appeal to governments as a means of financing investment. Gold and Myrvoda also find that ECP inflows have yielded macroeconomic benefits by raising private investment, particularly in the construction and real estate sectors; bolstering fiscal and current account balances; and strengthening bank liquidity. The authors caution, however, that growing reliance on these potentially volatile revenues can pose substantial challenges for small states. To contain risks, they argue that ECPs and their associated revenues should be managed prudently with priority given to saving, including through sovereign wealth funds; infrastructure investment; and paying off debt. The authors underscore the benefits of regional collaboration and coordination on administering ECPs to ensure the consistent and stringent screening of applicants, reduce costs and reputation risks, and avoid a "race to the bottom" through the easing of program conditions.

In Chapter 8, Okwuokei and van Selm assess the impact of recent debt-restructuring operations in the Caribbean. They focus on countries that have restructured their sovereign debt to commercial creditors since 2011. Some of these countries restructured their debt repeatedly, which, the authors argue, weakened their credibility and access to capital markets. For debt-restructuring operations undertaken in the context of an IMF-supported program, Okwuokei and van Selm find that restoring debt sustainability was the main objective, while in other cases, relieving immediate cash flow pressure was the focus. The authors document how the scope of restructuring across domestic and external debt differed, and how this difference reflected domestic financial stability considerations. They also identify factors that increased the likelihood of a successful debt restructuring, including features that created incentives for sustained prudent fiscal policy, increased investor participation rates, and included mechanisms that insulate government debt from the effects of natural disasters. The authors conclude by underscoring the importance of embedding debt restructuring in a credible program of fiscal consolidation and structural reform.

Figure 1.8. Financial Sector Indicators

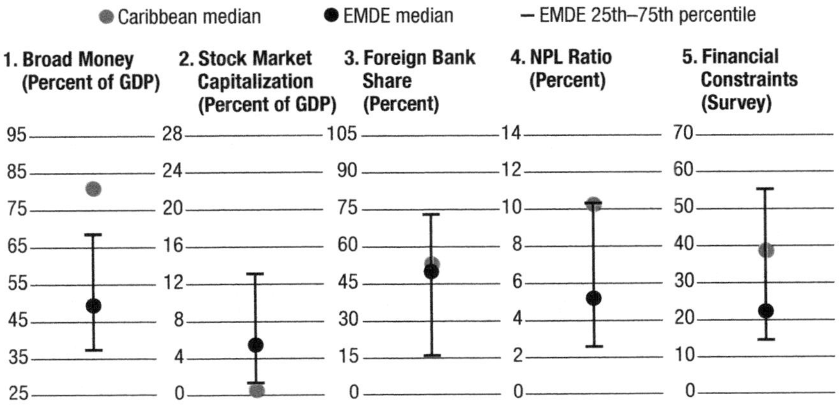
Caribbean median
EMDE median
EMDE 25th–75th percentile
1. Broad Money (Percent of GDP)
2. Stock Market Capitalization (Percent of GDP)
3. Foreign Bank Share (Percent)
4. NPL Ratio (Percent)
5. Financial Constraints (Survey)
95
85
75
65
55
45
35
25
28
24
20
16
12
8
4
0
105
90
75
60
45
30
15
0
14
12
10
8
6
4
2
0
70
60
50
40
30
20
10
0

Sources: Cull and others 2017; World Bank, *Enterprise Surveys*; World Bank, *World Development Indicators*; and IMF staff estimates.
Note: EMDE = emerging market and developing economy; NPL = nonperforming loan. Figure reports data for 2015 or most recent year available.

## BALANCING FINANCIAL SECTOR GROWTH, STABILITY, AND INCLUSION

The Caribbean banking system is relatively deep and interconnected, but external shocks, combined with institutional inefficiencies and rigidities, have caused persistent vulnerabilities and constrained access to credit. The depth of the financial system, when measured by the ratio of credit provided by financial institutions or broad money to GDP, is generally higher or comparable to that of peer economies (Figure 1.8). This depth, however, partly reflects the region's high government debt held by the public, while equity and corporate bond markets remain underdeveloped. Moreover, banks are saddled with high levels of nonperforming loans (NPLs), and a large share of nonfinancial firms cite access to credit as a major constraint.

To inform the debate about how to strengthen the Caribbean financial sector's resilience, as well as its ability to finance business investment and growth, the book addresses the following questions:

- What reforms could ease financial constraints facing Caribbean households and firms, and how would such reforms influence economic growth, inequality, and financial sector stability?
- How strongly interconnected is the Caribbean financial sector, to what extent have these links propagated financial distress across the region, and what reforms could limit the occurrence and transmission of such shocks?

- What factors explain the persistent rise of NPLs in the Caribbean, what is the effect of these NPLs on growth, and how can policymakers sever the adverse feedback loops between weak economic activity and weak asset quality?
- Why have Caribbean countries been losing correspondent banking relationships (CBRs), how has this loss affected the cost of international transactions and domestic financial intermediation, and what steps can regulators in the Caribbean and in advanced economies take to reduce CBR risks?

In Chapter 9, Wong investigates how deepening financial systems and expanding financial inclusion could support consumption and investment growth in the Caribbean. Wong finds that access to financial institutions has generally expanded over the past decade, with higher levels of deposits as a share of GDP and a larger nonbank financial sector. However, she also finds that Caribbean economies still lag behind their peers on indicators measuring credit availability to households and SMEs, with a high proportion of SMEs identifying access to credit as a major constraint. She argues that a careful deepening of financial systems and an expansion of financial inclusion that is mindful of the trade-offs between credit growth, inequality, and financial stability could bring significant benefits to Caribbean countries. To ease financial constraints, she proposes strengthening institutional and legal frameworks related to property rights and collateral, reducing information costs through stronger credit bureaus, and reducing operational costs through mobile networks. To safeguard the benefits of expanded financial inclusion without jeopardizing financial stability, Wong underscores the need for a strong framework for financial regulation and consumer protection.

Chapter 10, by Canetti and others, highlights the region's strong degree of financial connectivity, which, when coupled with insufficient regional oversight and regulatory controls, has amplified and spread financial distress. Canetti and his coauthors argue that the interconnectedness of the Caribbean banking, insurance, and other financial services sectors can promote international risk sharing, competition, and efficiency, but that it can also spread adverse shocks in unexpected ways. To assess the resilience of the regional system to financial and macroeconomic shocks, the authors conduct network simulations based on a unique data set on financial exposures. Their results confirm the systemic role of stability in the home financial sector of the region's largest conglomerates in limiting financial contagion. They also highlight the importance of strong capital positions in the region's banks and insurers. The authors conclude that national efforts to strengthen financial sector oversight need to be complemented with regional and global cooperation to strengthen resilience to cross-border shocks.

Beaton and others examine, in Chapter 11, the factors driving the rapid increase in NPLs across many Caribbean economies and propose a strategy for their resolution. They find that the high level of NPLs is, in large part, a legacy of the global financial crisis, but that their persistence reflects structural and institutional obstacles to their resolution. The authors also confirm the presence of an adverse feedback loop: NPLs depress growth of credit and economic activity, and this, in turn, further worsens asset quality. Beaton and her coauthors propose a multifaceted approach for severing this feedback loop: raising growth through macroeconomic policy support; strengthening supervisory frameworks to ensure financial stability and create incentives for NPL resolution; addressing deficiencies in information, insolvency, and debt-enforcement frameworks; and developing a pan-Caribbean market for distressed assets to facilitate the disposal of NPLs. Given the limits to institutional capacity in small Caribbean states, the authors conclude that there is a strong need to coordinate reforms and support these efforts with capacity-building assistance from international financial institutions.

Alleyne and others analyze, in Chapter 12, a recent development that has exacerbated the challenges facing the Caribbean financial system: the loss of CBRs. For many international banks, maintaining CBRs with banks in EMDEs has become less attractive given changes in the regulatory and enforcement landscape and higher compliance costs. In this context, banks in several Caribbean countries have lost CBRs over the past few years. The chapter authors find that this "de-risking" has raised the cost of international financial transactions and adversely affected services, such as international wire transfers, offshore financial services, and cash-intensive services. They estimate that, except for one case, countries have avoided major disruptions to financial intermediation, but caution that risks remain high. To address CBR risks, Alleyne and his coauthors urge Caribbean authorities to reinforce their anti-money laundering frameworks, and recommend that local banks explore ways to expand business volume available to their correspondent banks, including through mergers of small banks. The authors also urge advanced economy regulators to continue proactively communicating their regulatory expectations to correspondent banks, and call on international standards-setters to be mindful of unintended consequences on EMDEs of efforts to improve the resilience of the international financial system.

## STRUCTURAL IMPEDIMENTS TO GROWTH

Caribbean economies suffer from several structural impediments to growth that feed into and are an outcome of weak macroeconomic fundamentals. Three structural factors in particular—high energy costs, the emigration of skilled people ("brain drain"), and violent crime—in addition to the frequency and severity of natural disasters, are undermining the region's business climate. Most Caribbean economies fare poorly with respect to these factors when compared with other economies at a similar level of GDP per capita (Figure 1.9). The structural impediments weigh on the region's external competitiveness as well as on its ability to innovate, diversify, and grow. They also cause a vicious cycle by weakening financial and fiscal positions, which, in turn, hampers efforts to overcome the structural challenges. It is therefore imperative that policymakers address these structural weaknesses with a greater sense of urgency, including through targeted public intervention and infrastructure spending, in close

## Figure 1.9. Structural Impediments to Growth

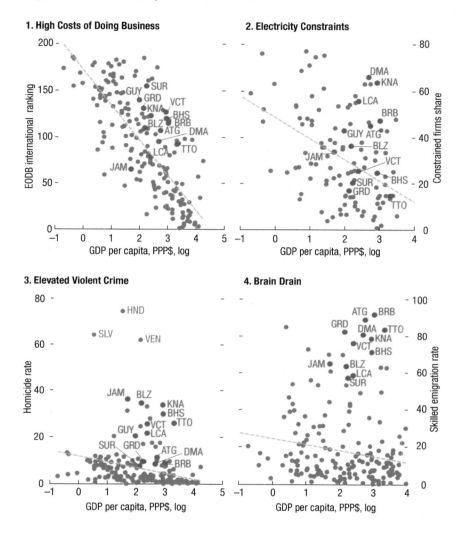

Sources: EM-DAT; Institute for Employment Research brain-drain data set (Brücker, Capuano, and Marfouk, 2013); World Bank, *Ease of Doing Business* (EODB) index; World Bank, *Enterprise Surveys*; World Bank, *World Development Indicators*; and IMF staff estimates.
Note: PPP = purchasing power parity. Electricity constraints measure share of firms reporting electricity as a major constraint; homicide rate is in homicides per 100,000; and skilled emigration rate is in percent of population of skilled nationals. Data labels in figure use International Organization for Standardization (ISO) country codes.

collaboration with the private sector. The book's last three chapters analyze each of these structural impediments.

McIntyre examines, in Chapter 13, how reducing the region's elevated energy costs could enhance the business climate, external competitiveness, and growth. He finds that Caribbean economies generally have high electricity costs, which reflect serious inefficiencies in the power sector and dependence on expensive imported petroleum products due to insufficient energy diversification. McIntyre cautions, however, that reducing these costs involves trade-offs: investment in energy reform would have long-term benefits, but raising public energy infrastructure investment would require increasing already-elevated debt-to-GDP ratios. He argues that greater private investment in energy infrastructure is needed, including through public-private partnerships, although such partnerships require strong institutional and legal arrangements to ensure successful implementation and limit contingent liability risks. McIntyre also proposes measures to enhance energy efficiency and encourage diversification toward renewable sources, and advocates establishing independent energy regulators to provide an environment conducive to private energy investment.

Wong analyzes, in Chapter 14, the role that brain drain and remittances have played in affecting Caribbean economic performance. She finds that in the Caribbean, the net effect on growth from emigration is negative for home countries. Reduced labor supply and productivity are the main channels. She also finds that remittances partly mitigate these negative effects, both by serving as a large and stable source of external financing and by helping to cushion the impact of shocks, including natural disasters. To address brain drain, Wong advocates reforms in home countries to improve the business climate and strengthen institutions, which would encourage people to stay while also facilitating the return of skilled and highly educated workers. In addition, given the role of remittances in financing and stabilizing economic activity, she proposes measures to reduce transaction costs associated with these transfers and to promote the use of formal channels of intermediation.

In Chapter 15, Sutton, Jaitman, and Khadan quantify the economic costs of the region's elevated violent crime rates and propose policies for reducing them. The authors focus on three costs: public spending on security and the criminal justice system, private spending on security, and social costs, including the income forgone because of victimization and incarceration. Using data from surveys recently conducted by the Inter-American Development Bank, the authors find that costs associated with crime in the Caribbean average nearly 4 percent of GDP per year, more than in most Latin American countries. The Caribbean economies with the highest costs of violent crime are The Bahamas, Jamaica, and Trinidad and Tobago. The authors estimate that reducing crime would significantly raise sales growth, particularly in the tourism sector. They recommend tackling crime by balancing suppression programs with prevention, including youth vocational training that increases job opportunities in the formal sector; targeting interventions in high-crime areas; and developing indicators that allow policymakers to more accurately monitor the effectiveness of anticrime programs.

## CONCLUSION

The chapters in this book provide a diagnosis of the central economic and financial challenges facing Caribbean policymakers and offer broad policy recommendations for promoting a sustained and inclusive increase in economic well-being. The analysis highlights the need for Caribbean economies to make a concerted effort to break the feedback loops between weak macroeconomic fundamentals, notably pertaining to fiscal positions and financial sector strains, and structural impediments, such as high electricity costs, limited financial deepening, violent crime, and brain drain, which have depressed private investment and growth.

A recurring theme in the book is the need for greater regional coordination in finding solutions to address the Caribbean's shared and intertwined macroeconomic and structural challenges. Coordination needs include, among others, reaching regional agreements to avoid a "race to the bottom" with regard to tax concessions for attracting foreign investment and ECPs, establishing a regional market for distressed assets, mitigating the risks of contagion from interconnected financial conglomerates through regional oversight and regulation, and pooling insurance coverage to deal with natural disasters.

The analysis in this book also suggests that strengthening regional and global market integration of Caribbean economies would provide an impetus to sustained growth in incomes and jobs. Related research, including for Caribbean economies, confirms that the free movement of capital, goods, labor, and services has positive effects on economic activity. Increasing market size, accelerating the acquisition and sharing of technological knowledge, and strengthening competition and efficiency are the main channels. Maximizing the benefits of regional and global integration requires, at the same time, providing support to those hurt by shifts in technology or trade, including through safety net programs such as time-bound income transfers and job retraining.

Greater regional and global economic integration of Caribbean economies would also facilitate structural transformation and a shift toward new economic activities, resulting in more diversified and less vulnerable economies. Structural transformation is already underway in the Caribbean, with entrepreneurs developing links from existing tourist destinations to local agricultural production, construction, and entertainment, and the development of medical tourism. Reforms to reduce the costs of doing business would reinforce this process.

A central challenge for the Caribbean is thus to come together as a region, overcome the limitations posed by size, and garner the benefits of globalization. Efforts should build on existing regional arrangements, such as the Caribbean Community—the region's most important trade initiative. Accelerating progress in implementing existing agreements, such as reduction of the common external tariff and completion of the single market and economy, particularly in relation to trade in services and the movement of labor, would stimulate trade. Policymakers could also promote deeper integration with Latin America and the rest of the world by pursuing new trade agreements, leveraging current agreements more effectively or deepening them to include areas beyond traditional trade issues, and developing port and transport infrastructure. Deepening international integration would also facilitate drawing on the experience of other countries dealing with similar challenges, which could yield significant dividends.

## REFERENCES

Brücker, Herbert, Stella Capuano, and Abdeslam Marfouk. 2013. "Education, Gender and International Migration: Insights from a Panel-Dataset 1980–2010." Institute for Employment Research, Nuremberg, Germany.

Cull, Robert, Maria Soledad Martinez Peria, and Jeanne Verrier. 2017. "Bank Ownership: Trends and Implications." IMF Working Paper 17/60, International Monetary Fund, Washington, DC.

# CHAPTER 2

# Reinvigorating Growth in the Caribbean

MARCOS CHAMON, JOSHUA CHARAP, QIAOE CHEN, AND DANIEL LEIGH,
WITH SUPPORT FROM FRANZ LOYOLA AND LULU SHUI

## INTRODUCTION

Growth in the Caribbean has been disappointing in recent decades. Averaging 2.1 percent per year since 2000, real GDP growth for the Caribbean has been half that of other emerging market and developing economies (EMDEs) and two-thirds that of non-Caribbean small states (Figure 2.1 and Table 2.1).[1] The growth weakness is concentrated among tourism-intensive Caribbean economies, which grew annually by only 1.6 percent (0.8 percent in per capita terms). Such low rates of growth complicate job creation, the raising of Caribbean wages and social conditions toward advanced economy levels, and management of the region's significant burden of public and private sector debt. Commodity exporters have seen faster growth during this period (3.7 percent per year), largely reflecting positive effects from the commodity price boom in the 2000s. More recently, however, growth in the commodity-exporting countries has also slowed or turned negative.

This chapter provides an overview of the conditions that have limited Caribbean growth by synthesizing insights from existing research and updating estimates on drivers of growth. It begins by comparing growth of Caribbean economies with that of peer groups, including countries at a similar level of development. To shed light on whether sluggish growth reflects slow accumulation of capital and labor or weak productivity growth, the chapter conducts a growth accounting exercise. Next, to highlight policy priorities for raising growth, the analysis ranks Caribbean economies and their peers according to 20 country characteristics relevant for growth. The chapter then provides estimates of the

---

[1] The analysis in this book focuses on 13 Caribbean economies, divided into two analytical groups: nine tourism-intensive economies (Antigua and Barbuda, The Bahamas, Barbados, Dominica, Grenada, Jamaica, St. Kitts and Nevis, St. Lucia, St. Vincent and the Grenadines) and four commodity exporters (Belize, Guyana, Suriname, Trinidad and Tobago). Following IMF (2016b), small states are defined as those with populations of less than 1.5 million that are not advanced market economies or high-income oil-exporting countries. Annex 2.1 provides further details on the data used in the analysis.

**Figure 2.1. Real GDP, 2000–15**
*(Cumulative; index, 2000 = 100; country-group medians)*

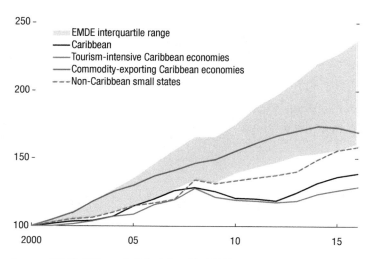

Sources: IMF, *World Economic Outlook*; Penn World Table; and IMF staff estimates.
Note: EMDE = emerging market and developing economy.

extent to which disappointing growth in tourism-intensive Caribbean economies can be explained by identified areas of weakness using growth equations estimated with the latest cross-country data. Finally, based on these growth equations, the chapter estimates the medium-term increase in growth that could come from addressing structural challenges, then discusses necessary policy reforms.

## CARIBBEAN GROWTH IN GLOBAL PERSPECTIVE

Since 2000, economic growth in all tourism-intensive Caribbean economies has been slower than for most EMDEs and non-Caribbean small states (Table 2.1). It has, on average, been even lower than for advanced economies, based on both overall GDP and on income per capita (converted at purchasing-power-parity exchange rates that more accurately reflect differences in the cost of living across countries). While the global financial crisis surely affected Caribbean economies severely, it is not an adequate explanation for their relatively weak average growth over this decade and a half. The shock of the global crisis may have amplified underlying domestic vulnerabilities. Commodity-exporting Caribbean economies have grown about as fast as non-Caribbean commodity exporters during this period—slightly slower in total GDP terms and slightly faster in per capita terms.

One may argue that the slow growth of Caribbean economies reflects the fact that they have reached a higher level of per capita income than most EMDEs, and

Table 2.1. Economic Growth, 2000–15

*(Percent per year; median)*

| Country | Real GDP Growth | |
|---|---|---|
| | Total | Per Capita |
| Caribbean | 2.1 | 1.2 |
| Tourism-Intensive Caribbean Economies | 1.6 | 0.8 |
| Antigua and Barbuda | 1.6 | 0.8 |
| The Bahamas | 0.6 | −0.4 |
| Barbados | 0.8 | 0.5 |
| Dominica | 1.7 | 2.1 |
| Grenada | 2.2 | 1.6 |
| Jamaica | 0.6 | 0.1 |
| St. Kitts and Nevis | 2.2 | 1.2 |
| St. Lucia | 1.3 | 0.6 |
| St. Vincent and the Grenadines | 2.1 | 2.0 |
| Commodity-Exporting Caribbean Economies | 3.7 | 3.0 |
| Belize | 3.4 | 0.9 |
| Guyana | 3.1 | 2.9 |
| Suriname | 4.2 | 3.0 |
| Trinidad and Tobago | 3.9 | 3.6 |
| Memorandum | | |
| Non-Caribbean EMDEs | 4.2 | 2.6 |
| Non-Caribbean Small States | 3.0 | 1.4 |
| Non-Caribbean Commodity Exporters | 4.2 | 2.4 |
| Advanced Economies | 1.9 | 1.1 |

Sources: IMF, *World Economic Outlook*; Penn World Table; and IMF staff estimates.
Note: EMDE = emerging market and developing economy.

therefore have less scope for rapid growth. This simple proposition is, however, not entirely valid for the Caribbean economies. The per capita income of Caribbean countries is well above the EMDE average, with a median level of US$10,600 in purchasing-power-parity terms as of the end of 2015, compared with the EMDE median of US$6,800. Standard growth theory predicts that these countries would grow more slowly because there is less of a gap with advanced economies to bridge through the accumulation of capital and technological leapfrogging. The experience of 179 economies since 2000 is consistent with the idea that countries at a higher income level grow more slowly (Figure 2.2).

Growth in tourism-intensive Caribbean economies has, however, been less than could have been expected on the basis of their per capita incomes. These countries should have grown at about 2.3 percent per year in per capita terms, as compared to the registered growth that has averaged 0.8 percent per year (Figure 2.3).[2] This puzzling weakness does not apply to commodity-exporting

---

[2]The prediction is based on the following equation, estimated for 148 advanced and emerging market and developing economies on the 2000–15 sample: $g_{it} = \alpha_t + \beta y_{it-N} + \varepsilon_{it}$, where $g$ is average per capita growth over each five-year period $t$ ($N = 5$), $y$ is initial (log) per capita income, and $\alpha_t$ is a time fixed effect capturing external (global) factors.

**Figure 2.2. Growth per Capita versus Initial per Capita Income, 2000–15**

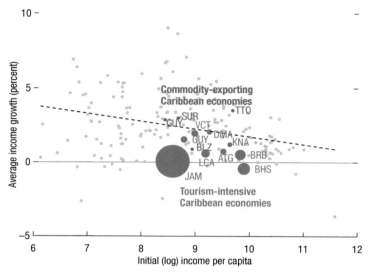

Sources: IMF, *World Economic Outlook*; Penn World Table; and IMF staff estimates.
Note: For tourism-intensive Caribbean economies, size of circles reflects population size.
Data labels in figure use International Organization for Standardization (ISO) country codes.

**Figure 2.3. Actual and Predicted Average GDP Growth per Capita, 2000–15**
*(Percent per year)*

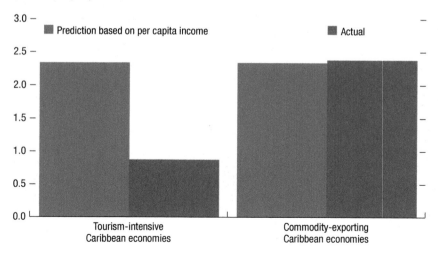

Sources: IMF, *World Economic Outlook*; Penn World Table; and IMF staff estimates.
Note: "Actual" denotes mean of sample available for estimating growth equation.

**Figure 2.4. Contributions to Average GDP Growth per Capita, 2000–15**
*(Percent per year)*

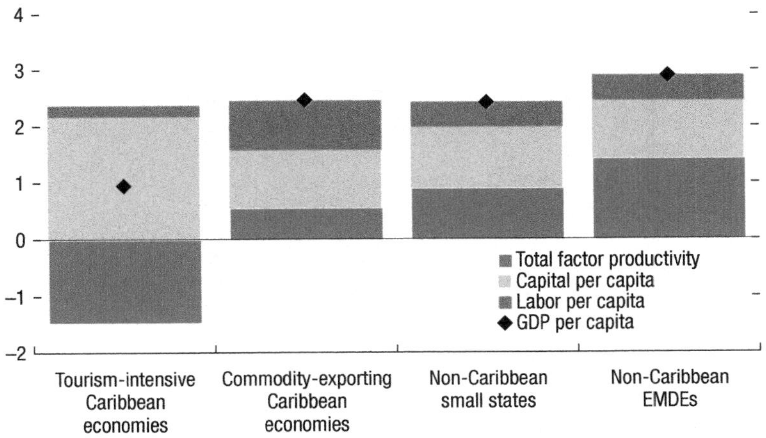

Source: Authors' calculations.
Note: Figure reports results for commodity-exporting Caribbean economies and tourism-intensive economies, non-Caribbean small states, and non-Caribbean EMDEs. EMDE = emerging market and developing economy.

Caribbean economies, which grew slightly faster than could have been expected during this period, reflecting the commodity boom of the 2000s.

A defining feature of Caribbean growth compared with that of other regions has been the weak contribution of total factor productivity (TFP), which measures the overall productivity of both labor and capital, and reflects such elements as technology. A simple growth decomposition exercise suggests that TFP growth since 2000 has been near zero or negative, unlike for non-Caribbean small states and other EMDEs (Figure 2.4).[3] On average, during 2000–15, TFP growth contributed –1.4 percentage points to annual growth for tourism-intensive Caribbean economies and 0.6 percentage points for commodity-exporting Caribbean economies, compared with larger positive contributions for non-Caribbean small states and EMDEs. This finding is consistent with other studies that point to falling or stagnating productivity in the Caribbean (for example, Ruprah, Melgarejo, and Sierra 2014; Thacker and others 2013) and with a recent study of productivity and innovation at the level of small and medium-sized Caribbean enterprises (Dohnert, Crespi, and Maffioli 2017).

---

[3]The analysis adjusts the usual approach for estimating TFP by accounting for the destructive effects of natural disasters on the capital stock (see Annex 2.2). Without this adjustment, the analysis would attribute disaster damage to TFP growth, resulting in even weaker TFP growth.

## WHAT'S THE HOLDUP?

To shed light on which country characteristics and policies may explain the slow growth of tourism-intensive Caribbean economies, this section proceeds in two steps. First, it compares performance with EMDE peer groups along dimensions that are relevant for growth and prosperity.[4] The second step uses estimated growth equations to quantify the extent to which growth underperformance could be attributed to the structural weaknesses identified in the first step.

### Diagnostic of Characteristics Relevant for Growth and Prosperity

A review of 20 country characteristics relevant for medium-term growth and prosperity reveals areas in which Caribbean economies rank poorly compared with other EMDE country groups (Table 2.2). For each of the 20 indicators, the color of each cell indicates the relative ranking of a country group compared with the others. Red indicates a less favorable ranking and green indicates a more favorable ranking. For example, the greater the ease of doing business compared with other country groups, the more green the cell color, and the higher the violent crime rate, the more red the cell color.

Notable structural and macroeconomic impediments to growth include the following:

- *Brain drain.* Caribbean countries stand out from their peers regarding outward migration of skilled human resources. The share of nationals with tertiary education (a proxy for high skills and knowledge) living abroad is about 76 percent, several times the rate for other EMDE regions, and 50 percent greater than the rate for non-Caribbean small states (Figure 2.5). Skilled emigration lowers growth by impairing the economy's stock of skills and knowledge (human capital).[5] IMF (2017b) finds that the exodus of skilled labor has contributed to rising wage costs, with negative effects on external competitiveness. Remittances from Caribbean emigrants have been sizable, supporting investment and education and fostering commercial

---

[4]Mapping how each of these determinants influences the contributions of capital and labor inputs and TFP is not straightforward. Nevertheless, there are reasons to expect that the variables under consideration influence investment, labor supply and demand, and TFP growth.

[5]Migration data for 182 countries during 1980–2010 yield the following estimation results:

$$\ln(H_{it}/H_{it-30}) = 38.4 - 17.6\ \ln(H_{it-30}) - 33.1\ \{\text{High-skill } E\}_{it-30:t} - 17.3\ \{\text{Medium-skill } E\}_{it-30:t} - 0.1\ \{\text{Low-skill } E\},$$

where $H$ denotes human capital and $E$ denotes emigration as a percentage of all country nationals. The measure of $H$ comes from the Penn World Tables and is based on the average years of schooling (from Barro and Lee 2013; Cohen and Leker 2014) and an assumed rate of return to education based on Mincer equation estimates (Psacharopoulos 1994). The results imply that countries with a lower initial level of $H$ had faster growth in $H$ (convergence). They also imply that the departure of the 30 percent of nationals with tertiary education from the Caribbean over this 30-year period has reduced Caribbean $H$ by about 10 percent.

Table 2.2. Heat Map: Characteristics Relevant for Growth and Prosperity
*(Ranking across country groups)*

| | Tourism-Intensive CRB Economies | Commodity-Exporting CRB Economies | Central America | South America | CEE | EM Asia | LICs | Non-CRB Small States |
|---|---|---|---|---|---|---|---|---|
| Violent Crime | | | | | | | | |
| Emigration | | | | | | | | |
| Skilled Emigration | | | | | | | | |
| Human Capital | | | | | | | | |
| Natural Disasters | | | | | | | | |
| Government Debt | | | | | | | | |
| Taxation | | | | | | | | |
| NPLs | | | | | | | | |
| Ease of Doing Business | | | | | | | | |
| Competitiveness | | | | | | | | |
| Bureaucracy | | | | | | | | |
| Regulatory Quality | | | | | | | | |
| Rule of Law | | | | | | | | |
| Control of Corruption | | | | | | | | |
| Trade Openness | | | | | | | | |
| Trade Tariff | | | | | | | | |
| Trade Connectivity | | | | | | | | |
| GVC Participation | | | | | | | | |
| High-Tech Export Share | | | | | | | | |
| Export Diversification | | | | | | | | |

Sources: Barro-Lee 2013 data set; IMF, Diversification database; IMF, *World Economic Outlook*; Institute for Employment Research, brain-drain data set; Penn World Table; World Bank, Ease of Doing Business Index; World Bank, *World Development Indicators*; World Bank, World Governance Indicators; and World Economic Forum, Global Competitiveness Index.
Note: See Annex Table 2.1.1 for data descriptions. Red = less favorable ranking; green = more favorable ranking. Table based on 2015 or most recent data. For natural disaster damage, table based on historical average (2000–15). CEE = Central and Eastern Europe; CRB = Caribbean; EM Asia = emerging market economies in Asia; GVC = global value chain; LICs = lower-income countries; NPLs = nonperforming loans.

linkages, but IMF (2017b) concludes that the overall impact of emigration on growth has been negative for Caribbean countries.

- *Natural disasters.* Caribbean countries are highly vulnerable to natural disasters because many of them are located in the cyclone and hurricane belts bordering the equator. Natural disasters reduce economic output by destroying crops, infrastructure, and, as Chapter 3 highlights, reducing tourism arrivals. Average annual physical damage from natural disasters amounted to 2.3 percent of GDP for tourism-intensive Caribbean economies since 2000, and 1.3 percent of GDP for commodity-exporting Caribbean economies, more than in non-Caribbean small states. Climate change is likely to exacerbate these challenges through rising sea levels (IMF 2016b).

- *Crime.* Caribbean economies have some of the highest violent crime rates in the world, with an average homicide rate of about 24 per 100,000 inhabitants in 2015, more than three times the rate in non-Caribbean small states.[6] Crime results in significant social costs, which tend to be

---

[6]The highest crime rates are found in The Bahamas, Jamaica, and Trinidad and Tobago.

### Figure 2.5. Emigration Rates, 2010
*(Share of country nationals living abroad)*

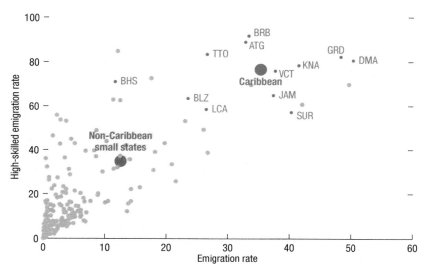

Sources: Institute for Employment Research, brain-drain data set; and IMF staff estimates.
Note: High-skilled emigration relates to nationals with tertiary education. Data labels in figure use
International Organization for Standardization (ISO) country codes.

concentrated among the most vulnerable members of society. As a detailed
study by the staff of the Inter-American Development Bank explains,
crime impedes economic growth by discouraging tourism and business
investment, reducing worker productivity, and diverting government
spending from investment in health, education, and productive infrastructure (Jaitman 2017). Jaitman (2017) estimates that direct crime-related
costs amount to about 3.6 percent of GDP for the Caribbean.[7] Violent
crime is a particularly acute challenge for tourism-dependent economies
because it depresses both demand for tourism and the supply side
of the economy.

- *Government debt burden.* Tourism-intensive Caribbean economies have
  accumulated the highest levels of government debt among EMDEs
  (Chapter III.1). Commodity-exporting economies have had lower levels of
  debt, but they recently saw a rapid increase. High debt presents costs and
  risks that weigh on medium-term growth, including distortions from high-

---

[7]The costs comprise lethal and nonlethal victimization and forgone income of prison populations, private spending on security by businesses and households, and public spending, including
the costs to the justice system, spending on police services, and spending on prisons.

er taxes needed to service the debt, displacement of productive government spending, and concerns associated with the possibility of default, which feeds uncertainty about future taxation and inflation. A number of studies have found a negative association between high government debt and growth for Caribbean economies, including, most recently, Thacker and others (2013).

- *Financial sector strains.* The banking sector in a number of Caribbean economies is burdened by high levels of nonperforming loans (NPLs), averaging 12 percent of the value of loans in tourism-intensive Caribbean economies, and 9 percent in commodity-exporting Caribbean economies, well above the levels for other EMDE groups. NPLs have a negative impact on bank profitability, increase bank vulnerability to shocks, and, in the absence of well-developed capital markets, constrain credit supply to finance productive investment and growth (Chapter IV.3). During 1995–2015, Caribbean economies underwent a number of episodes of financial stress, as documented by Laeven and Valencia (2013), which can have long-lasting effects on economic activity.

- *Business environment and competitiveness.* Stronger protection of property rights and better, simpler regulations for businesses are important for encouraging private investment and durable growth. The challenges in this area are greater for the commodity-exporting Caribbean economies than for the tourism-intensive ones, as is illustrated by their relatively poor rankings on the World Bank Ease of Doing Business Index, the Global Competitiveness Index of the World Economic Forum, and the World Bank Worldwide Governance Indicators (perceptions of corruption, law and order, regulatory quality, and bureaucratic efficiency).[8]

- *Trade integration.* Stronger trade links tend to raise long-term growth; the channels include enhanced competition and learning and productivity spillovers. The small size of Caribbean economies and the erosion of trade preferences extended to them (Cashin, Haines, and Mlachila 2010) accentuate the need for trade and market integration to overcome their constrained set of inputs, including the number of entrepreneurs, that can move to new and more productive activities as part of structural transformation and diversification (Hausmann and Klinger 2009). Caribbean trade openness—exports and imports as a share of GDP—is broadly comparable with other regions, but lower than could be expected based on the small size of Caribbean economies, which increases reliance on imports (Figure 2.6). Caribbean connectivity with the world trade network, as measured by the number of trading partners and their network centrality, as well as participation in global value chains (networks of production stages of goods and

---

[8]The Ease of Doing Business indicator used here is the "distance to frontier" overall index, which summarizes 41 indicators for 10 doing business topics.

### Figure 2.6. Trade Integration and Country Size

**1. Trade Openness versus Country Size**

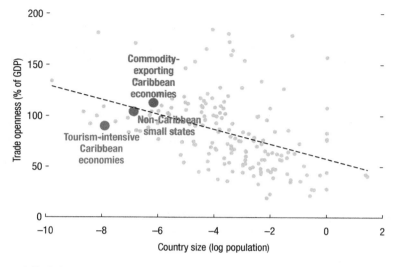

**2. Trade Connectivity Index**

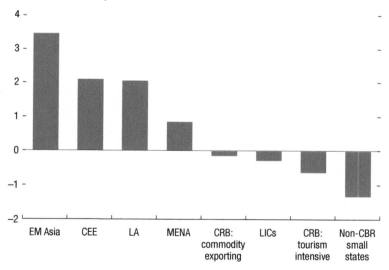

Sources: IMF, Direction of Trade Statistics; and IMF staff estimates.
Note: Trade openness defined as sum of exports and imports as a share of GDP. Trade connectivity measured by five indicators from IMF (2017a) covering number of countries traded with as well as their centrality in the world trade network, combined in a composite index. CEE = Central and Eastern Europe; CRB = Caribbean; EM Asia = emerging market economies in Asia; LA = Latin America; LICs = low-income countries; MENA = Middle East and North Africa.

services across borders) remains limited compared with other regions.[9] These limitations in part reflect the small size of Caribbean economies, but do constrain opportunities for diversifying and upgrading the complexity and technological content of exports.

Each of these factors matters individually, but their cumulative impact is compounded, with the potential to cause persistently weak growth. For example, violent crime may cause emigration and brain drain, which in turn can make it harder to cope with high debt burdens because fewer skilled workers remain to shoulder the debt service. By the same token, tackling one obstacle to growth can facilitate responding to others.

## Insights from Growth Equations

How much of the puzzlingly weak growth of tourism-intensive Caribbean economies can be explained by their structural challenges? Estimating medium-term growth equations using data for many countries can shed light on this question. The equations are estimated in the form of five-year non-overlapping intervals covering 1995–2015 for an unbalanced panel of up to 148 advanced and emerging market and developing economies, including the Caribbean economies under study.[10] Specifications for which data are limited are restricted to 2010–15. The estimated equations include a full set of time fixed effects to take account of global shocks such as shifts in commodity prices or the global business cycle. To address concerns about reverse causality, the values for the right-hand side variables are for the year preceding each five-year growth interval. Since natural disasters are independent of growth, they are included contemporaneously in the estimated equations. To guard against the undue influence of outliers, the estimation results are reported based on Cook's distance approach, as well as ordinary least squares.[11] See Table 2.3.

The estimation results for growth drivers that are beyond the control of policymakers are intuitive. A higher initial level of per capita income is associated

---

[9]Following IMF (2017a), trade connectivity is measured by five indicators, which are here combined into a single composite indicator (first principal component): the number of countries exported to, the number of countries imported from, centrality in the world trade network ("eigencentrality"), centrality among exporters in the world trade network ("out eigencentrality"), and centrality among importers in the world trade network ("in eigencentrality"). Caribbean economies' limited number of trading partners partially reflects the importance of tourism, given that trade in this sector is naturally more concentrated with regions of geographic proximity (North America and Europe).

[10]The equations estimated are as follows: $g_{it} = \alpha_t + \beta X_{it-N} + \varepsilon_{it}$, where $g$ is average per capita growth over each five-year period $t$ ($N = 5$), $X$ is a matrix of country characteristics, and $\alpha_t$ is a time fixed effect.

[11]Cook's distance measures how influential observations are on the estimated regression coefficients (Cook 1979; Hayashi 2000). Observations with Cook's distance greater than $4/N$, where $N$ is the sample size, are discarded.

## Table 2.3. Per Capita Real GDP Growth Equation Estimates

| | 1995–2015 | | 2010–15 | |
|---|---|---|---|---|
| | OLS | Cook's D | OLS | Cook's D |
| | (1) | (2) | (3) | (4) |
| Log of Initial Income per Capita | −1.267*** | −1.169*** | −1.690*** | −1.771*** |
| Trade Integration | 0.366* | 0.492*** | 0.435** | 0.525*** |
| Human Capital | 2.176*** | 2.479*** | −0.280 | 1.373** |
| Natural Disaster | −6.587** | −10.069** | −10.326 | −27.977** |
| Crime | −34.831*** | −25.274*** | −30.900** | −27.352*** |
| Government Debt | −0.487 | −0.683** | −1.058** | −1.303*** |
| Financial Crisis | −1.029*** | −1.037*** | | |
| NPLs | | | −1.351 | −5.909* |
| Ease of Doing Business | | | 6.464* | 5.715*** |
| Dummy, 2001–05 | −0.178 | −0.468 | | |
| Dummy, 2006–10 | −0.847*** | −1.003*** | | |
| Dummy, 2011–15 | −1.230*** | −1.349*** | | |
| Constant | 13.470*** | 12.170*** | 14.544*** | 14.312*** |
| Observations | 439 | 419 | 127 | 118 |
| $R^2$ | 0.193 | 0.255 | 0.297 | 0.418 |

Source: Authors' estimates.
Note: Outliers excluded using Cook's distance (D) method. Sample includes up to 148 advanced and emerging market economies (unbalanced panel). NPLs = nonperforming loans; OLS = ordinary least squares. *, **, and *** denote statistical significance at the 10, 5, and 1 percent level, respectively.

with slower growth, and the coefficient estimate is consistent with the literature. In addition, a number of external factors beyond the control of policymakers, captured by the equations' time fixed effects, had significant effects on growth. The global financial crisis of 2008–09 and its aftermath and the EMDE slowdown in more recent years are examples of adverse global factors that may explain the respective negative time fixed effect coefficient estimates.

Structural characteristics for which Caribbean economies rank unfavorably have the expected association with growth. Higher violent crime is associated with slower subsequent medium-term growth.[12] A higher level of human capital—measured based on the adjusted years of schooling of the population—is associated with faster growth. Natural disasters reduce growth over the five-year periods considered. A higher initial stock of government debt is associated with lower subsequent growth. Financial strains, whether measured by the occurrence of a banking, currency, or sovereign debt crisis (columns (1) and (2) in Table 2.3) or by the initial NPL ratio (columns (3) and (4)) are associated with weaker subsequent growth. A more favorable business climate is associated

---

[12]A rise in the homicide rate by 10 people in 100,000 (approximately equivalent to moving from the 25th to the 75th percentile of the sample) is associated with about 0.3 percentage point lower average growth over the subsequent five years in all the specifications estimated. The result is both statistically and economically significant, and is consistent with the findings of Demirci, Moreno, and Wong (forthcoming), who use an instrumental variables approach based on deportations from the United States.

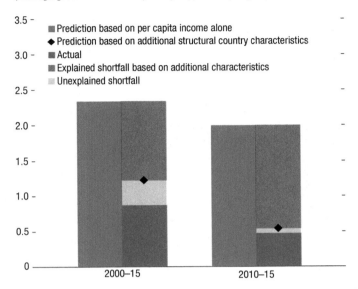

**Figure 2.7. Explaining the Growth Underperformance of Tourism-Intensive Caribbean Economies**
*(Average growth in real GDP per capita; percent per year)*

Sources: IMF, *World Economic Outlook*; Penn World Table; and IMF staff estimates.
Note: Estimates based on coefficients in Table 2.3 (columns (2) and (4), for 2000–15 and 2010–15, respectively).

with stronger growth, as is greater trade integration, measured by the ratio of trade to GDP.

The estimation results suggest that domestic structural challenges explain the bulk of the growth underperformance of tourism-intensive Caribbean economies (Figure 2.7). For 2000–15, the estimates based on the models reported in Table 2.3 explain more than 75 percent of the shortfall of actual growth below the rate predicted based on the level of income per capita alone. For the 2010–15 subsample, the models explain more than 95 percent of the shortfall.

## POLICIES FOR REINVIGORATING GROWTH

This chapter's analysis suggests ample scope for raising growth in the Caribbean by tackling the region's structural challenges. For illustrative purposes, the analysis simulates the increase in growth that would come from an improvement in the policy-related factors to the top decile of small states, based on the growth equation estimates (Table 2.4). The assumed adjustments should not be interpreted as overnight outcomes because they could take years or even decades to

### Table 2.4. Illustrative Medium-Term Growth Gains
*(Caribbean median)*

| | Baseline Level[1] | Illustrative Level (top decile of small states)[2] | Medium-Term GDP Growth Gain (percentage points)[3] |
|---|---|---|---|
| NPLs (percent of loans) | 10.94 | 2.33 | 0.51 |
| Ease of Doing Business (index) | 57.50 | 65.84 | 0.48 |
| Disaster Damage (annual, percent of GDP) | 2.24 | 1.12 | 0.33 |
| Crime (homicide rate per 100,000) | 20.98 | 10.49 | 0.29 |
| Government Debt (percent of GDP) | 80.65 | 60.00 | 0.28 |
| Human Capital (index) | 2.32 | 2.53 | 0.19 |
| Trade (percent of GDP) | 93.02 | 122.75 | 0.16 |
| Total | ... | ... | 2.23 |

Source: IMF staff estimates.

Note: NPLs = nonperforming loans.

[1] 2015 level except for disaster damage (historical average). Trade integration based on trade-to-GDP ratio. See Annex Table 2.1.1 for data descriptions.

[2] For crime and disaster damage, reduction by 50 percent is assumed. For government debt, reduction to 60 percent of GDP is assumed. For trade, a rise to the top quartile of non-Caribbean small states is assumed.

[3] Estimates based on coefficients in Table 2.3 (column (4)).

achieve.[13] Some of the reforms, such as government spending cuts or tax hikes aimed at reducing the stock of public debt, may even cause short-term negative effects on growth. For crime and disaster damage limitation, the simulations assume a reduction by one-half from the current level, and for trade integration, they assume an increase to the top quartile of small states. These are still ambitious goals, though less dramatic than improving to the top fifth percentile of small states. For government debt, a reduction to 60 percent of GDP is assumed.

The estimated illustrative growth gains associated with these structural adjustments vary across countries, reflecting their different challenges, but are in the range of 1–3 percentage points per year. Such an increase in growth would represent significant progress toward increasing prosperity (Figure 2.8). The policy priorities differ by country. In Jamaica, for example, the largest growth gains come from reducing government debt and crime. For St. Lucia, the largest gain comes from addressing NPLs, and for Suriname, from improving the business environment. The gains from greater intra- and interregional trade integration reported here complement the more detailed estimates of recent IMF research on the effects of expanding trade networks and achieving greater participation in global value chains for economies in Latin American and the Caribbean (IMF 2017a).

A set of self-reinforcing reforms, some of which Caribbean governments have already announced and are implementing, is needed to create an environment

---

[13]Costa Rica provides an example of significant gains in medium-term growth following reforms. The shift to faster growth in the 1990s was largely driven by Intel Corporation's decision to place its manufacturing plant in the country, which, in turn, was motivated by Costa Rica's high levels of educational attainment; economic openness; stable political, social, and macroeconomic environment; and strong doing business climate, reflecting decades of reforms, including investment in education (IMF 2016a).

**Figure 2.8. Reinvigorating Growth: Illustrative Medium-Term Growth Gains**
*(Percentage points per year; deviation from baseline)*

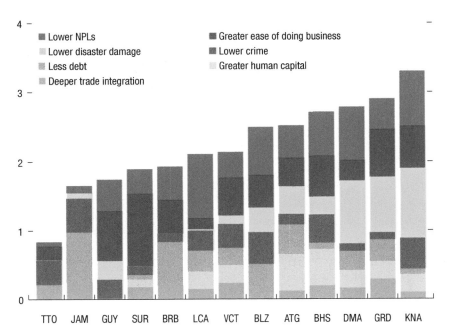

Source: IMF staff estimates.
Note: Estimates based on coefficients in Table 2.3 column (4). NPLs = nonperforming loans. Data labels in figure use International Organization for Standardization (ISO) country codes.

conducive to such medium-term gains. In conclusion, this chapter provides an overview of some of the main shared policy priorities for reinvigorating Caribbean growth.

- *Curbing and reversing brain drain.* A comprehensive strategy is needed to create an environment that encourages people to stay and provides incentives for return migration. To retain highly skilled workers, who tend to leave for technological or scientific "hubs," focusing on modernizing education and creating a critical mass of highly skilled workers is vital. Given the small size of Caribbean economies, achieving the required critical mass of skilled workers may require further promotion of labor market integration across the region.

- *Fighting crime.* More work is required to assess the effects of existing public policies and crime prevention programs in the Caribbean, but, as set out in a comprehensive study by the staff of the Inter-American Development Bank (Jaitman 2017), a greater emphasis on prevention, alongside suppression, is warranted. Prevention elements should be integrated into social programs in health and education, especially among the youth population. Some promising initiatives are based on adapting programs that were successful in other jurisdictions. Trinidad and Tobago adapted Chicago's CeaseFire program, which reduces violent crime through prevention and community-mobilization strategies, including intervention by "violence interrupters" who reach out to gang leaders and at-risk youth and mediate conflicts to reduce shootings and retaliatory violence (Ritter 2009). Jaitman 2017 also notes the effectiveness of moving toward restorative justice in Jamaica and Trinidad and Tobago, wherein victims and offenders mediate a restitution agreement. The criminal justice system should also be reformed to improve performance measurement and promote institutional accountability.

- *Deepening trade integration.* The Caribbean Community is one of the region's most important trade initiatives. Further progress toward the planned single market and economy in the Caribbean Community, which stalled in the aftermath of the global financial crisis, would lead to a further increase in trade. Caribbean economies would also be well served by greater integration with Latin American and the rest of the world. Interregional integration can be facilitated by new trade agreements, and there is scope in some cases to leverage current agreements more effectively, or deepen them to include areas beyond traditional trade issues. Deeper integration of Caribbean economies with global trade could also be achieved by reducing trade barriers, enhancing port infrastructure, fostering human capital formation, and supporting research and development (IMF 2017a).

- *Implementing sector-specific policies to support structural transformation.* A number of studies argue in favor of sector-specific public intervention to promote structural transformation where markets have failed (for example, Hausmann and Rodrik 2006). For Caribbean economies, Hausmann and Klinger (2009) suggest that if small market size is preventing firms from moving to new and more productive activities, proactive government intervention in the form of "strategic bets" may be appropriate, informed by an inclusive public-private consultation process. Such intervention needs to leverage comparative advantage and fill gaps in public goods such as infrastructure, education, and regulatory issues, and avoid "picking winners" and subsidizing low-productivity sectors or firms through tax exemptions and firm-specific subsidies. Examples include supporting the setup of new tourism destinations, including for medical tourism, through advertising activities, training, nature conservation efforts, and the provision of transportation infrastructure; and supporting agricultural productivity by upgrading feeder roads, land-holding laws, and phytosanitary standards. Unlike larger economies, small states cannot place several bets in the hope that some will work and pay for those that do not.

- *Enhancing the ease of doing business.* The policy priorities mentioned above would all help strengthen the ease of doing business in the Caribbean. The very small scale of most Caribbean economies makes removing barriers for businesses operating across these economies to achieve economies of scale particularly important. To promote financial development and access to credit, policy initiatives need to focus on institutional reforms, including strengthening property rights, enhancing the range of financial instruments, making credit information more available, and reducing the costs of financial intermediation.

# ANNEX 2.1. DATA SOURCES

### Annex Table 2.1.1. Data Sources

| Indicator | Source and Notes |
|---|---|
| Real GDP | PWT, extended based on WEO |
| Population | WEO |
| Capital Stock | PWT, extended based on WEO |
| Labor | PWT, extended based on WEO |
| Violent Crime | WDI; homicides per 100,000 inhabitants |
| Emigration | IAB brain-drain data set; share of nationals living abroad |
| Skilled Emigration | IAB brain-drain data set; share of nationals with tertiary education living abroad |
| Human Capital | PWT, Barro-Lee (2013) data set; years of schooling scaled by assumed rate of return to education based on Mincer equation estimates (Psacharopoulos 1994) |
| Disasters | EM-DAT; damage from natural disasters (percent of GDP) |
| Government Debt | WEO; general government debt in percent of GDP |
| Taxation | WDI; total revenue in percent of GDP |
| NPLs | WDI, augmented by data collected for Chapter 12 |
| Financial Crisis | Laeven and Valencia 2013 |
| Ease of Doing Business | World Bank Ease of Doing Business Index distance to frontier (0–100) |
| Competitiveness | World Economic Forum Global Competitiveness Index |
| Bureaucratic Efficiency | World Bank WGI; index |
| Regulation Quality | World Bank WGI; index |
| Rule of Law | World Bank WGI; index |
| Control of Corruption | World Bank WGI; index |
| Trade Openness | World Bank WGI; index |
| Trade Tariff | World Bank WDI; average trade tariff (percent) |
| Trade Connectivity | IMF 2017b |
| GVC Participation | IMF 2017b |
| High-Tech Export Share | World Bank WDI; percent |
| Export Diversification | IMF Diversification database; index |

Note: Data are 2015 or latest available. For natural disaster damage, distribution for 2010–15 is reported.
EM-DAT = International Disasters Database; GVC = global value chain; IAB = Institute for Employment Research (Brücker, Capuano, and Marfouk 2013); NPLs = nonperforming loans; PWT = Penn World Tables; WEO = IMF, *World Economic Outlook*; WDI = World Development Indicators; WGI = World Governance Indicators.

## ANNEX 2.2. GROWTH ACCOUNTING METHODOLOGY

The conventional Cobb-Douglas output production function is used to calculate each factor's contribution to growth. The analysis assumes that the production function includes capital and labor. The equation for output per capita is thus

$$\frac{Y}{P} = A\frac{K^{\alpha}}{P}\frac{L^{(1-\alpha)}}{P},$$

where $Y$ is output, $K$ is the physical capital stock, $L$ is employed labor, $P$ is population, and $A$ is total factor productivity (TFP). Differentiating with respect to time, and expressing the variables as growth rates yields the following:

$$\frac{Y}{P} = A + \alpha\frac{K}{P} + \left(1 - \alpha\right)\frac{L}{P}.$$

The contribution of each factor is calculated as its growth rate multiplied by its share, with TFP as the residual. The analysis is based on the conventional assumption that the share of capital, $\alpha$, is 0.35.

The physical capital stock is adjusted for the impact of natural disasters, which inflict significant damage on Caribbean countries. Without adjusting the capital stock, the contribution of capital would be overstated, and negative effects of natural disasters would be ascribed to TFP. Following Thacker and others (2013), the perpetual inventory method is used to compute the capital stock as follows:

$$K_{t+1} = \left(1 - \delta_t\right)\left(K_t - ND_t\right) + I_t,$$

where $\delta_t$ is the depreciation rate, $I_t$ is investment, and $ND_t$ is natural disaster damage to the capital stock in year $t$.

Data for $Y$, $K$, $L$, $P$, and $\delta$ are taken from the Penn World Tables (9.0). For 2015 and 2016, the latest *World Economic Outlook* data are used to extend the series. The Emergency Events Database is the source of the disaster damage estimates, which are available in U.S. dollars.

## REFERENCES

Barro, Robert J., and Jong-Wha Lee. 2013. "A New Data Set of Educational Attainment in the World, 1950–2010." *Journal of Development Economics* 104: 184–98.

Brücker, Herbert, Stella Capuano, and Abdeslam Marfouk. 2013. "Education, Gender and International Migration: Insights from a Panel-Dataset 1980–2010." Institute for Employment Research, Nuremberg.

Cashin, Paul, Cleary Haines, and Montfort Mlachila. 2010. "Caribbean Bananas: The Macroeconomic Impact of Trade Preference Erosion." IMF Working Paper 10/59, International Monetary Fund, Washington, DC.

Cohen, Daniel, and Laura Leker. 2014. "Health and Education: Another Look with the Proper Data." Unpublished, Paris School of Economics.

Cook, R. Dennis. 1979. "Influential Observations in Linear Regression." *Journal of the American Statistical Association* 74 (365): 169–74.

Demirci, Ozge, Edward Moreno, and Joyce Cheng Wong. Forthcoming. "Does Crime Hinder Growth: An IV Approach to Latin America and the Caribbean." IMF Working Paper, International Monetary Fund, Washington, DC.

Dohnert, Sylvia, Gustavo Crespi, and Alessandro Maffioli. 2017. *Exploring Firm-Level Innovation and Productivity in Developing Countries: The Perspective of Caribbean Small States.* Washington, DC: Inter-American Development Bank.

Hausmann, Ricardo, and Bailey Klinger. 2009. "Policies for Achieving Structural Transformation in the Caribbean." Private Sector Development Discussion Paper 2, Inter-American Development Bank, Washington, DC.

Hausmann, Ricardo, and Dani Rodrik. 2006. "Doomed to Choose: Industrial Policy as Predicament." Working Paper, Center for International Development, Harvard University, Cambridge, MA.

Hayashi, Fumio. 2000. *Econometrics.* Princeton, NJ: Princeton University Press.

International Monetary Fund (IMF). 2016a. "Jamaica: Staff Report for the 2016 Article IV Consultation, Eleventh and Twelfth Reviews under the Extended Fund Facility for Jamaica." IMF Country Report 16/181, Washington, DC.

———. 2016b. "Small State's Resilience to Natural Disasters and Climate Change—Role for the IMF." IMF Policy Paper, Washington, DC.

———. 2017a. "Cluster Report—Trade Integration in Latin America and the Caribbean." IMF Country Report 17/66, Washington, DC.

———. 2017b. *Regional Economic Outlook: Western Hemisphere.* Washington, DC, April.

Jaitman, Laura. 2017. *The Cost of Crime and Violence: New Evidence and Insights in Latin America and the Caribbean.* Washington, DC: Inter-American Development Bank.

Laeven, Luc, and Fabian Valencia. 2013. "Systemic Banking Crises Database." *IMF Economic Review* 61 (2): 225–70.

Psacharopoulos, George. 1994. "Returns to Investment in Education: A Global Update." *World Development* 22 (9): 1325–43.

Ritter, Nancy 2009. "CeaseFire: A Public Health Approach to Reduce Shootings and Killings." *National Institute of Justice Journal.* Issue No. 264 (November 2009).

Ruprah, Inder J., Karl Alexander Melgarejo, and Ricardo Sierra. 2014. *Is There a Caribbean Sclerosis? Stagnating Economic Growth in the Caribbean.* Washington, DC: Inter-American Development Bank.

Thacker, Nita, Sebastian Acevedo, Roberto Perrelli, Joong Shik Kang, and Melesse Tashu. 2013. "Economic Growth." In *The Eastern Caribbean Economic and Currency Union: Macroeconomics and Financial Systems,* edited by A. Schipke, A. Cebotari, and N. Thacker, 79–94. Washington, DC: International Monetary Fund.

# Caribbean Tourism in the Global Marketplace: Trends, Drivers, and Challenges

SEBASTIAN ACEVEDO, NICOLE LAFRAMBOISE, AND JOYCE WONG

## INTRODUCTION

The Caribbean region is highly dependent on tourism. The role of tourism in economic activity in the region increased steadily following the dismantling of the system of agricultural trade preferences in the late 1980s and early 1990s, and the tourism industry has proved to be resilient even as traditional output and export sectors waned. Beginning from a base of about 4 million tourists in 1970, the region now receives more than 26 million visitors a year. The sector accounts for a large share of many economies in the region, ranging from 7 percent to 90 percent of GDP, and 32 percent as a simple average (Figure 3.1). According to the World Tourism and Travel Council, the sector also directly accounts for, on average, almost 12 percent of total employment, and indirectly for another 20 percent.

Despite tourism's growing economic importance in the Caribbean, the region's share of the global tourism market has declined steadily since the 1990s, leveling off only in 2014–15 with a recovery in arrivals. The sector experienced a prolonged slump in many countries in the Caribbean following the global financial crisis in 2008–09, contributing to weak GDP growth, high unemployment, and a widening of fiscal and external current account deficits. Since the Caribbean economies are very open and highly dependent on major advanced economies as the source of tourist arrivals, they are extremely vulnerable to external shocks. This weakness is compounded by existing macroeconomic, structural, and geographical vulnerabilities in the region arising from an overhang of public debt, relatively high cost structures, and frequent natural disasters.

An understanding of whether tourism matters for growth is necessary to an assessment of whether the deceleration in the sector is perilous for the region. Although the literature analyzing this relationship is limited, some studies clearly suggest that tourism does indeed have a positive and significant impact on growth, particularly for low- and middle-income countries (Eugenio-Martín, Martín, and Scarpa 2004). A study by Thacker, Acevedo, and Perrelli (2012) that includes a

### Figure 3.1. Tourism's Total Contribution to the Economy, 2016
*(Percent of GDP)*

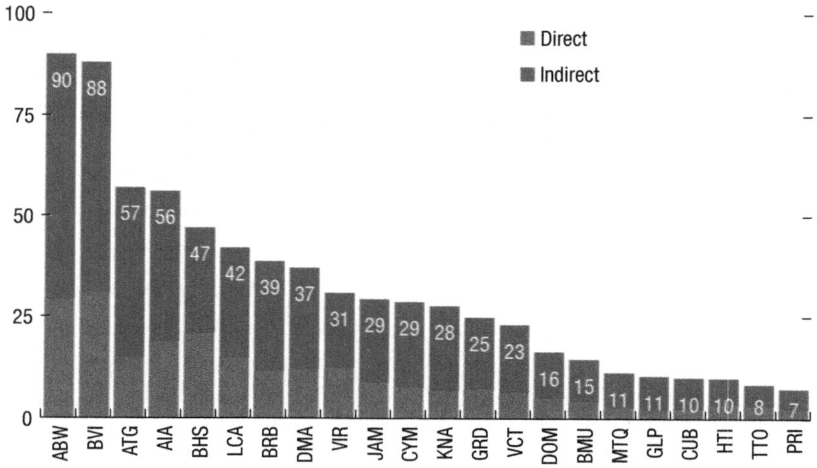

Sources: World Tourism and Travel Council; and authors' calculations.
Note: Data labels in figure use International Organization for Standardization (ISO) country codes.

large group of tourism-dependent small island states finds that tourism not only boosts economic growth, it also helps reduce growth volatility. Specifically, a 10 percent increase in tourist arrivals (as a share of a country's population) raises real per capita GDP growth by about 0.2 percentage point. Moreover, both tourist arrivals and higher-end tourism, as determined by tourists' average spending per day, are found to have a positive effect on productivity, with the former having a bigger impact. One could, therefore, argue with some conviction that the tourism sector is an important engine of growth for countries in the Caribbean.

In addition, the tourism industry also offers many backward links to the rest of the economy, such as agriculture, trade, transportation, communications, construction, and entertainment. The link between tourism and the domestic economy has not been fully developed in the Caribbean and offers immense scope for bringing about stronger, broader-based growth in tourism-dependent economies.

Against this backdrop, and with a focus on promoting growth resilience in the Caribbean, the IMF has been analyzing the performance and prospects for the tourism sector, notably by examining issues pertaining to competitiveness and the role of industry-specific factors. This chapter brings together these strands of research and their findings, which include the following:

- Relative tourism prices in the Caribbean, highlighting the cost differentiation of a beach holiday in the region compared with other beach destinations around the world

- The sensitivity of tourist arrivals and spending to price and income factors in the source markets
- The role of airlift, including an examination of how key factors of airlift supply affect U.S. tourist arrivals in the Caribbean
- The effects of hurricanes and hurricane-related damage on tourism

Based on these analyses, important policy implications are drawn to strengthen the performance of the tourism sector, as well as the overall productivity and competitiveness of tourism-based economies in the region.

Countries in the Caribbean will likely be faced with future challenges and opportunities arising from further rapprochement between the United States and Cuba, including the potential increase in U.S. tourist arrivals in Cuba, an issue that is analyzed in Chapter 4.

## STYLIZED FACTS

*Rising tourist arrivals.* The volume of tourists has more than doubled in the Caribbean, from 12 million in 1995 to 26 million tourists in 2014, fueled by steady growth in key advanced economies and strong inflows of foreign direct investment. The notable exception is The Bahamas, where tourist arrivals have remained mostly flat since the mid-1990s, largely because of the maturity of its market. The regional expansion, including in smaller countries, has taken place despite the very rapid growth experienced by the larger destinations (for example, Dominican Republic, Cancun,[1] and Cuba) over this period (Figure 3.2). The most rapid expansion took place in the 1990s, when tourist arrivals to the region increased by about 6 percent per year, and was followed by a marked slowdown in the 2000s, when the growth of tourist arrivals to the region declined sharply to 2.9 percent as the region was affected by the attacks of September 11, 2001; the dot-com bust in 2001–02; and most notably, the global financial crisis in 2008–09. Although growth in the sector has recovered in recent years, performance has been uneven (Figure 3.3)

*Declining global share.* Despite strong growth, the Caribbean share of the global tourism market has steadily declined, falling from about 2.6 percent in 1995 to about 2.1 percent in 2013 (Figure 3.4). Part of this loss reflects the surge in global tourism demand for relatively new markets such as China. However, even abstracting from this structural change (as denoted by the dotted counterfactual line in Figure 3.4, which is calculated on the assumption that tourism growth in Asia is capped at the same rate as in the rest of the world), the Caribbean's market share would have still declined. Within the Caribbean there have been significant shifts in market shares between 1995 and 2014, as Cancun, Cuba, and the Dominican Republic emerged as significant players with market share gains ranging from 5 percent to 10 percent (Figure 3.5, panel 2).

---

[1]Cancun is a large enough destination within Mexico that it competes directly with the Caribbean, particularly in the U.S. market, and thus is considered a separate market.

### Figure 3.2. Caribbean Tourist Arrivals, 1995–2014

**1. Caribbean Tourist Arrivals by Destination**
**(Millions)**

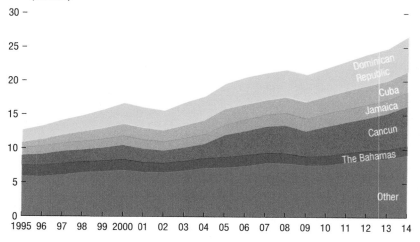

**2. Caribbean Tourist Arrivals by Source**
**(Million, average annual growth rate in parentheses)**

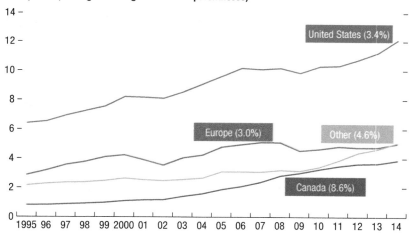

Sources: Acevedo, Alleyne, and Romeu 2016; and Caribbean Tourism Organization.
Note: In the case of destinations, "Other" includes Anguilla, Antigua and Barbuda, Aruba, Barbados, Belize, Bermuda, British Virgin Islands, Cayman Islands, Curaçao, Dominica, Grenada, Guyana, Haiti, Martinique, Montserrat, Puerto Rico, St. Kitts and Nevis, St. Lucia, Sint Maarten, St. Vincent and the Grenadines, Suriname, Turks and Caicos, and U.S. Virgin Islands. In the case of sources, "Other" includes the rest of the world.

**Figure 3.3. Caribbean Tourist Arrivals**
*(Year-over-year percent change)*

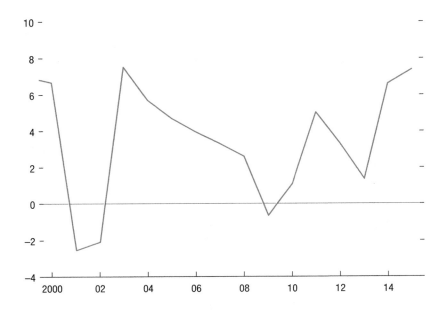

Sources: Caribbean Tourism Organization; and IMF staff estimates.

*Insufficient diversification of source markets.* Caribbean countries remain relatively undiversified in their tourism source markets (Figure 3.5, panel 1), although there have been some changes. In some countries, such as Aruba, The Bahamas, Cancun, Jamaica, and St. Kitts and Nevis, U.S. tourists make up more than 60 percent of total arrivals. The main growth market for the Caribbean has been Canada, while tourist arrivals from Europe have declined, likely owing to the prolonged recession there. Indeed, since early 2008, the share of U.S. tourists has held roughly steady, while the share of European tourists has fallen by a fourth, partially replaced by more tourists from Canada and other markets.

In addition, the lack of diversification in source markets has meant that economic cycles in advanced economies are easily transmitted to the Caribbean. This was particularly evident in the aftermath of the global financial crisis, as output contracted sharply in the United States, Canada, and the United Kingdom; unemployment in these countries remained at elevated levels for several years; and U.S. household net wealth dropped sharply. In 2009, 23 out of 28 destinations in the Caribbean experienced an average decline in tourist arrivals of about 8 percent. The only exceptions were Cuba, the Dominican Republic, Guyana, Haiti, and Jamaica, which managed to weather the crisis with price cuts. Although by 2010 most of the countries saw a recovery—with only 9 out of 28 destinations

**Figure 3.4. Caribbean Tourist Arrivals, Market Share**
*(Percent)*

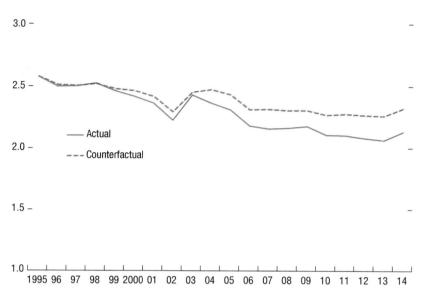

Sources: World Bank, World Development Indicators; and IMF staff calculations.

still suffering from the decline in demand—tourist arrivals remained weak until 2014. Coincidentally, the decline in the number of U.S. flights to the Caribbean following the financial crisis did not begin to change course until 2012. The global recession also left a more profound and lasting impact as weaker tourism demand pushed hotel occupancy rates down and hindered new investment.

*Relatively high pricing.* Tourism is a competitive market, and relative price comparisons indicate that vacationing in the Caribbean is substantially more expensive than in other parts of the world.[2] Based on an index—called the Week-at-the-Beach Index—LaFramboise and others (2014) show that the nominal cost of an average one-week beach holiday in the Caribbean (dark red bars in Figure 3.6) is higher than elsewhere in the world. This result is consistent across different data sources and indices (LaFramboise 2016).[3] To the extent the Caribbean

---

[2]LaFramboise and others (2014) and LaFramboise (2016) construct an index using online data from travel search engines such as Expedia. The index was inspired by the *Economist*'s "Big Mac Index," but instead of measuring hamburger prices, it compiles the prices of a basket of typical expenditures consumed during a beach holiday: hotel rates, taxi fares, beverages, and meals, excluding air travel. The sample includes many beach destinations in the Caribbean, Latin America, Asia, and Europe, and is constructed for three-star hotels and for a larger sample of three- to five-star hotel averages. Different indices were constructed for robustness, all of which showed consistency and fairly strong correlation.

[3]The index controls for "all-inclusive" hotels by ensuring a comparable share across markets.

## Figure 3.5. Evolution of the Caribbean Tourist Market, 1995–2014

### 1. Caribbean Tourist Arrivals by Source

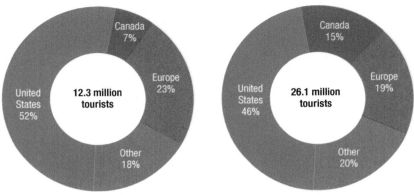

### 2. Caribbean Tourist Arrivals by Destination

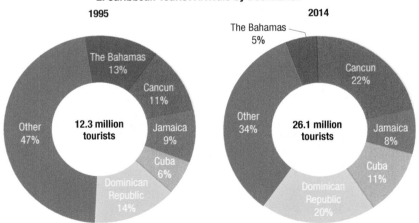

Sources: Acevedo, Alleyne, and Romeu 2016; and Caribbean Tourism Organization.
Note: In the case of destinations, "Other" includes Anguilla, Antigua and Barbuda, Aruba, Barbados, Belize, Bermuda, British Virgin Islands, Cayman Islands, Curaçao, Dominica, Grenada, Guyana, Haiti, Martinique, Montserrat, Puerto Rico, St. Kitts and Nevis, St. Lucia, Sint Maarten, St. Vincent and the Grenadines, Suriname, Turks and Caicos, and U.S. Virgin Islands. In the case of sources, "Other" includes the rest of the world.

### Figure 3.6. January 2017: Week-at-the-Beach Index—Expedia
*(Three- to five-star hotel average; The Bahamas = 100)*

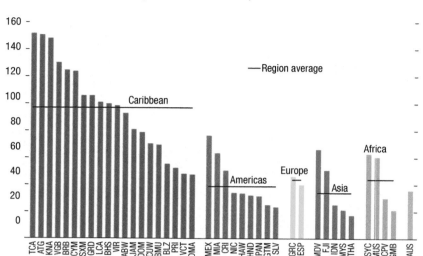

Sources: UNDP/UN Daily Subsistence Allowance Rates; and IMF staff calculations.
Note: Room rate: see https://www.travelocity.com, https://www.trivago.com; taxi, meals, water, beer, coffee: see https://www.numbeo.com/cost-of-living/ and https://www.worldcabfares.com/index.php. Total cost without tax = 7 x (3-star hotel) + 2 x (average taxi ride from main international airport to capital city) + 7 x (1 inexpensive meal + 2 mid-range meals) + 7 x (2 liters water) + 7 x (0.5 liter beer) + 7 x (coffee). Data labels in figure use International Organization for Standardization (ISO) country codes.

remains an attractive tourist destination, one could conclude that nonprice factors, such as superior beaches, clearer water, and proximity to its main market (the United States), make the marginal benefit of a beach holiday in the Caribbean high enough to exceed the elevated cost of a holiday there. However, the higher prices for Caribbean destinations have undoubtedly affected the region's competitiveness and capacity to attract more tourists, and could explain, in part, the declining global market share.

The Week-at-the-Beach index also shows that both Cuba and the Dominican Republic offer considerably lower cost vacations than the rest of the Caribbean, with costs comparable to those of Central America. This affordability not only makes both countries tough competitors in the regional tourism market, but may also pose challenges to the rest of the region if the United States decides to allow tourism travel to Cuba (see Chapter 4).

*Other risk factors.* The Caribbean is one of the most vulnerable regions in the world to natural disasters. In fact, 15 out of the top 25 countries worldwide with the most tropical cyclones per square kilometer are Caribbean islands (Figure 3.7). Hurricanes have caused major damage to hotel facilities and disrupted tourist arrivals, particularly since tourism infrastructure is usually concentrated in

**Figure 3.7. Natural Disasters, 1950–2014**
*(Number of disasters per 1,000 square kilometers)*

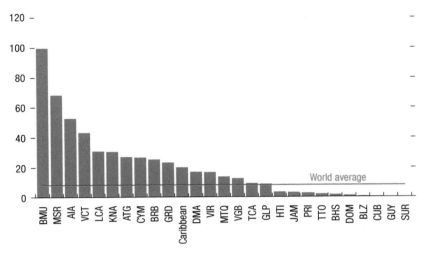

Sources: EM-DAT; and authors' calculations.
Note: Data labels in figure use International Organization for Standardization (ISO) country codes.

coastal areas, which are most exposed to hurricanes and floods. For example, when Hurricane Ivan hit Grenada in 2004, it damaged most hotels, while Hurricane Omar in 2008 essentially wiped out tourism in Nevis by damaging the main hotel on the island. In 2012, Hurricane Sandy caused severe disruptions to hotel operations in The Bahamas.

Given the declining global share of Caribbean tourism, the deceleration of the sector during the past decade, risks from weak diversification of source markets, and the role of natural disasters, a better understanding of tourism drivers, including the potential impact of economic cycles in source markets combined with the effects of domestic supply factors, is important to developing the right policy actions to tap the full potential of the sector.

## TOURISM IN THE CARIBBEAN—DEMAND AND SUPPLY FACTORS

Building on the work by Thacker, Acevedo, and Perrelli (2012) on the contribution of tourism to growth in the Caribbean, recent IMF research has focused on assessing the demand factors influencing tourist arrivals, as well as possible supply factors. Specifically, LaFramboise and others (2014) examine the factors that influence tourist arrivals to the Caribbean and whether these factors have changed since the 2008–09 global financial crisis.

They study the effects on tourist arrivals of demand variables like prices—based on the real effective exchange rate calculated using tourism source market weights—income and employment in the main source market countries; supply variables, such as the number of hotel beds in the region and the number of airlines flying to the Caribbean; and exogenous factors, such as natural disasters and crime. This chapter uses data for 16 Caribbean countries to estimate a dynamic panel regression with tourism arrivals and tourism expenditure from 2000 to the end of 2015 as the dependent variables. The sample is divided into "higher-end" and "lower-cost" destinations—as defined by the share of four- to five-star hotels in each market—to differentiate elasticities across destinations.

Consistent with earlier studies, the analysis shows that income factors in source markets play an important role in affecting tourist arrivals and expenditures.[4] Specific findings are provided below, with a focus on arrivals, for which data quality is superior relative to expenditure data.

### Estimated Price and Income Elasticities

An increase in price leads to a decline in arrivals, except in higher-end destinations. A 1.0 percent appreciation of the tourism-weighted real exchange rate is associated with a 0.17 percent decrease in arrivals in the baseline specification. In contrast, tourism arrivals and expenditure in higher-end tourism destinations are not sensitive to price.[5]

The analysis also shows that arrivals in the Caribbean are highly elastic to economic conditions in source countries. For example, a decrease in income or increase in unemployment in source country markets leads to an important decline in tourist arrivals. A 1.0 percent increase in the tourism-weighted unemployment rate in the source markets (which proxies the income effect) implies a 1.8 percent decrease in arrivals during 2000–15. The impact on arrivals is almost double (3.2 percent decline) in those markets deemed higher-end destinations (Annex Tables 3.1.1 and 3.1.2).[6]

---

[4]These estimates update those presented in LaFramboise and others (2014). The panel data in the original working paper covered the period to the end of 2013 but have been updated with data to the end of 2015. Compared with the 2014 estimates, elasticities are similar, with a marginal increase in price sensitivity in aggregate, and a marginal decrease in income sensitivity. This outcome appears to be consistent with the rebound in tourism flows those years and with improved economic conditions in some key source markets.

[5]Two criteria are used to classify the higher-end destinations: (1) the number of four- and five-star hotels as a share of the total (Anguilla, The Bahamas, Barbados, St. Kitts and Nevis), and (2) GDP per capita above US$15,000 (same group plus Trinidad and Tobago). The remainder in the sample of 16 countries are classified as lower cost.

[6]Endogeneity issues arising from the reverse causality between tourist arrivals and some of the explanatory variables were addressed using the Arellano-Bond estimation.

## Other Factors Influencing Tourist Arrivals and Expenditure

The panel regression incorporated a vector of time-varying explanatory variables including two tourism-supply factors—the number of airlines serving the Caribbean and the number of hotel rooms—and other factors including homicide rates in destination countries (a proxy for crime risks), a hurricane dummy, and a dummy for the September 11, 2001, terrorist attacks in the United States. The number of airlines was found to have a positive and statistically significant impact on arrivals (and expenditure), but the number of hotel rooms was found to have no statistically significant impact on arrivals or expenditure, even after controlling for reverse causality.

Other factors, such as hurricanes (see "Tourism's Vulnerability to Natural Disasters" below) and the September 11, 2001, terrorist attacks in the United States, were found to have negative and significant impacts on tourist arrivals and expenditures, but crime was found to have no significant impact. This outcome could reflect the perception that beach resorts in the Caribbean are physically well protected and secured, which mitigates tourists' exposure to crime risks.

## Implications

Policymakers could usefully integrate the sensitivity of tourist arrivals to economic conditions in source markets into their macroeconomic and fiscal planning frameworks. Efforts to diversify tourism markets would reduce vulnerability to the key advanced economies, which tend to follow the same economic cycle. In addition, risk-mitigation strategies such as regional coordination and better marketing of the "Caribbean brand" to make it attractive to a wider audience could help increase growth and the region's global market share.

In the higher-end destinations, where price does not appear to affect arrivals, countries should ensure that the physical plant of the tourism sector (for example, hotels, grounds, restaurants) and services remain of a quality commensurate with the higher-end brand. This requirement highlights the importance of ensuring that the supporting infrastructure and institutions provide quality public goods and services desired by higher-end tourists. In the lower-cost destinations, where arrivals are more price sensitive, the focus could be on reducing costs, particularly for labor and energy. The exchange rate could also be a useful shock-adjustment mechanism to help countries maintain or regain competitiveness (for countries with flexible exchange rate regimes), with due consideration to its broader economic and financial implications.

## The Role of Airlift in the Caribbean

Supply factors are a crucial determinant of tourism flows to the Caribbean. One such critical supply factor is airlift, which, given the small size of the Caribbean islands and their geographical separation from their large markets, plays a key role in connecting tourists with Caribbean destinations. Using a broad concept of airlift that includes supply factors such as the number of flights, seats, airlines, and departure cities, this section identifies airlift's effect on U.S. tourist arrivals to the Caribbean.[7,8]

Intuitively, better airlift between the United States and a Caribbean destination would promote tourism, but it is not immediately obvious which airlift factor contributes the most. Understanding this issue is important, not only because it has a large impact on tourism-intensive island economies, but also because Caribbean countries have at times struggled to get their desired level of airlift services, which has affected the region's tourist arrivals growth. Countries have resorted to incentive schemes for airlines involving minimum seat or revenue guarantees or marketing support in source markets for routes and airlines to a particular destination, all of which carry fiscal costs in these countries, many of which are already in a vulnerable fiscal situation.

Some interesting stylized facts emerge illustrating issues surrounding the U.S.-Caribbean airlift market. First, as expected, larger destinations (such as Cancun, the Dominican Republic, Jamaica, and The Bahamas) enjoy more flights, from more airlines, with direct connections to several U.S. cities (see Annex Table 3.2.1). However, after controlling for a country's land size or its hotel room capacity, the smaller islands have more airlift supply than the larger destinations (see Annex Table 3.2.2). In other words, despite their limited size and markets, the tourism sectors of the smaller islands appear to be adequately serviced by the airline industry, when compared with their larger neighbors.

Miami is the main U.S. hub for travel to the Caribbean, accounting for 20 percent of flights. American Airlines is the primary airline serving the Caribbean, accounting for 20 percent of flights to the region (Figure 3.8). Although the air travel market to the Caribbean region as a whole is competitive with regard to the number of airlines, some individual destinations have high market concentration in a few airlines. Moreover, air traffic connections with the United States to most of the smaller destinations are highly concentrated, leaving them vulnerable to service changes in a few airlines.[9]

## Estimation Results

To identify the effects of the different airlift supply factors on U.S. tourist arrivals to each Caribbean destination, a structural vector autoregression model (SVAR) is used. The SVAR model enables the disentangling of the reverse causality between tourist arrivals and airlift factors in which tourist arrivals are not only

---

[7]The analysis presented in this section is based on Acevedo and others (2016).

[8]The intraregional airline transportation market is also of great regional importance, particularly for tourism destinations that would like to promote more intraregional tourism. It is also important for developing multicountry destinations that require well-functioning regional air connectivity. A detailed analysis of this topic can be found in CDB (2015).

[9]The countries with the highest market concentration are Antigua and Barbuda, Barbados, Belize, Dominica, Grenada, St. Kitts and Nevis, and St. Lucia.

## Figure 3.8. U.S.-Caribbean Flights by Departing Cities and Airlines, 1990–2014

### 1. Airline Carriers
(Thousands)

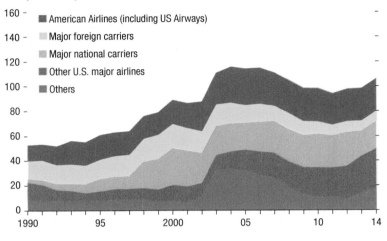

### 2. Departure Cities
(Thousands)

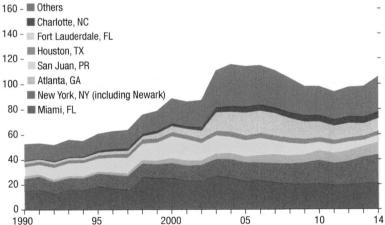

Sources: Air Carrier Financial Reports from United States Department of Transportation; and authors' calculations.

affected by the supply of airlift services but also have an impact on how much airlift the airlines are willing to provide.[10]

The results (Figure 3.9) for the panel SVAR show that all four airlift supply factors have a positive and significant impact on tourist arrivals to the Caribbean.

- The number of flights has the largest impact and seems to be the most effective way to increase arrivals to a country. A 1.0 percent increase in the number of flights to a destination instantly increases tourist arrivals by 0.3 percent, and the cumulative increase of tourist arrivals is estimated to be about 1 percent after 10 months.

- The airlift factor with the smallest impact on tourism is the number of U.S. cities with nonstop flights to the Caribbean.

To study possible differences across countries, individual countries' SVARs were also estimated. Table 3.1 shows the response of tourist arrivals to each airlift factor.

- For individual countries, the number of flights is once again the most important factor influencing tourism flows—it has not only the largest impact, but also the most persistent and significant effect on tourism.

- The other three demand factors are important and significant in only some destinations. For instance, increasing the number of airlines has an important bearing on tourist arrivals in St. Kitts and Nevis, but not in most other countries (except Bermuda and Cayman Islands).

- The least important airlift factor is the number of airlines, with the lowest impact on tourist arrivals and the lowest significance across countries.

This section also studies the dynamic effects between the variables using the SVAR. For example, although the number of airlines has a limited effect on tourist arrivals in most countries, adding more airlines results in an expansion of the number of cities and flights, which indirectly increases tourist arrivals. However, this connection appears to be short lived. It is interesting to note that an increase in the number of departure cities does not appear to increase the number of

---

[10]A full description of the identification strategy is in Acevedo and others (2016). The results presented are robust to different ordering of the variables and do not depend on the identification strategy. While tourist arrivals are assumed to be contemporaneously affected by all airlift supply variables (number of flights, seats, airlines, and departure cities to the Caribbean), changes in tourist arrivals will only affect airlift factors with a lag because short-term decisions to change flight schedules, airplane size, or departure cities are costly for airlines. Therefore, it is assumed that airlines adjust their supply to a destination to changes in demand only with a lag. As a first response, airlines will fly with more empty seats or will fill them to adjust to unexpected changes in demand, rather than changing airplanes or routes to maintain market share and retain customers. The model also controls for demand determinants (that is, U.S. unemployment), natural disasters, and the September 11, 2001, attacks that are exogenous to the model and are treated as such. The data on U.S. tourists are from the Caribbean Tourism Organization, and the airlift data are from the Air Carrier Financial Reports from the U.S. Department of Transportation. Unfortunately, the data from the U.S. Department of Transportation do not include information on airfares, an important factor in consumers' tourism decisions.

## Figure 3.9. Response of Tourist Arrivals to Different Shocks
*(Benchmark specification, panel SVAR)*

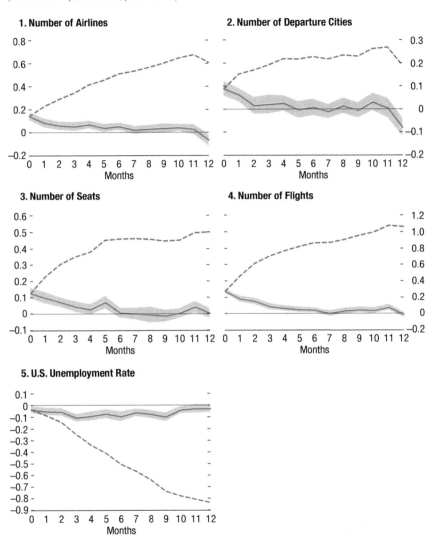

Source: Acevedo and others 2016, calculations based on the panel SVAR.
Note: The blue line represents the percentage deviation from the steady state of the response variable (tourist arrivals) to a 1 percent positive shock of the impulse variable. The shaded area is the 90 percent confidence interval and the red dashed line shows the cumulative percentage change of tourist arrivals. SVAR = structural vector autoregression.

**Table 3.1. Heterogeneity in the Response of Tourist Arrivals across Countries**

| | Immediate Impact of a 1% Shock to | | | | Cumulative Impact (Fifth month) of a 1% Shock to | | | |
|---|---|---|---|---|---|---|---|---|
| | Airlines | Cities | Flights | Seats | Airlines | Cities | Flights | Seats |
| **Average** | 0.11 | 0.11 | 0.37 | 0.13 | 0.27 | 0.29 | 1.19 | 0.51 |
| Antigua and Barbuda | 0.02 | 0.12 | 0.19 | 0.23 | 0.05 | −0.12 | 0.38 | 0.51 |
| Aruba | −0.04 | 0.21 | 0.35 | 0.18 | 0.17 | 0.90 | 1.68 | 0.54 |
| The Bahamas | 0.08 | −0.04 | 0.24 | 0.21 | 0.09 | −0.30 | 0.11 | 0.47 |
| Barbados | 0.17 | 0.12 | 0.31 | 0.17 | 0.00 | 0.57 | 0.85 | 0.60 |
| Belize | 0.06 | 0.31 | 0.14 | 0.07 | 0.29 | 1.13 | 0.94 | 0.31 |
| Bermuda | 0.12 | 0.17 | 0.48 | 0.02 | 0.51 | 0.27 | 0.84 | −0.09 |
| Cancun | 0.33 | 0.19 | 1.55 | −0.03 | 0.21 | 0.31 | 3.97 | 0.59 |
| Cayman Islands | 0.30 | 0.10 | 0.52 | 0.21 | 0.73 | −1.07 | 2.49 | 1.01 |
| Dominica | 0.02 | −0.17 | 0.19 | 0.12 | 0.21 | −0.08 | 0.43 | 0.46 |
| Dominican Republic | 0.09 | 0.10 | 0.25 | 0.14 | −0.13 | 0.58 | 1.06 | 1.10 |
| Grenada | 0.06 | 0.03 | 0.20 | 0.00 | 0.40 | 0.33 | 0.92 | 0.17 |
| Jamaica | −0.04 | 0.01 | 0.34 | 0.05 | −0.11 | 0.02 | 0.94 | 0.28 |
| St. Kitts and Nevis | 0.34 | 0.17 | 0.21 | 0.16 | 0.97 | 0.50 | 1.03 | 0.36 |
| St. Lucia | 0.06 | 0.19 | 0.21 | 0.29 | 0.45 | 1.07 | 0.97 | 0.80 |

Source: Authors' calculations based on country-specific structural vector autoregressions.
Note: The first four columns show the immediate response of tourist arrivals to a shock in the four airlift supply variables. The number in the cells indicates the immediate percent change in tourist arrivals after the shock. The green color indicates the significance. Dark green indicates that the response is different from zero for more than four periods; the lighter green for more than two periods.

flights. This result suggests that opening routes from new U.S. departure cities does not increase the overall frequency of flights to a destination because airlines instead shift flights from established routes to new ones, leaving the total number of flights unchanged.

## Implications

To boost tourist arrivals, policymakers across the Caribbean would benefit from focusing their efforts on increasing the number of flights to the region. Although all the other airlift factors have positive impacts on tourist arrivals, increasing the number of flights provides the most benefit. The implication is not that countries should limit themselves to only one airline with frequent flights—variety and diversification are also important and the results support that. However, given the choice between negotiating with an airline already serving the island to increase the frequency of flights or with a new airline to initiate flights to the island, the analysis indicates that countries would be better served by adding one more flight from an existing airline.

This finding is highly relevant since many destinations, particularly the smaller ones, provide subsidies or incentives of some kind to entice airlines to their islands. Without jeopardizing market competition, governments may find fiscal savings by negotiating with a smaller pool of airlines for more frequent flights rather than seeking to increase the number of airlines and direct connections.

# TOURISM'S VULNERABILITY TO NATURAL DISASTERS

The Caribbean countries, because of their size and geographical location, are exposed not only to policy and economic shifts in the United States and other large economies, but also to natural disasters, mostly hurricanes. This section discusses the economic impact of hurricanes, notably on tourist arrivals.

## The Costs of Disasters

Weather has a direct impact on tourists' decisions, particularly for the Caribbean's "sun, sand, and sea" type of tourism. For example, Forster and others (2012) find that 40 percent of surveyed tourists in Anguilla considered the hurricane season when making their travel plans. Not surprisingly, they also found that tourists are less willing to travel when the probability of a hurricane strike increases, or when the hurricane strength of a potential storm increases. Sookram (2009) estimates the effect of weather variables on tourist arrivals in the Caribbean, finding that higher average temperature and precipitation in a destination adversely affects tourism flows.

Hurricanes have a devastating effect on Caribbean economies. They destroy buildings and roads, damage crops, disrupt businesses, and upset tourism services. Since most of the tourism infrastructure in the Caribbean is located near the coast, and therefore highly vulnerable to hurricanes, the economic impact is enduring. For example, after Hurricane Ivan hit Grenada in September 2004, tourist arrivals fell by almost 34 percent in the following 12 months. More generally, LaFramboise and others (2014) find that a hurricane reduces tourist arrivals by 1.2 to 2.0 percent in the year of the disaster. Previous work by Granvorka and Strobl (2013) shows similar results, indicating that an average hurricane reduces tourist arrivals by 2 percent.

Acevedo and others (2016) distinguish between the effects of moderate and severe natural disasters (mostly hurricanes). A disaster is considered "moderate" if more than 0.01 percent of the population is directly affected, or "severe" if 1 percent or more of the population is affected. Figure 3.10 presents the responses of tourist arrivals to a natural disaster shock.[11] As expected, countries have different responses depending on the severity of the disasters they experience.

- In countries with more frequent and severe disasters, such as Antigua and Barbuda, The Bahamas, Grenada, and St. Kitts and Nevis, tourist arrivals drop significantly following a disaster. In the month that a severe disaster strikes, the immediate drop in tourist arrivals ranges from 25 to 50 percent relative to its average monthly growth, and on average the cumulative

---

[11]The information on natural disasters comes from the International Disaster Database. For a disaster to be included in the database, at least one of the following criteria must be met: (1) at least 10 people were killed, (2) at least 100 people were affected, or (3) a state of emergency was declared or a call for international assistance was made.

**Figure 3.10. Response of Tourist Arrivals to a Natural Disaster Shock**
*(Percent)*

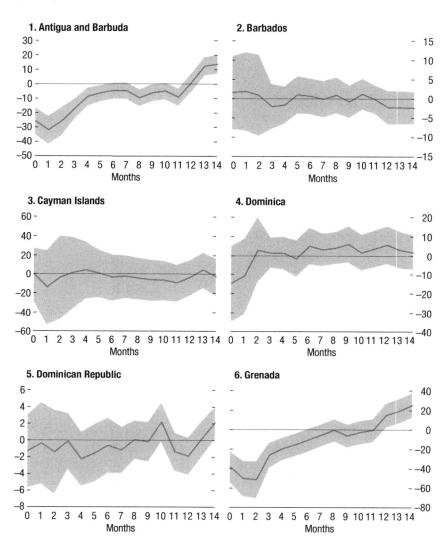

Source: Acevedo and others 2016, based on country-specific SVARs.
Note: Impulse: dummy variable for natural disasters. The shaded area is the 90 percent confidence interval. SVAR = structural vector autoregression.

**Figure 3.10.** *(continued)*
*(Percent)*

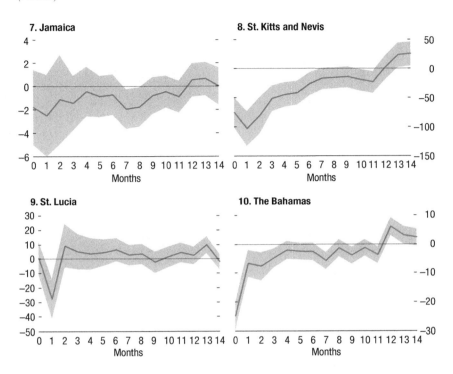

Source: Acevedo and others 2016, based on country-specific SVARs.
Note: Impulse: dummy variable for natural disasters. The shaded area is the 90 percent confidence interval. SVAR = structural vector autoregression.

decline in tourist arrivals during the next year exceeds 90 percent following a severe disaster, compared with a no-disaster situation. The sector usually starts to grow again only 10 to 12 months after the disaster.

• In contrast, in countries that commonly experience moderate disasters the impact on arrivals does not seem to be significant. This is the case for Barbados, the Cayman Islands, the Dominican Republic, and Jamaica, which tend to experience more moderate disasters.

## Implications

Natural disasters can have devastating socioeconomic effects. They damage or destroy physical structures and depress economic activity. The adverse effects, while directly felt by the tourism industry, have a broader and profound impact on the macroeconomy and growth. Thus, policy implications go beyond the tourism sector and include broader macroeconomic management and structural measures.

In a region that is highly susceptible to natural disasters and severe weather events such as the Caribbean, it is paramount that measures be taken to adapt to these vulnerabilities. These measures could involve, for example, upgrades to infrastructure, better zoning, improved insurance coverage, and better access to finance, especially for small businesses, to reduce the impact of disasters both on local communities and on the tourism sector. A detailed discussion of the broader effects of natural disasters and the associated policy recommendations is in Chapter 5, including improving economic activity and the countries' fiscal positions.

## CONCLUSIONS AND POLICY IMPLICATIONS

Steady growth in advanced economies and strong inflows of foreign direct invest-ment have helped tourism become a key growth engine in the Caribbean since the 1980s. However, since the 2008–09 global financial crisis and the ensuing collapse in external demand, the recovery in the tourism sector has been uneven across countries. With the Caribbean's relatively weak growth rates, declining share in global tourism, and exposure to natural disasters, it is now more import-ant than ever for stakeholders in the region to understand the drivers of and risks to tourism, such that policies could be geared toward accelerating growth in the sector and recovering some of the lost ground in the share of Caribbean tourism in the global market. Having a strong tourism sector and developing its backward linkages to the rest of the economy—an area for future research—would further support tourism as a strong source of growth.

The chapter highlights four key drivers of tourism in the Caribbean: (1) pricing and cost structures, which are high and undermine competitiveness in the global market for tourism; (2) income in source markets and expenditures, suggesting tourism recovery in the region will continue to be fragile until the main markets (United States, Canada, United Kingdom) experience stronger economic growth; (3) the number of flights serving the region, which has a positive effect on tourist arrivals; and (4) vulnerability to natural disasters, which entails significant costs to the industry and engenders slow recovery from disasters.

Given the potential for tourism to be a viable contributor to growth for the region, how should countries respond to build the sector? In the short term, countries should revisit options to maximize the number of flights serving their countries, which would also help minimize associated fiscal costs.

In the longer term, policymakers should focus on significant structural reforms to improve competitiveness, strengthen resilience, and increase the quality of the tourism product:

- Ensuring that the supporting infrastructure and institutions provide quality public services and security will foster continued arrivals to higher-end destinations. Focus on reducing energy, labor, and food costs through a more diversified energy matrix, labor laws that encourage labor market flexibility, and the strengthening of domestic sector links to hotels will improve competitiveness without resorting to fiscal incentives. Domestic sector links will help develop other economic sectors (for example, agriculture), which, in time, could become growth drivers themselves.

- Stronger physical infrastructure would not only help ensure quality while lowering costs but would also help strengthen resilience to natural disasters. Improving building codes and preparedness and better zoning laws will help countries weather large storms and speed up recovery. Improving access to finance (including lower transaction costs and better access to credit) and strengthening financial sector soundness would help improve businesses' safety nets and help them handle reconstruction costs.

- Diversifying markets (especially to emerging markets) and reducing reliance on the United States will greatly help the region protect against the longer-term impact of Cuba's development. In this regard, tapping into new markets and historical links, together with diaspora resources, could help provide a much-needed boost.

## ANNEX 3.1. REGRESSION RESULTS

Annex Table 3.1.1. Determinants of Tourism Arrivals and Expenditure

| Variables | 2014 WP Baseline | Updated Baseline | 2014 WP Baseline | Updated Baseline |
|---|---|---|---|---|
| | Ln(tourism arrivals) | | Ln(tourism expenditure) | |
| ΔLn(real exchange rate) | −0.158*** | −0.172*** | −0.101*** | −0.115** |
| | (0.010) | (0.016) | (0.003) | (0.038) |
| ΔTourism-Weighted Unemployment Rate | −2.081*** | −1.803*** | −3.707*** | −3.230*** |
| | (0.429) | (0.483) | (0.487) | (0.244) |
| ΔHurricane | −0.0138** | −0.0123* | −0.0226** | −0.0203** |
| | (0.006) | (0.007) | (0.008) | (0.008) |
| ΔSeptember 11 Terrorist Attacks | −0.0229*** | −0.0215*** | −0.0036*** | −0.0348*** |
| | (0.006) | (0.007) | (0.011) | (0.011) |
| ΔHomicide Rate | −0.0011 | −0.00113 | −0.00155 | −0.0015 |
| | (0.001) | (0.001) | (0.001) | (0.001) |
| ΔLn(number of airlines) | 0.0846*** | 0.0693*** | 0.0960*** | 0.0836*** |
| | (0.018) | (0.014) | (0.034) | (0.022) |
| ΔLn(number of hotel rooms) | −0.0104 | 0.000757 | 0.0365 | 0.0802 |
| | (0.066) | (0.065) | (0.007) | (0.068) |
| Observations | 141 | 167 | 141 | 171 |
| $R^2$ | 0.345 | 0.318 | 0.345 | 0.209 |

Note: "2014 WP" refers to LaFramboise and others 2014.
Robust standard errors in parentheses.
*** $p < 0.01$, ** $p < 0.05$, * $p < 0.1$

### Annex Table 3.1.2. High-End versus Lower-Cost Destinations

| Variables | Updated Higher End | Updated Lower Cost | Updated Higher End | Updated Lower Cost |
|---|---|---|---|---|
| | Ln(arrivals) | Ln(arrivals) | Ln(expenditure) | Ln(expenditure) |
| ΔLn(real exchange rate) | −0.142 | −0.162*** | −0.224* | −0.109** |
| | (0.069) | (0.016) | (0.086) | (0.041) |
| ΔTourism-Weighted Unemployment Rate | −3.365*** | −1.243*** | −2.692** | −3.141*** |
| | (0.284) | (0.223) | (0.530) | (0.416) |
| ΔHurricane | −0.0068 | −0.00968 | −0.00232 | −0.0168 |
| | (0.006) | (0.012) | (0.016) | (0.018) |
| ΔSeptember 11 Terrorist Attacks | −0.0354 | −0.0186*** | −0.0243 | −0.0325** |
| | (0.016) | (0.006) | (0.043) | (0.010) |
| ΔHomicide Rate | 0.000322 | −0.00199 | 0.00293 | −0.00223 |
| | (0.001) | (0.001) | (0.004) | (0.002) |
| ΔLn(number of airlines) | 0.0205 | 0.0704*** | 0.1 | 0.0848** |
| | (0.049) | (0.017) | (0.090) | (0.027) |
| ΔLn(number of hotel rooms) | −0.207** | 0.103* | 0.0473 | 0.0805 |
| | (0.051) | (0.053) | (0.049) | (0.138) |
| Observations | 52 | 115 | 51 | 120 |
| $R^2$ | 0.529 | 0.366 | 0.275 | 0.209 |

Note: Robust standard errors in parentheses.
*** $p < 0.01$, ** $p < 0.05$, * $p < 0.1$

# ANNEX 3.2 AIRLIFT TO THE CARIBBEAN

### Annex Table 3.2.1. U.S.-Caribbean Airlift Availability, 2014

| Country | ISO Three-Letter Code | Number of Flights | Number of Passengers | Plane Size (Average) | Departing U.S. Cities | Number of Airlines | Vacancy Rate |
|---|---|---|---|---|---|---|---|
| Antigua and Barbuda | ATG | 1,028 | 119,732 | 153 | 4 | 4 | 24 |
| Aruba | ABW | 4,822 | 646,257 | 159 | 10 | 9 | 16 |
| The Bahamas | BHS | 20,920 | 1,286,118 | 86 | 18 | 18 | 28 |
| Barbados | BRB | 1,306 | 197,440 | 178 | 3 | 4 | 15 |
| Belize | BLZ | 2,287 | 248,496 | 147 | 7 | 4 | 26 |
| Bermuda | BMU | 2,920 | 283,667 | 139 | 6 | 5 | 30 |
| Cancun | CAN | 25,360 | 3,426,071 | 160 | 33 | 14 | 16 |
| Cayman Islands | CYM | 4,005 | 400,035 | 139 | 11 | 6 | 28 |
| Dominica | DMA | 388 | 9,608 | 36 | 1 | 1 | 32 |
| Dominican Republic | DOM | 25,684 | 3,019,154 | 150 | 20 | 17 | 22 |
| Grenada | GRD | 440 | 54,427 | 154 | 2 | 3 | 19 |
| Jamaica | JAM | 13,327 | 1,591,018 | 151 | 16 | 12 | 21 |
| St. Kitts and Nevis | KNA | 1,621 | 84,198 | 74 | 5 | 6 | 30 |
| St. Lucia | LCA | 1,163 | 160,070 | 162 | 5 | 5 | 15 |

Sources: Air Carrier Financial Reports from United States Department of Transportation; and authors' calculations.
Note: The vacancy rate is defined as empty seats as percent of all seats. ISO = International Organization for Standardization.

## Annex Table 3.2.2. Rankings of U.S. Airlift Availability in the Caribbean Controlling by Size (1990–2014)

**Ranking of Airlift Availability per Land Area (km²)**

| Ranking | Flights | Seats | Passengers | Airlines | Cities | Combined |
|---|---|---|---|---|---|---|
| 1 | BMU | BMU | BMU | BMU | BMU | BMU |
| 2 | ABW | ABW | ABW | GRD | ABW | ABW |
| 3 | GRD | GRD | GRD | ABW | GRD | GRD |
| 4 | CYM | CYM | CYM | CYM | CYM | CYM |
| 5 | CAN | AIA | AIA | KNA | KNA | AIA |
| 6 | AIA | CAN | CAN | AIA | CAN | CAN |
| 7 | KNA | KNA | KNA | ATG | AIA | KNA |
| 8 | BRB | BRB | BRB | BRB | BRB | BRB |
| 9 | ATG | ATG | ATG | CAN | ATG | ATG |
| 10 | LCA | LCA | LCA | LCA | LCA | LCA |
| 11 | BHS | BHS | BHS | DMA | BHS | BHS |
| 12 | JAM | JAM | JAM | BHS | JAM | JAM |
| 13 | DMA | DMA | DMA | JAM | DMA | DMA |
| 14 | DOM | DOM | DOM | DOM | DOM | DOM |
| 15 | BLZ | BLZ | BLZ | BLZ | BLZ | BLZ |

**Ranking of Airlift Availability per Hotel Room**

| Ranking | Flights | Seats | Passengers | Airlines | Cities | Combined |
|---|---|---|---|---|---|---|
| 1 | BHS | BHS | BHS | KNA | KNA | BHS |
| 2 | BMU | BMU | BMU | BMU | BMU | BMU |
| 3 | AIA | AIA | AIA | AIA | CYM | AIA |
| 4 | KNA | KNA | KNA | CYM | ABW | KNA |
| 5 | CYM | CYM | CYM | ATG | BHS | CYM |
| 6 | CAN | CAN | CAN | GRD | AIA | CAN |
| 7 | ABW | ABW | ABW | ABW | CAN | ABW |
| 8 | DMA | DMA | DMA | DMA | ATG | DMA |
| 9 | ATG | ATG | ATG | BHS | GRD | ATG |
| 10 | JAM | JAM | JAM | LCA | DMA | JAM |
| 11 | BLZ | BLZ | BLZ | BLZ | LCA | BLZ |
| 12 | BRB | BRB | BRB | CAN | BLZ | BRB |
| 13 | LCA | LCA | LCA | BRB | BRB | LCA |
| 14 | GRD | GRD | GRD | JAM | JAM | GRD |
| 15 | DOM | DOM | DOM | DOM | DOM | DOM |

Sources: Air Carrier Financial Reports from United States Department of Transportation; Caribbean Tourism Organization; and authors' calculations.
Note: The combined ranking is a simple average of the rankings for each airlift factor, that is, flights, seats, and so on. Countries are indicated by International Organization for Standardization country codes.

# REFERENCES

Acevedo, Sebastian, Trevor Alleyne, and Rafael Romeu. 2017. "Revisiting the Potential Impact to the Rest of the Caribbean from Opening US-Cuba Tourism." IMF Working Paper 17/100, International Monetary Fund, Washington, DC.

Acevedo, Sebastian, Lu Han, Marie Kim, and Nicole LaFramboise. 2016. "Flying to Paradise: The Role of Airlift in the Caribbean Tourism Industry." IMF Working Paper 16/33, International Monetary Fund, Washington, DC.

Caribbean Development Bank (CDB). 2015. "Making Air Transport Work Better for the Caribbean." Caribbean Development Bank, St. Michael, Barbados.

EM-DAT: The OFDA/CRED International Disaster Database. Université Catholique de Louvain, Brussels, Belgium, www.emdat.be.

Eugenio-Martín, Juan, Noelia Martín, and Riccardo Scarpa. 2004. "Tourism and Economic Growth in Latin American Countries: A Panel Data Approach." Nota di Lavoro 26.2004 (Milan: Fondazione Eni Enrico Mattei).

Forster, Johanna, Peter Schuhmann, Iain Lake, Andrew Watkinson, and Jennifer Gill. 2012. "The Influence of Hurricane Risk on Tourist Destination Choice in the Caribbean." *Climate Change* 114 (3): 745–68.

Granvorka, Charley, and Eric Strobl. 2013. "The Impact of Hurricane Strikes on Tourist Arrivals in the Caribbean." *Tourism Economics* 19 (6): 1401–09.

LaFramboise, Nicole. 2016. "The Week-@-the-Beach Index." *The Caribbean Corner* Issue 6 (April): 9–10.

————, Nkunde Mwase, Joonkyu Park, and Yingke Zhou. 2014. "Revisiting Tourism Flows to the Caribbean: What Is Driving Arrivals?" IMF Working Paper 14/229, International Monetary Fund, Washington, DC.

Sookram, Sandra. 2009. "The Impact of Climate Change on the Tourism Sector in Selected Caribbean Countries." ECLAC, *Caribbean Development Report* 2: 204–44.

Thacker, Nita, Sebastian Acevedo, and Roberto Perrelli. 2012. "Caribbean Growth in an International Perspective, the Role of Tourism and Size." IMF Working Paper 12/235, International Monetary Fund, Washington, DC.

# CHAPTER 4

# Cuba Awakening: Potential Risks and Opportunities

SEBASTIAN ACEVEDO AND JOYCE WONG

## INTRODUCTION

The growth of Caribbean tourism other than to Cuba is partly a post–Cuban revolution phenomenon. After the Cuban revolution in 1959, U.S. travel restrictions in 1963 closed U.S. tourism to one of the preferred Caribbean destinations of U.S. travelers. In 1953, the last year of tourism statistics in Cuba before the revolution,[1] Cuba received almost half of all tourist arrivals to the Caribbean; by 1980 Cuba had less than 3 percent of the market compared with the same set of countries.[2] For example, in The Bahamas—despite a long history of tourism promotion that started with the Tourism Encouragement Act of 1851—it was the U.S. embargo on Cuba that provided "the main stimulus to the tourism industry," with U.S. tourists switching to The Bahamas (The Bahamas Ministry of Tourism 2016). Tourist arrivals to The Bahamas grew from about 150,000 in 1954 to more than a million in 1968. Mexico also followed suit with the directed development of Cancun as a tourism destination.

Just as the closing of U.S.-Cuba relations was a boon to other Caribbean tourism destinations, could the normalization of U.S.-Cuba relations reverse these gains? Since the announcement in December 2014 that the United States and Cuba were normalizing relations, the United States has relaxed travel restrictions to Cuba by allowing travel without prior authorization for 12 categories, while still banning outright tourism flows. Nevertheless, 2015 was a record year for Cuba's tourism sector, with growth in arrivals of 17.4 percent (including growth of 21.8 percent in the "other" category, in which the United

---

This chapter is partly based on Acevedo, Alleyne, and Romeu (2017), and on Wong (forthcoming).

[1] The Cuban revolution started in July 1953, and the rebel forces seized control in January 1959.

[2] In 1953 only seven Caribbean countries reported tourist arrivals to the World Tourism Organization: The Bahamas, Barbados, Cuba, the Dominican Republic, Haiti, Puerto Rico, and Trinidad and Tobago. In 1953 tourist arrivals to the Caribbean were 649,911, but by 1980 arrivals to these seven countries had reached 4 million.

States is grouped).[3] Despite this sharp increase in arrivals to Cuba, the rest of the region still fared quite well, with average growth of 6 percent from all tourism sources, and 6.6 percent growth in U.S. tourist arrivals.

These short-term effects are encouraging for the rest of the Caribbean; however, given Cuba's sheer size, complete removal of travel restrictions between the United States and Cuba could potentially entail a much deeper structural change to tourism flows from the United States to the Caribbean, with varying effects across Caribbean destinations and over time. Thus, the potential impact across each Caribbean island of U.S. tourists' switch to Cuba will depend on (1) each island's dependence on U.S. tourists, (2) its gain from the Canadian and European tourists displaced from the Cuban market, and (3) the extent to which more U.S. tourists shift toward the Caribbean, generating an overall growth in Caribbean tourism.

Against this background, this chapter estimates the potential impact from a full removal of U.S. travel restrictions using two approaches:

- An updated gravity model following the approach of Romeu (2008, 2014)
- A calibrated structural setup in which the Caribbean market is the outcome of preferences with constant elasticity of substitution across destinations

## STYLIZED FACTS

Cuba's tourism market has been dominated by Canada, whose tourists account for 40 percent of the 3 million visitors to Cuba annually. Canada has also been the fastest growing source market for Caribbean tourism in the past 20 years (Figure 4.1), which suggests that it is possible for tourist arrivals from a particular source market to expand rapidly in Cuba while also growing and benefiting all other countries in the region. Going forward, more tourism from the United States to Cuba will likely have a positive impact on the region's share in global tourism; however, it will also likely result in a rearrangement of market shares within the region. Caribbean destinations most affected by Cuba's possible rapprochement with the United States are likely to be those most dependent on the U.S. market (for example, The Bahamas, Bermuda, Jamaica, Belize, St. Kitts and Nevis).

The changes in U.S. policy toward Cuba since December 2014 are quite significant: travel has been facilitated under much more general licenses for 12 categories,[4] the permitted level of remittances to Cuba has been increased, and

---

[3]Cuba's office of statistics does not report a separate line for U.S. visitors, but the "other" category is a large residual after reporting the 17 largest source markets, and it is believed to be mostly U.S. visitors.

[4]These 12 categories comprise family visits; official business of the U.S. government, foreign governments, and certain intergovernmental organizations; journalistic activity; professional research and professional meetings; educational activities; religious activities; public performances, clinics, workshops, athletic and other competitions, and exhibitions; support for the Cuban people; humanitarian projects; activities of private foundations or research or educational institutes; exportation, importation, or transmission of information or information materials; and certain export transactions that may be considered for authorization under existing regulations and guidelines.

## Figure 4.1. Evolution of the Canadian and Cuban Tourism Market, 1995–2014

### 1. Canadian Tourists by Destination

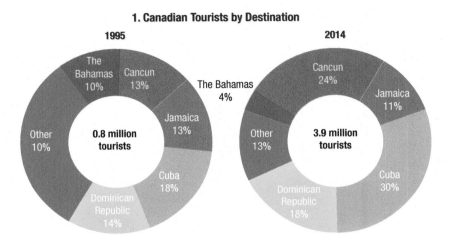

### 2. Cuban Tourist Arrivals by Source

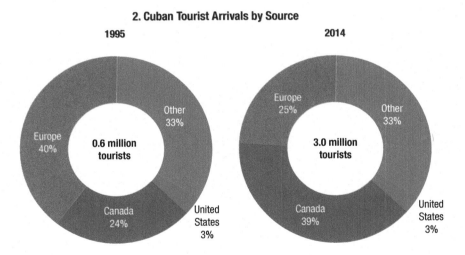

Sources: Acevedo, Alleyne, and Romeu 2017; Caribbean Tourism Organization; and World Tourism Organization.

Note: In the case of destinations, "Other" includes Anguilla, Antigua and Barbuda, Aruba, Barbados, Belize, Bermuda, British Virgin Islands, Cayman Islands, Curaçao, Dominica, Grenada, Guyana, Haiti, Martinique, Montserrat, Puerto Rico, St. Kitts and Nevis, St. Lucia, Sint Maarten, St. Vincent and the Grenadines, Suriname, Turks and Caicos, and United States Virgin Islands. In the case of sources, "Other" includes the rest of the world.

**Figure 4.2. Caribbean Tourist Arrivals by Source, 2014**
*(Percent of total)*

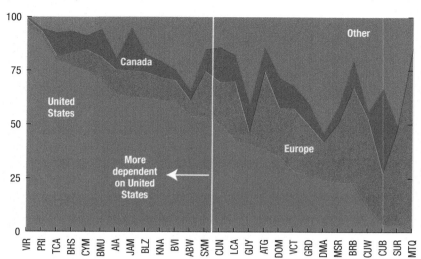

Sources: Acevedo, Alleyne, and Romeu 2017; Caribbean Tourism Organization; World Tourism Organization; and authors' calculations.
Note: "Other" includes the rest of the world. Data labels in figure use International Organization for Standardization (ISO) country codes.

commercial relations and authorized transactions have been broadened. However, tourism is still banned, although cruise ships and scheduled commercial airline traffic have resumed within the 12 categories of travel allowed. Although many of these changes are quite recent, 2015 was a record year for Cuba tourism—arrivals increased by 17.4 percent, with across-the-board increases in Canadian and European tourists, as well as U.S. visitors.

Some Caribbean destinations are more at risk of experiencing disruptions in their tourism sectors if a change in U.S. policy allows unrestricted tourism travel to Cuba, thereby increasing competition for U.S. tourists. Figure 4.2 shows the countries whose tourism source is predominantly the United States (that is, more than 50 percent). All the countries to the left of the white line depend heavily on U.S. tourists, with the U.S. Virgin Islands, Puerto Rico, Turks and Caicos, The Bahamas, the Cayman Islands, and Bermuda receiving more than 70 percent of their tourists from the United States. The tourism destinations on the right side of the white line, on the other hand, are more diversified away from the United States; hence, if the number of U.S. tourists visiting them were to decline, the shock would be smaller, and it would likely be easier for them to attract visitors from other countries to compensate for the decline in U.S. visitors.

**Figure 4.3. Caribbean Change in Share of Tourism Sources, 2000–14**
*(Percent)*

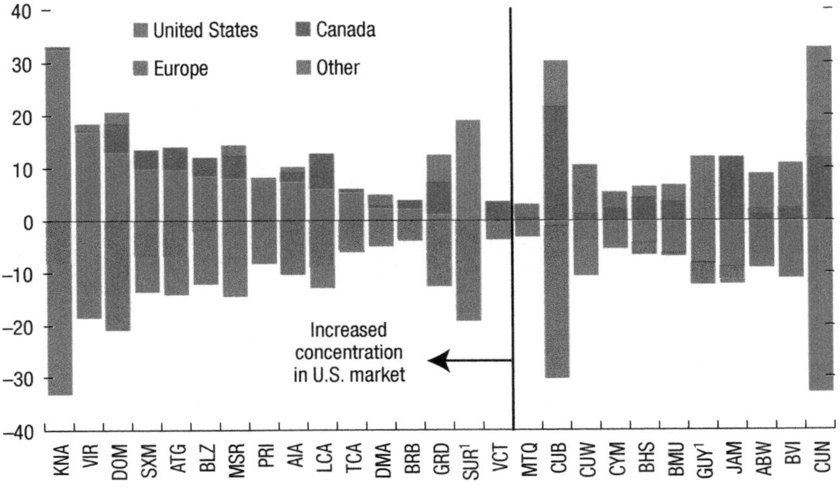

Sources: Acevedo, Alleyne, and Romeu 2017; Caribbean Tourism Organization; World Tourism Organization; and authors' calculations.
Note: "Other" includes the rest of the world. Data labels in figure use International Organization for Standardization (ISO) country codes.
[1]For Guyana the base year is 2001, and for Suriname the base year is 2006.

The extent to which a country's tourism strategy has recently concentrated on targeting the U.S. market matters as much as its current dependency on U.S. tourists. To study this aspect, the change in the share of tourists from all source markets was calculated, and is presented in Figure 4.3. All the countries to the left of the black bar have become more dependent on the U.S. tourism market since 2000. The countries to the right have diversified away from the United States, and thus are better prepared if a U.S.-Cuba opening were to result in a decline of U.S. tourists to the region. The countries to the left of the bar seem to have focused their efforts on attracting more U.S. tourists, so they are less prepared to diversify their visitor sources.

Not surprisingly, there is some overlap between the "most at risk" countries identified in Figures 4.2 and 4.3. Among those countries, the U.S. Virgin Islands, Puerto Rico, and Turks and Caicos stand out as the most vulnerable to a potential disruption in U.S. tourist flows. It is important to note that while some countries for which more than 50 percent of their visitors come from the United States have been diversifying away from the U.S. market (for example, The Bahamas and Bermuda), other countries with relatively low U.S. dependency (for example, Dominican Republic and Antigua and Barbuda) have actually been targeting the U.S. tourism market more in the past 15 years.

### Figure 4.4. U.S. Flights to Cuba and the Impact on the Rest of the Caribbean

**1. Direct Flights from the United States to Cuba (Thousands)**

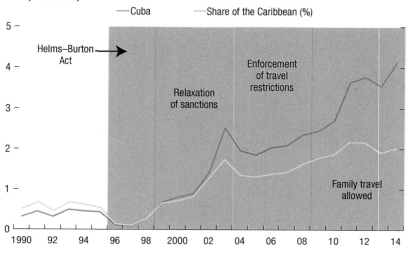

Sources: Bureau of Transportation Statistics; and authors' calculations.

**2. Response of Flights to the Rest of the Caribbean to an Increase in Flights to Cuba Shock**

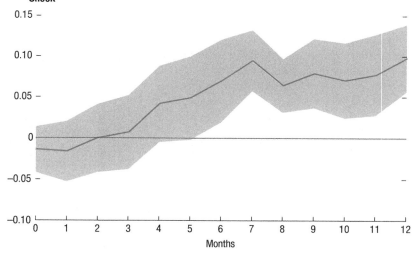

Source: Acevedo and others 2016, calculations based on the panel structural vector autoregression.
Note: Impulse is the number of flights to Cuba. The shaded area is the 90 percent confidence interval.

The enforcement—or relaxation—of U.S. travel restrictions to Cuba has had an important effect on the number of flights (panel 1 of Figure 4.4).[5] Thus, one of the concerns surrounding the opening of U.S.-Cuba travel is that air travel services might be diverted from the rest of the Caribbean to Cuba. Acevedo and others (2016) use a panel structural vector autoregression and find that more flights between the United States and Cuba has no statistically significant impact on the availability of flights to the rest of the Caribbean in the first few months (panel 2 of Figure 4.4).[6] Similar results were found for an increase in the number of U.S. flights to the rest of the region, suggesting that there is no substitution effect such that one destination's gain is another's loss. In other words, airlift supply between the United States and the Caribbean is not a zero-sum game.

Some possible explanations for the absence of a substitution effect could be that the airline industry expands its fleet to increase the number of flights to a Caribbean destination, airlines shift flights from other regions (domestic, Latin America), or they accommodate greater demand by scheduling more flights without requiring an increase in the fleet.

## POTENTIAL EFFECTS OF LIBERALIZING TOURISM BETWEEN THE UNITED STATES AND CUBA

This section examines the possible effects that a change in U.S. travel policy toward Cuba could have, not only on U.S.-Cuba tourism flow, but also on the rest of the Caribbean. Two methods—a gravity model and a structural model—are used to analyze these effects.

It is important to be mindful of some characteristics of the Cuban economy that could affect the transition:

- In the short term, Cuba will likely be constrained by capacity and hindered by its dual exchange rate system wherein tourists transact at a 1–1 exchange rate with the U.S. dollar, while locals transact at 24–1 with the U.S. dollar. Under such a setting, a large inflow of U.S. tourists (some of whom may substitute Cuba for other Caribbean islands) could potentially mean significant tourism-related price hikes in Cuba, potentially displacing current tourists from Canada and Europe. The winners and losers from this short-term switching effect across Caribbean islands will hinge on each country's dependence on U.S. tourists and the extent to which Canadian and European tourists are willing to substitute another island for Cuba (as discussed below).

- In the long term, as Cuba builds capacity, exchange rate adjustments take place, and the "curiosity factor" wanes for U.S. tourists, the region will likely settle into a new equilibrium determined by structural factors.

---

[5]Figure 4.4 also illustrates that there have been rapid changes in the supply and demand for flights between the United States and Cuba, which allows an estimate to be made of the impact in other Caribbean destinations of the changes in the number of U.S.-Cuba flights.

[6]Chapter 3 has a more detailed description of the work of Acevedo and others (2016).

Gradual changes are already taking place, and so far the region has coped well with the relaxation of travel restrictions from the United States to Cuba with little or no negative effects registered.

## Gravity Model

This modeling approach explicitly accounts for the U.S. travel restrictions to Cuba and then calculates a counterfactual scenario in which those restrictions are removed.[7] Bilateral tourist arrivals are a function of the distance between the destination and source country capitals, and factors that affect trade links such as cultural and historical relations (for example, whether the countries share a common language, have a colonial history or a common colonizer, or are part of the same country, such as the United States and Puerto Rico). To capture the effect of the travel restrictions imposed by the United States, the inquiry includes dummy variables that reflect periods when U.S. travel restrictions toward Cuba were more tightly enforced (1996–97 when the Helms–Burton Act increased sanctions, and 2004–08 when travel restrictions to Cuba were enforced more strongly).[8]

The results indicate that the full removal of travel restrictions would increase tourism flows from the United States to Cuba in the range of 3 million to 5.6 million people a year.[9] Most of the increase would come from new tourists to the region—that is, the overall number of tourists traveling to the Caribbean would increase. Nonetheless, some Caribbean destinations might see some temporary decline in U.S. arrivals (as is shown next). Table 4.1 suggests that part of Cuba's gain in U.S. tourism would be at the expense of other destinations (the ones with red cells in the U.S. column), but some Canadian and European tourists who currently visit Cuba could decide to visit other countries in the region once prices

---

[7] The idea behind gravity models is that trade flows are determined by trade costs; this approach can be applied to the movement of physical goods or to the movement of people for trade in tourism services. This chapter follows the work of Romeu (2014), which is based on the work of Anderson and Van Wincoop (2003) and Baldwin and Taglioni (2006).

[8] The model also controls for the participation of destination countries in different trade agreements (that is, CARICOM, the Central America Free Trade Agreement, and the Caribbean Basin Initiative) that facilitate travel and investment, including in tourism facilities. Also, to get a sense of the impact that U.S. tourists have on non-U.S. arrivals, this elasticity is estimated for each country. The model also includes destination-year and source-year indicators that capture nonsystemic tourism determinants of destination and source countries (for example, GDP). The model also controls for the effects of natural disasters; for the September 11, 2001, attacks that disrupted travel around the world; for the H1N1 outbreak in 2009; and for low-income country destinations that might have insufficient infrastructure capacity for a well-functioning tourism sector.

[9] The results of the estimations are presented in Annex Table 4.1.1, where column (1) shows the main estimation, and columns (2) and (3) show some alternative specifications that serve as robustness checks. To estimate the potential gain in U.S. tourist arrivals to Cuba we calculate a counterfactual scenario using these estimations. We set both variables measuring the restrictions to zero while at the same time setting the CBI variable for Cuba to one; that is, we assume that the United States includes Cuba as part of the CBI initiative. Model 1 predicts the highest gains (5.6 million), while Model 2 predicts gains of 3.2 million, and Model 3 predicts an increase of 3 million.

**Table 4.1. Actual versus Predicted Arrivals**

| Destination | United States | Canada | United Kingdom | Other | Total |
|---|---|---|---|---|---|
| | | | **Source** | | |
| Anguilla | | | | | |
| Antigua and Barbuda | | | | | |
| Aruba | | | | | |
| The Bahamas | | | | | |
| Barbados | | | | | |
| Belize | | | | | |
| Bermuda | | | | | |
| British Virgin Islands | | | | | |
| Cancun | | | | | |
| Cayman Islands | | | | | |
| Cuba¹ | | | | | |
| Curaçao | | | | | |
| Dominica | | | | | |
| Dominican Republic | | | | | |
| Grenada | | | | | |
| Guadeloupe | | | | | |
| Jamaica | | | | | |
| Martinique | | | | | |
| Miami | | | | | |
| Montserrat | | | | | |
| Puerto Rico | | | | | |
| Sint Maarten | | | | | |
| St. Kitts and Nevis | | | | | |
| St. Lucia | | | | | |
| St. Vincent and the Grenadines | | | | | |
| Suriname | | | | | |
| Trinidad and Tobago | | | | | |
| Turks and Caicos | | | | | |
| United States Virgin Islands | | | | | |
| Total | | | | | |

Note: The table compares actual tourist arrivals in 2013 with the predicted arrivals from model (1) in Annex Table 4.1.1. A red cell indicates that the model predicts fewer arrivals than the ones that actually took place in 2013, while a green cell indicates that the model predicts more arrivals than the actual.
¹ U.S. arrivals to Cuba based on the unrestricted model.

in Cuba start rising (countries with green cells in the Canada and U.K. columns). Interestingly, Miami could benefit from Canadian and U.K. visitors switching away from Cuba because it is the closest Caribbean destination to both source countries and has close cultural and historical ties.

Countries most vulnerable to possible spillovers from the U.S.-Cuba opening are (1) those with larger dependence on the United States as a source market in 2014, (2) those whose share of U.S. tourists has increased in recent years, and (3) those that could lose some U.S. tourists after a change in U.S. travel policy toward Cuba as identified by the gravity model. The results are summarized in the Venn diagram in Figure 4.5, identifying Anguilla, Belize, Sint Maarten, and the U.S. Virgin Islands as the more vulnerable group. This result does not imply that the other destinations are completely safe, or that this group will see declining U.S. tourism flows; it only highlights the countries that would need to be more alert to possible spillovers from changes in the U.S.-Cuba relationship.

## Figure 4.5. Destinations Most Vulnerable to a Change in U.S.-Cuba Travel Policy

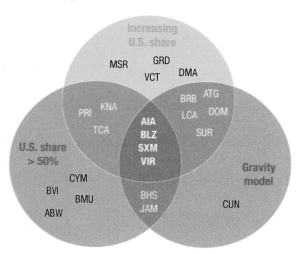

Sources: Acevedo, Alleyne, and Romeu 2017.
Note: Labels in figure use International Organization for Standardization (ISO) country codes.

### Structural Model: A Change in "Preferences"

A structural approach to examining the effects from the normalization of U.S.-Cuba relations confirms the findings above. In this setup, the United States, Canada, and Europe were assumed to have constant elasticity of substitution preferences[10] across Caribbean destinations:

$$\max u_j = \Sigma_{i = 1,...,I}(q_i visits_i^\rho)^{1/\rho} \text{ such that } \Sigma_i p_i visits_i = N,$$

where $q_i$ is the quality and preference indicator for destination $i$, $p_i$ is the price of a visit to destination $i$, and $visits_i$ is the number of visits to destination $i$.

Using data on visitors' arrivals from each market (United States, Canada, Europe) to each destination in the Caribbean and the Week-at-the-Beach Index (see Chapter 3 in this book) for prices at two times (2014 and 2016), three sets of implied "preferences" (United States, Canadian, European) for each Caribbean destination are calibrated ($\{q_1^*, \ldots, q_I^*\}_j, j = US, CAN, EUR$).[11]

---

[10]Constant elasticity of substitution preferences are widely used in the literature to convey a preference for a basket of different goods rather than homogeneous consumption ("taste for variety").

[11]"Preferences" should be used carefully in this setup: while the implied values for Canada and Europe likely reflect preferences for destinations, for the United States they also reflect the current institutional environment in which U.S. tourists are restricted from visiting Cuba; thus, the outcome of prices and numbers of visits reflects more than just market factors.

**Figure 4.6. Implied Preferences for Destinations**

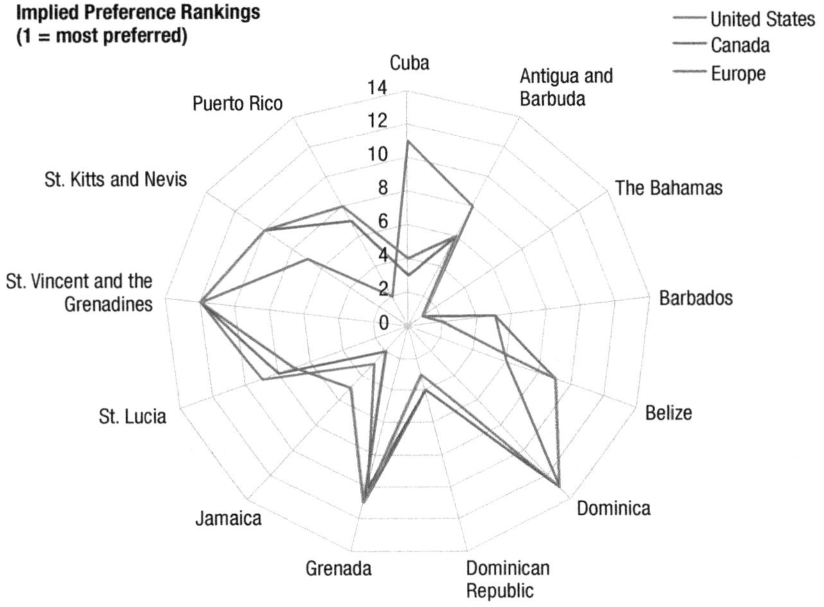

Sources: Caribbean Tourism Organization; and authors' calculations.

Each country's implied preference rankings are shown in Figure 4.6. In general, the preferences of the three markets are quite similar: The Bahamas ranks first for all three markets (United States, Canada, Europe) with Dominica and St. Vincent and the Grenadines ranking last. The places where U.S. preferences differ significantly are Puerto Rico (second for the United States and seventh and eighth for Canada and Europe, respectively) and, of course, Cuba (11th for the United States and third and fourth for Canada and Europe, respectively, where the U.S. ranking reflects the U.S. institutional ban).

The possible impact of U.S. tourists in the absence of any institutional restrictions is analyzed by assuming that U.S. tourists, in this case, would have the same preferences as Canadian tourists (including for Cuba), and Cuba is ranked third. In this case, arrivals to Cuba from the United States would increase by more than 3.3 million a year (from the current 96,000). Not all of this increase, however, would mean losses for other destinations: jointly the other 12 destinations would lose about 2 million visitors per year, with the largest losses in nominal terms coming from the main U.S. destinations.

Thus, out of Cuba's total gain in visitors, about 60 percent would be due to trade diversion while 40 percent would be due to trade creation. Why is there trade

**Figure 4.7. Change in U.S. Market Share**

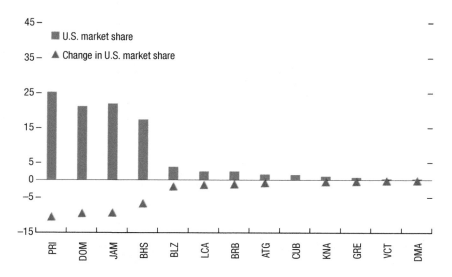

Source: Authors' calculations.
Note: Data labels in figure use International Organization for Standardization (ISO) country codes.

creation? Because of Cuba's relatively low prices: since the model assumes that the overall resource envelope for Caribbean destinations does not change, one trip to The Bahamas could be replaced by trips to Cuba and Belize, for example.

However, based on this simple model, the change in U.S. preferences would imply significant loss in market shares for Caribbean destinations highly dependent on U.S. tourists (Figure 4.7). Destinations most affected include the Dominican Republic, Puerto Rico, Jamaica, and The Bahamas (whose current U.S. market shares range from 17 to 27 percent), which could see their shares of the U.S. market drop by an average of 9 percentage points. Under the new preferences, Cuba would become the main U.S. destination, receiving more than 40 percent of U.S. tourists to the Caribbean. The results of this static analysis should be viewed with caution because (1) it fails to account for the duration of this transition, which, in turn, depends on Cuba's supply-side responses; and (2) it makes a simplifying assumption that the Caribbean islands currently receiving large proportions of U.S. tourists also make no supply-side responses to become more attractive and competitive destinations.

## CONCLUSIONS AND POLICY IMPLICATIONS

With the United States being the single largest tourism market for the Caribbean and, for most countries, the most important source of tourists, a full removal of U.S.-Cuba travel restrictions would undoubtedly bring about significant shifts in total tourists to the Caribbean and relative market shares. However, these shifts will not necessarily cause only negative outcomes for the rest of the Caribbean. There will be a period of adjustment and more intense competition, which, as in the past (when Cancun and the Dominican Republic became dominant tourist destinations), the Caribbean destinations must confront with sensible policies.

- In countries where the dependence on the U.S. market is large, a diversification strategy that targets other advanced economies and large emerging markets in Latin America would be beneficial. Tapping into new markets, historical links, and diaspora resources could help provide a much-needed boost.

- Improving competitiveness and reducing the costs of the tourism sector will be crucial. Supply-side reforms to decrease reliance on imports, increase domestic links (for example, with domestic agriculture and manufacturing), and strengthen physical infrastructure could support more market diversification.

- Upgrading quality and improving product marketing and differentiation (for example, by fostering cultural tourism instead of just "sun and sand") will help countries compete with a nascent low-cost provider like Cuba and attract tourists outside of the all-inclusive model.

- Finally, putting in place regional strategies to facilitate intraregional travel (for example, through a hub-and-spoke airline model) would help nurture the possibility of multidestination vacations. Such a model would help the rest of the Caribbean benefit from the new tourists who will start visiting the region when the United States opens free travel to Cuba.

It is encouraging that the region is actively addressing some of these challenges. The tourism authorities and local hoteliers are proactively embarking on efforts to enhance their tourism product by tapping into new markets, developing new products, promoting investment, forging new partnerships, and developing human capital. In addition, the Caribbean Hotel and Tourism Association has been actively engaging with Cuban authorities to explore partnerships in promoting multidestination initiatives. These various initiatives should mitigate the risk of decline in tourist arrivals from the United States to the Caribbean.

In addition, the whole process is likely to be gradual because Cuba will also need to adjust its economic policies to scale up investment and improve the quality of its tourism services. In the short term, higher U.S. tourism demand in Cuba may push prices up and potentially displace some Canadian and European tourists who would have otherwise visited Cuba but may instead travel to other Caribbean destinations. This displacement would partly offset any potential loss of U.S. tourists that some destinations might suffer in the adjustment phase to the new equilibrium. These shifts will provide support for other Caribbean destinations as they put in place reforms to adapt to the new equilibrium. In the long term, the change in U.S. policy is expected to benefit the whole region as aggregate tourism flows grow.

Nevertheless, the region should not be complacent about the changes that could come later. Many of the necessary reforms are significant and would take time to yield results; the earlier countries embark on these reforms, the readier they will be for Cuba's reopening.

# ANNEX 4.1

## Annex Table 4.1.1. Gravity Estimations

| Variables | (1) ln TA | (2) ln TA | (3) ln TA |
|---|---|---|---|
| Distance | −1.48*** | −1.55*** | −1.56*** |
| U.S.-Cuba Restrictions | −3.41*** | −3.61*** | −3.59*** |
| Tightening of Restrictions | −0.75*** | −0.73*** | −0.75*** |
| Common Language | 1.13*** | 1.08*** | 1.09*** |
| Common Colonizer | 0.51** | 0.54** | 0.53** |
| Colonial Ties | 1.36*** | 1.40*** | 1.41*** |
| Same Country | 1.19** | 1.15* | 1.11* |
| Europe | −0.16 | −0.17 | |
| Puerto Rico | 0.78 | 1.04 | |
| CAFTA | 0.40** | | 0.41** |
| CARICOM | −1.10* | | |
| CBI | 0.77 | | |
| H1N1 Epidemic | −0.12 | −0.18 | 0.10 |
| Natural Disasters | −1.81* | −2.20*** | −1.92*** |
| Low-Income Country | −1.18*** | −1.27*** | −1.37*** |
| 9/11 Attacks | −7.43*** | −7.53*** | −7.62*** |
| $\beta_{US}$ | | | |
|   Anguilla | −0.22*** | −0.22*** | −0.23*** |
|   Antigua and Barbuda | 0.04 | −0.03 | −0.04 |
|   Aruba | −0.14*** | −0.18*** | −0.19*** |
|   The Bahamas | −0.05 | −0.12*** | −0.12*** |
|   Barbados | 0.00 | −0.08* | −0.09** |
|   Belize | −0.06 | −0.12** | −0.13*** |
|   Bermuda | −0.17*** | −0.17*** | −0.18*** |
|   British Virgin Islands | −0.13*** | −0.18*** | −0.19*** |
|   Cancun | −0.08** | −0.09** | −0.08** |
|   Cayman Islands | −0.19*** | −0.19*** | −0.19*** |
|   Cuba | −0.14** | −0.15*** | −0.16*** |
|   Curaçao | −0.09 | −0.14*** | −0.15*** |
|   Dominica | −0.06 | −0.14** | −0.16** |
|   Dominican Republic | 0.03 | −0.02 | −0.02 |
|   Grenada | −0.07 | −0.16*** | −0.17*** |
|   Guadeloupe | −0.17*** | −0.17*** | −0.18*** |
|   Haiti | −0.15*** | −0.20*** | −0.20*** |
|   Jamaica | −0.03 | −0.10*** | −0.11*** |
|   Martinique | 0.02 | 0.02 | 0.01 |
|   Miami | 0.02 | 0.02 | 0.01 |
|   Montserrat | −0.20** | −0.30*** | −0.32*** |
|   Puerto Rico | −0.11 | −0.09 | −0.13*** |
|   Saba | −0.11 | −0.21*** | −0.22*** |
|   Sint Maarten | −0.07 | −0.13*** | −0.13*** |
|   St. Eustatius | −0.27*** | −0.35*** | −0.35*** |
|   St. Kitts and Nevis | −0.17** | −0.24*** | −0.26*** |
|   St. Lucia | −0.05 | −0.14*** | −0.15*** |
|   St. Vincent and the Grenadines | −0.07 | −0.16*** | −0.17*** |
|   Trinidad and Tobago | −0.16** | −0.25*** | −0.26*** |
|   Turks and Caicos | −0.30*** | −0.31*** | −0.32*** |
|   United States Virgin Islands | −0.24*** | −0.25*** | −0.26*** |
| Observations | 9,520 | 9,520 | 9,520 |
| $R^2$ | 0.92 | 0.92 | 0.92 |
| Adjusted $R^2$ | 0.90 | 0.90 | 0.90 |

Note: $\beta_{US}$ captures the effect of the log of U.S. tourist arrivals to each destination's other sources, that is, the elasticity of non-U.S. arrivals to a change in U.S. arrivals for each destination. CAFTA = Central America Free Trade Agreement; CARICOM = Caribbean Community; CBI = Caribbean Basin Initiative; TA = tourist arrivals.
*** $p < 0.01$, ** $p < 0.05$, * $p < 0.1$.

## Annex Table 4.1.2. Price and Visitor Data for Calibrated Model

| | | Visitors (per month) | | | | |
|---|---|---|---|---|---|---|
| | **Price Index** | **United States** | **Canada** | **Europe** | **Other** | **ALL** |
| Cuba | 0.92 | 8,000 | 94,328 | 83,026 | 119,032 | 304,386 |
| Antigua and Barbuda | 1.74 | 8,638 | 1,619 | 8,030 | 3,456 | 21,743 |
| The Bahamas | 2.52 | 92,368 | 10,417 | 7,554 | 9,415 | 119,754 |
| Barbados | 1.72 | 13,188 | 5,836 | 20,942 | 10,202 | 50,168 |
| Belize | 1.41 | 19,825 | 1,544 | 3,385 | 5,365 | 30,119 |
| Dominica | 1.15 | 1,507 | 237 | 1,091 | 3,220 | 6,055 |
| Dominican Republic | 1.15 | 112,508 | 28,126 | 59,900 | 104,711 | 305,244 |
| Grenada | 1.45 | 3,798 | 813 | 2,470 | 4,961 | 12,042 |
| Jamaica | 1.42 | 116,467 | 28,957 | 23,647 | 9,236 | 178,307 |
| St. Lucia | 1.21 | 13,216 | 2,515 | 6,653 | 6,196 | 28,580 |
| St. Vincent and the Grenadines | 1.23 | 1,920 | 632 | 1,805 | 2,127 | 6,483 |
| St. Kitts and Nevis | 2.21 | 5,442 | 382 | 849 | 2,431 | 9,103 |
| Puerto Rico | 1.46 | 134,184 | 1,693 | 3,720 | 10,843 | 150,440 |

Source: Caribbean Tourism Organization and author's calculations.

# REFERENCES

Acevedo, Sebastian, Trevor Alleyne, and Rafael Romeu. 2017. "Revisiting the Potential Impact to the Rest of the Caribbean from Opening US-Cuba Tourism." IMF Working Paper 17/100, International Monetary Fund, Washington, DC.

Acevedo, Sebastian, Lu Han, Marie Kim, and Nicole LaFramboise. 2016. "Flying to Paradise: The Role of Airlift in the Caribbean Tourism Industry." IMF Working Paper 16/33, International Monetary Fund, Washington, DC.

Anderson, J., and E. Van Wincoop. 2003. "Gravity with Gravitas: A Solution to the Border Puzzle." *American Economic Review* 93 (1): 170–92.

The Bahamas, Ministry of Tourism 2016 "The History of the Ministry of Tourism" http://www.tourismtoday.com/about-us/tourism-history

Baldwin, R., and D. Taglioni. 2006. "Gravity for Dummies and Dummies for Gravity Equations." NBER Working Paper 12516, National Bureau of Economic Research, Cambridge, MA.

Romeu, R. 2008. "Vacation Over: Implications for the Caribbean of Opening US-Cuba Tourism." IMF Working Paper 08/162, International Monetary Fund, Washington, DC.

Romeu, R. 2014. "The Vacation Is Over: Implications for the Caribbean of Opening US-Cuba Tourism." *Economía* 14 (2): 1–24.

Wong, Joyce Cheng. 2017. "A Giant Awakens: Structural Shifts to the Caribbean from Opening US-Cuba Tourism." Mimeo.

# CHAPTER 5

# Fiscal Challenges in the Caribbean: Coping with Natural Disasters

İNCI ÖTKER WITH FRANZ LOYOLA

## INTRODUCTION

The Caribbean economies face difficult fiscal challenges, reflected in their high and rising levels of deficits and debt. Large fiscal deficits and debt have been built up for a variety of reasons, ranging from lack of prudent macroeconomic policies and overspending by public enterprises, to costly financial crises that resulted in government intervention in the financial sector, to simply bad luck. In the Caribbean, like in many other small states and developing countries, bad luck includes frequent and severe natural disasters, which can result in a collapse of economic activity and erosion of fiscal buffers and undermine the sustainability of medium-term fiscal frameworks.

This chapter reviews the effects of natural disasters on economic growth and fiscal performance in the Caribbean. It draws on existing work within and outside the IMF to assess the impact of natural disasters on growth and fiscal performance and to identify how countries vulnerable to natural disasters and climate change can build resilience to disaster risk. It explores ways in which the Caribbean countries can reduce risks related to natural disasters and climate change, better prepare for them and mitigate their consequences when risks materialize, and respond to disasters in a way that facilitates rapid recovery.

## STYLIZED FACTS

The number of people affected by natural disasters around the world has been rising, making natural disasters an important source of fiscal challenge

---

The chapter draws heavily on IMF 2016a; LaFramboise and Loko 2012; Acevedo 2014; and World Bank 2013b.

**Figure 5.1. Number of Natural Disasters and Populations Affected, 1950–2016**

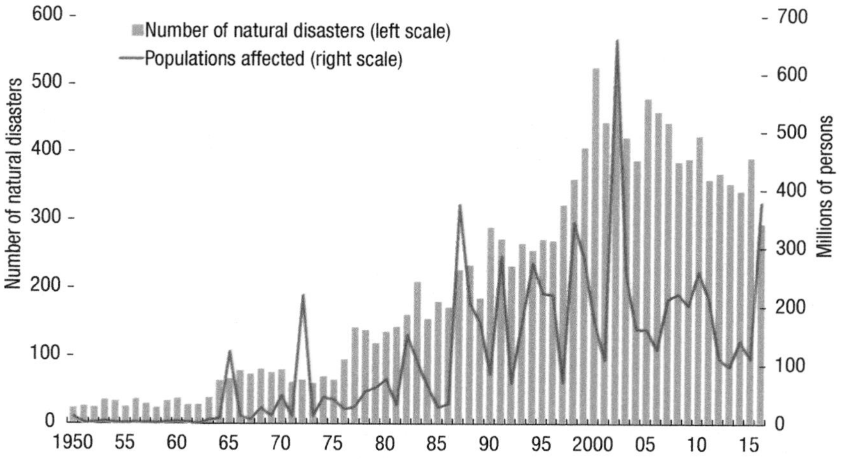

Sources: EM-DAT; and IMF staff calculations.

(Figure 5.1).[1] Since 1950, more than 12,000 natural disasters have been registered globally (182 disasters a year, on average), affecting more than 7.6 million people (Table 5.1). Direct economic damages from disasters over this period amounted to $525 million per year in constant 2009 U.S. dollars (Figure 5.2). Just like the number of people affected, economic damage (involving both direct and indirect costs) has been rising, from an estimated $70 billion per year, on average, in the 1990s to $113 billion per year since 2000. This upward trend is expected to continue as the frequency and severity of disasters increase and the number of people in areas more exposed to natural disasters and climate change becomes more highly concentrated.

Being in the cyclone and hurricane belts bordering the equator, where more frequent weather shocks are experienced, the Caribbean region has been highly exposed to natural disasters. Since 1950, the Caribbean has been hit by 324 natural disasters that killed close to 250,000 people and affected more than 24 million people, through injury or loss of homes, in addition to death. The economic impact of natural disasters has been substantial, exceeding $22 billion in constant

---

[1]In the commonly used global Emergency Events Database (EM-DAT), natural disasters are defined to include geophysical (earthquakes, volcanic activity, mass movement), meteorological (extreme temperature, fogs, storms), hydrological (floods, landslides, wave action), climatological (drought, wildfire), and biological (epidemic, insect infestation) events. EM-DAT covers disasters that involve at least 10 or more people reported killed, 100 or more people reported affected, a declaration of a state of emergency, or a call for international assistance.

## Table 5.1. Natural Disasters Worldwide: Occurrence and Impact

**World Excluding Caribbean**

| | Number of Occurrences | Number of Occurrences with Data on Deaths | Number of Deaths | Number of Occurrences with Data on Affected | Number of Affected | Number of Occurrences with Data on Damages | Total Damages (in thousands of 2009 U.S. dollars) |
|---|---|---|---|---|---|---|---|
| 1950–59 | 287 | 274 | 2,126,770 | 111 | 19,658,559 | 71 | 388,791 |
| 1960–69 | 565 | 475 | 1,750,121 | 419 | 199,337,760 | 350 | 970,629 |
| 1970–79 | 886 | 732 | 986,765 | 730 | 543,099,257 | 521 | 1,710,565 |
| 1980–89 | 1,790 | 1,495 | 796,631 | 1,526 | 1,241,458,242 | 1,011 | 3,338,391 |
| 1990–99 | 2,931 | 2,651 | 527,546 | 2,701 | 2,022,082,155 | 2,121 | 9,320,225 |
| 2000–09 | 4,423 | 4,152 | 839,245 | 4,252 | 2,281,785,389 | 2,753 | 9,624,746 |
| 2010–16 | 2,523 | 2,303 | 450,116 | 2,425 | 1,309,547,863 | 1,648 | 9,811,489 |
| Total | 13,405 | 12,082 | 7,477,194 | 12,164 | 7,616,969,225 | 8,475 | 35,164,836 |
| Average per Year | 200 | 180 | 111,600 | 182 | 113,686,108 | 126 | 524,848 |
| Average per Disaster | | | 619 | | 626,190 | | 4,149 |

**The Caribbean**

| | Number of Occurrences | Number of Occurrences with Data on Deaths | Number of Deaths | Number of Occurrences with Data on Affected | Number of Affected | Number of Occurrences with Data on Damages | Total Damages (in thousands of 2009 U.S. dollars) |
|---|---|---|---|---|---|---|---|
| 1950–59 | 11 | 9 | 1,079 | 3 | 270,200 | 4 | 82,000 |
| 1960–69 | 25 | 16 | 6,446 | 12 | 467,875 | 20 | 379,340 |
| 1970–79 | 21 | 10 | 188 | 16 | 1,508,930 | 9 | 67,709 |
| 1980–89 | 51 | 24 | 632 | 37 | 3,444,247 | 31 | 2,283,881 |
| 1990–99 | 58 | 27 | 1,521 | 47 | 3,918,138 | 34 | 2,351,577 |
| 2000–09 | 94 | 78 | 6,829 | 85 | 2,298,664 | 52 | 5,488,539 |
| 2010–16 | 64 | 44 | 230,675 | 57 | 12,367,507 | 38 | 11,839,152 |
| Total | 324 | 208 | 247,370 | 257 | 24,275,561 | 188 | 22,492,198 |
| Average per Year | 5 | 3 | 3,748 | 4 | 367,812 | 3 | 340,791 |
| Average per Disaster | | | 1,189 | | 94,457 | | 119,639 |

Sources: EM-DAT; and IMF staff calculations.

2009 U.S. dollars over the period 1950–2016, compared with $58 billion globally (including the Caribbean).

The Caribbean's vulnerability to natural disasters is highly typical of small states, which are proportionately more exposed (IMF 2016a). For small states (developing countries with population up to 1.5 million), the economic cost of the average natural disaster during 1950–2014 was equivalent to nearly 13 percent of GDP, compared with less than 1 percent of GDP for larger states (Figure 5.3). Nearly 10 percent of disasters caused damage of more than 30 percent of GDP in small states, compared with less than 1 percent in larger countries. An average disaster affects 10 percent of the population in small states, compared with 1 percent for other states. Among small states, the average annual damage

**Figure 5.2. Economic Damage from Disasters, 1950–2016**
*(Billions of U.S. dollars)*

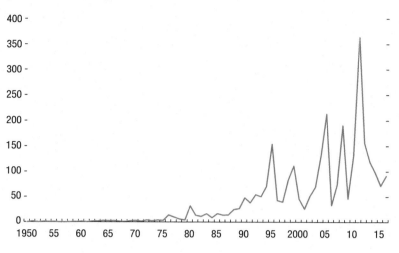

Sources: EM-DAT; and IMF staff calculations.

from disasters for the Caribbean is equivalent to 2.4 percent of GDP. The Caribbean small states have suffered more damage compared with other small states and larger states, and more populations have been affected in small states in general.

The average impact of disasters within a given region can mask the magnitude of devastation across individual countries. Economic losses from disasters may reach massive proportions (Figure 5.4). In Dominica, for instance, the 2015 floods cost an equivalent of 96 percent of GDP; in Grenada, the damage from the 2004 hurricane amounted to 200 percent of GDP; and the 1998 storms in St. Kitts and Nevis cost more than 100 percent of GDP. In 2016 alone, two major disasters with significant human and economic costs occurred: Hurricane Matthew (September–October 2016) was the costliest weather-related catastrophe, making landfall in Haiti, Cuba, and the Dominican Republic; an estimated 200,000 homes were damaged or destroyed; the official death toll reached 600; and the total economic loss amounted to $15 billion, only one-third of which was covered by insurance (Aon Benfield Analytics 2016). In 2016, Hurricane Earl also damaged portions of the Caribbean, Belize, and Mexico, with almost 70 people killed and 15,000 homes damaged.

Costly disasters in small states are also becoming more frequent (Figure 5.5, panel 1). Small states as a consolidated group experienced 511 disasters between 1950 and 2016, an average of about seven disasters each year (Figure 5.5, panel 2), compared with one disaster each year in eight countries with individual land areas similar to that of the combined small-states group. About half of these

Figure 5.3. Average Annual Effects of Natural Disasters

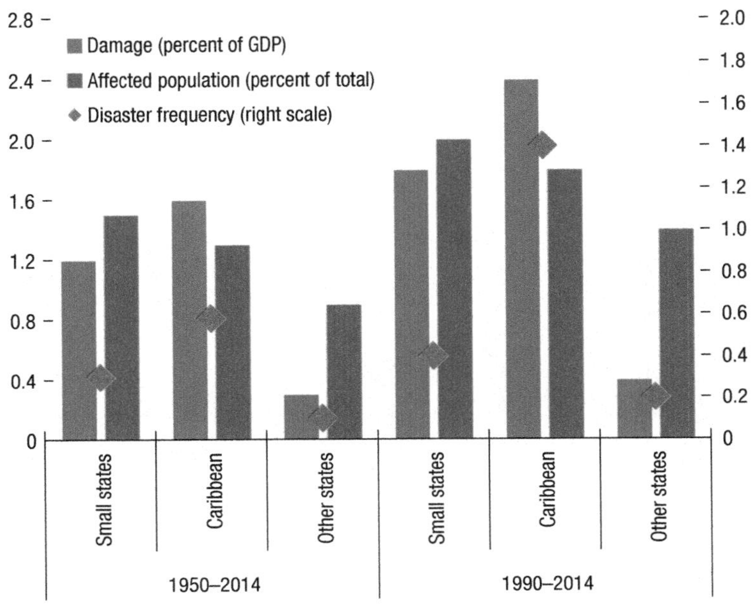

Sources: EM-DAT; IMF, *World Economic Outlook*; World Bank, World Development Indicators; and IMF staff calculations.
Note: Average annual disaster damage, affected population per 1,000 per square kilometers.

natural disasters in small states were in the Caribbean, with multiple disasters occurring in each country within a given year. Climate change is expected to exacerbate these effects by increasing the frequency and severity of natural disasters, notably through its impact on sea level and damage to biodiversity, agricultural and coastal areas, housing, and infrastructure that the tourism-based economies in particular rely on heavily. The impact of more frequent and costly natural disasters on the Caribbean economies can be substantial, including lower economic growth and worsening fiscal and external balances, as well as the implications for poverty and social welfare, with the most vulnerable populations particularly at risk (LaFramboise and Loko 2012).

# THE MACROECONOMIC IMPACT OF NATURAL DISASTERS

Natural disasters can be considered an extreme supply shock with potentially large and long-lasting macroeconomic effects. As IMF (2016a) and LaFramboise

**Figure 5.4. Annual Average Disaster Damage, 1970–2016**
*(Percent of GDP)*

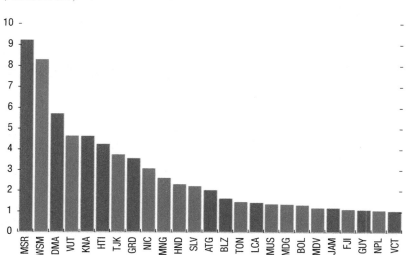

Sources: EM-DAT; and IMF, *World Economic Outlook.*
Note: Data labels in figure use International Organization for Standardization (ISO) country codes.

and Loko (2012) explain, the effects typically manifest themselves in three forms: (1) direct costs from the immediate loss of physical and human capital and destruction of infrastructure and property; (2) indirect, near-term loss of income from the disruption of economic activity in the public and private sectors, and costs incurred as individuals and businesses work around disruptions; and (3) recovery, with rebuilding and upgrading of infrastructure and replacement of damaged goods providing a temporary boost in activity and employment. The indirect impacts can spread throughout the economy over time and affect investment, growth, and fiscal and external accounts. The debt-to-GDP ratio can rise as the deterioration of the fiscal balance results in further debt accumulation and as growth slows. Periodic destruction of part of a country's productive assets acts as an implicit tax on capital and labor, deters investment, and lowers productivity and living standards on a sustained basis.

The Caribbean economies are highly vulnerable to these effects. An IMF study found five Caribbean countries at extreme risk of natural disasters (Grenada, Belize, St. Lucia, Dominica, St. Vincent and the Grenadines) and two countries (Antigua and Barbuda, St. Kitts and Nevis) at high risk, with vulnerability measured with respect to disaster frequency and effects of disasters (IMF 2016a). Belize has also been found highly vulnerable to climate change, with vulnerability assessed using an exposure index based on the analysis of the Intergovernmental Panel on Climate Change. Antigua and Barbuda

## Figure 5.5. Occurrence of Natural Disasters in the Caribbean

### 1. Occurrence of Natural Disasters, 1950–2016

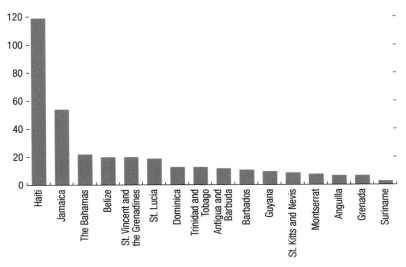

### 2. Number of Disasters in the Caribbean by Decade

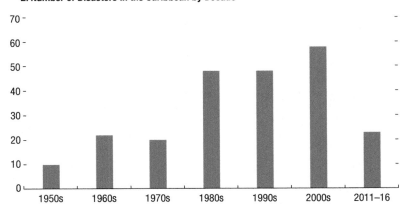

Source: EM-DAT.

and St. Kitts and Nevis have been found to be vulnerable to a rise in sea level. This vulnerability results from a large share of the population living in high-risk areas with weak infrastructure, greater reliance on sectors that depend directly on weather (for example, agriculture, tourism), and limited capacity and resources to manage risk and build resilience (LaFramboise and Loko 2012).

The existing literature summarized in IMF 2016a broadly supports the view that natural disasters have adverse effects on key macroeconomic outcomes. Small states are disproportionately affected because of their more frequent exposure:

- *Natural disasters have a clear temporary impact on growth*, though evidence on underlying long-term growth is mixed. Several studies point to significant negative short-term growth effects because damage to physical assets and commercial and financial infrastructure results in forgone production in the immediate aftermath of the disaster (Raddatz 2007; Noy 2009; Acevedo 2014; Cabezon and others 2015). Over a longer period, Loayza and others (2009) find reconstruction spending to have a positive impact on growth following small disasters, whereas several studies find a significant negative medium-term impact on growth following large shocks.[2] Event studies support the claim that hurricanes result in a jump in unemployment in the short term, followed by reversal to the baseline (Ewing and Kruse 2002). Cavallo and Noy (2010) find no significant long-term impact, while Cabezon and others (2015) find that for the Pacific islands, trend growth during 1980–2014 was 0.7 percentage point lower than it would have been without natural disasters.

- *Fiscal balances tend to be adversely affected*, but the extent of the deterioration typically depends on how governments respond to the disaster (LaFramboise and Loko 2012). The adverse impact on short-term activity tends to weaken the tax base and create higher volatility for tax revenue (see Cabezon and others 2015 for disaster-prone Pacific small states). Spending also tends to rise with relief and recovery programs.[3] Resulting fiscal imbalances worsen fiscal sustainability depending on how recovery costs are financed. More developed financial systems, with high rates of insurance penetration, have been found to limit output losses and expansion of fiscal deficits (Melecky and Raddatz 2011). In the absence of deep financial markets, disasters have been found to result in higher public debt

---

[2]Major disasters reduce real GDP per capita by about 0.6 percent on average (larger impact of 1 percent for lower-income countries (Hochrainer 2009; LaFramboise and Loko 2012). Disasters also produce an estimated 0.7 percentage point drop in a country's growth rate within the first year, on average, leading to a cumulative output loss, on average, of about 1.5 percent, in addition to the immediate direct losses (von Peter, von Dahlen, and Saxena 2012; LaFramboise and Loko 2012). The growth impact may differ across different types of disasters. Among climatic disasters, droughts have the largest average impact, with losses of 1 percent of GDP per capita and more than 2 percent per capita for lower-income countries (Raddatz 2009; Loayza and others 2009). In small island states, hurricanes have a larger estimated effect (on average, a 3 percent decline in GDP per capita) (Raddatz 2009).

[3]For middle- and upper-income countries, Melecky and Raddatz (2011) find that disasters boost expenditures by about 15 percent and lower revenues by about 10 percent, leading to an overall increase in budget deficits of 25 percent compared with initial levels.

(see, for example, Acevedo 2014 for the Caribbean).[4] Countries with deficits financed mostly with grants and donor support have adjusted more quickly (LaFramboise and Loko 2012).

- *Natural disasters also worsen external balances.* Damage to production and transportation capacity can reduce exports. In the short term, imports could decline with reduced economic activity, but may rise thereafter, supported by disaster relief and recovery programs. On balance, the trade balance could deteriorate (Rasmussen 2004; Cabezon and others 2015). External current accounts often deteriorate, although other elements of the balance of payments could offset the deterioration, including increased international aid and remittances in the short term (Bluedorn 2005), or insurance company payment inflows for damage insured or reinsured abroad (LaFramboise and Loko 2012).

- *Natural disasters typically have a disproportionate impact on the poor.* In developing countries and small states, low-income communities tend to live in the most vulnerable areas amid weak housing standards (World Bank 2003, 2016), and disasters can exacerbate social conditions. These communities typically have limited access to credit or insurance to help mitigate shocks (IMF 2003), and selling limited physical capital by the poor after disasters (including selling livestock to fund consumption) can lead to a long-term decline in productive capacity, reinforcing the vulnerabilities (LaFramboise and Loko 2012). Increased social spending by the government targeted to the most vulnerable populations, in turn, has fiscal implications.

## THE CARIBBEAN EXPERIENCE

An event analysis of 12 Caribbean countries broadly supports the findings of the previous studies, in that natural disasters have been associated with adverse effects on key macroeconomic outcomes. An examination of the disasters that had the largest damage-to-GDP ratios over the period 1950–2016 suggests that most countries experienced a decline in growth in the year of the disaster, but recovered in the subsequent year. Fiscal deficits also increased in the year of the disaster or subsequently in seven of the 12 countries. Debt-to-GDP ratios surged, and in some countries (The Bahamas, Barbados, Belize, St. Kitts and Nevis, St. Lucia, St. Vincent and the Grenadines) the disaster initiated an upward debt path that continued in subsequent years. External current account balances also deteriorated following disasters in most countries. The evolution of key macroeconomic variables around the very frequent natural disasters in some Caribbean countries (for example, The Bahamas and Jamaica) suggests that exposure to frequent disasters may be one of the key driving factors that interrupt a country's efforts to sustain high rates of growth and

---

[4]The fiscal impact of disasters may be understated, to the extent that aggregate spending data conceal a shift of resources toward disaster programs from other priorities.

improve fiscal balances, resulting, in turn, in gradually rising debt levels (Annex Figure 5.1.1).

Recent research on impediments to growth and strong fiscal performance in the Caribbean supports this possibility (Chamon and others, forthcoming). Policy-related structural challenges, including high exposure to natural disasters, explain the bulk of growth underperformance of the tourism-intensive Caribbean economies, along with other weaknesses, such as insufficient trade integration, gaps in human capital, crime, public indebtedness, ease of doing business, and financial strains. Addressing the various structural challenges to growth could provide important growth gains. The analysis suggests, for example, that reducing disaster damage by one-half could lead to significant growth gains for Dominica, Grenada, and St. Kitts and Nevis (about 1 percentage point higher GDP growth compared with baseline growth). These growth gains, in turn, could help break the negative debt-growth cycle and improve debt dynamics.

Climate change is expected to exacerbate the impact of natural disasters by making costly disasters increasingly more frequent and severe. Climate change increases the probability of large natural disasters (tropical storms) and raises mean damage (Acevedo 2016). Risks from sea-level rise and increased temperatures can affect growth through output losses in climate-sensitive sectors (such as forestry, tourism, agriculture, and coastal real estate) and through ecosystem disruption, damage to health, and water and food security risks, all with implications for long-term potential growth. Sea-level rise raises the risk of storm surges, tropical cyclones, and tsunamis, as well as the risk of persistent flooding and coastal erosion, affecting livelihoods, infrastructure, and habitability and posing a significant risk to growth and fiscal sustainability in tourism-dependent economies.[5] Stressed ecosystems could exacerbate poverty resulting from food insecurity, loss of productive assets, and limited savings (Hallegatte and others 2015).[6]

## THE POLICY RESPONSE

Differences in how natural disasters affect countries may reflect initial economic conditions and the country's structural characteristics and institutions. Institutions affect the efficiency of public intervention following disasters or have an indirect impact by shaping the private sector response. Higher literacy rates, greater financial sector depth, and a high degree of trade openness increase governments' ability to mobilize resources for reconstruction, mitigate the impact of the shock, and contain spillovers on the economy (Noy 2009). Economic diversification and availability of fiscal space to conduct countercyclical policy can also affect the

---

[5]Some small island states and coastal countries (for example, Guyana and Suriname in the Caribbean) could lose 10 percent of GDP or more under high sea-level scenarios (see, for example, Dasgupta and others 2007; World Bank 2013a).

[6]For Caribbean small states, a one-meter sea-level rise by 2080 is projected to result in losses and damage of about 8 percent of projected GDP (Simpson and others 2010; IMF 2016b; Farid and others 2016).

response and overall economic cost. Similarly, countries with large reserve buffers and access to domestic credit, but with less open capital accounts, are better able to cope with disasters. These messages have clear implications for how countries can better cope with natural disasters and climate change risks.

More specifically, countries can adopt policies that help reduce the human and economic costs of disasters and climate change, and build resilience to future shocks. To that end, public policies can focus on better preparation, mitigation, and response and explicitly build disaster and climate change risks into policy frameworks, including in the design of budgets, medium-term fiscal frameworks, public investment planning, debt and asset management policies, financial regulation and oversight, crisis management, and contingency planning. A range of approaches is needed to manage the risks both before disaster strikes and in the aftermath.

## Managing Risk Beforehand[7]

Identifying and assessing risks is the key starting point in managing disaster risk. Systems should be built to recognize the risks, assess their likelihood and potential impacts on macroeconomic outcomes and financial stability, and evaluate key vulnerabilities (for example, vulnerable infrastructure, communities, institutions, and populations). Where such risks are deemed high, countries should proactively improve the design of domestic policies to address the deficiencies and integrate these policies into investment, debt, and financial management frameworks. Governments, for instance, could prepare fiscal risk statements about the likelihood and potential impact of the risks and how they plan to manage the potential fiscal exposure to such disasters, which could, in turn, guide budget discussions and public financial management frameworks.

Reducing risk and preparing for it can be more effective than responding after the disaster strikes. Countries should invest in risk reduction, including by providing risk maps for high-risk areas and organizing information campaigns to raise risk awareness; setting up early-warning systems; implementing targeted public infrastructure projects (such as building seawalls along coastlines and maintaining and reinforcing roads and bridges); enforcing land use and zoning rules, building codes, and retrofitting requirements to reduce exposure to disaster damage; and providing incentives to encourage private sector investment in risk reduction (for example, through well-targeted subsidies for retrofitting properties or investing in drought-resilient crops).[8] Despite high returns to doing so (Figure 5.6)—potential benefits outweigh the costs—countries tend to underinvest in disaster risk reduction and prevention. Such underinvestment reflects a number of obstacles that public policy will need to address, ranging from moral hazard

---

[7]This section draws heavily on IMF 2016a, Otker-Robe 2014, and World Bank 2013b.

[8]For example, St. Lucia and St. Vincent and the Grenadines have enhanced disaster resilience through infrastructure projects, including more effective seawalls along urban coastlines, maintenance or reinforcement of bridges, and investments in urban resilience.

### Figure 5.6. Does It Pay to Prepare and Prevent?

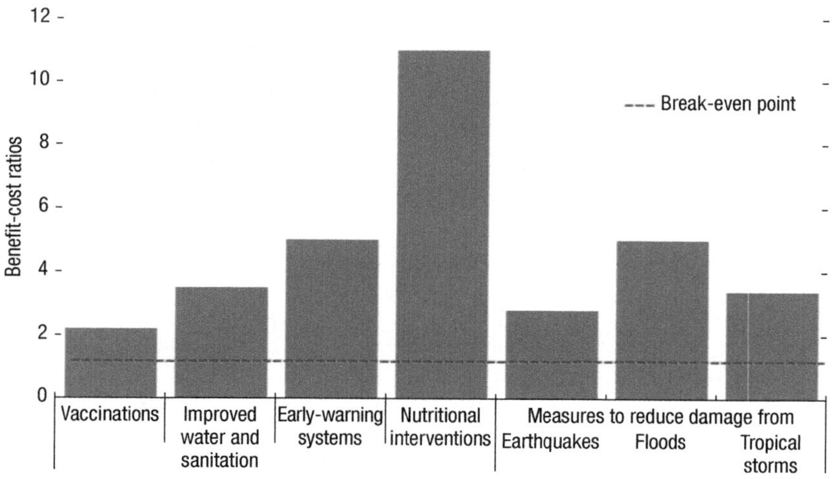

Source: Reproduced from World Bank 2013b.

(given the typical availability of ex post disaster funding) to capacity, information, or resource constraints in identifying, assessing, and managing risks, to political economy problems.

- *Capacity, information, and resource obstacles.* Insufficient resources and capacity make it difficult for developing countries, particularly the smaller Caribbean economies, to identify and assess disaster risks and take precautionary actions.[9] Similarly, shortfalls in funding the cost of climate change mitigation and adaptation have been an obstacle to taking action. Despite the available information on the evidence of climate change and disasters, individuals and governments continue to overlook their potential exposure to what they view as rare or distant events, underestimate the potential cost of inaction, and fail to take preventive action or insure against the events (Otker-Robe 2014; World Bank 2013b). Small-probability but high-impact risks are often ignored in the face of short-term challenges or priorities, resulting in underinvestment in preventive steps.

- *Moral hazard and political economy factors.* Availability of ex post disaster financing can create moral hazard and undermine incentives for prevention and preparation, including incentives to invest in warning systems or

---

[9]During 2007–12, for example, insurance covered less than 20 percent of total disaster losses in developing countries, on average, compared with about 60 percent in North America, according to SwissRe. Insurance intake is still low in many parts of the world, covering about one-third of natural disaster losses (Aon Benfield Analytics 2016).

enforce strict zoning and building regulations in disaster-prone areas, or for individuals to obtain insurance or avoid settling in when other alternatives are available (Clarke and Dercon 2016; IMF 2016b; World Bank 2013b). For governments, responding to disasters "after the event" may be judged to be more rewarding politically, compared with investing in generally costly hazard prevention and risk reduction, the rewards for which are less visible until disasters strike. Acting to reduce risk and prepare may also be undermined by political cycles, since preventive investments may span multiple administrations and make ownership difficult to attribute.

Public policy at national, regional, and international levels can help address the obstacles to effective management of disaster and climate change risks. Policy could aim to narrow existing information gaps and address behavioral biases, including through more systematic, frequent, and targeted dissemination of key information and best practices to build longer-term perspectives on rare, high-impact, or distant risks and raise awareness of the dangers of inaction. The international community could support capacity building and risk management actions to design contingency plans; set up monitoring, early-warning, and communication systems; develop insurance and hedging markets and make them more accessible to facilitate private sector risk-sharing solutions; and help countries diversify their economies to lessen the economic impact of disasters. Financing could be allocated to areas that build resilience and reduce vulnerabilities, and to those most exposed to shocks. Rewarding preparation and risk reduction by reducing premiums, making financing contingent on risk management, and providing technical assistance to build risk management capacity can limit moral hazard and encourage preparation that, over time, should reduce the need for future support (Otker-Robe 2014; World Bank 2013b).

Investing in risk mitigation is essential where risks cannot be prevented or reduced. Given the increasing cost and frequency of natural disasters, Caribbean governments can reduce their fiscal exposure by arranging for disaster financing before the event through a combination of (1) self-insurance (by building fiscal buffers or contingency funds), (2) risk-transfer arrangements (through catastrophe insurance or other capital market options, such as issuing catastrophe bonds, or participating in regional risk-sharing solutions), and (3) contingency financing.

- *Building fiscal buffers* provides self-insurance (IMF 2016a, 2016b). The appropriate size of the buffer can be established based on an assessment of disaster risks and their frequency and cost (Guerson 2016). Once the buffer is established, fiscal policy needs to ensure accumulation of savings, including through additional revenue measures or reduced spending if the buffer falls short, and a timeline for policy adjustment. Buffers can be accumulated in various ways and at various paces, and can be linked to medium-term fiscal objectives, considering the associated costs and benefits, especially when priority spending needs to be cut to boost savings and build buffers (IMF 2016a). "Looking through the cycle" may be needed in conducting fiscal policy, that is, a stronger fiscal stance may be needed in nondisaster years to accumulate buffers to offset the adverse impact when disasters hit. Fiscal rules can provide the discipline needed to sustain buffers and could be accompanied by an escape clause that allows for larger fiscal deficits as part of the response to natural disasters.[10] Debt-sustainability assessments should prevent an excessive rise in the overall debt burden and ensure a sustained period of strong fiscal performance to reduce debt ratios in disaster-prone countries.

- *Contingent lines of credit* can also help reduce ex ante disaster financing uncertainty. Ex ante financing agreements with bilateral, multilateral, and commercial creditors can be mobilized in the event of a disaster. For instance, at the bilateral level, the Marshall Islands, Micronesia, and Palau benefit from compacts with the United States offering access to emergency support from relevant U.S. agencies. At the multilateral level, the World Bank's Catastrophe Draw-Down Option offers a government immediate access to funds after a natural disaster, a time when liquidity constraints are usually highest.[11] Similarly, the IMF's emergency financing facilities, such as the Rapid Credit Facility and the Rapid Financing Instrument, are important sources of swift postdisaster liquidity support for small developing countries (IMF 2016a, 2017).

- *Disaster risk insurance* and related hedging tools also help protect governments from the economic burden of disasters and increase the capacity to respond. Governments can insure public assets and encourage insurance of private assets to reduce uncertainties associated with direct exposure to disaster risks. Encouraging private property insurance also reduces the risk that the public sector will be called on to cover private losses. Countries with more private and public insurance penetration experience lower output and income losses from disasters (Melecky and Raddatz 2011; von Peter, von Dahlen, and Saxena 2012; Munich Re 2013; Standard and Poor's 2015), but insurance coverage remains low globally (Swiss Re 2013; Aon Benfield Analytics 2016). Traditional indemnity insurance of physical assets is being used in a number of countries, although it is not widespread in small Caribbean economies given the high cost, especially where markets are underdeveloped and competition is limited (for example, in

---

[10]To build resilience to natural disasters, Grenada negotiated the inclusion of natural disaster clauses in several debt-restructuring agreements that allow for a delay in debt service following a qualifying natural disaster and provide important cash flow relief if a natural disaster materializes. Grenada also mandated contingency financing for natural disasters, with the Fiscal Responsibility Law requiring 40 percent of proceeds from the citizenship-by-investment (CBI) program to be transferred into the National Transformation Fund and saved. St. Kitts and Nevis is also in the process of establishing a Growth and Resilience Fund; deposits accumulated from CBI inflows are to be used to respond to external shocks, including natural disasters.

[11]The Catastrophe Draw-Down Option is available only to middle-income countries. A number of countries have used this instrument, including Colombia, Costa Rica, Guatemala, Peru, the Philippines, and Sri Lanka (World Bank 2011).

Belize and Grenada, insurance covered 4.5 percent of total damage in a recent large disaster; IMF 2016a).

- *Innovative approaches for sharing natural disaster risks* have also emerged over the past decade and could provide relief to governments in managing disaster risks. Parametric insurance, effectively an options contract, pays out in the event of a disaster that exceeds a pre-specified severity; triggers for payout are defined by storm, flood, or earthquake intensity and measured based on third-party data. While parametric insurance provides a quick relief, its cost can be high in a developing market. Economies of scale have been achieved by pooling cover at regional levels.[12] Catastrophe bonds that transfer the risk of a disaster to markets in exchange for a generous coupon payment allow the issuer to forgo repayment of the bond principal if a major disaster occurs. The forgone repayment releases resources from debt service to finance disaster response.[13] The market for catastrophe bonds is still developing, with challenges including the need to build investor expertise and confidence in these instruments and high cost.

Well-developed and well-functioning financial systems and markets are crucial to facilitating mitigation of natural disaster and climate change risks at affordable cost. More developed financial systems can enable a high rate of insurance penetration and offer hedging instruments, and help limit output losses and expansion of fiscal deficits (Melecky and Raddatz 2011). Access to credit, market insurance, and hedging products can provide the needed resources when disasters strike, helping mitigate the adverse effects on the private sector and reducing the burden on governments in reconstruction and recovery (Farid and others 2016; Fabrizio and others 2015). Well-developed financial markets can also help finance climate-change-risk adaptation efforts by funding projects that build resilience (for example, building floodgates, dykes, and other infrastructure, and investing in drought-resistant crops).

## Managing Postdisaster Risk

Building disaster response frameworks and contingency plans is crucial when risks cannot be averted or mitigated. Contingency plans are essential, since failure to plan can hamper the effectiveness of postdisaster intervention. Plans could focus on addressing the key risks and vulnerabilities (for example, emergency housing,

---

[12]These include, for example, the Caribbean Catastrophe Risk Insurance Facility, supported by the World Bank; a similar facility created for Pacific countries—the Pacific Catastrophe Risk Insurance Pilot; and African Risk Capacity, an Africa insurance pool for droughts (with flood risks to be added at a later date).

[13]Examples of such instruments include development, with collaboration with the World Bank, of a platform for a multicountry, multiperil catastrophe bond (the MultiCat Program with Mexico), which transfers risk to private investors and allows pooling of multiple risks to take advantage of diversification benefits (World Bank 2013a; Mahul and Cummins 2009; Mahul and Ghesquiere 2010).

**Table 5.2. Disaster Financing Risk-Layering Model**

| Probability or Frequency of Event (size of shock) | Ex Ante Financing | Ex Post Financing |
|---|---|---|
| 5 Percent or ≤ 20 Years (≤ 3 Percent of GDP) | Budgetary reserves | Emergency budget allocations |
| 3.33 Percent or ≤ 20–30 Years (≤ 5 Percent of GDP) | Contingent loans | Emergency loans |
| 1 Percent or ≤ 30–100 Years (≥ 5 Percent of GDP) | Insurance and reinsurance | – |
| 0.5 Percent or ≤ 100–200 Years (≥ 5 Percent of GDP) | Catastrophe bonds | Grants and humanitarian aid |
| Below 0.5 Percent or ≥ 200 Years (≥ 5 Percent of GDP) | Global partnerships for exogenous shocks and pandemics | Grants and humanitarian aid |

Source: Reproduced from IMF 2016a, based on Clarke and Deacon 2016.

compensation for the homeless, and restoration of key public infrastructure if hurricanes, cyclones, or earthquakes are the main risk, and food security and income support for farmers if drought is a key risk (Clarke and Dercon 2016; IMF 2016a). Putting in place necessary institutional frameworks could also provide spending flexibility for coping with natural disasters (for example, by allowing the government to exceed spending limits up to a defined amount in the event of a formally declared natural disaster, escape clauses in fiscal responsibility laws [as in Grenada] to allow the government to exceed targets if there were to be a major natural disaster, provision in the annual budget law for shifting resources following a major disaster, and setting up contingency space in the budget to cope with emergency needs).

Given the degree of exposure to disaster risk, policymakers could choose a mix of instruments to finance their contingent liability at the lowest economic opportunity cost. IMF (2016a) suggests that adopting the World Bank's risk-layered framework for optimizing disaster financing could be useful in this context (Table 5.2):

- Small but unpredictable financing needs can be met using self-insurance—either by reallocating spending or drawing down available government deposits.

- Moderate-sized disasters will generate financing needs that typically exceed buffers available from self-insurance, and will require access to external resources through contingent arrangements and risk-transfer options in which a third party takes over a portion of disaster-related financial risks in exchange for a fee or premium.

- For the largest disasters for which large-scale insurance is not cost-effective, sovereign catastrophe bonds can enable some risk transfer, though debt sustainability considerations may prevent large-scale use of borrowed resources, and there may be little alternative but to depend on grants and humanitarian assistance, where available.

# SUMMARY AND CONCLUSIONS

The Caribbean economies face formidable fiscal challenges, as evidenced by high levels of fiscal deficits and debt; many countries are trapped in a vicious circle of high-debt, low-growth performance. An important factor underlying this adverse feedback loop is the vulnerability of these countries to frequent and costly natural disasters. Since 1950, the region has been hit by hundreds of natural disasters (on average, seven disasters per year) that have killed hundreds of thousands of people and affected millions more. The economic impact of natural disasters is substantial; annual damage accounts for 40 percent of global damage, averaging 2.4 percent of GDP. Caribbean small states have suffered more damage at greater frequency than both other small and larger states. Climate change is expected to exacerbate these effects by increasing the frequency and severity of natural disasters, affecting the livelihood of the populations, and harming the essential assets their insufficiently diversified economies rely on.

Natural disasters have adverse effects on key macroeconomic outcomes. Most countries experience an immediate decline in growth in the year of the disaster, though generally recover in the subsequent year except for in the case of disasters. Fiscal deficits typically increase in the year of the disaster or subsequently, and debt-to-GDP ratios surge, in some countries initiating an upward path that continues for several years. External current account balances deteriorate in most cases. Exposure to frequent disasters may repeatedly interrupt a country's efforts to achieve high and sustainable rates of growth and improve fiscal balances and debt. Availability of aid, as well as more developed financial systems with high rates of insurance penetration, can help limit output losses and expansion of fiscal deficits and public debt.

Countries can adopt policies that help reduce the human and economic cost of disasters and climate change, and build resilience to future shocks. In this context, public policies can focus on better preparation, mitigation, and response and explicitly build disaster and climate change risks into their policy frameworks. Policies can address the obstacles to proactive management of disaster risk through risk reduction and preparation, including by reducing constraints on capacity, information, or resources; providing appropriate incentives; and countering political economy constraints. Where risks cannot be averted or reduced, risk mitigation using a combination of self-insurance, risk-transfer arrangements, and contingency financing is essential.

Policy at the regional and international levels could support countries' efforts by providing capacity building, tools for risk management, and financing. Technical assistance can help with designing contingency plans when risks cannot be prevented or mitigated; setting up monitoring, early-warning, and communication systems; developing insurance, financial, and hedging markets and making them more accessible to facilitate private sector risk-sharing solutions; and assisting countries with diversifying their economies to lessen the economic impact of disasters. Financing could target areas that reduce vulnerabilities and build resilience, and reward preparation and risk reduction. Given the degree of exposure to disaster risk, policymakers could choose a mix of instruments that finance their contingent liability at the lowest economic opportunity cost.

# ANNEX 5.1

Annex Figure 5.1.1. The Caribbean: Macroeconomic Effects of Natural Disasters before and after a Disaster Event

—— GDP growth     --- Government balance (percent of GDP)

—— Government debt (percent of GDP, right scale)   --- Current account balance (percent of GDP)

3. The Bahamas
(*t* = 2004)

4. Barbados
(*t* = 2004)

5. Belize
(*t* = 2000)

6. Dominica
(*t* = 2015)

**Annex Figure 5.1.1.** *(continued)*

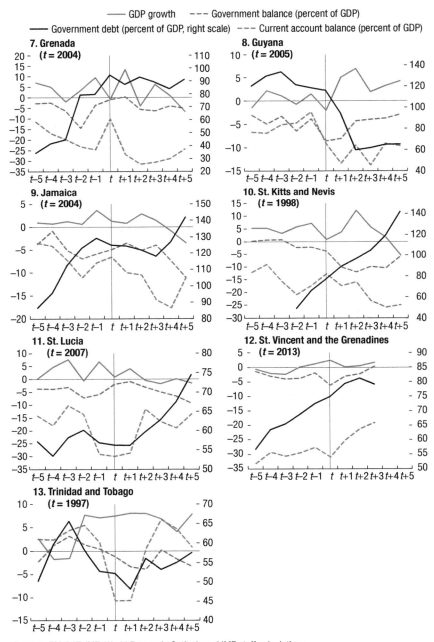

Sources: EM-DAT; IMF, *World Economic Outlook*; and IMF staff calculations.

# REFERENCES

Acevedo, S. 2014. "Debt, Growth and Natural Disasters: A Caribbean Trilogy." IMF Working Paper 14/125, International Monetary Fund, Washington, DC.

—. 2016. "Gone with the Wind: Estimating Hurricane and Climate Change Costs in the Caribbean" IMF Working Paper 16/199, International Monetary Fund, Washington, DC.

Aon Benfield Analytics. 2016. *2016 Annual Global Climate and Catastrophe Report*. London: Aon Benfield.

Bluedorn, J. C. 2005. "Hurricanes: Intertemporal Trade and Capital Shocks." Nuffield College Economics Paper W22.

Cabezon, E., L. Hunter, P. Tumbarello, K. Washimi, and Y. Wu. 2015. "Enhancing Macroeconomic Resilience to Natural Disasters and Climate Change in the Small States of the Pacific." IMF Working Paper 15/125, International Monetary Fund, Washington, DC.

Cavallo, E., and I. Noy. 2010. "The Economics of Natural Disasters: A Survey" IDB Working Paper Series 124, International Development Bank, Washington, DC.

Chamon, M., J. Charap, Q. Chen, D. Leigh, and F. Loyola. forthcoming "Growth in the Caribbean" In *Unleashing Growth and Strengthening Resilience in the Caribbean*. Washington, DC: International Monetary Fund.

Clarke, Daniel Jonathan, and Stefan Dercon. 2016. *Dull Disasters? How Planning Ahead Will Make a Difference*. Washington, DC: World Bank Group.

Dasgupta, S., B. Laplante, C. Meisner, D. Wheeler, and J. Yan. 2007. "The Impact of Sea Level Rise on Developing Countries: A Comparative Analysis." Policy Research Working Paper 4136, World Bank, Washington, DC.

Ewing, B., and J. Kruse., 2002. "The Impact of Project Impact on The Wilmington, North Carolina, Labor Market." *Public Finance Review* 30 (4): 296–309.

Fabrizio, Stefania, Rodrigo Garcia-Verdu, Catherine Pattillo, Adrian Peralta-Alva, Andrea Presbitero, Baoping Shang, Geneviève Verdier, Marie-Therese Camilleri, and others. 2015. "From Ambition to Execution: Policies in Support of Selected Sustainable Development Goals." IMF Staff Discussion Note 15/18, International Monetary Fund, Washington, DC.

Farid, M., M. Keen, M. Papaioannou, I. Parry, C. Pattillo, A. Ter-Martirosyan, and other IMF staff. 2016. "After Paris: Fiscal, Macroeconomic, and Financial Implications of Climate Change." IMF Staff Discussion Note 16/01, International Monetary Fund, Washington, DC.

Guerson, A. 2016. "Assessing Government Self-Insurance Needs against Natural Disasters—An Application to the ECCU." IMF Country Report 16/333, International Monetary Fund, Washington, DC.

Hallegatte S., B. Bangalore, L. Bonzanigo, M. Fay, T. Kane, U. Narloch, J. Rozenberg, D. Treguer, and A. Vogt-Schilb. 2015. *Shock Waves: Managing the Impacts of Climate Change on Poverty*. Washington, DC: World Bank.

Hochrainer, S. 2009. "Assessing the Macroeconomic Impacts of Natural Disasters—Are There Any?" World Bank Policy Research Working Paper 4968, World Bank, Washington, DC.

International Monetary Fund (IMF). 2003. "Fund Assistance for Countries Facing Exogenous Shocks." http://www.imf.org/external/np/pdr/sustain/2003/080803.pdf.

—. 2016a. "Small States' Resilience to Natural Disasters and Climate Change—Role for the IMF." Washington, DC.

—. 2016b. "Analyzing and Managing Fiscal Risks: Best Practices." Washington, DC.

—. 2017. "Large Natural Disasters—Enhancing the Financial Safety Net for Developing Countries." Washington, DC.

LaFramboise, N., and B. Loko. 2012. "Natural Disasters: Mitigating Impact, Managing Risks." IMF Working Paper 12/245, International Monetary Fund, Washington, DC.

Lee, D., P. Tumbarello, K. Washimi, and T. Zeinullayev (forthcoming). "Mind the Gap: Public Investment, Growth and Natural Disaster Risk in the Small States of the Pacific." International Monetary Fund, Washington, DC.

Loayza, N., E. Olaberria, J. Rigolini, and L. Christiaensen. 2009. "Natural Disasters and Growth." Policy Research Working Paper 4980, World Bank, Washington, DC.

Mahul, Olivier, and J. David Cummins. 2009. *Catastrophe Risk Financing in Developing Countries: Principles for Public Intervention.* Washington, DC: World Bank.

Mahul, Olivier, and F. Ghesquiere. 2010. "Financial Protection of the State against Natural Disasters: A Primer." Policy Research Working Paper 5429, World Bank, Washington, DC.

Melecky, M., and C. Raddatz. 2011. "How Do Governments Respond after Catastrophes? Natural-Disaster Shocks and the Fiscal Stance." Policy Research Working Paper 5564, World Bank, Washington, DC.

Munich Re. 2013. "Economic Consequences of Natural Catastrophes: Emerging and Developing Economies Particularly Affected—Insurance Cover Is Essential." Position Paper (October), Munich.

Noy, I. 2009. "The Macroeconomic Consequences of Disasters." *Journal of Development Economics* 88 (2): 221–31.

Otker-Robe, Inci. 2014. "Global Risks and Collective Action Failures: What Can the International Community Do?" IMF Working Paper 14/195, International Monetary Fund, Washington, DC.

Raddatz, C. 2007. "Are External Shocks Responsible for the Instability of Output in Low-Income Countries?" *Journal of Development Economics* 84 (1): 155–87.

———. 2009. "The Wrath of God: Macroeconomic Costs of Natural Disasters." Policy Research Working Paper, World Bank, Washington, DC., https://doi.org/10.1596/1813-9450-5039.

Rasmussen, T. 2004. "Macroeconomic Implications of Natural Disasters in the Caribbean." IMF Working Paper 4/224, International Monetary Fund, Washington, DC.

Simpson, M., D. Scott, M. Harrison, R. Sim, N. Silver, E. O'Keeffe, S. Harrison, and others. 2010. *Quantification and Magnitude of Losses and Damages Resulting from the Impacts of Climate Change: Modelling the Transformational Impacts and Costs of Sea Level Rise in the Caribbean.* Barbados, West Indies: United Nations Development Programme.

Standard and Poor's. 2015. "Storm Alert: Natural Disasters Can Damage Sovereign Creditworthiness." Ratings Direct. unepfi.org/pdc/wp-content/uploads/StormAlert.pdf.

Von Peter, G., S. von Dahlen, and S. Saxena. 2012. "Unmitigated Disasters?—New Evidence on the Macroeconomic Cost of Natural Catastrophes." BIS Working Paper, Bank for International Settlements, Geneva.

World Bank. 2003. "Caribbean Economic Overview 2002: Macroeconomic Volatility, Household Vulnerability, and Institutional and Policy Responses." Report No. 24165, LAC. World Bank, Washington, DC.

———. 2011. "Catastrophe Deferred Drawdown Option." Product Note, World Bank, Washington, DC. http://treasury.worldbank.org/bdm/pdf/Handouts_Finance/CatDDO_Product_Note.pdf.

———. 2013a. *Turn Down the Heat: Climate Extremes, Regional Impact and the Case for Resilience.* Washington, DC: World Bank.

———. 2013b. *World Development Report 2014—Risk and Opportunity: Managing Risk for Development.* Washington, DC: World Bank.

———. 2016. "Shock Waves: Managing the Impacts of Climate Change on Poverty." World Bank, Washington, DC.

# CHAPTER 6

# Tax Incentives:
# To Use or Not To Use?

MEREDITH A. MCINTYRE

## INTRODUCTION

Tax incentives are all too pervasive in the Caribbean and have been an integral part of the tax systems since the 1970s. They were enacted to attract private investment in tourism, manufacturing, and agro-industries in an attempt to diversify the economy away from primary commodity exports—sugar and bananas—that were adversely affected by the dismantling of preferential trading arrangements with Europe in the 1990s. Concessions for investment in sectors such as tourism and manufacturing have generally been provided through targeted legislation, such as the Fiscal Incentives Act, Aid to Pioneer Industries Act, and the Hotel Aids Act. Tax incentives granted for regional, social, and welfare reasons are provided in the Common External Tariff (CET) Act and in specific legislation covering statutory bodies and state enterprises.

An important reason often provided by authorities in the Caribbean for the widespread use of tax incentives, particularly in the tourism sector, is the increased competition in this market in the Caribbean. Every country feels compelled to offer generous incentives packages to both existing and potential investors, since they fear that otherwise these investors will move their existing or potential investment to a competing destination in the region. Another argument advanced in support of incentives schemes is that they strengthen competitiveness by compensating investors for distortions and inefficiencies in the economy. However, from the investors' perspective, evidence suggests that tax incentives themselves do not necessarily make a country more attractive; investment location decisions are driven more by overall cost competitiveness.

Experience in the Caribbean indicates that tax incentives have had a positive impact on foreign direct investment (FDI), particularly in the tourism industry. At the same time, however, such incentives have imposed significant costs on host economies because they have resulted in large revenue losses, exacerbating already-weak fiscal conditions, including rising public debt levels, in most countries. Indeed, a study by the Vale Columbia Center (2013) notes that by any

Table 6.1. Prevalence of Tax Incentives around the World

| | Number of Countries Surveyed (percent) | Tax Holiday or Tax Exemption (percent) | Reduced Tax Rate (percent) | Investment Allowance or Tax Credit (percent) | VAT Exemption or Reduction (percent) | R&D Tax Incentive (percent) | Super-Deductions (percent) | SEZ, Free Zones, EPZ, Freeport (percent) | Discretionary Process (percent) |
|---|---|---|---|---|---|---|---|---|---|
| East Asia and Pacific | 12 | 92 | 92 | 75 | 75 | 83 | 8 | 83 | 25 |
| Eastern Europe and Central Asia | 16 | 75 | 31 | 19 | 94 | 31 | 0 | 94 | 38 |
| Latin America and the Caribbean | 24 | 75 | 29 | 46 | 58 | 13 | 4 | 75 | 29 |
| Middle East and North Africa | 15 | 73 | 40 | 13 | 60 | 0 | 0 | 80 | 27 |
| OECD | 33 | 21 | 30 | 61 | 79 | 76 | 18 | 67 | 27 |
| South Asia | 7 | 100 | 43 | 71 | 100 | 29 | 57 | 71 | 14 |
| Sub-Saharan Africa | 30 | 60 | 63 | 73 | 73 | 10 | 23 | 57 | 47 |

Source: Vale Columbia Center 2013, 53.

Note: EPZ = export processing zone; OECD = Organisation for Economic Co-operation and Development; R&D = research and development; SEZ = special economic zone; VAT = value-added tax.

measure—whether percent of government revenues, percent of the value of the investment for which incentives are provided, or the cost per job created—these incentives have proved to be costly.

Against this backdrop, the IMF's policy advice has emphasized streamlining incentives schemes to minimize costs and reduce distortions by not favoring specific activities, while underscoring the importance of structural reforms to improve competitiveness and the domestic economic and business environment to attract private investment. These issues are further elaborated in this chapter.

The next section provides a brief synopsis of the typology of tax incentives in the Caribbean, and is followed by a discussion of their effectiveness. The subsequent section elaborates on policy recommendations, followed by a discussion of reform experiences based on two country case studies—Jamaica and Grenada. The final section provides concluding remarks.

## A TYPOLOGY OF TAX INCENTIVES IN THE CARIBBEAN

Tax holidays are widely used throughout the world. Table 6.1 indicates that tax holidays are commonplace in South Asia, Eastern Europe and Central Asia, and the East Asia Pacific countries, but less so in Organisation for Economic Co-operation and Development countries. This reflects the gradual shift away from the use of tax holidays over time in developed countries because of their ineffectiveness in increasing investments.

Tax incentives are widespread in the Caribbean. Virtually all countries in the region have special incentives regimes aimed at attracting and retaining private investment by compensating investors for high operating costs and low productivity. In the absence of an effective regional agreement on tax harmonization, intense tax competition occurs as countries vie with each other to attract private investment. Table 6.2 provides a snapshot of the various types of tax incentives or holidays being provided by countries in the Caribbean.

**Table 6.2. Summary of Tax Incentives in Caribbean Countries**

| Country | Tax Holidays | Other Incentives |
|---|---|---|
| **Antigua and Barbuda** | 3–20 years (general) 6–25 years (tourism, manufacturing, information and communications technology, financial services, health and wellness, energy, and creative industry) | Cabinet, at its discretion, may exempt persons or enterprises from any tax or duty<br>Carryforward on losses from tax holidays for up to seven years<br>Exemption from Antigua and Barbuda sales tax, customs duties, and revenue recovery charge on all capital items in tourism, manufacturing, information and communications technology, financial services, health and wellness, energy, and creative industries<br>Reduction in property tax rate of from 10 to 100 percent<br>Stamp duty reduction of from 10 to 100 percent<br>Exemption from environmental levy<br>Exemption from Antigua and Barbuda sales tax, corporate income tax, and withholding tax for international business corporations |
| **Barbados** | 11–15 years 10 years for renewable energy projects | Minister of Finance has substantial discretionary powers under Duties, Taxes and Other Payments (Exemptions) Act to grant exemptions to any person or business.<br>Reduced corporate tax rate (15 percent) on manufacturing and construction, and for small businesses<br>20–40 percent initial and investment allowances<br>Exemptions from VAT and customs duties on plant and equipment and raw materials for manufacturing, and small business<br>Exemptions from VAT and customs duties on building materials and supplies in hotels in the tourism industry<br>Export allowance provisions<br>*Deductions*<br>   Capital expenses are allowed 150 percent deduction for qualifying expenditures under the Tourism Development and Shipping Incentives Acts<br>   100 percent deduction on interest (150 percent for renewable energy)<br>   10 percent tax credit on qualified new employment<br>   35–93 percent tax credit on export and foreign currency earnings<br>   Losses carried forward for nine years |
| **Belize** | Up to 5 years | Reduced tax rate on customs duties and VAT<br>*Exemptions*<br>  Receipts of less than BZ$54,000 per year<br>  Rental receipts of less than BZ$1,650 per month and sole source of income<br>  Interest on savings<br>  Employment income<br>  Charitable contributions up to BZ$30,000 per year |
| **Dominica** | 5–20 years | VAT and customs duty waivers for machinery and equipment for manufacturing; VAT waivers for building materials (tourism)<br>VAT exemption for agricultural and fishing inputs<br>Accelerated depreciation of up to 20 percent upon expiration of tax holidays<br>No taxes for offshore banking and insurance<br>VAT and customs exemption on gifted items and building materials for schools<br>VAT and customs exemption on gifted items for churches, charitable organizations, private schools, and universities |

**Table 6.2.** *(continued)*

| Country | Tax Holidays | Other Incentives |
|---|---|---|
| **Grenada** | Tax legislation and Investment Act were revised in 2016. These acts establish a standardized statutory investment incentives regime for eligible priority sectors: tourism (accommodation, restaurants, services); agriculture and agribusiness; manufacturing; education and training; health and wellness; information and communications technology; energy; medical services; sports; creative industries. Reduced incentives apply to other eligible sectors (taxi and tour operators, student accommodation, and heavy equipment operators). | Automatic exemptions and tax concessions to eligible sectors include the following:<br>*VAT*—suspension of VAT applicable to all eligible sectors on imports of building and raw materials, and machinery and equipment. In addition, zero rating of VAT on local purchases of building materials and capital goods for priority sector projects exceeding EC\$30 million.<br>*Customs (Import) Duty*—applicable to eligible sectors, based on specified category of imported items by sectors, with waivers of from 50 to 100 percent.<br>*Customs Service Charge*— applicable only to raw materials for all manufacturers at reduced rate of 3 percent.<br>*Excise Tax*—same percentage exemption as duty exemption on raw materials and vehicles for qualifying investment in eligible sectors except student accommodation.<br>*Property Transfer Tax*—50–100 percent waiver, based on investment costs and geographic location, applicable only to priority sectors. For villas and condos, reduced rates of 1 percent and 5 percent for the developer and purchaser, respectively, on first sale; a rate of 2.5 percent for both buyer and seller on subsequent sales.<br>*Withholding Tax*—on interest charges and royalty fees, applicable only to tourism accommodation and health and wellness projects. Tiered waivers based on investment costs (50 percent for EC\$30 million to EC\$80 million; 100 percent for investments over EC\$80 million).<br>*Loss Carryforward*—100 percent of losses in any year carried forward for six years, applicable to tax-compliant companies in all eligible sectors.<br>*Investment Allowance*—at a rate of 100 percent of qualifying capital expenditure, applicable only to priority sectors.<br>*Tax Credit for Training*—deductible allowance at rate of 150 percent of qualifying training costs, to all eligible sectors.<br>*Tax Credit for Research and Development*—150 percent tax credit applicable only to agriculture and agribusiness. |
| **Guyana** | 5–10 years | Noncommercial companies face a 35 percent corporate income tax.<br>*Exemptions include the following:*<br>Import duty for all oil products, imports from CARICOM, fuel imports from Venezuela and Curaçao, vehicles for public servants, and certain manufacturing equipment and raw materials<br>Tax credit for VAT on goods imported for business, and zero rate on large working capital items<br>Up to 75 percent reduction in corporate income tax for exporters of nontraditional products outside the CARICOM area<br>Nontraditional agro-processing, communication technology, petroleum exploration and refining, mineral extraction, and tourism<br>Charitable organizations are exempt from CIT, withholding tax, and property tax.<br>*Exempted types of income*<br>50 percent of capital gain on developed property<br>25 percent of capital gain on undeveloped property<br>Interest and other income that is subject to withholding tax<br>Treasury bill discounts earned by commercial banks<br>Donations to companies, limited to 10 percent of their chargeable income.<br>*Transparency*<br>Tax exemptions are published annually, starting in 2004.<br>Exemptions are established at the legal level.<br>Some exemptions are given under the Customs Duties Orders. |

**Table 6.2.** *(continued)*

| Country | Tax Holidays | Other Incentives |
|---|---|---|
| **Haiti** | Up to 15 years | Tax holiday: Zero rate for up to 15 years, gradually increases thereafter starting at 15 percent. |
| | | Tax incentives are established by law, with no discretion. Available to both domestic and foreign investors. |
| | | Sectors: Exports and reexports, agriculture, craft, manufacturing, tourism and associated services, free trade zones. |
| | | Exemptions from turnover tax for local manufacturers that import their new material and export their production or sell to an exporter |
| | | Offshore banking, nonprofit organizations, and charitable organizations are exempt from customs and income tax. Export processing zones are exempt from royalties, local taxes (except license), VAT and other indirect taxes, and customs duties and fees on equipment imports. |
| **Jamaica** | No tax holidays. Corporate tax rate is 25 percent (excluding regulated industries, which continue to be taxed at a higher rate). | Cabinet approved *de minimis* cap on discretionary waivers of J$10 million per month. |
| | | Simplified capital allowances and tax depreciation rates aligned with economic life of assets for new investments |
| | | Enterprises in tourism industry could either retain exemptions under previous incentives regime (Hotels [Incentives] Act) or move to new regime. Grandfathered companies would pay VAT at standard rate of 16 percent (rather than reduced VAT rate for tourism of 10 percent) until their current set of incentives ends. |
| | | Employment tax credit for all statutory payroll levies (education tax, National Housing Trust, National Insurance, and Human Employment and Resource Training contributions) capped at 30 percent of the chargeable income tax |
| | | The Large-Scale Projects and Pioneer Industries Act permits the minister to grant unspecified tax concessions to qualifying investment projects up to 0.25 percent of GDP per year. |
| | | *Exemptions* |
| | |   Charitable, religious, scientific, and educational organizations |
| | |   Income and incentives on capital expenditure to an approved organization in a special development area |
| **St. Kitts and Nevis** | Up to 15 years | Cabinet, at its discretion, may exempt any person or enterprise from any tax or duty. |
| | | Exemption from VAT and customs duties on plant, machinery and equipment, and raw materials in manufacturing |
| | | Exemption from VAT and customs duties on building materials in tourism |
| | | VAT and customs duty exemptions for churches, charitable and sporting organizations, private schools, universities, and returning residents |
| | | Exemption from VAT of listed equipment for agriculture and fishing |
| | | Reduced property tax rate by up to 75 percent |

**Table 6.2.** *(continued)*

| Country | Tax Holidays | Other Incentives |
|---|---|---|
| **St. Lucia** | Up to 25 years (manufacturing) | Rebate on profits for exports outside CARICOM of from 25 to 50 percent of paid income tax |
| | Up to 15 years (tourism) | No taxes for offshore banking and insurance |
| | Up to 15 years (micro and small business) | Reduced corporate tax rate (20 percent) on residential complexes, conference centers, commercial buildings, and arts and cultural investments |
| | 5 years for yachting activity | Reduced VAT rate (8 percent) for goods and services provided by hotels |
| | 5 years in the Free Trade Zone, subsequently, 2–8 percent on chargeable income | Exemption from VAT and customs duties on machinery, plant and equipment, and raw materials in manufacturing |
| | | Exemption from customs duties on building materials for micro and small-scale enterprises |
| | | Exemption from VAT and customs duties on listed equipment for agriculture and fishing |
| | | Exemption from VAT and customs duties for churches, charitable organizations, sporting organizations, private schools, universities, and radio stations |
| | | Exemption from customs duties for yachting equipment and materials for five years |
| | | Cabinet-approved discretionary exemptions from VAT and customs duties to individuals and companies |
| **St. Vincent and the Grenadines** | Tax holidays up to 15 years | Losses carried forward for five years after tax holiday |
| | | Tax credit for exports (up to 50 percent) depending on the ratio of exports to total profits |
| | | Income from exports taxed at reduced rates (15–30 percent) depending on export destination |
| | | Exemption from corporate tax, VAT, and customs duties for companies engaged in development of tourism on Mustique, Canouan, and Quatre Isle Islands |
| | | Reduced VAT rate (10 percent) on tourism for accommodation, diving, and marine or land tour services |
| | | Exemption from VAT and customs duties on building materials and hotel equipment in tourism |
| | | Exemption from tax on income from farming and VAT and customs duties on agriculture and fishing inputs |
| | | Exemption from income tax from construction, sale, or lease of residential accommodation for up to 10 years |
| | | Exemption from corporate income tax on dividends |
| | | Exemption from CIT, customs duties, and property tax for small businesses |
| | | Exemption from custom duties and property tax, and 1 percent income tax for international companies |
| | | Cabinet at its discretion may exempt any individual or company from tax or duty. |

| Table 6.2. *(continued)* | | |
|---|---|---|
| Country | Tax Holidays | Other Incentives |
| **Suriname** | Up to 10 years | Holiday period depends on the value of the investment and employment generation. |
| | | Tax incentives are based on the Investment Law of 2001. |
| | | The Raw Material Act, based on a presidential resolution, is outside of the Investment Law. |
| | | Reduced rate on customs duties and sales tax |
| | | The exemption does not apply if the profits, after offsets for losses, amount to twice the invested capital. |
| | | Sectors: agriculture, fishery/aquaculture, mining, forestry, tourism (except casinos), construction, manufacturing, road transport, and trade. |
| | | *Exemptions from import duties and turnover tax for the following:* |
| | |     Imports of investment goods per Investment Law of 2001 |
| | |     Imports of project goods if they are financed by investment donors per the Tariff Act |
| | |     Imports of all goods from CARICOM that are wholly produced within the community, per the Tariff Act (with the exemption of sales tax) |
| | |     Imports of raw materials per the Raw Material Act |
| | | Nonprofit organizations and charitable institutions do not pay taxes. |
| | | Both domestic and foreign investors have the same incentives. |
| **Trinidad and Tobago** | Up to 5 years | Reduced rate on customs duties and VAT |
| | | Allowance to companies that export to countries outside of CARICOM: |
| | | - An allowance that equals 150 percent of all promotional expenses is deducted from profits. |
| | | - An allowance that equals 15 percent of capital cost |
| | | - An allowance that equals a maximum of 25 percent of the value of investment is deducted from chargeable profits |
| | | *Deductions* |
| | |     Wear and tear on plant and machinery and buildings used in the production of income |
| | |     Bad and doubtful debt |
| | |     Premium paid on fire insurance |

Source: Country authorities.
Note: CARICOM = Caribbean Community; CIT = corporate income tax; VAT = value-added tax.

Generally, tax incentives schemes are directed at a few sectors in the economy, mostly export-related industries, and the package typically consists of corporate income tax holidays and exemptions from value-added taxes (VAT) and customs duties. Holidays for corporate income taxes are the most widely used incentives in the region. Countries offer tax holidays ranging from five to 25[1] years. These holidays are typically granted to specific sectors, notably tourism and manufacturing, for which the Caribbean countries are viewed as having a comparative advantage. Many countries in the region also grant corporate income tax exemptions to offshore banking and insurance. In some countries, income tax laws include accelerated depreciation provisions and allow net operating losses to be carried forward for a certain period.

---

[1] A study by the Vale Columbia Center (2013) indicates that most countries offer a tax holiday for between three and eight years, suggesting that the Caribbean is overly generous compared with the rest of the world.

Import-related tax exemptions are also commonplace in the tax incentives schemes in the region. Like corporate tax holidays, these tax incentives exempt qualified investors from paying customs duties and VAT on imports for a defined period. In some instances, such exemptions could amount to almost 100 percent of taxes and duties owed. Import duty exemptions can be provided only for items listed in the Customs Tariff Legislation that are subject to the Caribbean Community (CARICOM) CET. In addition, a reduced VAT rate on tourism-related services, including hotel accommodation, is quite common in the region (for example, in Antigua and Barbuda, Barbados, Grenada, Jamaica, St. Kitts and Nevis); the reduced rate applies to tour operators and restaurants in St. Kitts and Nevis.[2] The scope of the VAT exemptions and zero-rated goods varies across individual countries, and the list usually includes items beyond basic staples and medicines.

Employment tax credits (to promote employment) and property tax exemptions, including preferential access to high-value land for investors in the tourism industry, are also frequently used. In addition, concessions to government agencies, statutory bodies, and nongovernmental organizations are also a common practice in the region. Typically, government imports are exempt from customs duties and excise taxes. In addition, statutory bodies, nongovernmental organizations, targeted private sector entities (for example, private universities in Grenada) and some utilities (electric power plants in Dominica and St. Lucia) receive customs duty exemptions.

It is important to note that, in almost all countries, the cabinet or the different ministries (finance, agriculture, commerce, tourism, and so on) have the authority to grant concessions, and in practice they have discretion in all aspects of the decision,[3] including, for example, whether the legal requirements are fulfilled in an application and what the terms of the concession should be. Thus, many concessions are provided on a case-by-case basis, based on nontransparent cabinet decisions that leave many investors concerned about unequal treatment and favoritism. This said, it is evident from Table 6.1 that discretionary administrative processes are also pervasive in other regions of the world.

## EFFECTIVENESS OF TAX CONCESSIONS: BENEFITS AND COSTS

An obvious question is whether tax incentives have encouraged private investment, particularly FDI, in the region. The Vale Columbia Center (2013) study points out that firms engaging in FDI do so for four main motives:

- *Market seeking*. Investors are in search of new consumers for their goods and services.
- *Resource seeking*. Investment is driven primarily by the availability of, and access to, natural resources, raw materials, or low-skilled labor in a host country.

---

[2]A reduced VAT rate also applies to hotel accommodation and food, beverages, and other related services by providers in the tourism sector (St. Lucia).

[3]Chai and Goyal (2008) find that tax legislation in the region typically did not provide detailed procedural rules or specific criteria for granting tax concessions.

## Table 6.3. Typology of FDI and Response to Tax Incentives

| Type of Investment | Factors that Drive Investment | Response to Investment Incentives |
|---|---|---|
| Resource-Seeking FDI | Location of natural resources, raw materials, low-skilled labor, agglomeration benefits | Low response. FDI driven primarily by nontax factors. |
| Market-Seeking FDI | Market potential<br>– Market dimensions<br>– Income per capita<br>– Customer-specific preferences<br>– Kind of goods and services to be provided | Low response. Level playing field between firms is critical (same tax system for all competitors). |
| Strategic-Asset-Seeking FDI | Acquisition of strategic assets<br>– Brands and market positioning<br>– Know-how<br>– Technology<br>– Distribution networks<br>– Human capital | Low response. FDI is driven by the location of the asset. However, lower taxes on capital gains reduce the cost of the transfer of these assets. |
| Efficiency-Seeking FDI | Lower costs<br>– Mostly export oriented<br>– Availability of skills at low costs<br>– Close to markets<br>– Low relocation costs | High response to tax incentives. Firms are expected to compete globally, hence, the lower the costs, the better their ability to compete globally. |

Source: Vale Columbia Center 2013, 15.
Note: FDI = foreign direct investment.

- *Strategic-asset seeking.* FDI is driven by a firm's desire to acquire tangible or intangible assets (for example, advanced technology owned by a target company) to strengthen its own position or weaken the position of its competitors.
- *Efficiency seeking.* Investment is motivated by firms seeking to decrease their costs of production by transferring production to locations with low labor costs or rationalizing their operations.

The study analyzes the impact of tax incentives on investors' investment decisions based on the four motives for FDI. A typology is developed to illustrate the effectiveness of tax incentives on investors' decisions varies by the nature of the business and its motive for FDI (Table 6.3).

Table 6.3 indicates that firms engaging in FDI to enter new markets or to acquire natural resources (or other strategic assets) are less influenced by tax incentives than are export-oriented, footloose firms investing in a country to take advantage of cheap labor and lower costs. The latter group seems most relevant to an understanding of FDI in the Caribbean and the role played by tax incentives in investment location decisions. Klemm and Van Parys (2012) find that Latin American and Caribbean countries competed over footloose investment; in some cases, tax holidays or a reduced tax burden were found to be effective in attracting FDI. Similarly, Cubbedu and others (2008) note that an earlier survey of multinationals in the Caribbean revealed that investment in the tourism sector is more sensitive, relative to other sectors, to tax incentives. In contrast, however, Chai and Goyal (2008), using a panel sample of Eastern Caribbean Currency Union countries for the period 1990–2003, find that tax incentives have a limited impact on FDI.

## Table 6.4. Revenue Losses from Concessions

*(Percent of GDP, unless otherwise indicated)*

| | Overall Forgone Revenue (percent of GDP) | | | | | *Of Which:* Discretionary | | | |
| | | | | | | Share (%) | | 2010–12 | |
| | 2010 | 2011 | 2012 | 2013 | 2010–12 | Minimum | Maximum | Minimum | Maximum |
|---|---|---|---|---|---|---|---|---|---|
| **Antigua and Barbuda** | . . . | 7.0 | 6.4 | 6.7 | 6.7 | . . . | . . . | 1.6 | 3.2 |
| VAT | . . . | 4.6 | 3.8 | 4.0 | 4.2 | 20 | 40 | 0.8 | 1.7 |
| Import Duties | . . . | 1.7 | 1.9 | 2.1 | 1.8 | 35 | 70 | 0.6 | 1.3 |
| Corporate Income Tax | . . . | 0.7 | 0.7 | 0.6 | 0.7 | 15 | 30 | 0.1 | 0.2 |
| Others | . . . | 0.0 | 0.0 | 0.0 | 0.0 | 20 | 40 | 0.0 | 0.0 |
| **Dominica** | 3.9 | 4.9 | 4.3 | . . . | 4.4 | . . . | . . . | 1.0 | 2.0 |
| VAT | 2.4 | 3.1 | 2.7 | . . . | 2.7 | 20 | 40 | 0.5 | 1.1 |
| Import Duties | 1.1 | 0.9 | 0.7 | . . . | 0.9 | 35 | 70 | 0.3 | 0.6 |
| Corporate Income Tax | 0.3 | 0.8 | 0.8 | . . . | 0.6 | 15 | 30 | 0.1 | 0.2 |
| Others | 0.1 | 0.1 | 0.1 | . . . | 0.1 | 20 | 40 | 0.0 | 0.0 |
| **Grenada** | 6.7 | 6.7 | 7.5 | . . . | 7.0 | . . . | . . . | 1.5 | 3.0 |
| VAT | 3.8 | 3.9 | 3.7 | . . . | 3.8 | 20 | 40 | 0.8 | 1.5 |
| Import Duties | 0.5 | 0.6 | 1.4 | . . . | 0.8 | 35 | 70 | 0.3 | 0.6 |
| Corporate Income Tax | 0.5 | 0.5 | 0.5 | . . . | 0.5 | 15 | 30 | 0.1 | 0.2 |
| Others | 1.9 | 1.7 | 1.9 | . . . | 1.8 | 20 | 40 | 0.4 | 0.7 |
| **St. Kitts and Nevis** | 5.4 | 5.4 | 4.8 | . . . | 5.2 | . . . | . . . | 1.4 | 2.8 |
| VAT | 1.7 | 1.6 | 1.4 | . . . | 1.6 | 20 | 40 | 0.3 | 0.6 |
| Import Duties | 2.8 | 2.8 | 2.3 | . . . | 2.6 | 35 | 70 | 0.9 | 1.8 |
| Corporate Income Tax | 0.9 | 0.9 | 1.0 | . . . | 0.9 | 15 | 30 | 0.1 | 0.3 |
| Others | 0.0 | 0.1 | 0.1 | . . . | 0.1 | 20 | 40 | 0.0 | 0.0 |
| **St. Lucia** | 6.4 | 5.7 | 7.3 | . . . | 6.5 | . . . | . . . | 1.5 | 3.0 |
| VAT | 2.7 | 2.2 | 3.7 | . . . | 2.9 | 20 | 40 | 0.6 | 1.1 |
| Import Duties | 2.0 | 1.8 | 1.8 | . . . | 1.9 | 35 | 70 | 0.7 | 1.3 |
| Corporate Income Tax | 1.5 | 1.4 | 1.5 | . . . | 1.5 | 15 | 30 | 0.2 | 0.4 |
| Others | 0.2 | 0.3 | 0.3 | . . . | 0.3 | 20 | 40 | 0.1 | 0.1 |
| **St. Vincent and the Grenadines** | 6.3 | 5.4 | 7.8 | 9.9 | 6.5 | . . . | . . . | 1.6 | 3.2 |
| VAT | 3.3 | 2.6 | 3.2 | 3.2 | 3.0 | 20 | 40 | 0.6 | 1.2 |
| Import Duties | 2.1 | 1.8 | 2.2 | 3.5 | 2.0 | 35 | 70 | 0.7 | 1.4 |
| Corporate Income Tax | 0.5 | 0.6 | 0.6 | 0.6 | 0.6 | 15 | 30 | 0.1 | 0.2 |
| Others | 0.4 | 0.4 | 1.8 | 2.6 | 0.9 | 20 | 40 | 0.2 | 0.3 |
| **Barbados** | . . . | 6.2 | 5.6 | 0.0 | 5.9 | . . . | . . . | 1.5 | 2.9 |
| VAT | . . . | 3.5 | 2.9 | . . . | 3.2 | 20 | 40 | 0.6 | 1.3 |
| Import Duties | . . . | 1.9 | 1.8 | . . . | 1.9 | 35 | 70 | 0.6 | 1.3 |
| Corporate Income Tax | . . . | . . . | . . . | . . . | . . . | 15 | 30 | 0.0 | 0.0 |
| Others | . . . | 0.8 | 0.9 | . . . | 0.8 | 20 | 40 | 0.2 | 0.3 |
| Discretionary Waivers | . . . | 0.3 | 0.4 | . . . | 0.3 | . . . | . . . | . . . | . . . |
| **Jamaica** | 6.1 | 5.9 | 7.8 | . . . | 6.6 | . . . | . . . | 1.5 | 3.0 |
| VAT | 3.6 | 3.2 | 3.6 | . . . | 3.5 | 20 | 40 | 0.7 | 1.4 |
| Import Duties | 1.2 | 1.2 | 1.4 | . . . | 1.3 | 35 | 70 | 0.4 | 0.9 |
| Corporate Income Tax | 0.4 | 0.5 | 0.6 | . . . | 0.5 | 15 | 30 | 0.1 | 0.2 |
| Others | 0.9 | 0.9 | 2.2 | . . . | 1.3 | 20 | 40 | 0.3 | 0.5 |

Source: Chai and Goyal 2008.
Note: VAT = value-added taxes.

**Figure 6.1. Tax Expenditures as a Percentage of GDP**
*(Select countries)*

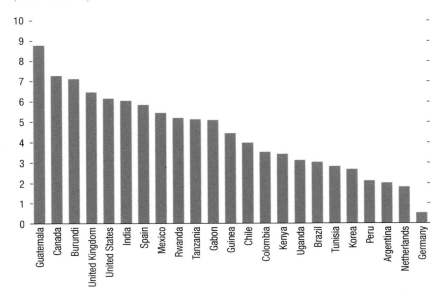

Source: James 2013.

While the available evidence indicates that tax incentives have attracted FDI, it is evident they also impose significant costs, including notably the erosion of the tax base, the direct loss of revenue, efficiency losses due to the preferential treatment of specific activities over others, administrative complexity, and social costs from corruption and unproductive rent-seeking activities.

Analytical work by the IMF has focused greater attention on revenue losses from the provision of tax incentives by countries in the region. IMF estimates[4] indicate that the total tax revenue forgone because of tax incentives, or the size of tax expenditures in the region, is between 4.4 and 7.0 percent of GDP, based on a sample of Caribbean countries in the period 2010–13 (see Table 6.4).[5] The size of tax expenditures is not significantly higher than that in other countries. The Vale Columbia Center (2013) study presents data for 22 countries, including several OECD countries, and the size of tax expenditures as a percentage of GDP (Figure 6.1) is similar to that for the Caribbean. Moreover, based on data from the same study, it is clear that incentives are also a costly way to generate jobs (Figure 6.2).

---

[4] Chai and Goyal (2008); Krelove and others (2014); Krelove, Crivelli, and Gendron (2014); Mullins and Hutton (2008); Norregaard and others (2015); and Taitt (2013).

[5] The data also indicate that revenue forgone because of discretion ranges between 1.6 and 3.2 percent of GDP.

**Figure 6.2. Incentives and Employment Costs**
*(Select countries)*

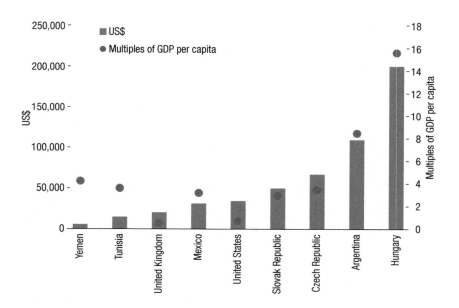

Source: Vale Columbia Center (2013).

In addition, assessments of the impact of tax incentives in the region (Chai and Goyal 2008; Cubbedu and others 2008) conclude that although tax incentives have some effect on FDI, the impact is far less significant than the impacts from improving the economic and institutional environment, particularly the quality of institutions, upgraded infrastructure, transparent regulatory arrangements, lower energy costs, and more flexible labor markets.

Moreover, based on survey data from the Vale Columbia Center (2013) study, tax incentives rank low in importance to investors (Figure 6.3), and they are likely to have made the investment anyway even without the incentive (Figure 6.4).

Notwithstanding these stylized facts, since the Caribbean countries are actively engaged in intense tax competition, the question is what can be done to rationalize tax incentives and address the high costs?

## POLICY RECOMMENDATIONS

IMF policy advice has advocated a significant streamlining of incentives, based on clear principles, notably (1) broadening the tax base while reducing the tax rate;

## Figure 6.3. Determinants of Investor Decisions

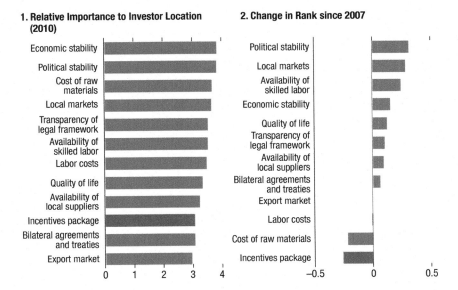

**1. Relative Importance to Investor Location (2010)**

**2. Change in Rank since 2007**

Source: Vale Columbia Center (2013).

and (2) eliminating or reducing the scope for discretion while moving to a transparent, rules-based system.

Specific recommendations for streamlining or reforming incentives schemes have included the following:

## Tax Holidays

- Limit the granting of tax holidays, for instance by scaling back holiday periods for new investments (for example, all holiday periods should be a maximum of 10 years, but previously granted holidays would be grandfathered), with no renewal (Norregaard and others 2015).

- Adopt investment-linked or performance-based incentives to encourage investment. As indicated in Table 6.2, some countries have already accelerated investment allowances, loss carryforward provisions, and accelerated depreciation allowances, which can be retained.

## Import-Related Concessions

- Rationalize the costly system of open-ended, discretionary duty concessions granted at the border. Key actions include (1) substantially cutting back

**Figure 6.4. Importance of Incentives to Investor Decisions**

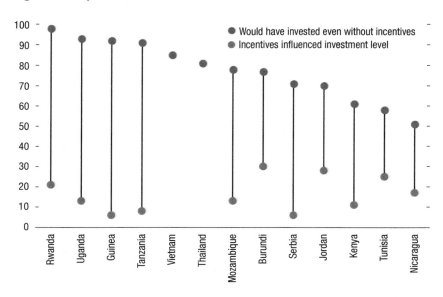

Source: Vale Columbia Center (2013).

eligible items on the list of conditional duty exemptions provided for under the CARICOM CET, (2) adopting an annual cap for aggregate duty exemptions and concessions, and (3) clearly specifying sunset clauses for all duty incentives.

- Rationalize the tariff structure through the introduction of a few simple tariff bands, with less dispersion and lower nominal rates. Lower tariff rates remove the main argument for incentives (that is, high tariffs), thereby relieving the pressure for duty concessions. In addition, broadening the base of the tax is likely to result in higher revenues.

## Other Incentives

- Eliminate provisions allowing concessions for property taxes, stamp duties, and environmental levies.

## Rules-Based System

- Move to a transparent, rules-based approach to granting incentives in the region.

- Consolidate tax incentives in one law (or alternatively in a few tax laws), available to all firms on the same terms to level the playing field. The granting of tax concessions would be through a transparent administrative process that does not permit discretion.

## Tax Expenditure Budgeting

- Initiate the reform process by moving to transparent and comprehensive accounting of the costs of incentives, so that tax expenditure budgeting would become an integral part of the annual budget.
- Introduce caps on tax expenditures to embed discipline and limit the use of tax incentives. Caps on the annual costs of tax incentives (as proposed above) can be introduced. Initially, the focus could be on phasing out discretionary exemptions that are granted by cabinets, while maintaining a cap on legislation-based tax incentives programs.

# REFORM EXPERIENCES—THE CASES OF JAMAICA AND GRENADA

Recent IMF-supported programs in Jamaica and Grenada provide case studies of credible efforts to reform tax policy, including tax incentives, in the region. The focus of the reforms was to broaden the tax base, reduce rates, and move to a transparent, rules-based system for granting incentives to narrow the scope for discretion.

## Jamaica

Beginning in 2009, in the context of two IMF programs, and with the aid of technical assistance from the IMF and the Inter-American Development Bank, Jamaica undertook a comprehensive tax policy reform aimed at addressing one of the major weaknesses in its tax system: the proliferation of sectoral and discretionary tax incentives. The goal was to put in place a uniform, broad-based, and low-rate tax system that applies to all entities. The most salient legislation during these reforms was the Fiscal Incentives Act (FIA) of 2013. The FIA reflected IMF advice to reduce both tax rates and tax expenditures by repealing several sectoral incentives programs[6] and by reducing the main corporate income tax rate from

---

[6]The FIA repealed the following legacy incentives: Export Industry (Encouragement) Act, Hotels (Incentives) Act, Resort Cottages (Incentives) Act, International Finance Companies (Tax Relief) Act, Petroleum Refining Industry (Encouragement) Act, Shipping (Incentives) Act, Cement Industry (Encouragement) Act, Motion Picture Industry (Encouragement) Act, Income Tax Act (Approved Farmer Rules), Industrial Incentives Act, and Industrial Incentives (Factory Construction) Act.

**Figure 6.5. Discretionary Waivers**
*(J$ million, per month)*

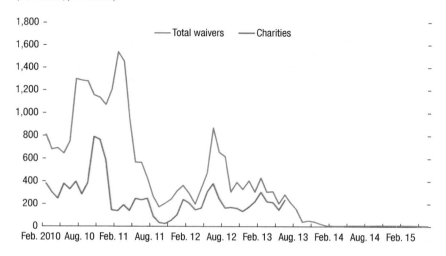

Source: Vale Columbia Center (2013).

33 1/3 percent to 25 percent (excluding regulated industries,[7] which continue to be taxed at a higher rate).

A key policy measure was the significant scaling back of discretionary waivers. Historically, these waivers were granted by the Ministry of Finance in accordance with provisions in tax-specific codes and reached nearly 2 percent of GDP in some years. As a first step, a cabinet decision established a *de minimis* cap to contain discretionary waivers to J$10 million per month; the cap remains in place (Figure 6.5). The reforms also reduced discretion by codifying requirements for becoming a charitable organization and thereby benefiting from associated tax concessions.

As an inducement, the FIA introduced an Employment Tax Credit (ETC) for companies in the nonregulated sector that migrated to the new incentives regime. The ETC is a nonrefundable tax credit totaling the sum of all statutory payroll levies (education tax, National Housing Trust, National Insurance, and Human Employment and Resource Training contributions) capped at 30 percent of the chargeable income tax. Maximum use of the ETC can reduce the effective corporate tax rate to as low as 17.5 percent. Adjustments were made to depreciation allowances and loss carryforwards. The reforms simplified capital allowances and better aligned tax depreciation rates with the economic life of assets.

---

[7] The corporate tax rate of 33 ⅓ percent was retained for the financial and telecommunications sectors.

**Figure 6.6. Tax Expenditures**
*(Percent of GDP)*

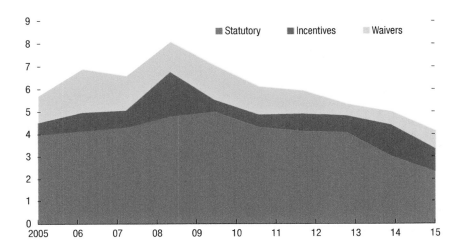

Source: Vale Columbia Center (2013).

The FIA used a "carrot-and-stick" approach to encourage incentives beneficiaries to make the transition to the new regime. This was particularly important for the tourism sector, which was benefiting from the Hotels (Incentives) Act. Existing projects were thus given the choice of either retaining their exemption, paying the general consumption tax (GCT) at the standard rate of 16.5 percent, and giving up access to the ETC, or moving to the new regime, continuing to enjoy a lower GCT rate of 10 percent, and accessing the ETC.

The customs tariff structure was also simplified. This effort reduced dispersion of tariff rates, with a medium-term objective of converging to a tariff rate of about 20 percent. Duties on a wide range of consumer goods were increased from 0 to 5 percent, while rates higher than 20 percent were mostly reduced. In accordance with CARICOM's CET, the rates on basic building materials, nonconsumer goods for productive use, and several goods acquired for health sectors were reduced to 0 percent.

Partly because of these reforms, tax expenditures (a key indicator of base broadening) have been dropping steadily since 2008. Tax expenditures have fallen from more than 8 percent of GDP in 2008 to 4 percent of GDP in 2015 (Figure 6.6). From an international perspective, Jamaica's tax expenditure has been reduced significantly (Figure 6.7). In addition to incentives reforms, this trend is also driven by other base-broadening measures, including broadening the base of the GCT to include government purchases, more foodstuffs, and electricity for businesses and some households

**Figure 6.7. Tax Expenditures**
*(Percent of GDP)*

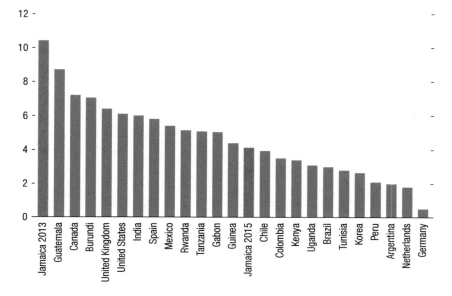

Source: Vale Columbia Center (2013).

Despite substantial progress, some sectoral incentives schemes were retained: the Urban Renewal Program, which encourages investment in poor communities, notably in downtown Kingston; the Bauxite and Alumina Industries Act; and export free zones (EFZs). However, the EFZs were repealed by the FIA and have been replaced by World Trade Organization–compliant special economic zones that enjoy tax incentives, including a 12.5 percent corporate income tax rate rather than the full exemption that was received by the EFZs.

Despite considerable progress, there have been some reversals with new, somewhat discretionary, tax incentives introduced at the end of 2013. For example, the Large-Scale Projects and Pioneer Industries Act was implemented, permitting the minister to grant unspecified tax concessions to qualifying investment projects up to 0.25 percent of GDP per year. The projects must be shown to be consistent with the strategic priorities of the government and to have a transformational impact on the economy.

## Grenada

Grenada undertook a comprehensive reform of the tax incentives regime with the introduction of the 2014 Investment Act and a series of amendments to the individual tax acts in 2015. The Investment Act streamlined investment procedures and codified investment requirements and incentives criteria. In addition, the legislative amendments removed discretion in the granting of tax incentives and codified specific incentives into Grenada's tax laws.

The new tax incentives framework is centered around tax relief provided under the Income Tax Act, targeted at qualifying investments in priority sectors, including agriculture, education, energy, health, housing, manufacturing, and tourism. It provides for a 100 percent investment allowance (usable over a 10-year period) for corporate income tax. In addition, the depreciation allowance permits investors to recover qualifying investment costs before paying corporate income tax on investment profits.

Income tax deductions were also provided, including the following:

- To stimulate growth, a 50 percent corporate income tax deduction for the cost of research and development in the agricultural sector
- To promote skills development of the labor force, a 50 percent corporate income tax deduction for qualifying training expenditure
- To assist investors in recovering their losses, extension of the period for carrying losses forward to six from three years

Incentives reforms also included changes to the VAT. To support investment in priority sectors, a VAT suspension regime was established for goods imported to undertake investment in a priority sector.

Finally, in consultation with CARICOM partners, Grenada removed discretion in the granting of customs duty exemptions by amending its list of conditional duty exemptions.

In summary, tax incentives reforms implemented in Grenada and Jamaica reflect the main elements of IMF advice to Caribbean countries. The focus has been on broadening the tax base by scaling back tax holidays, rationalizing the tariff structure, and reducing concessions in the VAT, together with moving to a rules-based, transparent system of granting tax concessions.

## A REGIONAL APPROACH TO TAX INCENTIVES

Although streamlining incentives will lower costs, it is essential that competition across countries in the region in providing incentives to attract investment is reduced to avoid a race to the bottom. While a country that succeeds in attracting a new investor may reap near-term benefits, the analysis in this chapter demonstrates it does so at a cost likely higher than it would have been in the absence of wasteful incentives competition. Currently, an offer and receipt of incentives has become the norm rather than the exception, benefiting investors at the expense of the country's welfare.

Tax competition is a problem of collective action. Individual countries in the region do not want to restrain their ability to use tax incentives to obtain an advantage over other countries in the region, especially for tourism investment, knowing that other countries have not similarly committed to restrict use of incentives. In the absence of regional coordination, each country pursues its own interests to attract investment, which can lead to a race to the bottom where everyone is worse off.

International experience suggests that a coordinated approach involving a regional agreement on best practices for business taxation and tax incentives can address these collective action problems. Cebotari and others (2013) examine regional agreements in the European Union, Central America, and East Africa and find that they included provisions to award tax incentives transparently to all investors and were based on legislation (thereby removing discretion). In addition, they eliminated existing tax incentives while grandfathering companies that had already been awarded incentives.

IMF policy advice has emphasized limiting tax competition by intensifying the harmonization of tax incentives among Eastern Caribbean Currency Union and CARICOM countries. Advice includes a recommendation that the region adopt a code of conduct for tax incentives. Cebotari and others (2013) point out that most codes of conduct used in other regions have some common characteristics:

- They are not legally binding. The code places a responsibility on the countries involved to be honor bound in observing the agreement. Institutional arrangements are put in place to monitor compliance and review complaints against noncompliant countries, but no sanctions can be applied.

- Tax systems are transparent, with all tax incentives specified in legislation, provided to investors on the same terms, and with no administrative discretion.

- Countries commit not to provide additional incentives or make existing incentives more generous, for example, by lengthening their duration.

- Incentives that are inconsistent with the code are eliminated, although companies that have already been granted incentives are grandfathered until the expiration of the incentives.

Earlier efforts at harmonizing tax incentives, notably the Harmonized Scheme of Fiscal Incentives introduced in the 1970s by CARICOM, failed primarily because individual countries continued to perceive a benefit by deviating from an agreed framework. In addition, there was no strong regional institution with a clear political mandate to supervise and enforce the agreement.[8] In contrast, the success of tax coordination in the European Union reflects each country's political commitment to participate and support enforcement.[9] Therefore, an important first step would be to establish an organizational home in a regional institution for developing and monitoring the implementation of policy on regional harmonization of tax incentives.

---

[8]More recently, CARICOM had been working on an Investment Code, but it seems to be dormant.

[9]The European Union code of conduct for business taxation is nonbinding, but it does have political force through the commitment of member states.

It is vital that the region ramp up efforts to achieve regional coordination, drawing on international best practice as highlighted above. It may be best to begin by taking stock of existing incentives and examining their cost to the individual economies. The transparent reporting of tax expenditures could provide the needed impetus for reform and regional cooperation as policymakers and key actors see in clear terms that the costs of tax incentives are undermining their fiscal frameworks and not moving their economies toward fiscal and debt sustainability.

Finally, IMF policy advice recommends attaching greater importance to the implementation of structural reforms vital to improving the domestic business and economic environment, thereby strengthening competitiveness and promoting investment. Generally, IMF staff have emphasized the importance of pursuing structural reforms to achieve greater labor market flexibility, lower energy costs through energy diversification, increase efficiency in the delivery of public services, and eliminate cumbersome bureaucratic procedures that harm the investment climate.

## CONCLUSION

For a variety of reasons, including private sector lobbying in individual countries, pressures remain to maintain tax incentives to encourage investment in the Caribbean. Tax incentives have been helpful in attracting investment to the region, especially in tourism, but at substantial cost, particularly revenue losses that worsen already-vulnerable fiscal situations and undermine macroeconomic stability. Moreover, incentives create an unlevel playing field, even for similar businesses.

IMF policy advice recommends structural reforms to strengthen competitiveness and improve the business environment together with significantly streamlining existing tax incentives to minimize costs and enhance transparency. Specific recommendations emphasize centralizing legal provisions in one incentives law or alternatively in tax laws and adopting a rules-based, transparent system to minimize discretion. Also, income tax holidays should be scaled back and tax incentives for investment should be provided, including through accelerated depreciation allowances and loss carryforward provisions. To reduce the pressure for import-related concessions, the tariff duty structure should be rationalized by introducing a few simple tariff bands, with less dispersion and lower nominal rates. Finally, collective action is required across all countries to establish a regional approach to the harmonization of tax incentives that will limit tax competition and avoid a race to the bottom.

## REFERENCES

Caner, Selcuk, Martin Grote, Russell Krelove, and Pierre-Pascal Gendron. 2015. "St. Lucia: Review of Income Taxation and VAT Performance for Fiscal Sustainability." Unpublished, International Monetary Fund, Fiscal Affairs Department, Washington, DC.

Cebotari, Aliona, Melesse Tashu, Selcuk Caner, Denise Edwards-Dowe, Brian Jones, Vinette Keene, Robert Mills, and Sumiko Ogawa. 2013. "Enhancing Fiscal Revenue." In *The Eastern Caribbean Currency Union: Macroeconomics and Financial Systems*, edited by Alfred Schipke, Aliona Cebotari, and Nita Thacker. Washington, DC: International Monetary Fund.

Chai, Jingqing, and Rishi Goyal. 2008. "Tax Concessions and Foreign Direct Investment in the Eastern Caribbean Currency Union." IMF Working Paper 08/257, International Monetary Fund, Washington, DC.

Cubbedu, Luis, Andreas Bauer, Pelin Berkmen, Magda Kandil, Koffie Nassar, and Peter Mullins. 2008. "Tax Incentives and Foreign Direct Investment: Policy Implications for the Caribbean." In *The Caribbean: Enhancing Economic Integration*, edited by Andreas Bauer, Paul Cashin, and Sanjaya Panth. Washington, DC: International Monetary Fund.

International Monetary Fund (IMF). 2013. "Jamaica: Staff Report for the Request for a New Extended Fund Facility Program." IMF Country Report 13/126, International Monetary Fund, Washington, DC.

———. 2014. "Grenada: Staff Report for Article IV Consultation and Request for a New Extended Credit Facility Program." Washington, DC.

———. 2015. "Grenada: Staff Report for the Second Review of the Extended Credit Facility Program." Washington, DC.

James, S. 2013. *Tax and Non-Tax Incentives and Investments: Evidence and Policy Implications*. World Bank Investment Climate Advisory Services, September.

Klemm, Alexander, and Stefan Van Parys. 2012. "Empirical Evidence on the Effects of Tax Incentives." *International Tax Public Finance*. 19: 393–423.

Krelove, Russell, Selcuk Caner, Steven Clark, and Jemma Lafeuilee. 2014. "Grenada: Tax Reform for Fairness, Growth and Simplicity." Unpublished, International Monetary Fund, Fiscal Affairs Department, Washington, DC.

Krelove, Russell, Ernesto Crivelli, and Pierre-Pascal Gendron. 2014. "Barbados: A Tax Reform Roadmap for Simplicity and Revenue Buoyancy." International Monetary Fund, Fiscal Affairs Department, Washington, DC.

Mullins, Peter, and Eric Hutton. 2008. "Commonwealth of Dominica: Review of VAT and Excises." Unpublished, International Monetary Fund, Fiscal Affairs Department, Washington, DC.

Norregaard, John, David Bevan, and Alexander Klemm. 2008. "Jamaica: A Strategy for Reform of Tax Incentives." Unpublished, International Monetary Fund, Fiscal Affairs Department, Washington, DC.

Norregaard, John, Ernesto Crivelli, Russell Krelove, Arthur Swistak, and Riel Franzsen. 2015. "ECCU: Tax Incentives and Property Taxation in the ECCU." International Monetary Fund, Fiscal Affairs Department, Washington, DC.

Palomba, Geremia, Mario Mansour, and Eric Hutton. 2009. "St. Vincent and the Grenadines: Reforming the Income Tax and the System of Tax Incentives." Unpublished, International Monetary Fund, Fiscal Affairs Department, Washington, DC.

Tait, Robert. 2013. "Antigua and Barbuda: Strengthening the Customs Administration." Unpublished, Caribbean Regional Technical Assistance Center, Customs and Excise Division.

Vale Columbia Center. 2013. "Investment Incentives: The Good, the Bad, and the Ugly." Background paper for the Eighth Columbia International Investment Conference, Columbia University, New York, November 13–14.

Van Parys, Stefan, and Sebastian James. 2010. "The Effectiveness of Tax Incentives in Attracting FDI: Evidence from the Tourism Sector in the Caribbean." Gent University Working Paper 675, Gent, Belgium.

# CHAPTER 7

# Managing Economic Citizenship Program Inflows: Reducing Risk and Maximizing Benefits

JUDITH GOLD AND ALLA MYRVODA

## INTRODUCTION

The number of economic citizenship programs (ECPs) has surged in recent years. An increasing number of countries, especially in the Caribbean, are offering opportunities to obtain citizenship or residency in exchange for a substantial financial contribution to the domestic economy. Following recent large inflows to St. Kitts and Nevis and Dominica under these programs, three other Eastern Caribbean Currency Union (ECCU) countries—Antigua and Barbuda, Grenada, and St. Lucia—launched their own ECPs during 2013–15. ECPs (also referred to as citizenship-by-investment programs) are particularly attractive to small states, for which inflows can be so large as to have a significant economic and fiscal impact. An increasing number of advanced economies are also offering economic residency programs. These programs are being mainstreamed because high-net-worth individuals consider citizenship or residency to be a means for improving international mobility, tax planning, and family security while also seeking investment opportunities.

Given the shared advantages for interested individuals and host jurisdictions, ECPs are likely to continue to grow, but with important spillovers and downside risks for small states and the international community. In small states, the inflows to the private sector can have a sizable impact on economic activity, while the fiscal revenues, like other large windfall revenues from abroad, can be quite substantial. In St. Kitts and Nevis and Dominica, the inflows have led to an improvement in the fiscal outcome, facilitated repayment of debt, and spurred economic growth. However, poor management of the revenue upsurge could exacerbate vulnerabilities. If large and persistent, investment and fiscal flows may lead to adverse macroeconomic consequences associated with Dutch disease, including higher inflation and loss of competitiveness, and the crowding out of other private sector activity. Moreover, program inflows may be subject to sudden-stop risk related to rapid changes in advanced economies' immigration policies. Finally, if not administered with due diligence, ECPs can lead to security breaches and possibly facilitate illicit activities such as tax evasion and money laundering, raising concerns for the international community and exposing the host jurisdiction to reputational risks.

This chapter reviews recent experience with ECPs in the Caribbean, discusses their macroeconomic implications, and proposes a prudent management framework. Such a framework would aim to save the bulk of the inflows to the public sector—improving the fiscal and external positions—as well as regulate inflows to the private sector. The chapter addresses the importance of adopting a strong institutional and governance framework to prevent possible abuse of such programs. Large and persistent inflows may warrant a dedicated mechanism to manage large savings, including through a sovereign wealth fund (SWF). The chapter is organized as follows: The next section provides an overview of recent developments in the economic citizenship domain and discusses selected ECPs. The following two sections discuss macroeconomic implications and the risk associated with ECP inflows, and are followed by a section that proposes the appropriate policy response to address risks in each sector. The final section concludes.

## THE NATURE AND SCOPE OF ECPS

Many economic citizenship or residency programs around the world provide citizenship or residency in exchange for substantial financial transfers. Programs vary substantially in their design, conditions, and cost (see Table 7.1). However, they all either allow direct citizenship or provide a route to citizenship in return for a sizable financial transfer, which can be in the form of an investment in the economy or a contribution to the public sector. Small states, like those in the Caribbean, offer a direct route to citizenship without, or on the basis of very limited, residency requirements. Advanced economies such as Canada, the United Kingdom, and the United States have had "immigrant investor programs" dating back from the mid-1980s to the mid-1990s.[1] These programs grant residency status leading to citizenship in return for substantial investment, either in public debt instruments (as in Canada) or in the private sector.[2] All of these programs purport to stimulate growth and employment by attracting more foreign capital and investment by way of offering citizenship or residency status to high-net-worth individuals.

The number of countries offering such programs, including in the Caribbean, has increased markedly recently. During 2013–15, Antigua and Barbuda, St. Lucia, and Malta launched new citizenship programs, while Grenada revived its previously retired program. Several European countries, including France, Greece, Hungary, Latvia, the Netherlands, Portugal, and Spain, have also recently

---

[1] The number of U.S. EB-5 investor visas increased fivefold from 2010 to 2016, but still represent only 2 percent of annual immigration to the United States.

[2] The federal Canadian program was abolished in the 2014 federal budget because the program was found to have limited economic benefit, but some provinces operate their own programs.

Table 7.1. Selected Citizenship- and Residency-by-Investment Programs Worldwide

| | Country | Inception Year | Minimum Investment[1] | Residency Requirements[2] | Citizenship Qualifying Period[3] |
|---|---|---|---|---|---|
| **Citizenship Programs** | Antigua and Barbuda | 2013 | US$250,000 | 5 days within a 5-year period | Immediate |
| | Cyprus | 2011 | €2.5 million | No (under revision) | Immediate |
| | Dominica | 1993 | US$100,000 | No | Immediate |
| | Grenada | 2014 | US$250,000 | No | Immediate |
| | Malta | 2014 | €1.15 million | 6 months | One year |
| | St. Kitts and Nevis | 1984 | US$250,000 | No | Immediate |
| | St. Lucia | 2016 | US$100,000 | No | Immediate |
| **Residency Programs** | Australia | 2012 | $A 5 million | 40 days/year | 5 years |
| | Bulgaria | 2009 | €500,000 | No | 5 years |
| | Canada[4,5] | Mid-1980s | Can$800,000 | 730 days within a 5-year period | 3 years |
| | Canada-Quebec[5] | n.a. | Can$800,000 | 730 days within a 5-year period | 3 years |
| | France | 2013 | €10 million | n.a. | 5 years |
| | Greece | 2013 | €250,000 | No | 7 years |
| | Hungary | 2013 | €250,000 | No | 8 years |
| | Ireland | 2012 | €500,000 | No | n.a. |
| | Latvia | 2010 | €35,000 | No | 10 years |
| | New Zealand | n.a. | $NZ 1.5 million | 146 days/year | 5 years |
| | Portugal | 2012 | €500,000 | 7 days/year | 6 years |
| | Singapore | n.a. | S$2.5 million | No | 2 years |
| | Spain | 2013 | €500,000 | No | 10 years |
| | Switzerland | n.a. | Sw F 250,000/year | No | 12 years |
| | United Kingdom | 1994 | £1 million | 185 days/year | 6 years |
| | United States | 1990 | US$500,000 | 180 days/year | 7 years |

Sources: Arton Capital; Country authorities; Henley and Partners; U.K. Migration Advisory Committee Report; and other immigration services providers.
Note: n.a. = not applicable or not available.
[1]Alternative investment options may be eligible.
[2]Explicit minimum residency requirements under immigrant investor schemes; residency criteria to qualify for citizenship may differ.
[3]Including the qualification period for permanent residency under residency programs.
[4]Program suspended since February 2014.
[5]Although not specific to the immigrant investor program, retaining permanent residency requires physical presence of 730 days within a five-year period.

introduced new residency programs by way of a significant investment. About half of the European Union member states now have dedicated immigrant investor routes.[3] These residency visas, dubbed the "Golden Visa" following the Portuguese program that carries the name, allow recipients access to all 26

[3]The Austrian government can confer immediate citizenship to foreign persons in cases of extraordinary merit, which can include substantial investments in the country under Article 10 (6) of the Austrian Citizenship Act. However, the Austrian government indicated that no citizenships have been granted under this provision since mid-2011.

Schengen countries.[4] Furthermore, some countries are also revising their existing programs to improve their competitiveness and appeal, while others are trying to increase the programs' potential economic or fiscal contributions (MAC 2014).[5] Cyprus amended its program to provide more investment options, including in government bonds, bank deposits, and other financial instruments, in addition to its original real estate or other private investment option. In the Caribbean, Dominica recently introduced a real estate investment option in addition to its original requirement of a direct contribution to the government and subsequently lowered government fees for the real estate investment option, while St. Lucia has reduced the minimum required investment.

The launch of new citizenship programs in the Caribbean has intensified competition, creating pressure to ease conditions (IMF 2016). After peaking in 2014, inflows to St. Kitts and Nevis weakened in 2015 and declined further in 2016; meanwhile, applicants' preferences continued to shift further toward the real estate option. Inflows to Antigua and Barbuda, after the initial surge following introduction of the program, fell in 2016. Inflows to Dominica surged on account of very competitive conditions and extensive marketing activities, which cost the equivalent of 1.1 percent of GDP in fiscal year 2015/16. Demand growth in Grenada has remained steady but relatively modest, while the newly established program in St. Lucia met with only limited success in its first year of operation owing to its relatively high pricing and political uncertainty in an election year (IMF, forthcoming).[6]

The surge in interest in these programs may reflect a combination of growing wealth in emerging markets and an increase in global uncertainties and security issues. The increasing number of high-net-worth individuals outside advanced economies would appear to be the critical factor on the demand side. The main reasons for the rise in demand from this group include (1) the desire for easier travel (see Figure 7.1) in the face of growing travel restrictions and encumbrances for nationals of non-advanced economies after the September 11, 2001, attacks; (2) the search for a safe haven in the context of a deteriorating geopolitical climate and increased security concerns; and (3) other considerations, such as estate and tax planning (Xu, El-Ashram, and Gold 2015).[7] Although accurate statistics are sparse, press reports and observations of trends in several countries indicate a surge in clients from China, followed by Russia, along with a steady rise in

---

[4]The Schengen Agreement permits Schengen visa holders to travel freely within the Schengen area as well as across Iceland, Liechtenstein, Norway, and Switzerland.

[5]For example, the U.K. Migration Advisory Committee was asked by the U.K. government to review whether specific features of the program were delivering "significant economic benefits" to the nation.

[6]During the first year of operation, six applications were approved under the real estate option, but none of them had reached investment stage by the end of 2016; 14 applications were accepted under the donation option for a total of US$1.4 million; and five applicants were approved under the bond option for US$2.7 million. No interest was shown in the enterprise investment option.

[7]A *Financial Times* article, "Sea, Sun and Easy Visas Lure China Buyers" (Wise 2014), cites concerns about political changes, economic crises, and the pursuit of a safe haven as key motivations for Chinese citizens seeking a Golden Visa in Portugal.

## Figure 7.1. Visa-Free Access of Selected Countries with an ECP
*(Index)*

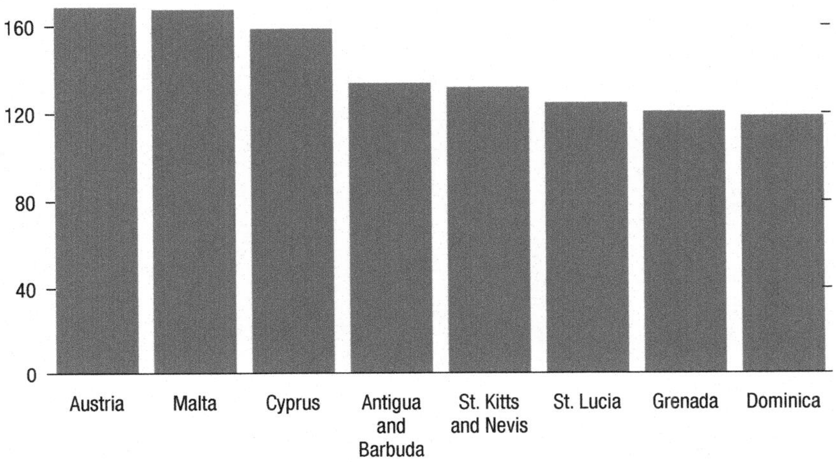

Source: The Henley & Partners Visa Restriction Index 2016.
Note: ECP = economic citizenship program. A higher ranking reflects a higher number of countries accessible without a visa.

investors from the Middle East, although to a much lesser degree.[8] In Antigua and Barbuda, for instance, Chinese applicants were by far the largest share of passport recipients (41 percent), followed by investors from Lebanon and Russia (about 5 percent each of total applicants) (Figure 7.2).

Citizens from advanced economies also represent an important share of applicants to some citizenship programs, and are generally motivated by more generous tax regimes. For instance, ECP passport recipients in Antigua and Barbuda originating from Canada, the United Kingdom, the United States, and Western Europe jointly accounted for more than 9 percent of total applicants since program inception through the end of 2016. Many small states have historically acted as tax havens, offering low or zero tax rates on personal or corporate income, secrecy laws on banking, and few or no restrictions on financial transactions. Some ECPs have marketed their country's favorable tax treatment to attract high-net-worth clients seeking global tax planning benefits. This strategy includes countries in the Caribbean as well as several European Union (EU) members that offer relatively more favorable tax

[8]Chinese nationals have reportedly received 75–80 percent of Portugal's Golden Visas, and 81 percent of the U.S. EB-5 investor visas in 2013. A report by the *Economist* magazine (March 1, 2014) indicates that about half of the U.K.'s "economic" visas between 2009 and 2013 were granted to Chinese and Russian citizens. St. Kitts and Nevis reports similar trends.

**Figure 7.2. Antigua and Barbuda: Number of ECP Applications by Country of Birth**
*(Percent of total, program inception through 2016)*

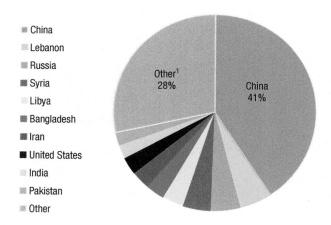

- China
- Lebanon
- Russia
- Syria
- Libya
- Bangladesh
- Iran
- United States
- India
- Pakistan
- Other

Sources: Country authorities; and IMF staff estimates and calculations.
Note: ECP = economic citizenship program.
[1]"Other" includes countries with less than 2 percent of total in each category.

treatment within the EU to resident firms and individuals.[9,10] However, tax havens have come under increasing pressure from the Organisation for Economic Co-operation and Development and the Group of Twenty to share tax and banking information to combat international tax avoidance, money laundering, and the financing of terrorism. Thus, the use of citizenship or residency investor schemes for purposes of tax avoidance may become more difficult as more advanced economies adopt anti-avoidance provisions in their tax legislation and enact financial transparency laws similar to the U.S. Foreign Account Tax Compliance Act. Increased reporting requirements by foreign financial institutions has made it harder for U.S. taxpayers to conceal assets in offshore accounts. In the Caribbean economies with ECPs, FATCA Model 1 Intergovernmental Agreements have become operational in St. Kitts and Nevis and St. Lucia, and have been signed by Antigua and Barbuda and Grenada, while an agreement in substance is in place in Dominica.[11]

---

[9]Economic citizenship programs in Cyprus and Malta as well as investor residency programs in Bulgaria, Hungary, Ireland, and Portugal feature preferential tax treatment. For example, in 2008 Bulgaria introduced a 10 percent flat tax rate on all income levels, one of the lowest in the EU, while in Portugal, investor residents may enjoy tax exemptions on foreign income, including pensions, for up to 10 years under specific circumstances.

[10]Slemrod (2008) characterizes both tax havens and citizenship programs, among others, as examples of the commercialization of state sovereignty that is more prevalent in small states where alternative means of raising revenues are hard to find.

[11]U.S. Department of the Treasury, resource center (https://www.treasury.gov/resource-center/tax -policy/treaties/Pages/FATCA.aspx), accessed May 9, 2017.

**Figure 7.3. Inflows under Citizenship-by-Investment Programs**

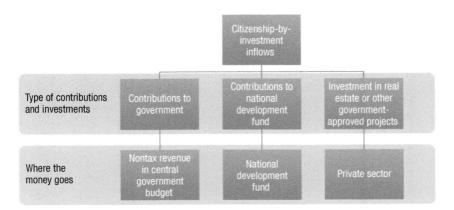

The rise in demand has coincided with, or perhaps has been in response to, an increase in service providers. Several international firms are now providing legal and other services to individuals, facilitating the process of obtaining a second passport or a residency visa. These firms hold frequent conferences around the world, providing a forum for discussion and marketing among interested clients and intermediaries. The firms offer comparative analyses of the relative merits of various programs and provide a rating system. Some of these firms also have close relationships with ECP countries, advising them on the design and administration of such programs. The Investment Migration Council, based in Geneva, was launched in October 2014 by a group of service providers to assist in setting high quality standards for their services and to facilitate further growth and expansion of this industry (Xu, El-Ashram, and Gold 2015).

## THE MACROECONOMIC IMPACT OF ECP INFLOWS

ECPs generate a variety of inflows. Depending on the program, there are mainly three types of inflows: (1) contributions to the government relating to registration or application fees, as well as fees to cover processing and due diligence costs; (2) nonrefundable contributions to government or quasi-government funds (such as national development funds [NDFs]); and (3) investments in the private or public sector, which can often be sold or redeemed after a specific time (Figure 7.3). Investments in the private sector are mainly in the form of real estate, but can also be in other government-approved projects. Some ECPs also include options for buying public debt instruments. Programs can consist of just one of these options, or any combination of them. For example, in Dominica, until recently, the ECP allowed only for contributions to the government.

The growth in ECP-associated inflows to the Caribbean has already had important consequences. Region-wide on-budget ECP inflows in the Caribbean increased

## Figure 7.4. ECP Fiscal Revenues—On Budget

### 1. Percent of Regional GDP[1]

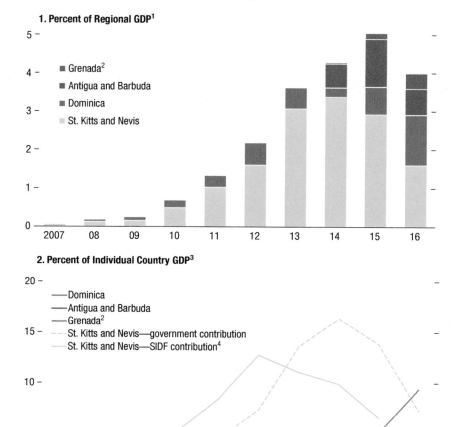

Sources: Country authorities; and IMF staff calculations.

Note: ECP = economic citizenship program; SIDF = Sugar Industry Diversification Foundation.

[1]ECP fiscal revenues as a share of the total nominal GDP of Antigua and Barbuda, Dominica, Grenada, and St. Kitts and Nevis. May include projected figures for 2016 because fiscal year duration varies. Excludes estimates for St. Lucia due to small size.

[2]Figure for Grenada includes National Transformation Fund.

[3]Data shown in fiscal years. May include projected figures for 2016 because fiscal year duration varies.

[4]On-budget flows exclude SIDF contribution to St. Kitts and Nevis, which is added for comparison.

**Figure 7.5. St. Kitts and Nevis: ECP Inflows and Fiscal Balance**
*(Percent of GDP)*

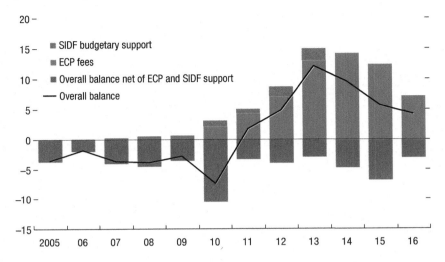

Sources: St. Kitts and Nevis authorities; and IMF staff estimates.
Note: ECP = economic citizenship program; SIDF = Sugar Industry Diversification Foundation. Data
shown in fiscal years. Projected figure for fiscal year 2016.

from virtually zero in 2007 to a peak of 5.1 percent of regional GDP (excluding St.
Lucia) in 2015 (Figure 7.4).[12] St. Kitts and Nevis's and Dominica's ECPs—the
oldest Caribbean programs, established in 1984 and 1993, respectively—experienced
a surge starting in 2010. In St. Kitts and Nevis, ECP receipts, largely in the form of
fees to the budget, increased from less than 1 percent of GDP in 2008 to a peak of
14 percent of GDP in 2014, followed by a gradual deceleration to an estimated
7 percent of GDP in 2016 (Figure 7.5). Inflows to Dominica remained more moderate until recent efforts to promote the program and to allow real estate development, leading to on-budget ECP revenue estimates of 9.5 percent of GDP in 2016
(Figure 7.6). In addition to budget contributions and private sector inflows into real
estate development, a significant portion of ECP inflows is accumulated off budget.
In St. Kitts and Nevis, for instance, ECP inflows to the Sugar Industry
Diversification Foundation (SIDF) were equivalent to another 5 percent of GDP in
2016. In Dominica, recorded off-budget revenues equated to about 12 percent of
GDP in fiscal year 2015/16. Inflows under some of the newer programs in the
region also have been sizable and macro-relevant (IMF, forthcoming).

---

[12]Includes ECPs in Antigua and Barbuda, Dominica, Grenada, and St. Kitts and Nevis. St. Lucia
was excluded because inflows to date have been negligible. If St. Lucia was included, total revenues
would have peaked at 3.7 percent of regional GDP.

**Figure 7.6. Dominica: ECP Inflows and Fiscal Balance**
*(Percent of GDP)*

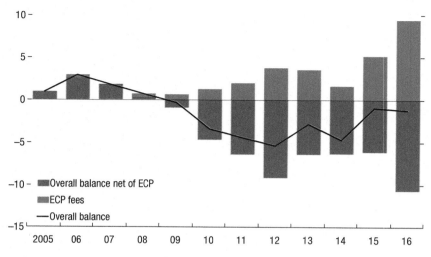

Sources: Dominica authorities; and IMF staff estimates.
Note: ECP = economic citizenship program. Data shown in fiscal years. Projected figure for fiscal year 2016.

The macroeconomic impact of the inflows depends on the design of the program, the magnitude of the inflows, and their management. In small states, large ECP inflows could have significant spillovers to nearly every sector. Although comprehensive data are not readily available, as noted above, the inflows to St. Kitts and Nevis and Dominica have had sizable benefits. Programs with private investment options could have a direct real sector impact, particularly on the construction and real estate sectors, including through the development of tourist accommodation. Contributions to the government and to the NDF, when spent or invested, could also affect the real economy. At the same time, to the extent that contributions to the public sector are saved, they can yield measurable improvements in key macroeconomic balances, in particular the fiscal balance. The external accounts are also affected, mainly the capital account, which would benefit from increased private capital transfers (contributions to NDFs) and foreign direct investment (ECP-related real estate investment).

Significant ECP inflows have supported economic recovery in some of the Caribbean economies. The large inflows to St. Kitts and Nevis and Dominica, and to a lesser extent to Antigua and Barbuda, are a significant share of GDP, affecting aggregate demand. In St. Kitts and Nevis, these inflows have benefited real estate and tourism development, and fueled a pickup in construction, thereby stimulating economic activity. This impact, combined with the authorities' efforts to boost employment through the public employment program, helped lower the unemployment rate in St. Kitts and Nevis to well below the Caribbean average. In Dominica, public capital investment financed by ECP inflows continues to provide a significant source of funding to infrastructure rehabilitation after Tropical Storm Erika;[13] meanwhile, several large-scale projects partly funded by ECP inflows are expected to underpin improved medium-term growth prospects (Guerson and others, forthcoming).

ECP inflows in the Caribbean have facilitated significant budgetary outlays while improving fiscal balances. St. Kitts and Nevis saved a large share of ECP receipts and SIDF income, and also prepaid a portion of its external debt while still accommodating support to the budget (including by SIDF transfers to the budget). The country's overall fiscal surplus rose to more than 12 percent of GDP in 2013, one of the highest in the world. Moreover, at the end of 2016, accumulated central government deposits totaled about 29 percent of GDP, and additional SIDF assets were an estimated 20 percent of GDP. In Dominica, ECP receipts have provided an important source of funding for the authorities to implement their budget priorities. Since Tropical Storm Erika, ECP funds have largely been used for reconstruction and debt servicing. Specifically, the largest outlay helped finance the post-Erika emergency infrastructure works at the Douglas Charles Airport, while a significant share of ECP revenues helped finance the National Employment Program. Dominica's authorities also intend to save a portion of future ECP inflows in a vulnerability fund. In accordance with legislation in Grenada, funds have been used to pay budgetary arrears, accumulate savings in the contingency fund, and finance investment projects.[14] In St. Lucia, the authorities intend to save the proceeds from the citizenship program in an SWF and use the fund to finance capital projects and to repurchase debt, but as noted earlier inflows to date have been very modest.

Large program inflows can also have a significant impact on a country's external accounts. The budgetary revenues can improve the country's current account deficit, substantially so if they are saved, and the capital account can be strengthened by external transfers to development funds and higher foreign direct investment. But increased domestic spending as a result of higher government expenditures and investment will substantially boost imports, particularly in small open economies, offsetting some of the initial improvement in the balance of payments.

Large ECP inflows can also boost bank liquidity, especially if the bulk of the budgetary receipts are saved in the banking system. For instance, by the end of 2016 ECP inflows to St. Kitts and Nevis and Dominica contributed to the build-up of government deposits in the banking system of more than 29 percent and 26 percent of GDP, respectively (Figure 7.7). Although some improvement in

---

[13]Tropical Storm Erika hit Dominica August 27, 2015, resulting in loss of life and substantial damage to crops and infrastructure, estimated at US$483 million or 96 percent of GDP, of which 65 percent was attributed to public sector reconstruction costs.

[14]Legislation in Grenada requires that starting in January 2016, 40 percent of ECP receipts must be placed in a contingency fund for the purposes of clearing arrears, repaying or restructuring debt, and dealing with natural disasters.

**Figure 7.7. Banking System Liquidity**
*(Percent of GDP)*

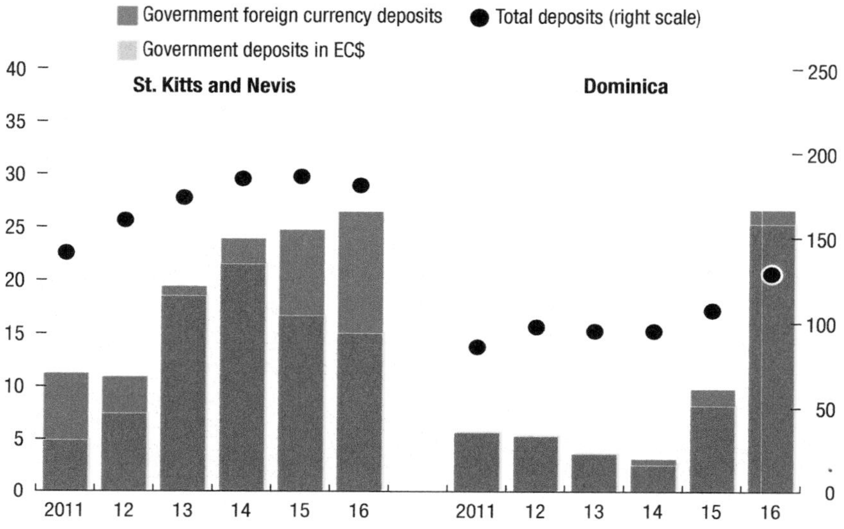

Sources: Country authorities; Eastern Caribbean Central Bank; and IMF staff estimates.

bank liquidity is welcome, the small size of the economies and limited lending opportunities and undiversified options for credit expansion will put pressure on bank profitability and asset liability management. This may also manifest itself in a sizable increase in net foreign assets as banks seek alternative channels for investment.[15]

## POTENTIAL RISKS OF ECP INFLOWS

Inflows under ECP programs are potentially volatile and may be vulnerable to sudden-stop risks, exacerbating macroeconomic vulnerabilities in small states. The underlying asset generating these inflows is the visa-free access or residency rights granted to foreign investors through the program, the potential loss of which could trigger a sudden stop. For example, a change of visa policy in advanced economies is a significant risk that can suddenly diminish the appeal of these programs and, if concerted action is taken, can even lead to the suspension of their operation. Increasing competition from similar programs in other

---

[15]In St. Kitts and Nevis, net foreign assets of the commercial banking system increased more than sixfold between 2010 and early 2015, peaking at more than 70 percent of GDP in April 2015, and remain relatively high at 54 percent of GDP as of December 2016.

**Figure 7.8. Magnitude and Volatility of GDP Growth**

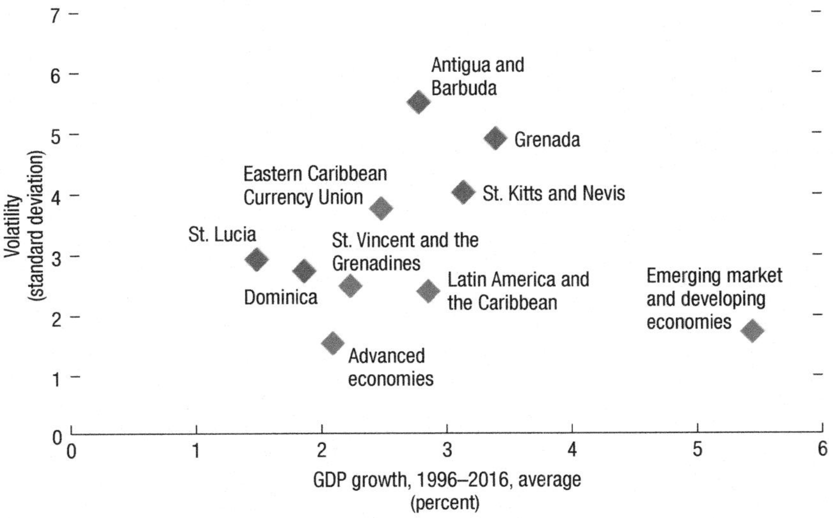

Sources: IMF, *World Economic Outlook*, and IMF staff estimates.
Note: Red markers refer to selected small state economies with economic citizenship programs.

countries or a decline in demand from source countries can also rapidly reduce the number of applicants.

The potential volatility of inflows can generate a host of real, fiscal, external, and financial sector vulnerabilities, while the risk of sudden stop presents yet another challenge to small states. These countries already face higher volatility in economic growth and fiscal revenues, well above the world average, reflecting their higher risk of natural disasters and the openness of their economies (Figure 7.8).

Indeed, there are early signs of a "race to the bottom." As noted earlier, Dominica amended its program requirements by lowering the government fee applicable to the real estate investment option to stimulate hotel development. Subsequently, in December 2016, Dominica lowered the government contribution fee for the real estate investment option.[16] St. Lucia has also eased the conditions for access to its citizenship program (Table 7.2), substantially reducing the cost to make the program more competitive and generate more revenue.[17] This

---

[16]It also raised dependents' age limit.

[17]The main changes to St. Lucia's ECP include (1) removal of a minimum personal wealth requirement (which had been US$3 million), (2) reduction of the required contribution from US$200,000 to US$100,000 for single applicants (with a similar reduction in fees for applicants with dependents), and (3) removal of the cap of 500 citizenships per year. The bond option, which

action puts the conditions of St. Lucia's citizenship program broadly on par with that of Dominica, and may generate additional demand, but it may also attract investors who otherwise would have invested in the other Caribbean ECPs. Regardless, it is unlikely that the ECP in St. Lucia will become as important a source of revenue as are the programs in Dominica and St. Kitts and Nevis owing to the much larger size of the St. Lucian economy (Figure 7.9).

These inflows can also present significant fiscal management challenges. Like those caused by windfall revenues from natural resources (Gupta, Segura-Ubiergo, and Flores 2014), such revenues can increase pressure for higher government spending, including higher public sector wages, social spending, and other recurrent commitments, even though the underlying revenues may be volatile and difficult to forecast. The resulting increase in dependence on these revenues could lead to sharp fiscal adjustments or an acute increase in debt if or when the inflows diminish. Although ECP revenues in the Caribbean have largely been used for general budget financing, debt consolidation, and reconstruction after natural disasters, they have also been used to support expansion of current spending. For example, in Antigua and Barbuda, while these resources have been used for debt servicing and general financing purposes, a portion of funds—largely off budget—has been used to support the social security system and state-owned enterprises. In St. Kitts and Nevis, revenues have contributed to funding a broad spectrum of expenditures, including social programs and grants.

Poor management of ECP inflows can also pose a risk to external sustainability. Increased public and private spending will lead to growing external imbalances. Risks to the exchange rate and foreign currency reserves are also magnified as these inflows become a major source of external financing reflecting potential volatility. Rising inflation from economic overheating can also cause the real exchange rate to appreciate, lowering external competitiveness over the long term.

Large increases in banking sector liquidity can also pose risks to financial stability. Rapid buildup of deposits in the banking system, leading to a rise in liquidity, can cause a deterioration of credit standards or significant currency or maturity mismatches. Risks to financial stability may be magnified if banks face excessive exposure to construction and real estate sectors that are already propped up by investments from the ECP. In that case, a sharp decline in program inflows could prompt a correction in real estate prices, with negative implications for banks' assets, particularly if supervision is weak.

Governance presents yet another challenge to sustainability. Cross-border security risks associated with the acquisition of a second passport are likely to be the main concern of advanced economies. Reputational risks are also magnified: weak governance in one country could easily spill over to others given that advanced economies are less likely to differentiate between citizenship programs. In addition, poor or opaque administration of programs and their associated inflows—including inadequate disclosure of the number of passports issued,

---

was considered the most advantageous portion of the program before the changes, is now discouraged with a new administrative fee of US$50,000.

Table 7.2. Investment Requirements of Economic Citizenship Programs in the Caribbean[1]

*(U.S. dollars)*

| | Option I | | | | Option II | | | |
|---|---|---|---|---|---|---|---|---|
| | **Government Fee** | **and** | **Contribution to National Development Fund** | | **Government Fee** | **and** | **Redeemable Investment[2]** | |
| **Type of Application** | **Single Applicant** | **Family** | **Single Applicant** | **Family** | **Single Applicant** | **Family** | **Single Applicant** | **Family** |
| Antigua and Barbuda[3] | 50,000 | 150,000 | 200,000 | 200,000 | 50,000 | 150,000 | Real estate: 400,000 Business: 1,500,000 | Real estate: 400,000 Business: 1,500,000 |
| Dominica[4] | 100,000 | 200,000 | ... | ... | 25,000 | 75,000 | Real estate: 200,000 | Real estate: 200,000 |
| Grenada | ... | ... | 200,000 | 200,000 | 50,000 | 50,000 | Real estate: 350,000 | Real estate: 350,000 |
| St. Kitts and Nevis[5] | ... | ... | 250,000 | 300,000 | 50,000 | 125,000 | Real estate: 400,000 | Real estate: 400,000 |
| St. Lucia[6] | ... | ... | 100,000 | 190,000 | 50,000 | 50,000 | Government bonds: 500,000 | Government bonds: 550,000 |

Sources: Arton Capital; Citizenship-by-Investment Units Guidelines; Country authorities; and Henley and Partners.
[1]Depicts minimum investment requirements for single versus family applications (a couple with up to two dependents under the age of 18). Additional due diligence and processing fees apply.
[2]For most programs, a minimum holding period of five years is required for redeemable investment options. Assets may be eligible for resale to future applicants under the citizenship-by-investment program.
[3]A limited time offer that remained valid from the launch of the program in 2013 through year-end April 2016 allowed for a flat government processing fee of US$100,000 for a family of four, waiving the processing fees for the two dependents.
[4]Dominica amended program requirements effective December 2016. Changes include higher age limit of young dependents and lower government fees for real estate investment option.
[5]Although an explicit government application fee is not required in the national development fund option of St. Kitts and Nevis, about 25 percent of the contribution is retained by the government as budgetary fees.
[6]Business investment must fall under one of the following categories: specialty restaurants; cruise ports and marinas; agro-processing plants; pharmaceutical products; ports, bridges, roads, and highways; research institutions and facilities; or offshore universities. In early 2017, St. Lucia made an announcement to change its program requirements. The required contribution to the economic fund was reduced from US$200,000 to US$100,000 for single applicants, and from US$250,000 to US$190,000 for a family (applicant with a spouse and up to two dependents). The cap of 500 citizenships per year was removed. An administrative fee of US$50,000 was introduced for the bond option. The remaining two options were left unchanged.

revenues collected, and mechanisms governing the use of generated inflows—could prompt strong public and political resistance, complicating, or even terminating, these programs.

Significant governance and integrity challenges have emerged in the past, jeopardizing some programs and causing others to be discontinued.[18] Risks

---

[18]Van Fossen (2007) provides an extended summary of governance and corruption issues that plagued the Pacific Islands' experience with the sale of passports through ad hoc schemes.

### Figure 7.9. Number of Main Applicants Needed to Generate Inflows of 1 Percent of GDP[1]
*(Percent of GDP, 2016)*

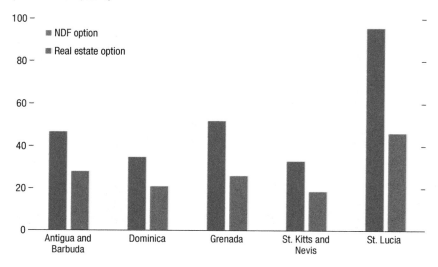

Sources: Citizenship-by-Investment Units; IMF, *World Economic Outlook*; and IMF staff estimates and calculations.
[1]Based on minimum investment requirements per country for the national development fund (NDF) and real estate options. Assumes equal weights to the composition of applications (single versus family applications). Based on 2016 figure for nominal GDP.

related to international security and financial integrity are reported to have contributed to the discontinuation of citizenship programs in Belize, Grenada, and Nauru after the September 11, 2001, attacks (Table 7.3).[19] Ireland also discontinued its ECP in 1998 and initiated a parliamentary review that concluded that the program did not provide sufficient economic benefits to justify its reintroduction.[20] Reports have arisen reflecting integrity concerns with some programs. The Financial Crimes Enforcement Network issued an advisory in May 2014 relating to concerns about the St. Kitts and Nevis program, and the Canadian government imposed visa requirements on citizens of St. Kitts and Nevis in November 2014. More recently, in June 2016, Canada also imposed visa requirements on Antigua and Barbuda's citizens, reportedly as a result of its concerns about the

---

[19]Grenada revived its economic citizenship program in 2013.

[20]However, Ireland introduced an economic residency program in 2012. A debate in the Irish Upper House of Parliament pointed to issues with the conduct of the original citizenship program (Seanad Éireann Debates 1998).

**Table 7.3. Suspended Citizenship Programs**

| Country | Period | Reason for Suspension |
|---------|--------|----------------------|
| Ireland | 1980s–1998 | Insufficient economic benefit |
| Grenada | 1997–2001 | Security concerns after 9/11 |
| Belize | 1995–2002 | Security concerns after 9/11 |
| Nauru | 1990s–2003 | Security concerns after 9/11 |

Sources: Press reports; and country authorities.

management of the program.[21] The rapid emergence and growth of such programs may exacerbate risks of abuse and corruption, and raise the possibility of curtailed visa-free access to advanced economies.

# PRUDENT POLICY FRAMEWORK FOR ECP INFLOWS

Appropriate government policies can reduce and contain the risks to small states of large inflows from ECPs while allowing these economies to capitalize on the possible benefits. Where inflows are significant and expected to continue for a few years, a prudent management framework could improve fiscal management, giving priority to capital spending, debt reduction, and saving, and help deal with the potential volatile and unpredictable nature of ECP receipts (Xu, El-Ashram, and Gold 2015). Specifically,

- Prudent management of government spending has an important role in containing the impact of these inflows on the real economy, but it should be accompanied by sufficient oversight and regulation to pace inflows, particularly to the private sector. For example, annual caps on the number of applications or the size of investments would limit the influx of investment to a country's construction sector. A regulatory framework for the real estate market would reduce risk and limit the potentially damaging effects of price distortions and segmentation in the domestic property market resulting from investment minimums imposed by these programs. Compiling relevant real estate data to monitor the impact of these programs should be a priority.

- Changing key parameters of the program, such as increasing the cost of the real estate option, thereby making direct contribution to the NDF relatively more attractive, can also be an effective way to redirect investment to the public sector, allowing countries to save the resources for future use, including for debt repayment and investment in infrastructure.

- Building sufficient fiscal buffers should be a priority. Large fiscal revenue windfalls could potentially trigger unsustainable expansions in expenditure

---

[21]The statement issued by Canada indicated that "After carefully monitoring the integrity of Antigua and Barbuda's travel documents, the Government of Canada has determined that Antigua and Barbuda no longer meets Canada's criteria for a visa exemption" (Travelwirenews 2017).

that leave the economy exposed if the revenue stream dries up. Given the potentially volatile nature of these inflows, ECP countries—and small economies in particular—need to build buffers by saving the inflows.

- Reducing high public debt in highly indebted countries to sustainable levels is also important (Figure 7.10). Reducing debt is particularly relevant given that, in some cases, the debt-service cost on some of the public debt can exceed the potential rate of return on savings.[22] Reducing debt could lessen the negative impact of the debt overhang on growth, expand borrowing capacity, and improve the fiscal balance. Trade-offs between increasing savings and reducing debt depend on the cost of debt, the return on saved assets, institutional capacity to manage growing financial wealth, and sound debt management principles (IMF 2014). Other factors may include the need for a certain level of sovereign debt instruments to promote financial market development and to provide investment and liquidity-management instruments for domestic financial institutions and social security funds, which face very limited investment options in small states.

- Prudent management of citizenship revenue inflows would allow for a sustainable increase in public investment and accommodate countercyclical spending and relief measures in the face of natural disasters. Recent literature demonstrates that, in credit-constrained, capital-scarce developing economies, productive domestic capital spending could yield higher returns than foreign investment (including by an SWF), and should also be considered as part of an optimal strategy to manage a resource revenue windfall (Takizawa, Gardner, and Ueda 2004; Venables 2010; van der Ploeg and Venables 2011; Araujo and others 2012). This should be done through a sustainable investment approach—in which a combination of raising public investment and saving some of the resources in a stabilization fund to support ongoing maintenance is used to preserve investment efficiency.[23] A conservative scaling-up schedule for public investment that is consistent with both development needs and macroeconomic conditions would allow some of the revenue windfall to be saved in a stabilization fund.[24] Indeed, St. Kitts and Nevis announced in December 2016 its intention to establish in 2017 a Growth and Resilience Fund to manage

---

[22]This may not be true for countries where debt is mostly concessional and where large deficits in infrastructure may allow for an overall return on investment that is higher than the cost of debt.

[23]For example, in Grenada proposed guidelines for investment operations funded by ECP resources require that spending on a project be undertaken only after sufficient funds are secured to finance the project to completion and its maintenance over the medium term.

[24]IMF staff simulations for Dominica (Guerson and others, forthcoming) show that additional capital expenditure would help close the infrastructure gap and permanently raise the level of income in the economy, saving accumulation would provide for a smooth transition when or if ECP revenues come to a sudden stop, and debt reduction would help reduce the debt-servicing burden and allow for faster attainment of the regional debt target of 60 percent of GDP by 2030.

**Figure 7.10. Public Debt of Selected Countries with ECPs**
*(Percent of GDP, 2016)*

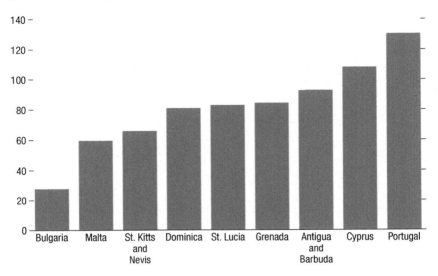

Sources: Country authorities; and IMF staff estimates.
Note: ECPs = economic citizenship programs.

the large accumulated liquid assets that are currently being held in the baking system.[25]

- Fiscal revenue from ECPs should be channeled through the country's budget. In St. Kitts and Nevis, contributions to the SIDF—the country's NDF—are not reported on budget. In Antigua and Barbuda, only NDF resources are managed on budget; the Citizenship by Investment Program Unit surplus from application fees to the government is managed at the cabinet's discretion, outside the budget framework. Similar information gaps exist in Dominica, where ECP revenues are accumulated in commercial bank accounts and transferred on-budget on an as-needed basis. Starting in fiscal year 2017/18, however, Dominica's authorities intend to fully reflect all ECP revenues on budget. Funding fiscal or quasi-fiscal operations from outside the budget weakens the assessment of the underlying

---

[25]The announcement was made in the context of the 2017 budget speech. Prime Minister Harris indicated that "The medium-term macroeconomic objective of this strategy is to use the accumulated savings to build policy buffers against exogenous shocks that could result from hurricanes, downturns in key tourism markets and adverse developments related to the CBI [Citizenship-by-Investment] inflows" (Caribbean News Now 2016).

### Box 7.1. Treatment of Economic Citizenship Program Inflows in Fiscal Accounts

The surge of economic citizenship program inflows has created a new revenue stream that needs to be accurately reflected in the fiscal accounts. These recommendations are in line with best practices.

- **Application fees**, in line with the *Government Finance Statistics Manual 2001*, should be recorded transparently in government budgets as nontax revenue. These are revenues earned on account of providing this asset, of which a small part reflects fees for service, covering the cost of government processing, due diligence, and the like. Similarly, government spending to deliver these services should be identified transparently in expenditures, under goods and services.
- **Contributions to national development funds (NDFs)** are public sector revenues that should also be booked in government accounts when they are first received. Such payments should be recorded transparently and recognized as increasing government's earning capacity. The mechanism in some existing programs, whereby these contributions go directly to NDFs rather than being channeled through the budget, means that the full stream of income to government is not fully captured. In general, best practice would be to record all contributions to government directly in the budget, and then channel them to be spent (or saved) in line with government priorities, as direct government expenditure or—in the case of NDFs, for instance—as budget transfers to off-budget agencies.
- **Inflows to the private investor** will affect public finances to a much lesser extent. The main channel will be through an increase in stamp duty for the transfer of real estate assets. Notwithstanding the small fiscal impact, records of the size of private sector transactions should be maintained by the government, so that their impact on activity and on the balance of payments can be fully understood. Other fiscal impact will be through the increase in income tax (from construction companies and real estate agents) and personal income tax (from construction workers).

fiscal stance and provides incomplete information about the actual size of the government's spending commitments. A broader fiscal perimeter, reflecting all ECP-related revenues and expenditures, is needed to properly analyze the true fiscal policy stance in ECCU countries with ECPs. This broader perimeter would provide for a transparent accounting of the inflows and reduce the risks of intensifying demand pressures and funding of low-priority public investment projects. The role of development funds financed by ECPs should be properly defined and their operations and investment should be fully integrated into the budget (Box 7.1).

- Effective management of inflows, combined with prudent fiscal administration, will also reduce risk to the external sector. Managing and regulating inflows to the private sector, while curbing the expansion of public sector spending, would contain the increase of imports, limit the rise in wages and the real exchange rate, and contribute to accumulating international reserves—to serve as a buffer in case of a sharp slowdown in ECP receipts.

- Financial sector oversight will also need to be strengthened. As ECP resources make their way through the system, bank balance sheet exposures need to be carefully monitored to safeguard against the emergence of weak credit standards or significant currency or maturity mismatches. This oversight is particularly relevant as ECP beneficiaries, including the government and real estate developers, rapidly accumulate deposits in the system. Strengthening banking sector oversight and prudential regulation will be important to preserve banks' financial soundness indicators, and should include appropriate stress testing of banks' exposures to the risk of real estate market corrections, to moderate risks arising from the rapid influx of resources to the financial system. Caps on credit growth, restrictions on foreign currency loans, or simply tighter capital requirements may be needed to dampen the procyclical flow of credit.

- Investing ECP-related fiscal savings abroad would enhance financial stability and help preserve the quality of invested assets. As noted, government saving of large ECP inflows has already resulted in substantial growth of government deposits in the domestic banking system in St. Kitts and Nevis and in Dominica. Investing the bulk of these savings abroad under a formalized investment framework, such as an SWF, would ease the profitability pressures at domestic banks and safeguard their balance sheets against maturity and currency mismatches (Table 7.4). Additionally, the savings would not be exposed to the same idiosyncratic risks, which would help the government tap these assets swiftly in the event of large shocks, like natural disasters, without creating pressure on the domestic banking system. Equally important, the quality of invested assets is more likely to be preserved through a more comprehensive investment process, which should ideally be subject to a prudent governance framework, and adequate oversight of regulatory and legislative bodies. A comprehensive process would also help deal with fluctuations in program revenues and stabilize the impact on the economy, possibly also providing scope for intergenerational transfers. However, other less costly options may also be possible, such as having the saved assets managed by the central bank or the Bank for International Settlements (Table 7.4).

- Rigorous due diligence of the process for citizenship applications is essential to preserve the credibility of the ECP and preclude potentially serious integrity and security risks. A comprehensive framework is needed to curtail the use of investment options as routes for money laundering and financing criminal activity. Such safeguards are integral to the success of ECPs and would also increase protection against the risk of the withdrawal of correspondent banking relationships by global banks (see Chapter 12). A high level of transparency regarding ECP applicants would further enhance the programs' reputation and sustainability. Complying with international guidelines on the transparency and exchange of tax information would reduce the incidence of program misuse for purposes of tax

**Table 7.4. Summary of Potential Investment Channels for ECP Savings in Small State Economies**

| Investment Channels | Benefits | Considerations |
|---|---|---|
| A Central Bank–Managed Investment Account | – Existing expertise and established investment and risk management frameworks<br>– High accessibility and less time-consuming to set up<br>– Management costs are likely to be lower than external managers. | – Investment returns are likely to be commensurate with those earned on the general central bank reserve account. |
| World Bank Treasury-Reserve Advisory and Management Program | – Broader asset management experience<br>– Established methodology and standard investment guidelines<br>– Targeted technical assistance to build domestic capacity for investment monitoring and management<br>– World Bank mission to assess best investment strategy | – Management fees may be higher than the central bank, lowering net nominal returns.<br>– Minimum portfolio size is US$100 million.<br>– Cap on size of managed portfolio of about 20 percent of international reserve balance |
| Bank for International Settlements (Bis) | – Investment in a broader asset pool under a specific investment mandate or in an open-end fund (BIS investment pool) | – Accessible only through an account with the central bank or monetary authority |

Note: ECP = economic citizenship program.

evasion or other illicit activities and minimize the risk of adverse international pressure.

- Stopping further reductions in investment requirements and other program conditions would also be important to safeguarding future inflows. A regional approach could ensure the adoption of best practices across the region, promote information sharing and transparency, and prevent applicants who do not pass due diligence in one country from applying elsewhere. Joint management of ECP applications would also help achieve economies of scale and reduce costs while averting a race to the bottom. Some progress on this front has already been made. The authorities of ECCU countries have recently granted to the Organisation of Eastern Caribbean States the mandate to coordinate regional cooperation on ECP programs. Moreover, the Citizenship-by-Investment Programs Association was formed in 2015 under the auspices of the Organisation of Eastern Caribbean States intended to strengthen the regulatory framework and promote collaboration on due diligence.

- In addition to all of the above, pursuing deeper structural reforms to address fundamental institutional weaknesses are necessary for achieving sustained growth objectives. Reliance on ECP flows—which could be volatile—is not a panacea for addressing a country's macroeconomic and growth challenges. Attracting durable private and foreign investment to sustain long-term growth requires creating an attractive business environment and improving competitiveness (see Chapter 2).

- Finally, to help garner and maintain public support for these programs, the economic benefits should accrue to the whole nation. The programs should be viewed as a national resource that may not be renewable if the nation's reputation is tarnished by mismanagement. A clear and transparent framework for the management of resources is necessary, including a well-defined accountability structure that includes oversight and periodic financial audits. Information on the number of people granted citizenship and the amount of revenue earned—including its use and the amount saved, spent, and invested—should be publicly available.

## CONCLUSION

ECPs create potential benefits, but also risks, particularly for small states. Inflows under these programs can be substantial, with their impact widely felt across all economic sectors. They can significantly boost private sector investment and economic activity in small states, many of which are still recovering from the repercussions of the 2008–09 global financial crisis. They can also increase fiscal revenues and contribute to improving overall fiscal performance. However, if not managed carefully, these inflows will lead to challenges like those that have confronted resource-rich economies for decades, including possible boom-bust cycles and loss of external competitiveness. Moreover, the high sudden-stop risk of these inflows poses an even greater challenge than the high volatility associated with resource revenues.

Prudent management of the ECP and its associated financial inflows, combined with parallel structural reforms, can contain these risks while allowing countries to benefit from their positive impact. Critical measures include monitoring and regulating the inflows into the private sector to ensure that the magnitude of the inflows is consistent with economic absorptive capacity to contain price pressures. The bulk of fiscal revenues should be saved, to alleviate excessive demand pressures and to prevent the buildup of fiscal dependence on these inflows. ECP-generated savings can be channeled into precautionary balances to help these countries deal with exogenous shocks—which small states are significantly more vulnerable to—and more rapidly reduce high levels of public debt. Scaling up public investment in a sustainable manner may also increase potential growth, but projects should be subject to careful screening to ensure they deliver sufficiently positive economic and social return, and that they are consistent with macroeconomic sustainability. Finally, prudent management should carefully address governance and integrity risks by implementing a rigorous due diligence process, a strong anti-money laundering/combating the financing of terrorism framework, and transparent administration of the program.

Establishing an SWF to manage large ECP fiscal savings, such as the GRF being established in St. Kitts and Nevis, could further strengthen fiscal management and safeguard financial stability while providing for the potential to enhance returns on accumulated savings. If established in line with best practices, an SWF would reinforce a strong governance framework in the management and investment of saved resources, and increase transparency. An SWF could raise the credibility of ECPs within host nations, improve prospects for better management of the inflows, and allow for the future sustainable use of these resources for the benefit of the citizens of the host country.

Finally, particularly in the context of the ECCU, a regional approach to ECPs should be adopted. Collaborating on and coordinating the administration of these programs, especially with regard to ensuring stringent screening of applicants, could reduce costs and diminish reputational risks. It may also provide the best safeguard against a race to the bottom, which, if not addressed, would ultimately significantly reduce the potential from these inflows to the region.

# REFERENCES

Araujo, J., B. Grace Li, M. Poplawski-Ribeiro, and L. Zanna. 2012. "Current Account Norms in Natural Resource Rich and Capital Scarce Economies." IMF Working Paper 13/80, International Monetary Fund, Washington, DC.

Guerson, A., B. Csonto, A. Myrvoda, and M. Mendes Tavares. Forthcoming. "Optimal Management of Citizenship-by-Investment Program Revenues in Dominica; Dominica Selected Issues Papers." International Monetary Fund, Washington, DC.

Gupta, Sanjeev, Alex Segura-Ubiergo, and Enrique Flores. 2014. "Sharing the Wealth." *Finance and Development* 51 (4): 52–55.

International Monetary Fund (IMF). 2012. "Macroeconomic Policy Frameworks for Resource-Rich Developing Countries." IMF Policy Paper, Washington, DC.

———. 2014. "Sovereign Asset-Liability Management-Guidance for Resource-Rich Economies." IMF Policy Paper, Washington, DC.

———. 2016. "Eastern Caribbean Currency Union: 2016 Discussion on Common Policies of Member Countries—Press Release and Staff Report." IMF Country Report 16/333, International Monetary Fund, Washington, DC.

———. Forthcoming. "Eastern Caribbean Currency Union: 2017 Discussion on Common Policies of Member Countries." Washington, DC.

Kälin, C. H. 2014. *Global Residence and Citizenship Handbook*. 4th Edition. Zurich: IDEOS Publications.

Seanad Éireann Debates. Motion on Passports for Investment. Vol. 154 No. 11, March 4, 1998.

Slemrod, J. 2008. "Why Is Elvis on Burkina Faso Postage Stamps?" *Journal of Empirical Legal Studies* 5 (4): 683–712.

St. Kitts and Nevis Citizenship-by-Investment Unit website http://www.ciu.gov.kn/.

St. Kitts and Nevis Sugar Industry Diversification Foundation website http://www.sknsidf.org/.

Takizawa, H., E. Gardner, and K. Ueda. 2004. "Are Developing Countries Better Off Spending Their Wealth Upfront?" IMF Working Paper 04/141, International Monetary Fund, Washington, DC.

U.K. Migration Advisory Committee (MAC). 2014. "Tier 1 (Investor) Route: Investment Thresholds and Economic Benefits." London. https://www.gov.uk/government/publications/the-investment-limits-and-economic-benefits-of-the-tier-1-investor-route-feb-2014.

Van der Ploeg, F., and A. Venables. 2011. "Harnessing Windfall Revenues: Optimal Policies for Resource-Rich Developing Economies." *Economic Journal* 121 (551): 1–30.

Van Fossen, A. 2007. "Citizenship for Sale: Passports of Convenience from Pacific Island Tax Havens." *Commonwealth and Comparative Politics* 45 (2): 138–63.

Venables, A. 2010. "Resource Rents: When to Spend and How to Save." *International Tax and Public Finance* 17 (4): 340–56.

Wise, P. 2014. "Sea, Sun and Easy Visas Lure China Buyers." *Financial Times*, October 8. https://www.ft.com/content/d7c1b472-44a6-11e4-ab0c-00144feabdc0.

Xu, X., A. El-Ashram, and J. Gold. 2015. "Too Much of a Good Thing? Prudent Management of Inflows under Economic Citizenship Programs." IMF Working Paper 15/93, International Monetary Fund, Washington, DC.

# CHAPTER 8

# Debt Restructuring in the Caribbean—The Recent Experience

JOEL CHIEDU OKWUOKEI AND BERT VAN SELM

## INTRODUCTION

Many economies in the Caribbean region have been caught in a low growth–high debt trap for decades. Debt has been built up over the years through large fiscal deficits, the costs associated with natural disasters, public enterprise borrowing, and off-balance-sheet spending, including for financial sector bail-outs. High levels of debt have, in turn, had a negative impact on growth, notably because high debt contributes to macroeconomic uncertainty and because the high cost of debt service reduces the fiscal space for investing in human and physical infrastructure that would support growth.[1]

In the years leading up to the 2008–09 global financial crisis, moderate growth helped some countries stabilize and reduce their debt levels, but the crisis reversed this trend (Figure 8.1). A number of Caribbean countries are now among the most highly indebted in the world. At the end of 2016, four countries in the region (Jamaica, Barbados, Antigua and Barbuda, Belize) had debt-to-GDP levels close to, or even above, 100 percent of GDP (Figure 8.2). In commodity-exporting countries, such as Trinidad and Tobago and Suriname, lower global commodity prices have led to large fiscal deficits and rapid debt accumulation in recent years, with public debt-to-GDP ratios now about 50 percent, and on the rise.

The Caribbean region has seen several episodes of sovereign debt restructuring to commercial creditors over the past few years (Annex Tables 8.1.1. and 8.1.2). This chapter looks at the four countries in the region that have engaged in such restructuring since 2011: Jamaica, Belize, Grenada, and St. Kitts and Nevis.[2]

---

The authors thanks Chuan Li for excellent research assistance.

[1]Several studies have looked at the high indebtedness of the Caribbean region, including CDB 2013; Jahan 2013; McIntyre and Ogawa 2013; and Amo-Yartey and Turner-Jones 2014.

[2]Older cases, such as Dominica's 2004 debt restructuring and that of Antigua and Barbuda in 2010, are discussed in Jahan 2013. In both cases, both domestic and external debt were restructured in the context of IMF programs.

**Figure 8.1. The Caribbean: Total Government Debt, 2000–16**
*(Percent of GDP, weighted average)*

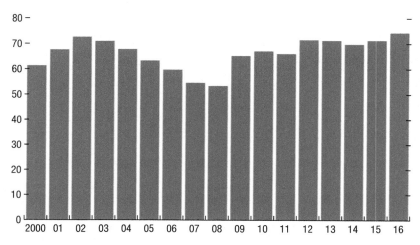

Sources: IMF, *World Economic Outlook*; and IMF staff estimations.

**Figure 8.2. The Caribbean: Total Government Debt, 2016**
*(Percent of GDP)*

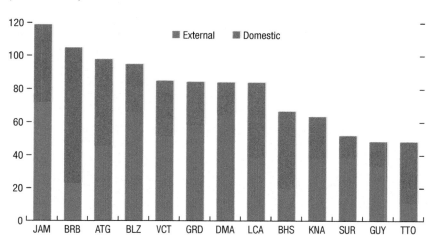

Sources: IMF, *World Economic Outlook*; and IMF staff estimates.
Note: Data labels in figure use International Organization for Standardization (ISO) country codes.

Three of these cases entail examples of a second or even third restructuring of what is essentially the same debt to private creditors: Jamaica (domestic debt twice—2010 and 2013), Belize (external debt three times—2006–07, 2012–13, and 2016–17), and Grenada (both domestic and external debt were restructured twice—in 2004–06 and in 2013–15). Among the recent episodes, St. Kitts and Nevis's 2011–12 restructuring is the only one that was not a repeat operation.

The chapter looks at ways to assess the relative successes of these operations, including impact on debt sustainability, debt-to-GDP ratios, and developments in yields and market access.[3] In other words, the "success" of the debt operation is looked at through the perspective of debt-related indicators rather than broader growth indicators that are typically influenced by general domestic reforms and policies as well as external factors. The inquiry also discusses factors that may have contributed to success, including (1) the size of the restructuring (principal haircut or not; impact on the net present value [NPV] of the debt); (2) the type of debt selected for restructuring (external, domestic, or both); (3) the role of debt modalities, including collective action clauses (CACs), hurricane and clawback clauses, and step-up and step-down clauses; and (4) the sustained implementation of a supporting macroeconomic reform program. A concluding section draws key policy lessons.

## JAMAICA: JDX AND NDX

Jamaica has restructured its debt to private creditors twice in recent years: in the 2010 Jamaica Debt Exchange (JDX), and then again in 2013, in an operation labeled National Debt Exchange (NDX). The design choices for these operations and their outcomes—their immediate and medium-term impact on public debt and their impact on financial markets—contain valuable lessons for the design of successful debt-restructuring operations.

Both JDX and NDX were embedded in, and executed at the start of, IMF-supported economic reform programs—the 2010 Stand-By Arrangement (SBA), and the 2013 Extended Fund Facility (EFF), respectively. In fact, both operations were prior actions for IMF Executive Board approval of the broader, IMF-supported reform program, including IMF financing (300 percent of quota under the 2010 SBA and 225 percent of quota under the 2013 EFF). Both programs aimed to put public finances on a sustainable footing with a combination of fiscal consolidation, measures to boost growth, and debt restructuring. Performance under these programs was different: while the 2010 SBA went off track after three quarterly reviews owing to fiscal slippages, the 2013 EFF remained on track for the duration of the program, until November 2016, with 13 reviews completed and targets for the 14th review met. Under the EFF, Jamaica maintained a primary surplus of 7 percent of GDP or higher for four

---

[3]To ensure comparability with IMF country reports, this chapter uses the definitions of public debt used in those individual reports.

**Figure 8.3. Jamaica: Public Debt, 2013**
*(Percent)*

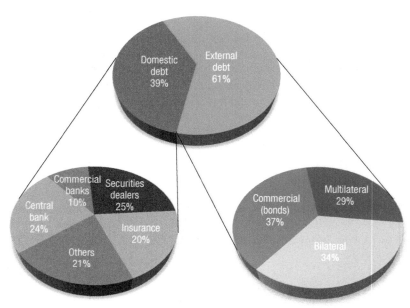

Sources: Country authorities; and IMF staff calculations.

years in a row—2013 through 2016—and these targets continued to be sustained in the 2016 SBA. In contrast to the 2010 SBA, the 2013 EFF managed to put public debt on a clear downward path and restore debt sustainability.

In both cases, the Jamaican authorities opted to restructure domestically issued debt only (Figure 8.3). The exchanges excluded bonds issued in foreign jurisdictions or held by nonresidents—a choice guided by the Jamaican authorities' emphasis on the voluntary nature of the operation (Grigorian, Alleyne, and Guerson 2012, 8). Even so, in both JDX and NDX, participation rates ended up being very high, at 99 percent or more (Grigorian, Alleyne, and Guerson 2012, 12; IMF 2013a,14). Both JDX and NDX targeted lower coupon rates and extensions of maturities, with no principal haircut. Under JDX, the rate on Jamaican dollar–denominated debt with an average interest rate of 19 percent was reduced to an initial rate of 12.5 percent, and the average maturity of domestic debt was increased from 4.7 to 8.3 years, resulting in significant immediate fiscal savings for the government (Grigorian, Alleyne, and Guerson 2012, 11–12). Under NDX, coupons were reduced by 1–5 percent and maturities extended by three to 10 years, depending on the instrument; NDX also served to address a large bunching of maturities at the end of February 2013 (IMF 2013a, 13–14).

JDX and NDX were also similar in that they targeted a limited reduction in the NPV of the public debt. The immediate reduction in the NPV of public debt was a bit higher under JDX (an estimated 15–20 percent) than under NDX (8.6 percent of GDP reduction against 2020 GDP).[4] Concerns about the impact of the debt restructuring on the stability of the domestic financial sector—and in particular, the relatively large securities dealers sector, with total assets equivalent to 40 percent of GDP in 2013, and a significant portion in government bonds— played an important role in this element of the design of JDX and NDX (see, for example, Wynter 2016, 3). To help mitigate this risk, in both cases, a Financial Sector Support Fund was set up to provide liquidity support, if needed, to individual financial institutions that might experience difficulties as a result of the debt exchange. Both the 2010 SBA and the 2013 EFF also included measures to strengthen the securities dealers sector's capital and liquidity buffers and improve its legal and prudential framework.

Despite these similarities in design, the impact of JDX on domestic financial markets was very different from the impact of NDX. No individual financial institutions applied for Financial Sector Support Fund resources under either JDX or NDX. But while trading in government bonds quickly resumed after JDX, the market for government bonds remained inactive for three years after NDX, until February 2016, when the government issued domestic bonds for the first time after NDX (Schmid 2016, 6–7 and Figure 8.4). This evidence from Jamaica's domestic bond market points to the importance of getting it right the first time—including by underpinning the restructuring with a sustained fiscal consolidation program. Repeated restructuring of what is essentially the same debt will lead creditors to anticipate the likelihood of similar operations in the future, and is thereby detrimental to market development.

The Jamaican authorities' decision to restructure domestic bond debt twice while leaving external bond debt untouched led investors to perceive domestically issued bonds as a higher risk than bonds issued in foreign jurisdictions. As a result, the external credit channel was able to reopen much earlier after the NDX than the domestic bond market, with the issuance of a new US$800 million (about 6 percent of GDP) Eurobond in July 2014. This channel was again used in July 2015, with a US$2 billion issuance that supported the buyback of Jamaica's US$3 billion debt to Venezuela, accumulated under the PetroCaribe program, at a sharp (about 50 percent) discount. This debt restructuring with Venezuela reduced Jamaica's debt-to-GDP ratio by about 10 percentage points in a single operation. Having the external credit channel available relatively quickly after NDX thus played a critical role in Jamaica's ability to manage and reduce its public debt (Figure 8.5).

With access to global capital markets but not to domestic markets for several years, the share of Jamaica's external, United States dollar-denominated debt in overall public debt gradually increased, with United States dollar-denominated

---

[4]The 2013 EFF program specified the prior action for debt restructuring against projected 2020 GDP.

### Figure 8.4. Secondary Government Bond Market Activities

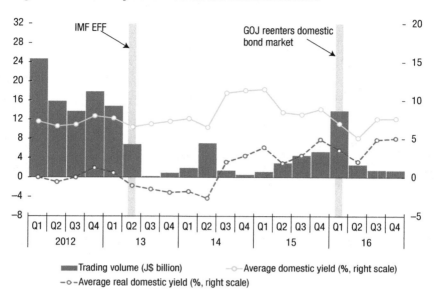

Sources: Country authorities; and IMF staff calculations.
Note: EFF= Extended Fund Facility; GOJ=government of Jamaica.

debt now well over half of overall public debt. This has made debt dynamics more vulnerable to exchange rate developments—a clear downside to Jamaica's "domestic-only" approach to sovereign debt restructuring.

Another important difference between JDX and NDX was that after NDX, starting in 2013, implementation of the reform program supporting the debt exchange was monitored not just by an IMF-supported program with quarterly reviews, but also by a domestic monitoring mechanism with monthly reviews (including a monthly report in national newspapers and a monthly press conference by the private sector co-chair). The Economic Program Oversight Committee was set up at the initiative of the government's four largest domestic creditors who were affected twice by the debt restructurings, and included representatives of labor unions and government as well as sectoral interests (for example, agriculture). Broad-based program ownership by various stakeholders, including the private sector, public sector, media, unions, academia, think tanks, civil society, and opposition, provided an environment for the Economic Program Oversight Committee to effectively hold the government to its commitments. With this broad support, Jamaica was able to sustain an exceptionally high primary surplus—initially 7½ percent of GDP, and 7 percent of GDP starting in 2016—over a prolonged period. Four years after NDX, it became clear that the broader

**Figure 8.5. Jamaican Bond Spreads**
*(Percent)*

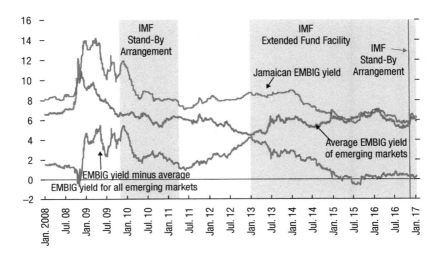

Source: Bloomberg.
Note: EMBIG = JPMorgan Emerging Market Bond Index Global.

strategy, of which the 2013 NDX was an important part, put Jamaica's debt on a firm downward trajectory (Figure 8.6).

In sum, three key lessons stand out from Jamaica's recent experience. First, debt restructuring *can* help put debt on a downward trajectory, but only when it is an element of a broader, well-executed strategy that includes fiscal consolidation and policies to support economic growth. Second, debt restructuring works best as a single-shot operation—repeated restructurings undermine the credibility of the government and will lead investors to anticipate similar operations in the future, with a negative impact on market development. Third, effective monitoring of the supporting reform program that reinforces the debt restructuring is critically important, and can be facilitated by a credible domestic monitoring mechanism that involves key domestic stakeholders. The Jamaican experience shows that sustained implementation of the underlying reform plan is key— NDX secured a smaller NPV gain than JDX, yet it was the 2013 NDX operation that marked the turning point toward debt sustainability.

## BELIZE: TOWARD SUPERBOND 3.0

Belize completed its third debt restructuring in a decade in 2017. On November 9, 2016, the Belizean authorities announced their decision to seek a restructuring of Belize's debt to holders of United States dollar-denominated bonds (US$526 million,

**Figure 8.6. Jamaica: Public Debt-to-GDP Ratio**
*(Percent)*

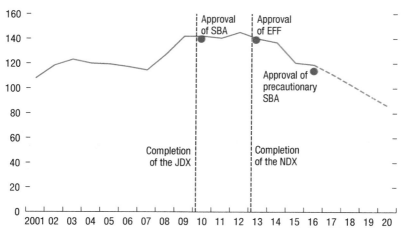

Sources: IMF, *World Economic Outlook*; and IMF staff estimations.
Note: EFF = Extended Fund Facility; JDX = Jamaica Debt Exchange; NDX= National Debt Exchange; SBA= Stand-By Arrangement.

or about 30 percent of GDP), following similar operations in 2006–07 and 2012–13 (Figure 8.7). In their press release, they attributed their decision to "serious economic and financial challenges currently facing the country," and referred to low growth, rising fiscal deficits, U.S. dollar strength, Hurricane Earl, and higher-than-anticipated arbitration awards, among other factors.[5] A little more than four months later, on March 15, 2017, the Belizean authorities announced that they had reached agreement with private external bondholders. The new agreement reduced the interest rate on the bonds to 4.9375 percent (the rate was set to step up from 5 percent to 6.767 percent in August 2017), and amended the principal repayment schedule by pushing back principal repayments to 2030–34 (instead of starting semiannual installments in August 2019). The final maturity date of the bond was brought forward from 2038 to 2034.

Ten years earlier, in 2006–07, Belize first exchanged various external debt instruments for a single United States dollar-denominated bond ("Superbond") with a face value of US$547 million. This initial exchange lengthened maturities, extended the grace period (with no principal repayment until 2019), and lowered interest rates, but did not reduce the face value of the debt (no principal haircut). The operation was driven by an acute liquidity shortage (Asonuma and others

---

[5]In June 2016, a ruling by the Permanent Court of Arbitration increased total compensation payments for the nationalized Belize Telecom Limited to US$275 million, equivalent to about 16 percent of 2016 GDP.

**Figure 8.7. Belize: Central Government Public Debt, 2016**
*(Percent)*

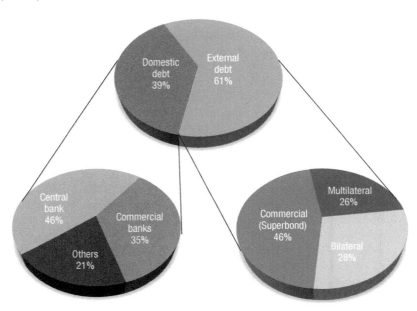

Sources: Country authorities; and IMF staff calculations.

2014, 4). Participation in the exchange was high, reaching 98 percent after the activation of a CAC on one of the bonds. The NPV haircut of the operation has been estimated to be 24 percent (Asonuma and others 2014, 10).

Similarly, when this debt was again rescheduled in 2012–13, the focus of the operation was on improving the government's cash flow over the near-to-medium term rather than on longer-term debt sustainability considerations. The maturity of the bond was lengthened again (from 2029 to 2038), and the interest rate was reduced. There was a modest haircut (3 percent of the principal amount), and the NPV gain of the operation was estimated to be 29 percent (Asonuma and others 2014, 19). Execution of the CAC raised the participation level from 86 percent to 100 percent (Asonuma and others 2014, 18).

Both Superbond 1.0 (the 2006–07 operation) and Superbond 2.0 (the 2012–13 operation) built in significantly more demanding debt-servicing terms after an initial period of low interest rates (a *step-up coupon*) and no principal repayments. The first operation set interest rates at 4.25 percent until 2010 but had rates jump to 8.5 percent after 2012. Similarly, the design of the second operation included an increase in the coupon rate from 5 percent to 6.767 percent starting in 2017, and maintained a grace period (no principal payments) until 2019. This design feature of the first two debt-restructuring operations (debt service becoming more onerous over time) may have contributed to the three-in-a-row scenario that eventually played out (Asonuma and others 2014, 9–10). The 2017 Superbond 3.0 avoids a step-up coupon but does concentrate principal repayments in the final five years of the loan, so that debt service becomes more onerous toward the end of the life of the bond.

Over the period of the three restructurings, economic policies and outcomes changed little despite a turbulent global environment. A small primary surplus was maintained in most years (1.2 percent, on average, over 2007–16), corresponding to a small overall deficit (1.9 percent of GDP). Growth remained anemic, at 2.1 percent, on average, since 2007. Meanwhile, the exchange rate peg of the Belizean dollar to the U.S. dollar ensured low inflation (1.4 percent, on average, over the period). With these trends, the debt-to-GDP ratio remained high—in the range of 75–100 percent over the period (Figure 8.9).

As in Jamaica, Belize has repeatedly targeted the same debt for restructuring—in this case, its external debt (denominated in U.S. dollars, and issued under U.S. law) to bondholders. This focus on external commercial debt is partly explained by domestic financial stability concerns (Asonuma and others 2014, 8), which in turn has implications for market access—Belize has not been able to issue new debt to international bondholders in a long time, but retains the ability to issue domestic debt to domestic financial entities. After the government announced the third debt restructuring, the yield on the Superbond shot up to more than 20 percent (Figure 8.8).

Neither the first nor the second debt restructuring was supported by a sustained fiscal consolidation program and growth-supporting initiatives—Belize's most recent IMF program expired in 1986, long before these debt restructurings. The focus of the two restructurings on improving the government's immediate cash flow issues, rather than on longer-term debt sustainability, has meant that neither the 2006–07 nor the 2012–13 operation managed to place government finances on a sound footing, and neither operation put the debt-to-GDP ratio on a clear downward trajectory. On the eve of the third debt restructuring, at the end of 2016, public debt remained about 100 percent of GDP.

The 2017 agreement with bondholders is anchored by fiscal adjustment, but the adjustment is not ambitious enough to restore debt sustainability. The authorities have committed to tighten the fiscal stance by 3 percentage points in fiscal year 2017/18, and to maintain a primary surplus of 2 percent of GDP for the subsequent three years (fiscal years 2018–21), implying no additional adjustment effort after 2017/18. The agreement also includes a monitoring mechanism for the fiscal adjustment effort: if Belize fails to meet the 2018–21 primary surplus target, the authorities will submit a report to the National Assembly to explain why the target was missed. In addition, if this occurs, Belize has committed to requesting an IMF technical assistance mission to determine why the primary surplus target was missed and recommend remedial measures.[6] The authorities

---

[6]The IMF has not committed to provide such technical assistance.

**Figure 8.8. Belize: Superbond Price Developments**
*(U.S. dollars)*

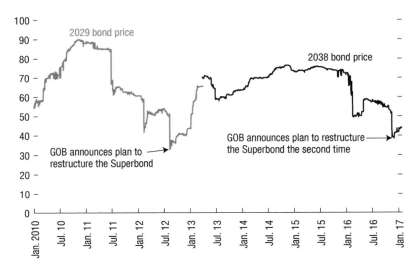

Source: Bloomberg.
Note: GOB = government of Belize.

**Figure 8.9. Belize: Public Debt-to-GDP Ratio**
*(Percent)*

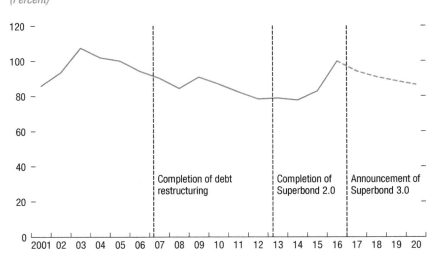

Sources: IMF, *World Economic Outlook*; and IMF staff estimations.

have also committed to publishing the findings of any such IMF technical assistance. Furthermore, if the primary surplus target is missed, interest payments on the bond will become payable on a quarterly rather than semiannual basis (for the subsequent 12 months after the target is missed).

These repeated efforts to restructure private debt risk undermine Belize's credibility and access to international capital markets for an extended period, in turn hurting prospects for strong and sustainable growth. The authorities appear to be well aware of this issue: as the government indicated in its December 2016 solicitation of comments from bondholders, "No one—least of all the Government of Belize—wishes to contemplate the prospect of a fourth restructuring of these instruments." The first two operations made clear that ambitious fiscal consolidation is critical to underpinning any debt rescheduling and to establishing credibility with the markets. Absent such adjustment, any debt rescheduling is likely to be only a temporary palliative.

To secure durable gains, the 2017 debt restructuring needs to be supported by a medium-term strategy that combines more ambitious, and high-quality, fiscal consolidation with structural measures to boost growth. Although the debt rescheduling provides meaningful cash flow relief, and the agreed upon fiscal tightening is a step in the right direction, the agreement is just one element of a more comprehensive package needed to lift Belize out of high debt and low growth. The agreement reduces the cost of servicing a relatively expensive part of external debt, and the NPV gain is significant, at 28 percent.[7] However, the overall level of public debt remains very high. Further fiscal adjustment—targeting a primary surplus that is greater than 2 percent of GDP—will be necessary to put debt on a clear downward trajectory. Containing government spending on wages and pensions, which is already high by international standards and projected to increase over the medium term, will be important. Concrete steps to improve the business climate, including by making it easier to start a business and get credit, could help foster growth.

## GRENADA: HURRICANE CLAUSE

Grenada has restructured its sovereign debt to private (and bilateral official) creditors twice since 2004: first during 2004–06, after a devastating hurricane (Ivan, with estimated damage equivalent to 200 percent of GDP) and then again during 2013–15. Both operations were complicated and took considerable time to complete—much longer than the Jamaican and Belizean experiences discussed above. Both operations were also eventually accompanied by IMF-supported reform programs, as in Jamaica, although in Grenada the debt operations were not a formal condition for IMF support (that is, they were not a prior action for program approval).

---

[7]Including fees and using an exit yield of 9.1 percent on March 15, 2017. NPV gain calculated as (1–NPV new/face value existing).

**Figure 8.10. Grenada: Public Debt-to-GDP Ratio**
*(Percent)*

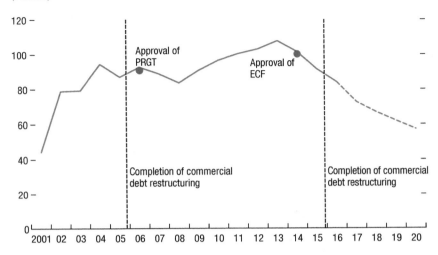

Sources: IMF, *World Economic Outlook*; and IMF staff calculations.
Note: ECF=Extended Credit Facility; PRGT=Poverty Reduction and Growth Trust.

Hurricane Ivan struck Grenada on September 7, 2004, and the Grenadian authorities announced their intention to seek "the cooperation of creditors" three weeks later, on October 1. The stated objective was to return Grenada to a position of economic stability and debt sustainability (Asonuma and others, 2017, 9). Both external and domestic debt to private creditors, as well as official bilateral debt, were targeted, excluding Treasury bills and debt to multilateral institutions. The commercial debt rescheduling agreed to more than a year later, on November 15, 2005, encompassed US$77 million of domestic debt and US$172 million of external debt (both partly denominated in Eastern Caribbean dollars and partly in U.S. dollars) and featured (1) no principal haircut; (2) extension of final maturity (to 2025); (3) a significant NPV haircut, estimated at about 38 percent; and (4) importantly, lower interest rates, but also a *step-up coupon rate*: 1 percent until 2008, 2.5 percent until 2011, 4.5 percent until 2013, 6 percent until 2015, 8.5 percent until 2018, and 9.0 percent until maturity. As in Belize's first and second debt restructurings, this design feature makes debt service more onerous over time. The exchange achieved 91 percent participation (without using CACs), and was followed by a Paris Club agreement with bilateral creditors in May 2006 (Asonuma and others 2017, 16). Losses incurred by Paris Club creditors were substantially smaller than private sector creditors' losses (Asonuma and others 2017, 17). With no nominal haircut, debt remained high at about 90 percent of GDP in 2005.

**Figure 8.11. Grenada: Public Debt, 2013**
*(Percent)*

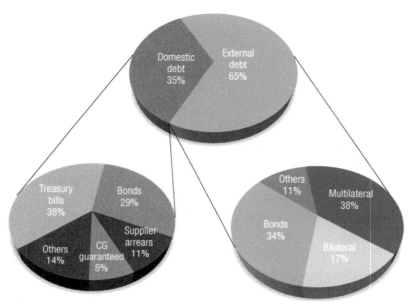

Sources: Country authorities; and IMF staff calculations.
Note: CG = central government.

Although the IMF provided emergency assistance not long after Ivan (in November 2004), negotiations on an IMF-supported program to help address Grenada's challenges took until April 2006 to complete. The debt exchange with commercial creditors thus took place independent of an IMF-supported program.

Although the 2004–06 restructuring achieved liquidity relief, Grenada's debt sustainability was not restored (Asonuma and others 2017, 18). Two IMF-supported economic reform programs—a 2006–10 Poverty Reduction and Growth Facility and a 2010–13 Extended Credit Facility—made limited headway in improving debt dynamics; a 2014 Ex Post Assessment evaluated performance under these programs as weak (see IMF 2014b, 1). Public debt once again increased to more than 100 percent of GDP at the end of 2012 because the government tried to use fiscal policy to counteract the negative impact of the global financial crisis on Grenada (mostly the reduced numbers of tourists but also a decline in foreign investment). The government's cash flow came under severe pressure as multilateral financing dried up and domestic banks limited their exposure to the government. This set the scene for a second round of debt restructuring, conducted over 2013–15 and announced by the Grenadian authorities on March 8, 2013 (Figure 8.12).

**Figure 8.12. Grenada: Commercial Bond Price Development**
*(U.S. dollars)*

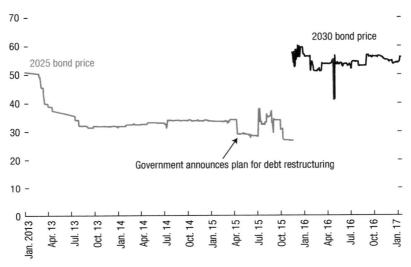

Source: Bloomberg, L.L.C.

As in Jamaica and Belize, Grenada's second round focused on the same debt as the first one: public debt to both private and official creditors, with the exception of Treasury bills and debt to multilaterals (Asonuma and others 2017, 23; Figure 8.11). The bulk of the restructured debt in this operation was debt to external bondholders (as in the earlier operation)—US$194 million. Agreement with these private creditors was reached in March 2015—a full two years after the initial announcement, with the formal closing of the agreement another eight months later, in November 2015. This extended negotiation period is at least partly explained by the Grenadian authorities' capacity constraints. For these bonds, a principal haircut of 50 percent was agreed to, interest rates were fixed at 7 percent, and the maturity of the debt was extended by five years, to 2030. The NPV haircut amounted to 49 percent. Activation of a CAC increased participation from 94 percent to 100 percent. As with the first restructuring, Paris Club agreement on debt rescheduling (in November 2015) accompanied the commercial debt rescheduling. Similar to previous experience with the 2004–06 debt restructuring, losses incurred by official creditors were lower than those incurred by private creditors.

A three-year, IMF-supported, "home-grown" reform program was approved by the IMF Executive Board in June 2014, after one year of discussions that occurred in parallel with debt negotiations. The program targets significant up-front fiscal consolidation accompanied by broad and deep reform of the legislative framework—including a fiscal responsibility law—to install a more permanent framework for fiscal prudence and debt sustainability. Performance under this program has been strong to date, with the government meeting fiscal targets and completing reviews on a regular basis. Implementation of structural benchmarks under the program has been solid, though usually with some delay, often related to capacity constraints. As in Jamaica, monitoring of program implementation has been complemented by a domestic monitoring mechanism, with broad participation. Grenada now appears to be on the right track: the November 2016 IMF staff report notes that the debt-to-GDP ratio is now on a clear downward trajectory, projected to fall to 57.5 percent by 2020, thereby meeting the 60 percent Eastern Caribbean Currency Union target (IMF 2016b; Figure 8.10). To achieve that, sustained fiscal prudence will be required and the government will need to conclude restructuring of its remaining debt on terms comparable to those already received.

Grenada's new bonds include a two-step nominal haircut stipulating that half of the haircut agreed to at the time of the exchange would be contingent on, and granted after, the successful completion of the IMF program (in 2017). This provision provides an incentive for the government to continue to pursue prudent macroeconomic, and in particular fiscal, policies and should help ensure that debt remains on a sustainable track.[8] Another interesting feature of Grenada's new government bond is the inclusion of a risk-transfer element in the form of a "hurricane clause" that would defer payment of all debt service in the event of a qualifying hurricane. This clause was also a feature of Grenada's debt restructuring with Taiwan Export-Import Bank, where it appeared first. The clause provides for deferred payments for up to 12 months, deferred interest is capitalized, and deferred principal is distributed equally on top of scheduled payments until final maturity (Asonuma and others 2017, 27). This new clause would provide significant cash flow relief for Grenada if there were to be a natural disaster, with qualifying criteria determined by an outside entity and triggered when the government's accident insurance policy is activated by the Caribbean Catastrophe Risk Insurance Facility. This improved debt design should help reduce the need for and likelihood of a follow-up debt restructuring. The November 2015 Paris Club deal also includes a hurricane clause, though in much weaker terms of relief since it allows only "for creditors to consider further debt relief in the event of a natural disaster," without automaticity or specifics, and with additional criteria such as evidence of "imminent default."

Key lessons learned from Grenada's two recent debt restructurings can be summarized as follows: First, without a credible, ambitious, front-loaded, multiyear fiscal consolidation effort accompanied by priority structural reforms to enhance growth prospects, debt restructurings will not lead to debt sustainability because it is just one element of a broader strategy needed to put public debt on a sustainable footing. Second, debt design matters: hurricane clauses can help the

---

[8]A similar clause was also included in the 2009–10 restructuring of Seychelles' debt, and in St. Kitts and Nevis as discussed below.

**Figure 8.13. St. Kitts and Nevis: Public Debt-to-GDP Ratio**
*(Percent)*

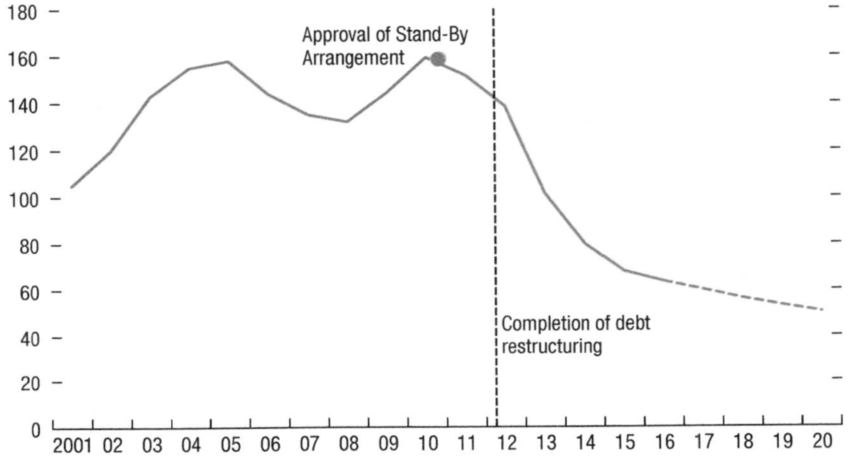

Sources: IMF, *World Economic Outlook*; and IMF staff estimations.

government manage cash flows and smooth consumption and investment follow-ing natural disasters, thereby minimizing output losses and making debt more sustainable over time; and phased debt relief (the two-step nominal haircut) can strengthen incentives for sustained policy and fiscal reform.

## ST. KITTS AND NEVIS: SUCCESS STORY?

St. Kitts and Nevis's case differs in important respects from the three country cases discussed above. First, a large principal haircut secured a significant imme-diate reduction in the debt-to-GDP ratio, after which debt has remained on a declining trend (Figure 8.13). The 2016 IMF staff report estimates the debt-to-GDP ratio at 68 percent at the end of 2015, down from 159 percent in 2010. Rapid real GDP growth (more than 6 percent in both 2013 and 2014) and strong implementation of the supporting reform program (a 2011–14 SBA) ensured that gains in achieving debt sustainability were maintained; large government revenue from a successful citizenship-by-investment program sup-ported a fiscal consolidation effort. Second, this episode could be viewed as an example of getting it right the first time: it did not involve a repeat restructuring of already restructured debt.

At the end of 2010, St. Kitts and Nevis faced dire macroeconomic conditions and an imminent debt crisis. GDP had fallen by a cumulative 7½ percent since 2009. The country sought IMF support through a program, and public announcement of a debt restructuring was a prior action for that program (IMF

**Figure 8.14. St. Kitts and Nevis: Government Public Debt, 2010**
*(Percent)*

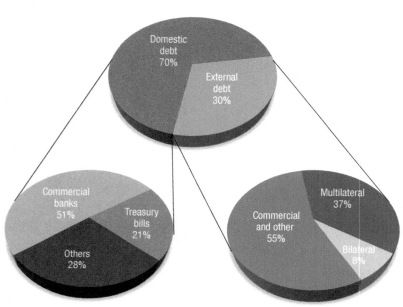

Sources: Country authorities; and IMF staff calculations.

2011, 45). The program approved by the IMF Executive Board in July 2011 included front-loaded fiscal adjustment along with measures to safeguard financial stability and boost growth. The objective of the debt restructuring was to address the debt overhang and restore debt sustainability.

A comprehensive debt restructuring, including all public debt except Treasury bills and debt to multilateral creditors, was announced in June 2011 (Figure 8.14). A debt exchange with external commercial creditors was completed in April 2012; a total of US$135 million was eligible to be exchanged in this operation. Participation was initially at 97 percent, and then increased to 100 percent using CACs. One-third of creditors opted for a "par bond"—an Eastern Caribbean dollar–denominated, 45-year, mortgage-style instrument, with a 1.5 percent coupon. The remaining two-thirds preferred a "discount bond": a United States dollar-denominated bond with a 50 percent cut in face value. Interestingly, the latter instrument has a *step-down coupon*, in sharp contrast to the step-up coupons found in Belize and Grenada. It carried a 6 percent coupon for the first four years, which then steps down to 3 percent. Obviously, this is a modality that promotes debt sustainability over the medium and long term. The aggregated NPV haircut on the total exchange was large, at 65 percent (IMF 2012b, 7; IMF 2015, 43).

The 2012 St. Kitts and Nevis restructuring with external commercial creditors featured a number of innovative attributes. The restructured debt contains a partial guarantee from the Caribbean Development Bank—an important creditor in this case, holding 85 percent of multilateral debt. The CDB had provided an earlier guarantee on a bond issued by the government in 2008, and this guarantee facility was restructured with the debt (Jahan 2013, 270).[9] The restructured debt also contains a clawback feature, which provides for creditors to be issued additional bonds if the authorities failed to implement the underlying reform program (specifically tied to completing the sixth review under the SBA by a certain date). As in Grenada, the size of the haircut was made contingent on reform program implementation, thereby building in a clear incentive for the country authorities to stay the course and continue to pursue prudent fiscal policies. The debt exchange with commercial creditors was followed by a flow restructuring with Paris Club creditors.

Given the large holdings of domestic debt by commercial banks, financial sector stability considerations loomed large in the design of the domestic part of the debt restructuring. The SBA program that supported the restructuring involved establishing a banking sector reserve fund to ensure the stability of the financial system (similar to the Financial Sector Stability Fund set up in Jamaica to support JDX and NDX). A debt-for-land swap played a key part in the restructuring of domestic debt: government land was placed in a special purpose vehicle, and funds received from sales were used to settle creditors' (mostly domestic banks') claims. This part of the debt restructuring took a long time to execute—in fact, five years afterward, it was still a work in progress. In the 2016 Article IV report, it was noted that "establishing a clear framework for completing the debt-land swap is crucial to preserve the credibility of the debt restructuring and hard-earned gains in debt sustainability, while protecting financial stability" (IMF 2016e, 14).

## INNOVATIONS AND POLICY LESSONS

Recent attempts in the Caribbean to restructure debt to commercial creditors have had mixed results. On the basis of impact on debt-to-GDP ratios, yields, and market access, some episodes can be labeled a success, in that they resulted in a decisive break in the debt-to-GDP trend. Jamaica 2013, Grenada 2013–15, and St. Kitts and Nevis 2011–12 all fall into this group. Other episodes have had less success in achieving stated objectives (Jamaica 2010, Belize 2006–07 and 2012–13, Grenada 2004–06).

Two of the recent cases—St. Kitts and Nevis 2011–12 and Grenada 2013–15—saw some innovative features built into new debt contracts. The clawback feature included in the former case and the two-step haircut approach in the

---

[9]Seychelles' 2009–10 debt restructuring was the first time a guarantee from a multilateral organization—the African Development Bank—was offered in the context of a sovereign debt restructuring (Jahan 2013, 243).

latter provide incentives for sustained prudent fiscal policy, and are thus conducive to successful debt restructuring. In addition, the hurricane clause included in Grenada's new debt provides automatic liquidity relief if there were to be future misfortune. Innovative solutions tailored to individual country circumstances can help to put and keep public debt on the right trajectory.

More traditional elements of debt design also play an important role. CACs matter: in several cases in the Caribbean in which external bond debt was restructured, CACs were instrumental in overcoming holdout investors and increasing participation rates to 100 percent. Step-up or step-down coupons can have an important bearing on the ability of the sovereign to remain current on its debt obligations.

The cases analyzed in this chapter suggest that the size of the debt restructuring (as measured by NPV) is not necessarily a decisive factor in securing debt sustainability, although of course a large haircut can help bring debt down quickly, as the St. Kitts and Nevis restructuring shows. More important is to embed the restructuring in a credible fiscal-consolidation and growth-boosting program that is well designed and implemented, with adequate monitoring.

Finally, the analysis shows that getting it right the first time helps—repeatedly restructuring the same debt is detrimental to market development and access and to government credibility. Maintaining access to credit, or quickly regaining access to capital markets after a restructuring operation, is critically important for the continued ability to manage public debt, as the Jamaica PetroCaribe buyback operation shows.

# ANNEX 8.1. FEATURES OF CARIBBEAN DEBT RESTRUCTURING

Annex Table 8.1.1. Caribbean: Public Debt Composition Prior to Restructuring

| | Belize | | | Grenada | | Jamaica | | St. Kitts and Nevis |
|---|---|---|---|---|---|---|---|---|
| | 2006 | 2012 | 2016 | 2005 | 2012 | 2009 | 2012 | 2010 |
| **Debt (US$ million)** | | | | | | | | |
| Domestic Debt | 149.9 | 194.9 | 526.2 | 173.5 | 286.1 | 8,879.7 | 11,419.1 | 769.8 |
| External Debt | 985.6 | 1,047.3 | 1,197.5 | 392.2 | 540.5 | 7,553.0 | 8,133.4 | 331.2 |
| Multilateral | 211.4 | 327.8 | 327.8 | 116.7 | 214.7 | 2,468.9 | 3,224.7 | 124.3 |
| Bilateral | 213.2 | 170.6 | 312.5 | 76.4 | 77.0 | 940.1 | 801.5 | 30.1 |
| Commercial | 561.0 | 548.9 | 557.2 | 199.2 | 199.1 | 4,144.0 | 4,107.2 | 176.8 |
| Other[1] | 0 | 0 | 0 | 0 | 49.7 | 0 | 0 | 0 |
| **Debt (percent of total)** | 100.0 | 100.0 | 100.0 | 100.0 | 100.0 | 100.0 | 100.0 | 100.0 |
| Domestic Debt | 13.2 | 15.7 | 30.5 | 30.7 | 34.6 | 54.0 | 58.4 | 69.9 |
| External Debt | 86.8 | 84.3 | 69.5 | 69.3 | 65.4 | 46.0 | 41.6 | 30.1 |
| Multilateral | 18.6 | 26.4 | 19.0 | 20.6 | 26.0 | 15.0 | 16.5 | 11.3 |
| Bilateral | 18.8 | 13.7 | 18.1 | 13.5 | 9.3 | 5.7 | 4.1 | 2.7 |
| Commercial | 49.4 | 44.2 | 32.3 | 35.2 | 24.1 | 25.2 | 21.0 | 16.1 |
| Other | 0 | 0 | 0 | 0 | 6.0 | 0 | 0 | 0 |

Sources: Authorities; and IMF staff estimates.
[1]For Grenada, central government guaranteed debt, external arrears on interest, and overdue membership dues.

## Annex Table 8.1.2. Caribbean: Key Features of Recent Debt-Restructuring Cases

| | Targeted Debt | Preemptive or Post Default | Announcement of Restructuring | Start of Negotiation | Final Exchange Offer | Date of Exchange | Total Duration (months) | Debt Exchanged[1] (US$ billion) | IMF Program | Cut in Face Value[2] (%) | Outstanding Instruments Exchanged | New Instruments |
|---|---|---|---|---|---|---|---|---|---|---|---|---|
| Belize | External bonds and loans | Preemptive | Aug. 2006 | Aug. 2006 | Dec. 2006 | Feb. 2007 | 6 | 0.52 | No | 0.0 | Seven bonds, eight loans | One bond |
| Belize | External bonds | Preemptive | Aug. 2012 | Aug. 2012 | Feb. 2013 | Mar. 2013 | 7 | 0.55 | No | 10.0 | One bond | One bond |
| Belize[3] | External bonds | Preemptive | Dec. 2016 | Dec. 2016 | ... | ... | ... | ... | No | 0.0 | No exchange | No exchange |
| Grenada | External and domestic bonds and loans | Preemptive | Oct. 2004 | Dec. 2004 | Sep. 2005 | Nov. 2005 | 13 | 0.21 | Yes | 0.0 | Seven external bonds, nine domestic bonds, two external loans, six domestic loans | One US$ bond and one EC$ bond |
| Grenada | External and domestic bonds and loans | Post default | Mar. 2013 | Apr. 2013 | Nov. 2015 | Nov. 2015 | 31 | 0.26 | Yes | 50.0 | One US$ bond and two EC$ bonds | One US$ bond and two EC$ bonds |
| Jamaica | Domestic bonds | Preemptive | Jan. 2010 | Jan. 2010 | Jan. 2010 | Feb. 2010 | 8 | 7.8 | Yes | 0.0 | About 350 US$- and J$-denominated domestic bonds | 25 US$- and J$-denominated domestic bonds |
| Jamaica | Domestic bonds | Preemptive | Feb. 2013 | Feb. 2013 | Feb. 2013 | Feb. 2013 | 1 | 8.9 | Yes | 0.0 | 11 external bonds, two domestic bonds, four loans | One US$ bond and one EC$ bond |
| St. Kitts and Nevis | External bonds and loans, and domestic bonds and loans | Preemptive | Jun. 2011 | Aug. 2011 | Feb. 2012 | Mar. 2012 | 10 | 0.14 | Yes | 32.8 | 28 US$- and J$-denominated domestic bonds and loans | 26 US$- and J$-denominated domestic bonds and loans |

Sources: Authorities' websites; Das, Papaioannou, and Trebesch 2012; IMF 2013b; and IMF staff reports.

[1] Total eligible debt to be restructured in the debt operation.

[2] Excludes past due interest; for Belize, missed coupon payments were added to the face value of the new bond (about 7 percent), resulting in a net face value haircut of about 3 percent.

[3] Negotiations to change the amortization schedule and coupon rate were completed on March 15, 2017.

# REFERENCES

Amo-Yartey, Charles, and Therese Turner-Jones. 2014. "Fiscal Consolidation and Debt Reduction in the Caribbean: An Overview." In *Caribbean Renewal: Tackling Fiscal and Debt Challenges*, edited by C. Amo-Yartey and T. Turner-Jones, 1–24. Washington, DC: International Monetary Fund.

Asonuma, T., Mike (Xin) Li, Michael G. Papaioannou, Saji Thomas, and Eriko Togo. 2017. "Sovereign Debt Restructuring in Grenada: Causes, Processes, Outcomes, and Lessons Learned." IMF Working Paper 17/171, International Monetary Fund, Washington, DC.

Asonuma, T., G. Peraza, K. Vitola, and T. Tsuda. 2014. "Sovereign Debt Restructurings in Belize: Achievements and Challenges Ahead." IMF Working Paper 14/132, International Monetary Fund, Washington, DC.

Caribbean Development Bank (CDB). 2013. *Public Sector Debt in the Caribbean: An Agenda for Reduction and Sustainability*. Bridgetown, Barbados: Caribbean Development Bank.

Das, U., M. Papaioannou, and C. Trebesch. 2012. "Sovereign Debt Restructurings 1950–2010: Literature Survey, Data, and Stylized Facts." IMF Working Paper 12/203, International Monetary Fund, Washington, DC.

Grigorian, D. A., T. Alleyne, and A. Guerson. 2012. "Jamaica Debt Exchange." IMF Working Paper 12/244, International Monetary Fund, Washington, DC.

International Monetary Fund (IMF). 2011. "St. Kitts and Nevis: 2011 Article IV Consultation and Request for Stand-By Arrangement: Staff Report; Staff Supplements; Public Information Notice and Press Release on the Executive Board Discussion; and Statement by the Executive Director for St. Kitts and Nevis." IMF Country Report 11/270, Washington, DC.

———. 2012a. "St. Kitts and Nevis: First Review under the Stand-By Arrangement and the Financing Assurances Review, and Request for Waivers of Applicability and Modification of Performance Criterion: Staff Report and Press Release." IMF Country Report 12/51, Washington, DC.

———. 2012b. "St. Kitts and Nevis: Second Review under the Stand-By Arrangement and the Financing Assurances Review, and Request for Waivers of Applicability: Staff Report and Press Release." IMF Country Report 12/196, Washington, DC.

———. 2013a. "Jamaica: Request for an Extended Arrangement under the Extended Fund Facility." IMF Country Report 13/126, Washington, DC.

———. 2013b. "Sovereign Debt Restructuring—Recent Developments and Implications for the Fund's Legal and Policy Framework." Washington, DC, April.

———. 2014a. "The Fund's Lending Framework and Sovereign Debt," Washington, DC.

———. 2014b. "Grenada: Ex Post Assessment of Longer Term Program Engagement." IMF Country Report 14/19, Washington, DC.

———. 2014c. "Grenada: 2014 Article IV Consultation and Request for an Extended Credit Facility Arrangement—Staff Report; and Press Release." IMF Country Report 14/196, Washington, DC.

———. 2015. "St. Kitts and Nevis: Ex Post Evaluation of Exceptional Access under the 2011 Stand-By Arrangement." IMF Country Report 15/297, Washington, DC.

———. 2016a. "Belize 2016 Article IV Consultation—Press Release; Staff Report; and Statement by the Executive Director for Belize." IMF Country Report 16/334, Washington, DC.

———. 2016b. "Grenada: Fifth Review under the Extended Credit Facility, Request for Modification of Performance Criteria, and Financing Assurances Review—Press Release; and Staff Report." IMF Country Report 16/389, Washington, DC.

———. 2016c. "Jamaica: Request for Stand By Arrangement and Cancellation of the Current Extended Arrangement under the Extended Fund Facility—Press Release and Staff Report." IMF Country Report 16/350, Washington, DC.

———. 2016d. Jamaica: Thirteenth Review under the Arrangement under the Extended Fund Facility—Press Release and Staff Report." IMF Country Report 16/297, Washington, DC.

————. 2016e. "St. Kitts and Nevis: 2016 Article IV Consultation—Press Release; and Staff Report." IMF Country Report 16/250, Washington, DC.

Jahan, S. 2013. "Experiences with Sovereign Debt Restructuring: Case Studies from the OECS/ ECCU and Beyond." In *The Eastern Caribbean Currency Union: Macroeconomic and Financial System*, edited by A. Schipke, A Cebotari, and N. Thacker. Washington, DC: International Monetary Fund.

McIntyre, Arnold, and Sumiko Ogawa. 2013. "Public Debt." In *The Eastern Caribbean Currency Union: Macroeconomic and Financial System*, edited by A. Schipke, A Cebotari, and N. Thacker, 111–29. Washington, DC: International Monetary Fund.

Schmid, Juan Pedro. 2016. "Addressing Debt Overhang: Experiences from Two Debt Operations in Jamaica." IDB Policy Brief, Inter-American Development Bank, Washington, DC.

Wynter, Brian. 2016. "Challenges Faced by Jamaica in Recent Debt Management Initiatives and Lessons for Small, Open Economies Managing High Levels of Sovereign Debt." Keynote Address, First Annual Interdisciplinary Sovereign Debt Research and Management Conference, Institute for International Economic Law, Georgetown University Law Centre, Washington, DC, January 21.

# CHAPTER 9

# Financial Development and Inclusion in the Caribbean

JOYCE WONG

## INTRODUCTION

Financial development, by providing agents with better market access, liquidity, and diversity of instruments, has the potential to unleash new growth sources and help countries reap the benefits of globalization and make the transition to higher income levels. Although Figure 9.1 simply shows a correlation, an extensive literature has documented the mostly positive impact from financial development on countries' income levels and growth. Efficient financial systems help channel funds to productive uses, provide insurance against shocks, reduce information asymmetries, and can potentially alleviate poverty and inequality (Beck, Demirgüç-Kunt, and Levine 2004). Sound financial systems can also foster innovation and entrepreneurship through risk diversification (King and Levine 1993).

Recent focus has also been on ensuring that gains from financial development are reaped across the population. This effort has brought into the spotlight financial inclusion and its promise of boosting growth while reducing poverty and inequality (Beck, Demirgüç-Kunt, and Levine 2007; Clarke, Xu, and Zou 2006). Financial inclusion helps mobilize savings, provides households and firms with greater access to the resources needed to finance consumption and investment, and helps insure against shocks. Financial inclusion also fosters labor and firm formalization—that is, it helps reduce informality—and has been positively linked with job creation, growth, and innovation (Beck, Demirgüç-Kunt, and Maksimovic 2005; Aiyagari, Demirgüç-Kunt, and Maksimovic 2007). These, in turn, boost government revenues and strengthen social safety nets.

The Caribbean region has many characteristics that may pose challenges to financial development and inclusion:[1] the countries' small size and scale, prolonged low growth, high debt, and vulnerability to external shocks and natural

---

[1]Caribbean countries included are Antigua and Barbuda (ATG), The Bahamas (BHS), Barbados (BRB), Belize (BLZ), Dominica (DMA), the Dominican Republic (DOM), Grenada (GRE), Guyana (GUY), Haiti (HTI), Jamaica (JAM), St. Kitts and Nevis (KNA), St. Lucia (LCA), St. Vincent and the Grenadines (VCT), Suriname (SUR), and Trinidad and Tobago (TTO).

### Figure 9.1. Financial Development and PPP GDP per Capita
*(EM Asia and LAC countries, 1995–2013)*

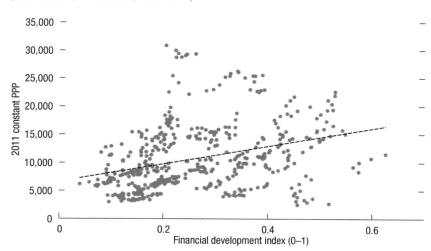

Source:
Note: EM = emerging market; LAC =  Latin America and the Caribbean; PPP = purchasing power parity.

disasters. While small scale does not appear to directly hamper growth in the short term (Easterly and Kraay 2000), it could foster relatively concentrated and small banking sectors, with weak competition and poor service delivery. However, some Caribbean countries have developed large offshore financial centers and others have undergone significant financial market development, particularly of their sovereign debt markets, to support large government borrowing.

Given the region's challenges of high debt and exposure to external shocks, both of which hinder development prospects (Armstrong and Read 2003; Charvériat 2000; Greenidge and others 2012; Thacker and Acevedo 2010), a careful development of financial systems and expansion of financial inclusion could help generate sustained and inclusive growth (Holden and Howell 2009; Aghion and others 2005). Such development could also bring insurance benefits by helping the countries (at the aggregate level) and households (at the micro level) cope with shocks. Deeper financial systems promote diversification and growth and have been found to be linked to financial stability (Sahay and others 2015; Heng and others 2016).

Against this background, this chapter examines the current state of financial development and inclusion in the Caribbean from several different perspectives:

- This inquiry uses the financial development index developed in Heng and others (2016) to examine the financial market and financial institution development in the region compared with the rest of the Latin America and Caribbean (LAC) region. This is a new approach using a broad-based index that improves upon the previous narrower measures of financial develop-

## Figure 9.2. Financial Development Index

| Financial Development Index | | | | | |
|---|---|---|---|---|---|
| **Institutions** | | | **Markets** | | |
| **Access** | **Depth** | **Efficiency** | **Access** | **Depth** | **Efficiency** |
| ➤Bank branches per 100,000 adults<br><br>➤ATMs per 100,000 adults | ➤Domestic bank deposits to GDP (%)<br><br>➤Insurance company assets to GDP (%)<br><br>➤Mutual fund assets to GDP (%)<br><br>➤Domestic credit to private sector to GDP (%) | ➤Bank concentration (%)<br><br>➤Bank lending-deposit spread<br><br>➤Overhead cost to total assets<br><br>➤Bank net interest margin<br><br>➤Non-interest income to total income | ➤Total number of issuers of debt (domestic and external, NFCs and financial)<br><br>➤Market capitalization excluding top 10 companies to total market capitalization | ➤Stock market capitalization to GDP<br><br>➤Stock market total value traded to GDP (%)<br><br>➤Stock of government debt securities in % of GDP<br><br>➤Debt securities of financial sector by local firms in % of GDP<br><br>➤Debt securities of nonfinancial sector by local firms in % of GDP | ➤Stock market turnover ratio (value traded to stock market capitalization) |

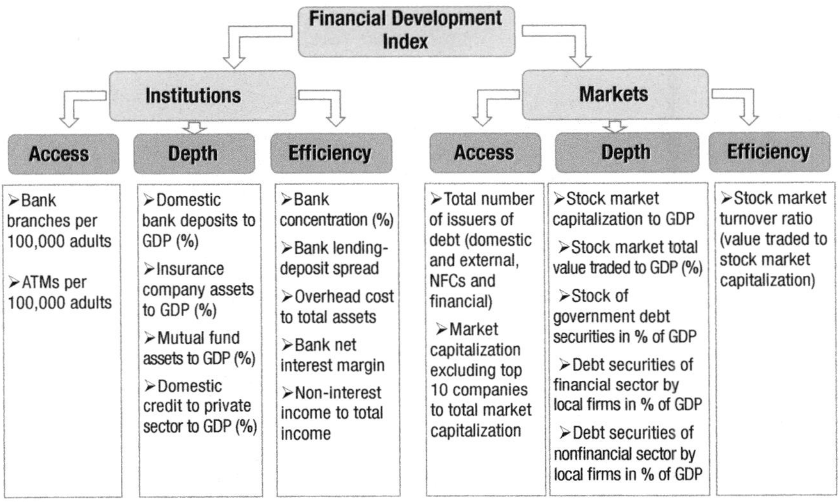

Source: Heng and others (2016).
Note: ATM = automated teller machine; NFC = nonfinancial corporation.

ment such as the private-credit-to-GDP ratio, the ratio of liquid liabilities of the financial system to GDP, stock market capitalization as a share of GDP, and the market turnover ratio (Levine 1997, 2005).

- Next, it examines the region's level of financial inclusion for households and small and medium enterprises (SMEs), which are significant drivers of growth and employment. Data availability, however, constrains the analysis for the Caribbean to a narrower set of indicators.

- It then uses a quantitative model based on Dabla-Norris and others (2015), calibrated for several Caribbean countries, to examine the trade-offs between inequality and growth when constraints to financial inclusion are loosened for enterprises.

- Finally, it analyzes Jamaica to illustrate potential policy considerations in a country where several financial constraints are binding.

# STYLIZED FACTS ON CARIBBEAN FINANCIAL DEVELOPMENT

Using the broad-based index developed in Heng and others (2016), the analysis examines the financial development of four large Caribbean countries: The Bahamas, Barbados, Jamaica, and Trinidad and Tobago. The index contains two major components: financial institutions and financial markets. Each component is broken down into access, depth, and efficiency subcomponents (Figure 9.2).

These subcomponents, in turn, are constructed based on several underlying variables that track development in each area.

The overall financial development index shows that all four countries—The Bahamas, Barbados, Jamaica, and Trinidad and Tobago—improved between 1995 and 2013, and their relative order remained unchanged (Figure 9.3). The Bahamas and Barbados have relatively high levels of financial development, while Trinidad and Tobago and Jamaica lag somewhat. The following provides more detail:

- Overall financial market development in the Caribbean is driven by strong performance of the depth subcomponent (Figure 9.4). In fact, Barbados, Jamaica, and The Bahamas all figure in the top four in financial market depth in the LAC region, ahead of much more financially developed countries such as Chile, Brazil, and Peru. This strong performance is driven by debt issuances from several sectors: international issuances of the public sector (Jamaica is in third position for LAC), the financial sector (Barbados and The Bahamas are in the top three), and the corporate nonfinancial sector (where The Bahamas, Barbados, and Jamaica are the top three). On the other hand, Caribbean countries severely lag the rest of LAC in financial market access and efficiency, driven by relatively shallow equity markets with only a few issuers.

- As for financial institutions, the Caribbean broadly compares favorably with the rest of LAC. Barbados has a high deposits-to-GDP ratio and a significant nonbank financial sector. The Bahamas surpasses the LAC average in both access and efficiency, thanks to strong performance in the number of automated teller machines (ATMs) and bank branches per capita and high levels of credit to GDP. Trinidad and Tobago is broadly on par with the rest of LAC in depth and efficiency although it lags in access. In all, these three countries have relatively good financial institutions, although with room for improvement. However, Jamaica lags behind its Caribbean neighbors in overall financial institution development, driven by low levels of physical access, low ratios of deposits and credit to GDP, high interest rate spreads, high operating costs, and a concentrated banking market.

## ZOOMING IN: HOUSEHOLDS AND SMEs

The three key determinants of access to finance for households are (1) physical barriers (for example, long distance to a bank branch, poor transportation), (2) eligibility barriers (for instance, documentation requirements, literacy), and (3) affordability (such as minimum balances and fees). Although the last two determinants are at least as important as the first, physical access is a precursor to the other factors, especially in a region where mobile banking remains underdeveloped. Furthermore, data for the Caribbean on physical and eligibility barriers remain scarce and not comparable across countries. Thus, to maximize the sample of Caribbean countries, this section examines a measure of physical access to financial services (see Dabla-Norris and others 2015) constructed as a composite

## Figure 9.3. Financial Development Index, 2013 versus 1995

■ Overall financial development — Financial markets — Financial institutions

**1. LAC: Financial Development Index, 1995**

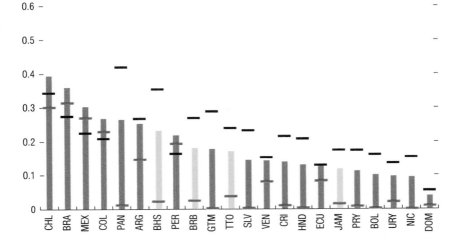

**2. LAC: Financial Development Index, 2013**

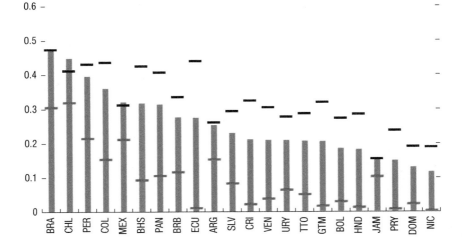

Source: Based on index developed in Heng and others (2016).
Note: LAC = Latin America and the Caribbean. Data labels in figure use International Organization for Standardization (ISO) country codes.

### Figure 9.4. Financial Institutions and Markets: Subcomponents
*(Normalized such that maximum of the group = 1)*

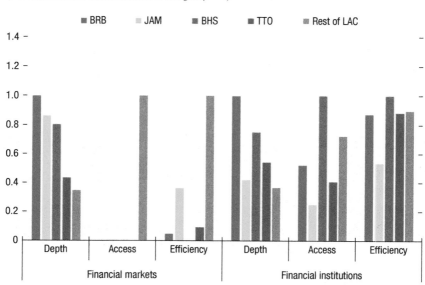

Source: Based on index developed by Heng and others (2016).
Note: LAC = Latin America and the Caribbean. Other data labels in figure use International Organization for Standardization (ISO) country codes.

index that aggregates information on the presence of both ATMs and branches by geographical and population units.

Data suggest that about half of the Caribbean countries in this larger sample are "underserved" when compared with the LAC average (Figure 9.5). For the Eastern Caribbean Currency Union, small country size helps generate a higher level of measured access to financial services. The strong performance of Jamaica and The Bahamas is likely linked to proliferation of banking access points in tourism areas, illustrating a potential weakness with the measurement of physical access: ATMs and branches could be highly concentrated in some areas, leading to high measured access that does not necessarily reach everyone in the population.

The World Bank's Enterprise Surveys show that the proportion of SMEs that identify access to credit as a major constraint is much larger in the Caribbean than in the rest of LAC (Figure 9.6). Nearly 40 percent of SMEs in larger Caribbean countries such as Jamaica and Barbados cite credit access as a major issue. However, the difference in the proportion of firms with credit access is striking—only 26 percent in Jamaica versus over 55 percent in Barbados. This difference reflects constraints that are local to the Jamaican economy (as discussed in section

**Figure 9.5. Caribbean: Index of Physical Access to Finance**

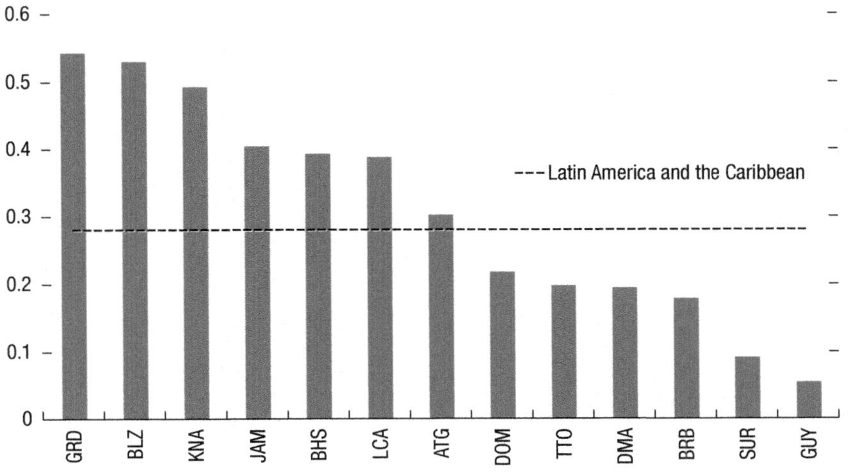

Sources: World Bank Enterprise Survey; and IMF staff calculations.
Note: Data labels in figure use International Organization for Standardization (ISO) country codes.

"Case Study: Jamaica"), combined with a history of support for SMEs in Barbados, including through programs such as the Barbados Investment Fund and the Export Rediscount Facility, which have supported microenterprises and SMEs in the tourism and export sectors.

Caribbean countries are aware of these constraints and some have begun to implement policies to ease them. For example, the central bank in Suriname has classes for the proprietors of SMEs to educate them on basic accounting and knowledge transfer. The country has also been quite innovative in using television series to promote financial inclusion (similar to South Africa). In Trinidad and Tobago, where SMEs have relatively good access to finance, the central bank offers booklets on money management, homeownership, budgeting, insurance, and consumer protection services, all of which are available to the wider public.

An extensive menu of policies for fostering financial inclusion and development is available. What should guide policymakers when determining the right combination and sequencing of policies for their own countries? Given the risks of financial sector development happening "too fast" (see Heng and others 2016 for a discussion of these risks), how can policymakers ensure that policies that help one outcome (growth, for instance) do not generate negative outcomes (such as inequality or instability) in other areas? The next section uses a structural framework to provide a better understanding of some of these trade-offs.

### Figure 9.6. SME Access to Credit in the Caribbean

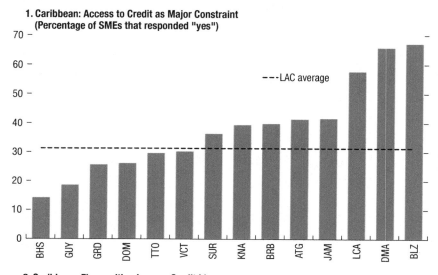

**1. Caribbean: Access to Credit as Major Constraint
(Percentage of SMEs that responded "yes")**

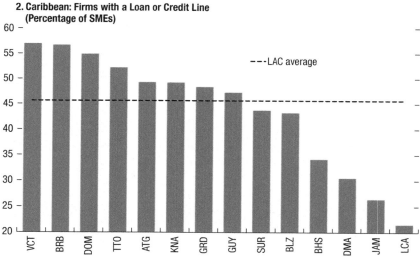

**2. Caribbean: Firms with a Loan or Credit Line
(Percentage of SMEs)**

Sources: World Bank Enterprise Survey; and IMF staff calculations.
Note: LAC = Latin America and the Caribbean; SME = small and medium enterprises. Data labels in
figure use International Organization for Standardization (ISO) country codes.

# GROWTH-INEQUALITY TRADE-OFFS

This section uses a micro-founded structural model borrowed from Dabla-Norris and others (2015) to examine the implications for growth and inequality of relaxing various constraints to firms' financial inclusion. This model features agents who are born with different levels of wealth and talent and who make choices between being workers or entrepreneurs. Agents can save without extra cost, but borrowing entails a fixed "participation cost." Once that cost is paid, the total amount that the agent can borrow will depend on the collateral posted. The "price" of borrowing will be determined by the economy's spread between deposit and loan interest rates.[2]

The model is calibrated for three Eastern Caribbean Currency Union countries (Antigua and Barbuda, St. Lucia, St. Kitts and Nevis) and five larger countries (The Bahamas, Barbados, Dominican Republic, Jamaica, Trinidad and Tobago). In the model, constraints to firms' financial inclusion are grouped into three categories:[3]

- *Participation costs* typically reflect banks' high documentation requirements, which impede access to finance (for example, for opening, maintaining, and closing accounts, and for loan applications). Other barriers, such as red tape and the need for guarantors, can also be captured. These costs are modeled as fixed costs, capturing the fact that documentation requirements, while they might be somewhat more onerous for very large scale projects, do not directly grow with loan or firm size.

- *Borrowing constraints* are proxied by collateral requirements that regulate the leverage of firms in the credit system. These collateral requirements depend on factors such as creditors' rights, information disclosure requirements, and contract enforcement procedures.

- *Intermediation costs* (for example, high interest rates and fees) can reflect information asymmetries between banks and borrowers and limited competition in the banking system.

The model's key parameters are calibrated to simultaneously match the moments of firm distribution, such as the percentage of firms with credit and the firm employment distribution, as well as the economy-wide nonperforming loan ratio and interest rate spread.

As seen in Figure 9.7, when compared with advanced economies (which serve as proxies for the frontier), most countries in the Caribbean lag in these indicators. For example, only 48 percent of firms, on average, have access to credit in

---

[2]For more details, please see Dabla-Norris and others (2015).

[3]Note that although each constraint is described separately, the equilibrium outcome for each of them is endogenously determined in the model.

### Figure 9.7. Country-Specific Financial Constraints

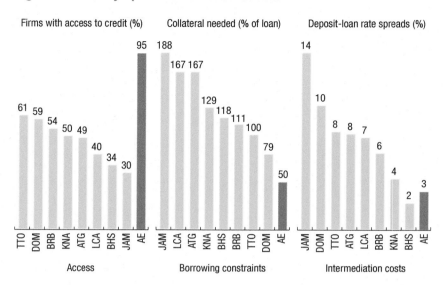

Source: World Bank Enterprise Surveys.
Note: AE = advanced economies. Data labels in figure use International Organization for Standardization (ISO) country codes.

the Caribbean, about half of the advanced economy average of 95 percent.[4] There are also significant differences across countries:

- Constraints are especially severe in Jamaica, which has the highest intermediation cost and collateral requirements and the lowest proportion of firms with access to credit.

- Two notable cases are those of Trinidad and Tobago and the Dominican Republic, with the lowest collateral requirements in the region and the most firms with access to credit. Nevertheless, interest rate spreads are high in both countries, reflecting inefficiencies such as the lack of a unified and modern asset registry, which exacerbates information costs for the lender. Thus, intuitively, firms can access credit and leverage up, but must pay dearly for it: price is used as a differentiating tool.

- By contrast, The Bahamas has higher collateral requirements and very few firms with access to credit, but very low interest rate spreads. In this case, credit market entry costs are high—but leverage is kept at low rates, so funding is relatively cheap for those that can access it.

---

[4]Note that figure 9.7 plots the proportion of all firms with access to credit, which differs from Figure 9.6, which includes only SMEs.

## Figure 9.8. Relaxing Collateral Requirements

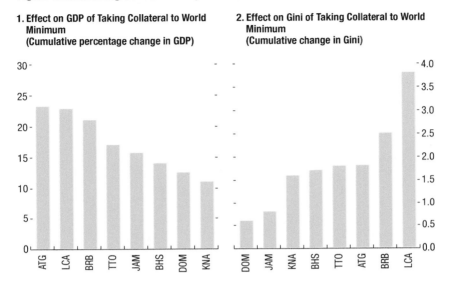

1. **Effect on GDP of Taking Collateral to World Minimum**
   **(Cumulative percentage change in GDP)**

2. **Effect on Gini of Taking Collateral to World Minimum**
   **(Cumulative change in Gini)**

Source: IMF staff calculations.
Note: Data labels in figure use International Organization for Standardization (ISO) country codes.

What are the effects on GDP and inequality of "removing" each of these constraints? To answer this question, three policy experiments are conducted:

- Relaxing collateral requirements to the world minimum
- Reducing participation costs to zero
- Reducing interest rate spreads to zero

These policy changes are significant and would take time to phase in.[5] For ease of comparison, each of the economies is modeled before and after the full transition, that is, we examine "steady states." The numbers presented should thus be interpreted as cumulative changes to GDP and the Gini coefficient across several years, driven by the implementation of each of these policies alone. Across all countries for which the model is calibrated, the loosening of any of the three constraints generates positive effects on GDP (Figures 9.8–9.10), while only the loosening of participation costs generates lower inequality. Each of these constraints is discussed in detail below.

---

[5]The lowering of spreads and participation costs to zero should be interpreted as an idealized frontier to ease comparison. In practice, it is unlikely that all barriers to credit could be eliminated or that there would be a zero margin to financial intermediation services.

### Figure 9.9. Lowering Participation Costs

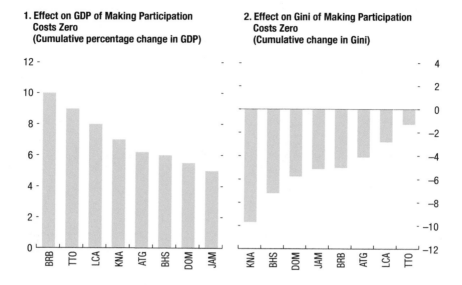

**1. Effect on GDP of Making Participation Costs Zero**
(Cumulative percentage change in GDP)

**2. Effect on Gini of Making Participation Costs Zero**
(Cumulative change in Gini)

Source: IMF staff calculations.
Note: Data labels in figure use International Organization for Standardization (ISO) country codes.

## Relaxing Collateral Requirements

The largest GDP gains accrue from lowering collateral requirements (Figure 9.8). The model predicts that total cumulative expansion of the Caribbean countries' GDP could range between 10 and 20 percent if all collateral requirements were lowered to 50 percent, which is the lowest level of collateral across countries in the World Enterprise Surveys. The magnitude of the GDP gain across countries, however, depends on the levels of other constraints. For instance, Antigua and Barbuda and St. Lucia are the biggest gainers in the sample, driven by a combination of currently high levels of collateral and moderate constraints in other areas. Thus, when collateral constraints are loosened in these economies, firms can take full advantage since the other constraints are relatively benign. This is not the case in Jamaica, for example, because even after collateral requirements are lowered, firms still face high spreads and high participation costs.

Lowering collateral requirements will, however, exacerbate inequality. Although everybody benefits from borrowing more against the same level of collateral, productive firms in the economy benefit more because they have the most to gain from expanding the scale of their operations. Higher leverage leads to more investment for larger companies, which generates a higher scale of production, thereby boosting growth. These gains, however, accrue more to the top of the distribution (larger, wealthier firms), thereby worsening inequality.

## Figure 9.10. Lowering Intermediation Costs

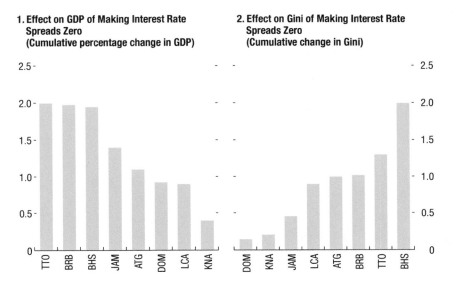

1. **Effect on GDP of Making Interest Rate Spreads Zero**
   (Cumulative percentage change in GDP)

2. **Effect on Gini of Making Interest Rate Spreads Zero**
   (Cumulative change in Gini)

Source: IMF staff calculations.
Note: Data labels in figure use International Organization for Standardization (ISO) country codes.

## Lowering Participation Costs

Reducing participation costs to zero also has a significant positive effect on GDP for all Caribbean countries, with average gains of about 7 percent (Figure 9.9). These gains are higher for countries where small enterprises account for a larger portion of the economy. For example, Barbados, where the largest 5 percent of firms employ only 22 percent of total labor (compared with an average of 39 percent of total labor in the other countries), reaps the highest GDP benefits from loosening participation costs. Moreover, these gains are also supported by low spreads and collateral requirements prevailing in the country, which allows the smaller firms to take full advantage of the credit market once they enter.

The participation cost, which is a fixed cost reflecting regulatory requirements, documentation, and red tape, is a more binding constraint for smaller firms (Krešić, Milatović, and Sanfey 2017), and therefore unambiguously improves inequality when lowered. In a sense, this is the most binding constraint on an extensive margin because it largely determines how many firms have credit access but not directly how much credit. The size of the impact on inequality, once again, depends on the way in which country-specific factors interact with financial sector characteristics. For example, the large reduction in inequality for St. Kitts and Nevis is driven partly by the dominance in the country of small firms

### Figure 9.11. Loosening All Three Constraints

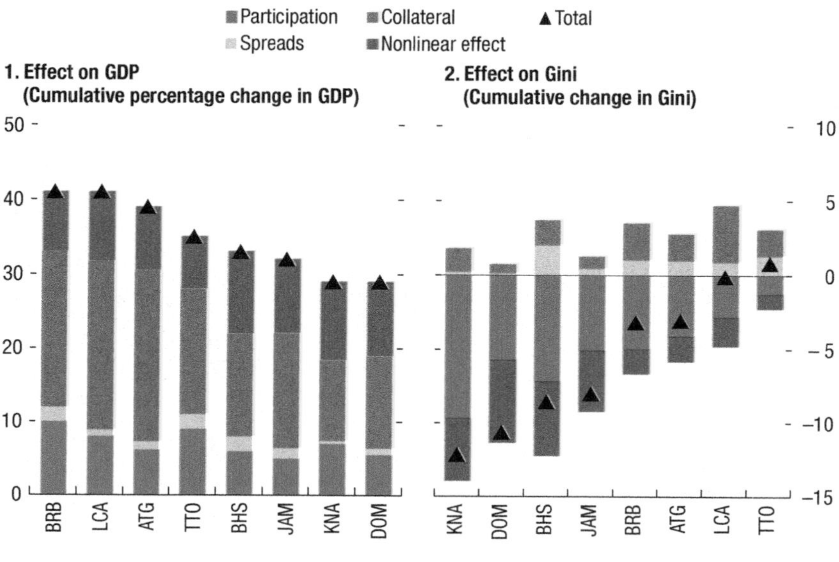

Source: IMF staff calculations.
Note: Data labels in figure use International Organization for Standardization (ISO) country codes.

(the largest 5 percent of firms employ only 32 percent of labor) whereas the strong effect for The Bahamas comes from its current low levels of participation.

## Lowering Intermediation Costs

In this sample of countries, growth and inequality both are the least responsive to lowering the interest rate spread (Figure 9.10). Just as for collateral requirements, loosening this constraint mostly benefits those firms that already have access to credit, generating a positive impact on growth but a worsening of inequality. Contrary to collateral requirements, however, lower spreads make credit cheaper without directly expanding the amount of leverage; the impact is strongest among medium-sized firms for which these costs were a larger proportion of their profits. Thus, loosening this constraint does little to help the smallest firms that are currently outside the credit market for other reasons (for example, participation constraints)—hence worsening inequality—and does not significantly affect the most productive firms in the economy (which were already bearing the higher spreads), resulting in a smaller impact on growth.

## Combined Effect of All Constraints

The analysis above, based on relaxing individual constraints, shows that the benefits come with trade-offs. Although the model suggests that relaxation of the collateral requirement will generate the highest increase in growth, it could also *exacerbate* inequality; lowering participation costs will also boost growth, but by a little less, and will *reduce* inequality.

So, what happens when all three constraints are loosened concurrently? The various constraints interact such that the joint effect on GDP is more than the additive effect of loosening each constraint in isolation (Figure 9.11, panel 1). Inequality also declines, on net, for most of the countries in the sample (Figure 9.11, panel 2). Note, however, that in this case the nonlinear effect may help exacerbate inequality (that is, loosening collateral constraints and spreads both exacerbate inequality, and their joint effect is stronger than the sum of their isolated effects).

Finally, and while not directly included in the model, stability factors should inform the decision about which constraints to loosen. Policies such as reducing collateral constraints and lowering participation costs, while beneficial for growth and inequality, could also expose the economy to instability. For example, high leverage levels and entry of lower productivity–higher risk firms into the credit market could increase nonperforming loans, which are already at relatively high levels in some countries. Thus, a strong regulatory and supervisory environment will be paramount to ensure continued financial stability as inclusion policies unfold.

# CASE STUDY: JAMAICA

## Facts

As discussed in the previous section, there is no "one-size-fits-all" solution to financial inclusion; the most binding constraints and drivers vary by country. This section takes an in-depth look at Jamaica and several of its constraints to examine potential policies. This case study could serve as a template for examining constraints to financial development and inclusion, and could be applied to other Caribbean countries as data become available.

As shown in Figure 9.12, Jamaica's financial development has been broadly stable albeit declining since the mid-2000s. Although development of financial institutions has been sluggish since 1995, financial market development improved until the 2008–09 global financial crisis. The stagnation of financial institution development in Jamaica is likely a legacy of the crisis experienced by the country in the early 1990s, which virtually halted growth of nonbank financial institutions (for example, insurance companies). The crisis had a severe impact on the country's public debt, which in turn encumbered private sector balance sheets and crowded out private credit. The financial system, which had more than 100 institutions in 1995, became more concentrated, to the point where the two largest banks in 2015 accounted for three-quarters of the banking system's assets.

Despite this history, financial inclusion indicators, especially for household usage of financial services, point to significant potential that could be tapped in Jamaica. Almost 78 percent of households report having an account at a financial institution, one of the highest rates in the world, versus only

## Figure 9.12. Financial Development and Inclusion in Jamaica

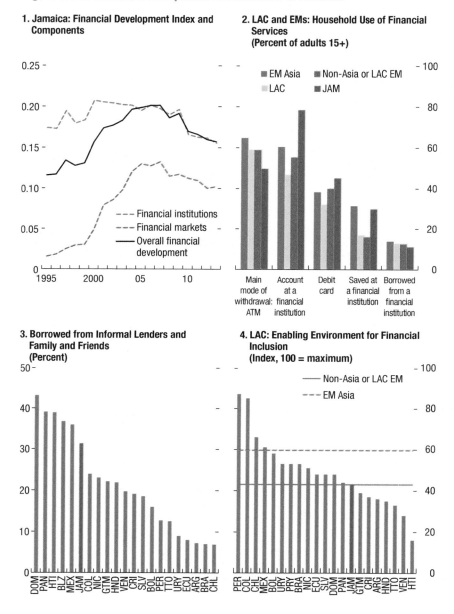

1. Jamaica: Financial Development Index and Components

2. LAC and EMs: Household Use of Financial Services
(Percent of adults 15+)

3. Borrowed from Informal Lenders and Family and Friends
(Percent)

4. LAC: Enabling Environment for Financial Inclusion
(Index, 100 = maximum)

Sources: Consensus Economics; IMF, Primary Commodity Price System; and IMF staff estimates.
Note: ATM = automated teller machine; EM = emerging market; LAC = Latin America and the Caribbean. Data labels in figure use International Organization for Standardization (ISO) country codes.

47 percent in LAC. Furthermore, Jamaica is also a leader in the number of people who report saving at a financial institution and the proportion of households that use a debit card.

Nevertheless, this significant coverage blurs weaknesses in the provision of credit by the formal financial system. More than 30 percent of households report borrowing through informal channels (friends, family, or informal lenders)—one of the highest proportions in a region where informal borrowing is already high. At the same time, only 11 percent of households surveyed report borrowing from a formal financial institution.

According to the 2014 Global Microscope Survey, recent reforms have helped improve Jamaica's environment for financial inclusion but results will take time to be realized. For example, the nascent credit bureau system will help lower intermediation costs, but weaknesses in information sharing between bureaus and other entities (such as tax administration, banks, and other lenders) imply significant gaps in use of the system. A registry for movable collateral has been established, and the new framework for electronic retail payment services will provide a boost to mobile payments. Nevertheless, prudential oversight and reporting requirements over credit unions and small micro-lenders (which play a significant role in the country and in the region more generally) could still be strengthened.

## Quantitative Model

In addition to GDP and the Gini coefficient, the quantitative model discussed in section "Growth-Inequality Trade-Offs" also has implications for variables such as total factor productivity (TFP), interest rate spread, percentage of firms with credit, and number of entrepreneurs in the economy. A thorough discussion for all eight Caribbean countries would be voluminous; therefore, this section provides an example of how such an analysis could be undertaken using Jamaica— chosen because of its severely binding constraints.

Table 9.1 summarizes the outcomes for each of the abovementioned variables when each of the three constraints (participation costs, borrowing constraints, and intermediation efficiency) is loosened. A few dynamics in the model warrant attention:

- Lowering participation costs (first row of Table 9.1) will lower the economy's average productivity level as smaller (and less productive) firms enter the market. Note that while this is true in the model by assumption, this may not be true in practice as highly productive firms often remain outside credit markets and lower participation costs enable their entry.
- Lower collateral constraints (second row) will increase average TFP (as productive firms become even larger), but with negative consequences for competition as the number of firms (proxied by entrepreneurs in the model) drops.
- The loosening of both participation and borrowing constraints endogenously increases spreads (fourth column). In the first case, this increase is driven

**Table 9.1. Effects of Loosening Constraints**

| | Variable | | | | | |
|---|---|---|---|---|---|---|
| Constraint | GDP | TFP | Gini | Spreads | Firms with Credit | Number of Entrepreneurs |
| Participation cost | ↑ | ⇩ | ⇩ | ↑ | ↑ | ↑ |
| Borrowing constraints | ↑ | ↑ | ↑ | ↑ | ↑ | ⇩ |
| Intermediation costs | ↑ | 0 | ↑ | ⇩ | ↑ | 0 |

Note: TFP = total factor productivity.

by the entry of less talented entrepreneurs whose firms are riskier. In the second case, the increased leverage of large firms concentrates credit risk in the economy; if any of these large firms fail, the lender will incur significant losses. These endogenous changes in spreads illustrate the need to combine various financial inclusion policies to achieve the desired final outcomes.

## Combined Effect of Joint Loosening

Recall from section "Combined Effect of All Constraints" that the effect of joint loosening of constraints is larger than the additive effect of loosening each in isolation. The path to this final effect may not be monotonic, however. As an illustration, Figure 9.13 plots the combined effect of reducing both collateral constraints and participation costs for Jamaica, and how the final values previously shown in Figure 9.11 are derived. The combined relaxation of participation and borrowing constraints ameliorates the latter's effect on increasing inequality and produces an outcome that generates higher GDP (nearly 30 percent) with a decrease in the Gini coefficient of 0.06 (the circles in each panel indicate the point at which both constraints are fully loosened). GDP increases monotonically in every direction on the surface (panel 1). However, for inequality (panel 2), if participation costs remain above a certain level, any further loosening of collateral constraints could worsen inequality. Thus, policies to loosen collateral constraints should be phased in in tandem with steps to ease participation constraints.

# CONCLUSIONS AND POLICY IMPLICATIONS

*Caribbean financial systems are relatively well developed, but financial inclusion could be improved.* Some countries have deep markets as a result of government debt while others have developed offshore financial centers with some positive— but limited—spillovers to domestic markets and smaller clients.

*Financial development could be improved.* The financial development levels of The Bahamas, Barbados, Jamaica, and Trinidad and Tobago remain in the mid range of LAC. There is scope for further financial development, but care should be taken to safeguard financial stability. Policies that may be pertinent for these countries include strengthening institutional and legal frameworks related to

## Figure 9.13. Lower Participation Costs and Collateral Requirements

**1. Combined Effect on GDP Growth**

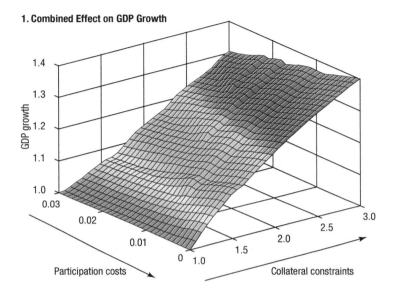

**2. Combined Effect on Inequality**

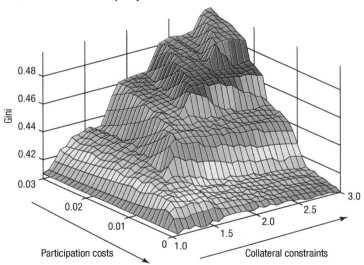

Source: Author's calculations.

property rights and collateral registries, as well as improving the credibility of financial systems and deposit insurance, enhancing capital and liquidity buffers, and addressing balance sheet mismatches.

*Policies to support SMEs are warranted.* Key supporting measures include understanding the determinants of banks' fees and charges, examining the existence of and eliminating predatory practices, and reviewing the adequacy of banking sector competition (including the framework for entry). As financial inclusion improves and more users enter the market, measures to reduce information costs (strong credit bureaus), efforts to reduce operational costs (using mobile networks and correspondent banking), and measures to improve the efficiency of courts and collateral recovery systems are necessary.

*There is no silver bullet solution to easing financial constraints.* There are trade-offs between growth, inequality, and financial stability; all should be considered when policies are designed. For example, even though policies aimed at lowering collateral requirements (such as strengthening the legal framework for managing and seizing collateral, reducing the size of collateral requirements, and creating modern collateral registries) are mostly beneficial for growth, they may also lead to higher inequality as marginal benefits accrue to the top of the distribution. In contrast, policies aimed at reducing participation costs (for example, lowering documentation requirements and reducing red tape and the need for informal guarantors to access finance) could help reduce inequality but may not yield comparable growth benefits.

*Synergies from a multipronged approach.* The joint loosening of multiple constraints is likely to yield larger returns (higher growth and lower inequality) than the sum of loosening several constraints sequentially. However, the transition to that final state may also entail temporary increases in inequality. Hence, tailored policies require a clear understanding of country-specific constraints, priorities, and timelines. Last, significant care should also be taken to ensure that a strong framework for financial regulation and consumer protection is in place to safeguard the benefits of expanded financial inclusion without jeopardizing financial stability.

*Significant data gaps hamper analysis for most countries in the region.* Good data are key to understanding the met and unmet needs of the users of financial services, their socioeconomic and demographic characteristics, and how financial constraints affect them. As an immediate first step, the Caribbean could focus on the collection of demand-side data to help diagnose problems, identify constraints, design targeted policies, and then monitor their impact.

## REFERENCES

Aghion, P., N. Bloom, R. Blundell, R. Griffith, and P. Howitt. 2005. "Competition and Innovation: An Inverted-U Relationship." *Quarterly Journal of Economics* 120 (2): 701–28.

Aiyagari, M., A. Demirgüç-Kunt, and V. Maksimovic. 2007. "Firm Innovation in Emerging Markets." World Bank Policy Research Working Paper 4157, World Bank, Washington, DC.

Armstrong, H. W., and R. Read. 2003. "Microstates and Subnational Regions: Mutual Industrial Policy Lessons." *International Regional Science Review* 26 (1): 117–41.

Beck, T., A. Demirgüç-Kunt and R. Levine. 2004. "Finance, Inequality and Poverty: Cross Country Evidence." NBER Working Paper, No. 10979.

Beck, T., A. Demirgüç-Kunt, and R. Levine. 2007. "Finance, Inequality and the Poor." *Journal of Economic Growth* 12 (1): 27–49.

Beck, T., A. Demirgüç-Kunt, and V. Maksimovic. 2005. "Financial and Legal Constraints to Growth: Does Firm Size Matter?" *Journal of Finance* 60 (1): 137–77.

Clarke, G. R., L. C. Xu, and H. F. Zou. 2006. "Finance and Income Inequality: What Do the Data Tell Us?" *Southern Economic Journal* 72 (3): 578–96.

Charvériat, C. 2000. "Natural Disasters in Latin America and the Caribbean: An Overview of Risk." Research Department Publication 4233, Inter-American Development Bank, Washington, DC.

Dabla-Norris, M. E., Y. Ji, R. Townsend, and D. F. Unsal. 2015. "Identifying Constraints to Financial Inclusion and Their Impact on GDP and Inequality: A Structural Framework for Policy." IMF Working Paper 15/22, International Monetary Fund, Washington, DC.

Easterly, W., and A. Kraay. 1999. "Small States, Small Problems?" World Bank Policy Research Working Paper 2139, World Bank, Washington, DC.

Economist Intelligence Unit, 2014. "Global Microscope 2014: The Enabling Environment for Financial Inclusion," sponsored by MIF/IDB, CAF, ACCION and Citi. EIU, New York.

Greenidge, Kevin, Roland Craigwell, Chrystol Thomas, and Lisa Drakes. 2012. "Threshold Effects of Sovereign Debt: Evidence from the Caribbean." IMF Working Paper 12/157, International Monetary Fund, Washington, DC.

Heng, Dyna, Anna Ivanova, Rodrigo Mariscal, Uma Ramakrishnan, and Joyce Wong. 2016. "Advancing Financial Development in Latin America and the Caribbean." IMF Working Paper 16/81, International Monetary Fund, Washington, DC.

Holden, P., and H. Howell. 2009. *Institutions and the Legal Framework for Business Development in the Caribbean*. Washington, DC: Inter-American Development Bank.

King, R. G. and R. Levine. 1993. "Finance, Entrepreneurship and Growth." *Journal of Monetary Economics* 32 (3): 513–42.

Krešić, A., J. Milatović, and P. Sanfey. 2017. "Firm Performance and Obstacles to Doing Business in the Western Balkans." EBRD Working Paper 200, European Bank for Reconstruction and Development, London.

Levine, R. 1997. "Financial Development and Economic Growth: Views and Agenda." *Journal of Economic Literature* 35 (2): 688–726.

———. 2005. "Finance and Growth: Theory and Evidence." In *Handbook of Economic Growth*, Vol 1, 865–934. Amsterdam: Elsevier.

Sahay, R., M. Cihak, P. N'Diaye, A. Barajas, D. Ayala Pena, R. Bi, Y. Gao, A. Kyobe, L. Nguyen, C. Saborowski, K. Svirydzenka, and R. Yousefi. 2015. "Rethinking Financial Deepening: Stability and Growth in Emerging Markets." IMF Staff Discussion Note 15-8, International Monetary Fund, Washington, DC.

Thacker, Nita, and Sebastian Acevedo. 2010. "A Cross-Country Perspective on Growth in the Caribbean: The Role of Tourism and Debt." In *Regional Economic Outlook: Western Hemisphere: Heating up in the South, Cooler in the North*. Washington, DC: International Monetary Fund.

# CHAPTER 10

# Financial Interconnectedness in the Caribbean: Challenges for Financial Stability

ELIE CANETTI, KIMBERLY BEATON, QIAOE CHEN, FABIO DI VITTORIO, UDI ROSENHAND, AND KALIN TINTCHEV

## INTRODUCTION

The global financial crisis of 2008–09 and, in the Caribbean, the crisis stemming from the collapse of Trinidad and Tobago–based CL Financial Group in 2009, raised awareness of risks to financial stability from financial interconnectedness. Even though interconnectedness can promote international risk sharing, competition, and efficiency (Claessens and others 2010), it can also spread adverse shocks in unexpected directions, and sometimes in an unexpectedly virulent manner (Kaminsky and Reinhart 2000). For instance, when CL Financial Group, which had assets of US$16 billion at the end of 2007 (about 30 percent of the Caribbean's regional GDP), collapsed, the adverse impact spilled over to all the Caribbean Community and Common Market (CARICOM) member states except Jamaica and Haiti, with claims on CL Financial as high as 17 percent of GDP in the Eastern Caribbean Currency Union (ECCU).[1]

Against this backdrop, the IMF launched the Caribbean Regional Financial Project (CRFP) in 2013 to gain a better understanding of financial interconnectedness in the region to determine the level of resilience of the regional financial system to financial and macroeconomic shocks (Box 10.1). Central to achieving these aims was the collection of unique data on financial exposures among banks, insurers, and sovereigns in the Caribbean, which facilitated the mapping of financial interconnections and simulations to assess financial spillovers. This chapter lays out the key

---

This chapter draws on the Caribbean Regional Financial Project, which was directed by Elie Canetti supervising a team led by Kimberly Beaton and comprising Qiaoe Chen, Fabio di Vittorio, Udi Rosenhand, and Kalin Tintchev. Xiaodan Ding, Anayo Osueke, and Xin Xu made additional contributions.

[1]See IMF 2011b, Box 1.

---

**Box 10.1. The Caribbean Regional Financial Project**

As part of a regional effort to strengthen financial stability following the CL Financial crisis, central bank governors in Caribbean Community (CARICOM) requested IMF assistance to develop a better understanding of the interconnections within the Caribbean financial system as one element of the region's broad effort to strengthen regional financial surveillance. An agreement between CARICOM governors and the IMF in May 2013 launched the Caribbean Regional Financial Project (CRFP) with the following objectives:

- To identify factors creating financial stability risks due to interconnections involving ownership, common funding, and exposures to regional sovereigns and firms
- To assess the resilience of the regional financial system to key macroeconomic shocks
- To strengthen the current policies and practices of the financial stability framework, including regional supervision and crisis management and resolution

To achieve these objectives, data on the exposures of jurisdictions' bank and insurance sectors to each other and to Caribbean sovereigns were collected to map financial interconnections and assess the potential for spillovers across the regional financial system. The financial systems examined covered the banking systems of The Bahamas, Barbados, Belize, the Eastern Caribbean Currency Union (ECCU), Guyana, Jamaica, Suriname, and Trinidad and Tobago as well as the insurance sectors of Barbados, Belize, Guyana, Jamaica, Suriname, and Trinidad and Tobago. For ECCU banking systems, aggregate data for the ECCU as a whole were used.

The final results were presented at the CARICOM governors' meeting in November 2015. The interconnectedness maps were presented in the first *Caribbean Regional Financial Stability Report* (Caribbean Center for Money and Finance 2016). The results of the network simulations are presented in this chapter.

---

findings of the CRFP exercise, including a granular assessment of the vulnerabilities in the financial system based on network simulations and policies that could help improve both national and regional financial regulation and supervision.

The first section provides an overview of the Caribbean financial system, followed by a discussion in the second section of financial integration in the region based on a mapping and risk analysis. Based on this analysis, the third section contains a discussion of the priorities for financial regulation and supervision for the Caribbean region.

# THE CARIBBEAN FINANCIAL SYSTEM: AN OVERVIEW

The Caribbean financial system has undergone significant development over the past few decades, shaped by the region's desire to achieve closer financial integration. In 2001, the Revised Treaty of Chaguaramas established the Caribbean Single Market and Economy and required the removal of restrictions on the provision of banking, insurance, and financial services as well as the free movement of capital across national borders.[2] Moreover, CARICOM continues to

---

[2]To date, Antigua and Barbuda, Barbados, Belize, Dominica, Grenada, Guyana, Haiti, Jamaica, St. Kitts and Nevis, St. Lucia, St. Vincent and the Grenadines, Suriname, and Trinidad and Tobago have joined the Caribbean Single Market and Economy.

work toward integration of capital markets as an explicit objective of its drive to create a common economic space. Closer financial integration has shaped recent developments in the Caribbean financial system, as evidenced by the fallout from the failure of a large regional insurer, CLICO (part of CL Financial Group), and has presented new challenges with the emergence of large and complex financial institutions.

Caribbean financial sectors are large relative to the size of their economies and are dominated by banks (Figure 10.1; Annex 10.1). Commercial banks account for the largest share of financial system assets, and The Bahamas and Barbados have significant offshore banking sectors.[3] The nonbank financial sector is also prominent in some of the larger economies in the region. In Jamaica, securities firms have assets under management of about 30 percent of GDP, while insurance companies are sizable in Barbados, Trinidad and Tobago, and, to a lesser extent, Jamaica and The Bahamas. Financial conglomerates have an important presence in the region: many nonbank financial institutions are subsidiaries or affiliates of commercial banks. The Caribbean also has one of the highest credit union penetration ratios (measured as the ratio of membership to total population) in the world, at about five times the world average, although these institutions represent only about 6 percent of total financial system assets.[4]

Foreign banks, notably from Canada, play an important role in the region's banking system (Figure 10.2). Some 60 percent of the region's total banking system assets are held by foreign banks.[5] These banks are primarily Canadian owned, with three Canadian banking groups accounting for about 45 percent of the region's total banking system assets.[6] Close business and financial links between Trinidad and Tobago and the broader Caribbean have also encouraged the cross-border expansion of Republic Bank, its largest indigenous bank, while First Citizens Bank of Trinidad and Tobago and the Eastern Caribbean Financial Holding Company (ECFH) in St. Lucia also have cross-border exposures within the Caribbean.[7,8] These banks are also interconnected: Republic Bank holds close to a 20 percent ownership stake in ECFH. Barbados, as the regional headquarters for the Canadian banks operating in the eastern Caribbean, and Trinidad and

---

[3]Offshore assets are not included in the data cited in this chapter, including in charts and tables.

[4]As of 2014, 371 credit unions operated in the region. About 15 percent of the population belong to a credit union.

[5]According to Bankscope. Data were the latest available as of 2014.

[6]Three Canadian banking groups—the Canadian Imperial Bank of Commerce (CIBC), Royal Bank of Canada, and Scotiabank—have sizable operations in the Caribbean. CIBC's operations are through its majority ownership in FirstCaribbean International Bank.

[7]ECFH is the sole owner of the largest bank in St. Lucia, the majority owner in the largest bank in St. Vincent and the Grenadines, and the second-largest shareholder in Eastern Caribbean Amalgamated Bank of Antigua and Barbuda.

[8]The National Bank of Dominica has cross-border exposure through its ownership stake in Caribbean Union Bank of Antigua and Barbuda.

### Figure 10.1. Financial Sector Assets
*(Percent of GDP)*

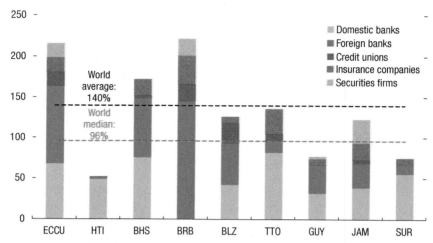

Sources: Country authorities (latest available); and IMF staff estimates.
Note: ECCU = Eastern Caribbean Currency Union. Data labels in figure use International Organization for Standardization (ISO) country codes.

Tobago, site of the largest Caribbean bank with cross-border exposures, have emerged as banking hubs for the region.[9]

Regional financial conglomerates dominate the Caribbean insurance sector. Sagicor Financial Corporation, headquartered in Bermuda since 2016 (but a Barbadian conglomerate when the analysis for this chapter was conducted), has the largest insurance network in the region, with subsidiaries in eight Caribbean countries.[10] As of the end of 2016, Sagicor had US$6.5 billion in assets. Guardian Group, headquartered in Trinidad and Tobago, is the second-largest insurer in the region with operations in nine Caribbean countries.[11] As of the end of 2016, it had US$3.6 billion in assets. Following the collapse of CL Financial, the Caribbean insurance industry has become highly concentrated in these two

---

[9]Royal Bank of Canada's regional holding company is registered in Trinidad and Tobago, while CIBC's regional holding company is headquartered in Barbados. Scotiabank's Caribbean operations have a more dispersed structure with no unique regional holding company.

[10]The holding company Sagicor Financial Corporation has subsidiaries in Aruba, The Bahamas, Barbados, the Cayman Islands, Costa Rica, Jamaica, St. Lucia, Trinidad and Tobago, and the United States.

[11]Guardian Group has subsidiaries in Aruba, The Bahamas, Barbados, Bermuda, Curaçao, Grenada, Jamaica, St. Lucia, Trinidad and Tobago, and Europe.

**Figure 10.2. Foreign-Owned Banks' Market Shares**
*(Percent of banking assets, 2014)*

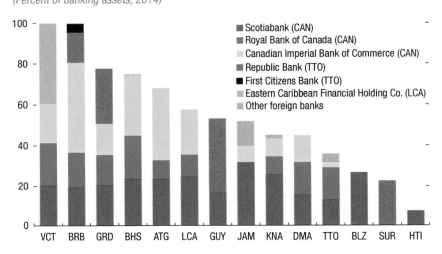

Sources: Bankscope; banks' annual reports; country authorities; and IMF staff estimates.
Note: Data labels in figure use International Organization for Standardization (ISO) country codes.

financial conglomerates, with their combined assets equivalent to some two-thirds of the insurance sector's total assets in the region.[12]

Regional financial conglomerates are also active in offering additional investment products. The region's nonbank non-insurer financial institutions are primarily concentrated in Jamaica, where securities firms have flourished in recent years, and in Trinidad and Tobago, where mutual funds manage assets in excess of bank deposits. Assets under management of Jamaican securities firms comprised about 30 percent of Jamaican GDP in 2016, of which some 55 percent were government bonds. The growth is mainly based on the repo business—short-term borrowing from households through hold-in-custody repurchase arrangements to fund investments in long-term government bonds. Securities dealers thus have significant exposure to government risk. The nature of dealers' profitability, generated by the interest differential between short- and long-term rates, also makes the sector vulnerable to interest rate and rollover risk.[13] The Jamaican authorities are undertaking regulatory reforms to address risks in this sector. In Trinidad and Tobago, the rapid growth of the collective investment scheme industry has been driven by attractive

---

[12]However, some of the two insurance companies' assets are held outside the Caribbean, notably in Sagicor's U.S. subsidiary, which held assets of US$1.9 billion at the end of 2016.

[13]A rise in long-term interest rates reduces the value of existing fixed-rate assets, and a sharp rise in short-term rates negatively affects profitability, given the need to roll over repo agreements with households.

returns relative to bank deposits. Many of these nonbank financial intermediaries, particularly the region's largest mutual funds, are affiliated with banks.

Caribbean capital markets remain in the early stages of development. Although stock exchanges exist throughout most of the region, the number of listed companies and market capitalization of most exchanges remain limited, and most markets are fairly illiquid. Similarly, bond markets are underdeveloped and dominated by government securities, with limited corporate issuance and secondary market activity.

# FINANCIAL INTEGRATION IN THE CARIBBEAN: MAPPING AND RISK ANALYSIS

The interconnections in the Caribbean financial system have the potential to transmit financial and economic shocks throughout the region. This section examines cross-border exposures across the region's financial sectors and with the global financial system, drawing on the June 2013 data set collected for the CRFP. Network maps are used to provide a visual representation of these exposures, while the resilience of the regional financial system to financial and economic shocks and the potential for cross-country spillovers are assessed with network simulations. The analysis is conducted for both banks and insurers, consistent with the CRFP data set (see Box 10.2).

## Direct Exposures

The Caribbean financial sector is highly interconnected, both within the region and with global institutions and markets. The data collected for the CRFP showed that Caribbean banks' cross-border claims in aggregate (including their exposures to sovereigns, banks, and insurers) were large, representing, on average, 12 percent of total assets (Figure 10.3).

Caribbean banks reported significant claims on global banks, mostly in the form of deposits, likely because of the dominant presence of Canadian banking groups (Figure 10.4). Banks' cross-border claims within the Caribbean were less important.[14] The exception was Barbados, which had significant deposits in ECCU banks, reflecting that country's importance as a banking hub for the ECCU. Banks' cross-border claims on sovereigns represented a relatively small share of total assets and were primarily concentrated in the larger sovereigns of the region, although Barbadian banks were also heavily exposed to ECCU sovereigns (Figure 10.5). Only Trinidad and Tobago had significant claims on global sovereigns, with about 4 percent of their reported assets held in the form of claims on the United States.[15] Banks' reported cross-border claims on insurers were negligible, well under 1 percent of their total assets in all cases.

---

[14]Respondents were instructed to classify claims held on a branch or office of a financial institution under the country of the incorporated parent.

[15]Somewhat surprisingly, the within-Caribbean cross-border exposures of banks from Trinidad and Tobago, another Caribbean banking hub, were reported to be relatively minor.

## Box 10.2. The Caribbean Regional Financial Project Data Template

Designing the Caribbean Regional Financial Project data template required addressing issues regarding the level of aggregation, the perimeter of coverage, "data crossings," and the risk concept to be used.

**Level of Aggregation.** The ideal level of aggregation is institution to institution. Given nonlinearities in financial contagion episodes (for example, because of feedback effects), financial stresses, particularly in highly connected individual institutions, may lead to broad financial crises even when (in aggregate) a financial sector may appear sound. In addition, stress tests on aggregate data require implausibly large shocks to make an entire financial sector insolvent. Finally, the greater granularity of individual institution data allows for a more accurate tracing of potential contagion paths, thereby serving as a more specific guide to where financial supervisors should require buffers or erect firewalls. Nonetheless, concerns that legal obstacles to information sharing could not be quickly overcome led to the decision to collect data at the aggregate sectoral level in this pilot project. Considering this decision, participants were instructed that exposures should be classified by the country of incorporation of the entity on which the exposure exists (if known). Thus, exposures to a branch or office of a financial institution should be classified under the country of the incorporated parent.

**Perimeter of Coverage.** The perimeter of coverage required two separate decisions. The first decision was from which institutions would data be collected; the second was on which institutions and sectors would data be collected (since, for example, one could gather information on connections between banks and securities firms by collecting data just from banks). Because complete exposure data can only be collected from the institutions to be surveyed, those institutions (in aggregate form) would end up forming the "nodes" of the network, in effect, the units of analysis. However, from those nodes, one could then collect information on exposures vis-à-vis other sectors. In the end, cost-benefit considerations dictated surveying only banks and insurance companies. In selected jurisdictions, some nonbank financial institutions (in Jamaica, for example) or credit unions (for instance, in the Eastern Caribbean Currency Union) could conceivably be of systemic importance, at least within that jurisdiction, but the cost of comprehensive data collection from the large number of such institutions suggested that the benefits of perhaps uncovering systemically connected institutions were unlikely to be worth the undertaking. Thus, data were collected only from banks and insurers, but among the information collected were their exposures to credit unions, to other nonbank financial institutions, to sovereigns, and to central banks. To construct economic stress tests, data were also collected on exposures to economic sectors including tourism, oil and energy, construction, real estate (residential and commercial), households, and offshore banks.

**Data Crossings.** Every datum in a financial context is inherently multidimensional. Connected with any specific exposure is a currency of denomination, a maturity, a nationality and sector of the counterparty, and the type of instrument (for example, bond, equity, loan, deposit). To be sure, richer experiments can be conducted on data the more multidimensional they are. For instance, one could model currency shocks, or shocks to risk appetite, that affect the demand for equities or equities and bonds, but not deposits. However, the more data "crossings" that are collected, the exponentially more costly it is to collect. For instance, a five-way crossing with x categories in each (for example, x currencies or x maturity buckets) would require $x^5$ separate data entries per node. Accordingly, it was decided to confine data crossings, for the most part, to sector and country. Maturity information was collected only on holdings of government maturities (short term of less than one year versus maturities of greater than one year). In addition, for exposures to economic sectors, it proved difficult for banks and insurers to identify the nationality of the

> **Box 10.2. The Caribbean Regional Financial Project Data Template** *(continued)*
>
> exposure, so in the end, most sectoral exposure data (except to governments) were collected on a global rather than a country- or region-specific basis.
>
> **Risk Transfers.** In principle, one can try to collect data on a "final risk" basis. This concept takes into account that an exposure on a balance sheet may have been transferred elsewhere via collateral, reinsurance, or some form of hedge, whether via a third-party guarantee or derivative. There are conceptual and practical problems in collecting data on a final risk basis, including that the risk transfer may be contingent (for derivative hedges, although derivatives markets are virtually nonexistent in the Caribbean) and that valuing collateral can be challenging, especially for collateral such as real estate that had become fairly illiquid in many Caribbean jurisdictions. Hence, only data on government guarantees were collected.

Caribbean banks' credit portfolios were concentrated in real estate and household loans. Residential and commercial real estate loans accounted for, on average, about 40 percent of total credit, and loans to households for 25 percent. Lending for tourism and construction stood at 20 percent of total loans. In several banking systems, holdings of government bonds (including domestic sovereign bonds) exceeded 100 percent of their capital. Caribbean sovereign exposure as a percentage of bank capital was especially large in Barbados, Jamaica, and the ECCU.

**Figure 10.3. Banks' Claims on Sovereigns, Banks, and Insurers**
*(Percent of total assets)*

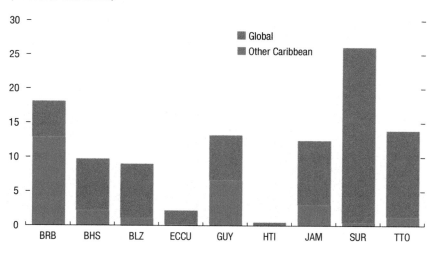

Sources: Country authorities; and IMF staff calculations.
Note: ECCU = Eastern Caribbean Currency Union. Excludes claims on nonfinancial private sector. Data labels in figure use International Organization for Standardization (ISO) country codes.

## Figure 10.4. Banks' Claims on Banks
*(Percent of total assets)*

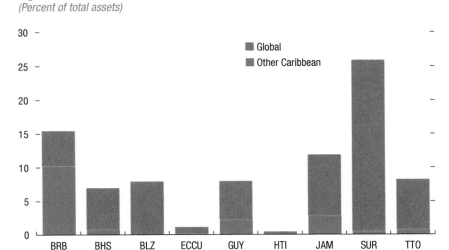

Sources: Country authorities; and IMF staff calculations.
Note: ECCU = Eastern Caribbean Currency Union. Data labels in figure use International Organization for Standardization (ISO) country codes.

## Figure 10.5. Banks' Claims on Sovereigns
*(Percent of total assets)*

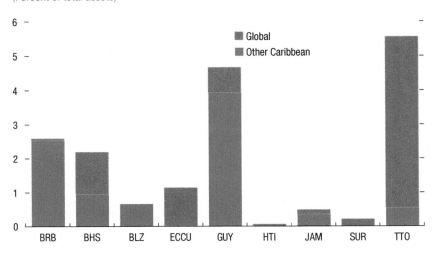

Sources: Country authorities; and IMF staff calculations.
Note: ECCU = Eastern Caribbean Currency Union. Excludes claims on nonfinancial private sector. Data labels in figure use International Organization for Standardization (ISO) country codes.

Banks were generally well capitalized, with most banking systems in the region having had risk-weighted capital adequacy ratios in excess of 15 percent (see Table 10.1); nonperforming loans were elevated, averaging 18 percent of total loans in the ECCU, and ranging between 12 percent and 16 percent in The Bahamas, Barbados, and Belize at the end of 2013.[16]

Caribbean insurers appeared more interconnected than banks; their cross-border claims were considerably larger as a share of their total assets than were those of banks. However, given the smaller relative size of the insurance sector, insurers' cross-border claims are smaller relative to the size of the economy (at only 5 percent of GDP) than those of banks. Given the presence of regional insurance conglomerates in Barbados and Trinidad and Tobago, cross-border claims of insurers in those countries represented a greater share of both economic activity and insurers' assets than for other countries, and these claims, including both equity and deposit claims, were primarily concentrated within the Caribbean. Insurers in Barbados, Jamaica, and Trinidad and Tobago had significant exposure to other Caribbean sovereigns and, to a lesser extent, global sovereigns. By contrast, insurers' cross-border claims on banks were negligible except in Barbados where they constituted about 5 percent of total assets. Insurers had significant cross-border claims on global insurers, primarily concentrated in Europe, presumably representing claims on reinsurers. Intra-Caribbean cross-border claims for insurers are small (except for Barbadian insurers). All Caribbean insurance sectors reported capitalization ratios well above 20 percent of total assets.

## Network Maps

Indirect exposures magnify the interconnectedness in the Caribbean financial system. By also including indirect exposures, network analysis provides a more complete picture of interconnectedness than direct exposures alone. For instance, banking system A may be directly exposed to banking systems B and C. However, banking system A may also be indirectly exposed to banking system C through banking system B's claims on banking system C. The value added of network analysis is that it considers all direct and indirect exposures.

Network maps provide a vivid visual description of the interconnections in the Caribbean financial system. A directional circular network of the Caribbean financial system (Figure 10.6) shows that financial connections were concentrated among only a subset of jurisdictions. Banks generally appear more highly interconnected than insurers, with the most significant connections being with their own sovereigns. In Figure 10.6, the thickness of the lines reflects the aggregate size of the exposures, which, since they are in nominal terms, will be larger for larger banking and insurance sectors. Banking systems in several countries stand out as fairly interconnected, while in some others, such as Belize, Haiti, and Suriname,

---

[16]Chapter 11 considers asset quality in the region and proposes a comprehensive strategy to address impediments to the resolution of problem loans.

### Table 10.1. Economic Scenario Results: Domestic Impact
*(Percent; postshock CARs below 8 percent are bolded)*

| | Barbados | Belize | ECCU | Guyana | Jamaica | Suriname | The Bahamas | Trinidad and Tobago |
|---|---|---|---|---|---|---|---|---|
| Initial CAR[1] | 18.7 | 23.5 | 10.5 | 28.9 | 15.4 | 11.9 | 31.3 | 28.0 |
| Postshock CARs | | | | | | | | |
| **Shocks to Total Credit Portfolio** | | | | | | | | |
| Loss rate of 2.5 percent of total loans | 16.2 | 21.4 | **7.0** | 27.4 | 13.3 | 10.0 | 29.0 | 26.2 |
| Loss rate of 5 percent of total loans | 13.7 | 19.2 | **3.5** | 25.8 | 11.1 | 8.1 | 26.6 | 24.4 |
| **Sovereign Shock** | | | | | | | | |
| 5 percent haircut | 15.8 | 22.1 | 9.2 | 26.2 | 12.3 | 11.5 | 29.8 | 24.9 |
| 10 percent haircut | 13.0 | 20.7 | **7.9** | 23.5 | 9.2 | 11.1 | 28.3 | 21.8 |
| 20 percent haircut | **7.3** | 17.9 | **5.3** | 18.0 | **3.0** | 10.4 | 25.3 | 15.5 |
| 30 percent haircut | **1.6** | 15.1 | **2.7** | 12.5 | **−3.1** | 9.6 | 22.3 | 9.2 |
| **Tourism Shock** | | | | | | | | |
| Loss rate of 5 percent of total loans | 18.1 | 23.2 | 9.7 | 28.9 | 15.1 | 11.7 | 31.2 | 28.0 |
| Loss rate of 10 percent of total loans | 17.5 | 22.9 | 8.9 | 28.8 | 14.7 | 11.6 | 31.0 | 27.9 |
| Loss rate of 15 percent of total loans | 16.9 | 22.5 | 8.1 | 28.7 | 14.4 | 11.5 | 30.8 | 27.9 |
| **Construction Shock** | | | | | | | | |
| Loss rate of 5 percent of total loans | 18.3 | 21.8 | 9.9 | 28.7 | 15.1 | 11.3 | 31.3 | 27.8 |
| Loss rate of 10 percent of total loans | 17.9 | 20.0 | 9.2 | 28.4 | 14.8 | 10.8 | 31.2 | 27.5 |
| Loss rate of 15 percent of total loans | 17.5 | 18.3 | 8.6 | 28.2 | 14.4 | 10.2 | 31.1 | 27.2 |
| **Real Estate Shock** | | | | | | | | |
| Loss rate of 5 percent of total loans | 16.6 | 22.8 | **7.4** | 26.8 | 14.1 | 10.5 | 29.1 | 27.0 |
| Loss rate of 10 percent of total loans | 14.5 | 22.1 | **4.3** | 24.7 | 12.8 | 9.1 | 26.9 | 25.9 |
| Loss rate of 15 percent of total loans | 12.4 | 21.4 | **1.2** | 22.5 | 11.5 | **7.7** | 24.6 | 24.8 |
| **Household Lending Shock** | | | | | | | | |
| Loss rate of 5 percent of total loans | 16.9 | 22.2 | 8.6 | 28.3 | 13.7 | 11.1 | 29.3 | 27.9 |
| Loss rate of 10 percent of total loans | 15.1 | 20.9 | **6.7** | 27.7 | 11.9 | 10.3 | 27.2 | 27.7 |
| Loss rate of 15 percent of total loans | 13.2 | 19.6 | **4.8** | 27.0 | 10.2 | 9.5 | 25.1 | 27.5 |
| **Energy Sector Shock** | | | | | | | | |
| Loss rate of 5 percent of total loans | 18.6 | 23.4 | 10.4 | 28.9 | 15.3 | 11.8 | 31.3 | 27.9 |
| Loss rate of 10 percent of total loans | 18.6 | 23.4 | 10.4 | 28.9 | 15.2 | 11.7 | 31.3 | 27.7 |
| Loss rate of 15 percent of total loans | 18.6 | 23.3 | 10.3 | 28.9 | 15.1 | 11.7 | 31.3 | 27.6 |
| Simultaneous Shocks | | | | | | | | |
| **Tourism and Construction Shocks** | | | | | | | | |
| Loss rate of 5 percent of total loans | 17.7 | 21.4 | 9.1 | 28.6 | 14.8 | 11.2 | 31.1 | 27.7 |
| Loss rate of 10 percent of total loans | 16.7 | 19.4 | **7.6** | 28.3 | 14.1 | 10.5 | 30.8 | 27.4 |
| Loss rate of 15 percent of total loans | 15.7 | 17.3 | **6.2** | 28.0 | 13.5 | 9.8 | 30.6 | 27.1 |
| **Tourism and Sovereign Shocks** | | | | | | | | |
| Loss rate of 5 percent of total loans | 15.2 | 21.8 | 8.4 | 26.1 | 12.0 | 11.4 | 29.6 | 24.9 |
| Loss rate of 10 percent of total loans | 11.8 | 20.1 | **6.3** | 23.3 | 8.6 | 10.9 | 28.0 | 21.7 |
| Loss rate of 15 percent of total loans | 8.3 | 18.3 | **4.2** | 20.5 | **5.2** | 10.4 | 26.3 | 18.5 |
| **Tourism, Construction, and Sovereign Shocks** | | | | | | | | |
| Loss rate of 5 percent of total loans | 14.9 | 20.0 | **7.8** | 25.9 | 11.7 | 10.8 | 29.6 | 24.6 |
| Loss rate of 10 percent of total loans | 11.0 | 16.6 | **5.0** | 22.8 | **8.0** | 9.7 | 27.8 | 21.1 |
| Loss rate of 15 percent of total loans | **7.2** | 13.1 | **2.3** | 19.7 | **4.2** | 8.7 | 26.1 | 17.7 |

Sources: National authorities; and IMF staff estimates.
Note: CAR = capital adequacy ratio; ECCU = Eastern Caribbean Currency Union.
[1]Risk-weighted CAR.

### Figure 10.6. Cross-Sectoral Connections in the Caribbean Financial Sector: Circular Network View

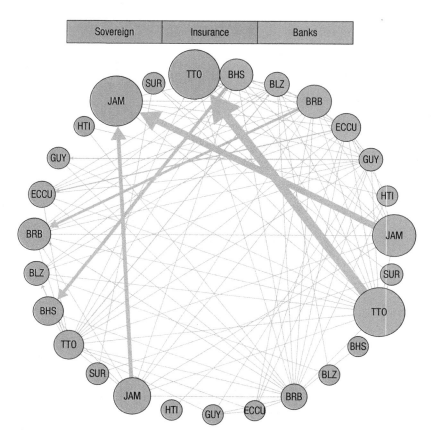

Sources: Country authorities; and IMF staff calculations.
Note: Color of node (circle) represents the type of sector (bank, insurer, or sovereign) with the country of domicile identified by its International Organization for Standardization (ISO) country code. The area of each node represents the size of its total balance sheet (assets plus liabilities, except for sovereigns, for which the size is based on the reported claims of banks and insurers on each sovereign). Each line represents the balance sheet connection between two nodes, with the width reflective of the size of the connection (in nominal terms) and the direction indicating whether the connection is based on a claim (asset) or liability. The node from which the arrow emanates has a claim on the node to which the arrow points. In some cases, the size of the connection is too small for the directionality to be observed. Claims of sovereigns on banks and insurers are not included because they were not collected in the Caribbean Regional Financial Project data set.

they appear to have relatively few and small connections to the rest of the regional financial system. Within insurance, Barbados and Trinidad and Tobago stand out as the jurisdictions with the most interconnectedness, reflecting the presence of the regionally important insurers in those jurisdictions. Finally, among sovereigns, Barbados, Trinidad and Tobago, and the ECCU appear to be the sovereigns on which the most other nodes have claims, although claims on the Jamaican sovereign (from the Jamaican bank and insurance sectors) appear quantitatively large (as do the claims of Bahamian, Barbadian, and Trinidadian banks on their respective sovereigns).[17]

The Trinidadian and Barbadian financial systems appear to be at the center of the Caribbean financial system. The map of the regional financial system using a centrality view (Figure 10.7) clearly indicates that some sectors are central to the Caribbean financial system, whereas others appear peripheral. The physical placement of each node on the network map (Figure 10.7) indicates its degree of interconnectivity and centrality to the system.[18] Both the banking and insurance sectors of Barbados and Trinidad appear at the center of the system. The key sovereign connections are with Barbados, Jamaica, Trinidad and Tobago, and the ECCU, with the Bahamian sovereign appearing somewhat less central. The financial systems of Belize, Haiti, and Suriname are on the periphery, with Guyana in between, having few significant connections with insurers or the sovereign, but some significant interconnectedness of the Guyanese banking system. The map also reveals that bank-insurer and insurer-sovereign links are quantitatively important for Barbados, Jamaica, and Trinidad and Tobago. Overall, the network visualization is consistent with the structure of the regional financial system discussed in the previous section.

## Systemic Spillover Analysis

This section examines two broad types of shocks and assesses how the nature of interconnectedness found in the data can lead to spillovers through balance sheet connections. First, the analysis looks at shocks of a financial origin, ignoring the underlying economic cause of the shock to a particular financial sector. The exercise assumes that the capital of one national financial system at a time becomes significantly impaired, then traces the resultant impact on the broader regional financial system.[19] Shocks to specific economic sectors at a Caribbean-wide level are then modeled, pursuant to the same methodology for assessing spillovers.

---

[17]Because data were not collected from sovereigns, the directional map shows only claims on sovereigns, but not claims of sovereigns on either the banking or insurance sectors.

[18]More technically, the map uses the Fruchterman-Reingold Algorithm. It is based on unweighted bilateral financial flows and tends to put the country with the most links (or edges) in the center and the less connected ones on the periphery. The position of the node does not consider the magnitude of a bilateral flow, but only whether there is an actual flow. See Fruchterman and Reingold (1991).

[19]It is assumed that the risk-weighted capital ratio (CAR) of the trigger banking system falls below 4 percent.

**Figure 10.7. Cross-Sectoral Connections in the Caribbean Financial Sector: Centrality View**

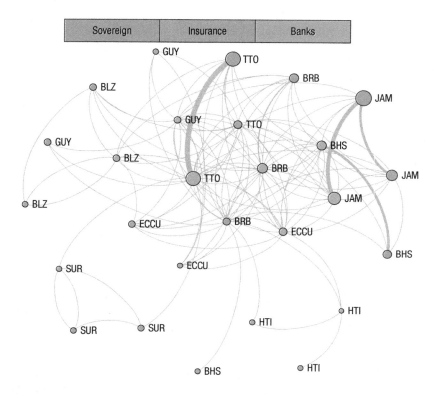

Sources: Country authorities; and IMF staff calculations.

Note: The color of the node (circle) represents the type of sector (bank, insurer, or sovereign) with the country of domicile identified by its International Organization for Standardization (ISO) country code. The placement of each node on the network map indicates its degree of interconnectivity and centrality to the system, with node position determined by the number of links it is attached to. Nodes with more links are placed toward the center. The area of each node represents the size of its total balance sheet (assets plus liabilities, except for sovereigns, for which the size is based on reported claims of banks and insurers on each sovereign). Each line represents the balance sheet connection between two nodes, with the width reflective of the size of the connection. Direction is indicated by following the connection in a clockwise direction (that is, following a node to the node to which it is connected in a clockwise direction indicates the claim is from the originating node to the destination node) and the direction indicating whether the connection is based on a claim (asset) or liability. Claims of sovereigns on banks and insurers are not included because they were not collected in the Caribbean Regional Financial Project data set.

## Financial Shocks

### Methodology

The CRFP's simulations of spillovers aimed to gauge financial systems' (banks and insurers) systemic importance within the Caribbean financial system as transmitters and recipients of spillovers. The systemic importance of each country's banking and insurance sector was assessed based on its potential to trigger regional systemic spillovers.[20] A financial system's vulnerability to spillovers was defined as the frequency of inward spillovers received in the simulations. Both a financial system's systemic importance and its vulnerability to spillovers are a function of its interconnectedness. Financial systems' vulnerability to spillovers is also a function of its initial capital buffers.

The analysis separately and jointly examined solvency and liquidity shocks for both banking and insurance sectors. The methodology, building on Espinosa-Vega and Sole (2010), posits an initial default of a banking or insurance sector and then studies the resulting path of defaults of other banking or insurance sectors based on their interconnections. To be clear, this stylized exercise was done to judge the potential role of each banking system in a potential contagion crisis, and implies nothing about the probability of any individual banking system falling into crisis. Specifically, each national banking or insurance sector is modeled to default, by assumption, on 60 percent of its cross-border borrowing from other banking systems, and to fail to roll over its cross-border lending.[21] On the solvency side, banking sectors that end up with capital shortfalls following the initial shock can trigger further rounds of spillovers if they lead to new capital shortfalls. The spillover path continues until no more banking sectors end up with capital shortfalls, at which point the simulation concludes and there are no more spillovers. On the liquidity side, the trigger institution is assumed to withdraw its funding of other institutions, thus forcing those institutions to sell assets at a loss. Those losses accrue to the affected institutions' capital, thereby possibly setting off further spillovers.

Espinosa-Vega and Sole's (2010) methodology was adapted for the aggregate country-level bank and insurance sector data included in the CRFP data set. Because it would be unrealistic to assume that the capital of an entire banking or insurance sector would become negative, even in a systemic crisis, a systemic crisis and a systemic financial spillover are modeled as a capital shortfall rather than a total loss of capital. For banks, solvency shocks use the Basel I hurdle rate of capital falling below 8 percent of risk-weighted assets; for insurers, solvency shocks use a hurdle rate of 8 percent of total assets to reflect insurers' large holdings of zero-risk-weighted government assets.

---

[20]A systemic spillover is defined as a fall in the recipient banking system's capital ratio (CAR) (or the insurance system's non-risk-weighted capital ratio) below the Basel I minimum of 8 percent (see methodology below).

[21]This implicitly assumes that the capital adequacy ratio of the trigger banking system or insurance sector falls below 4 percent. See methodology below.

The use of aggregate data may mask individual problem institutions and it also constrained this analysis of the dynamics of systemic crises because, for instance, the analysis is not able to assess the extent to which an individual institution could have a large, nonlinear impact on the overall financial system. The use of aggregate country-level data also prevented more granular analysis of the sources and paths of contagion. Some additional caveats are in order. The analysis does not capture indirect ownership links, for example, institutions from different Caribbean countries owned by a common foreign entity. In addition, data were not collected directly from nonbank non-insurance financial institutions, so any systemic risks associated with such institutions could only be assumed, not modeled. Critically, the spillover analysis captured only shock propagation through financial links and would miss any purely panic-driven contagion. Finally, there were significant internal and cross-jurisdiction inconsistencies and gaps in countries' submissions.

Once a financial sector's capital ratio falls below the assumed 8 percent threshold, subsequent spillovers depend on the capital shortfall of the affected financial system. The exercise assumed that a financial system would incur losses of 20 percent of its cross-border lending to a borrower banking system if the capital adequacy ratio (CAR) of the borrower falls to the 6–8 percent range. The loss rate increases to 40 percent if its CAR drops to 4–6 percent and to 60 percent if its CAR falls below 4 percent. Since these figures are at the system level, the declines in capital can be thought of as mapping to a smaller or larger number of individual financial institution defaults within the system. For liquidity shocks, the analysis assumes that financial systems with CARs of less than 4 percent would fail to roll over cross-border lending. To raise additional funding to offset the shock, borrowers are assumed to liquidate an equivalent amount of assets at a loss rate of 35 percent. These loss rates were determined based on stress-testing practices in Financial Sector Assessment Programs and expert judgment and are considered severe but plausible shocks.

The risk of regional financial spillovers depends on financial systems' interconnectedness and capital buffers. Financial systems with large debts to multiple countries are more likely to cause spillovers when they experience capital shortfalls. In addition, systems with exposures that are significant relative to capital are more susceptible to spillovers. For banks, the ratio of cross-border lending to the lender's capital, which helps detect vulnerability to solvency (credit) spillovers, and the ratio of cross-border liabilities to borrower's capital, which helps detect susceptibility to liquidity (funding) spillovers, provide a preliminary indication of sources of vulnerability and spillovers in the regional financial system. Figure 10.8 shows such lending and funding concentrations in excess of 15 percent of either the lender's or borrower's capital. By these measures, Barbados and the ECCU appear most susceptible to solvency and liquidity spillovers.[22]

---

[22]The ratios for the ECCU may overstate actual exposures because both domestic and international banks' exposures are included in the numerator while only capital for national banks is included in the denominator.

Figure 10.8. Large Interbank Lending and Funding Concentrations

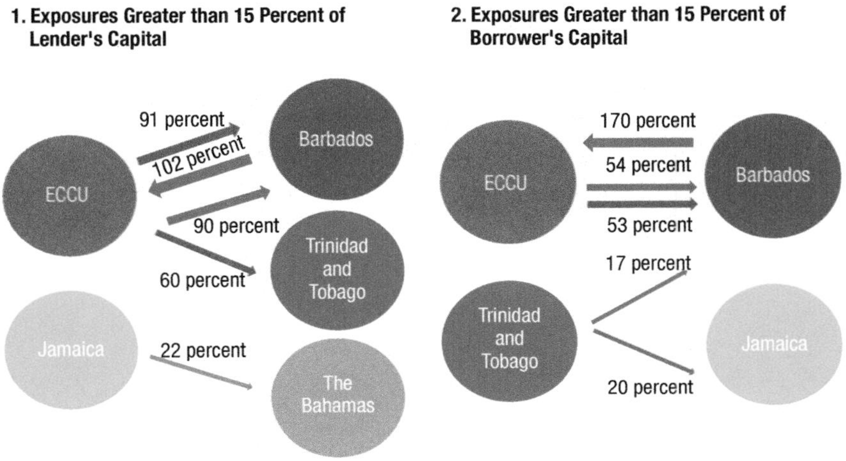
1. Exposures Greater than 15 Percent of Lender's Capital
ECCU
Barbados
Trinidad and Tobago
Jamaica
The Bahamas
91 percent
102 percent
90 percent
60 percent
22 percent
2. Exposures Greater than 15 Percent of Borrower's Capital
ECCU
Barbados
Trinidad and Tobago
Jamaica
170 percent
54 percent
53 percent
17 percent
20 percent

Sources: National authorities; and IMF staff estimates.
Note: Blue arrows indicate deposits, red arrows indicate loans, green arrows indicate equity stakes. Arrows point from lender to borrower. ECCU = Eastern Caribbean Currency Union.

## Results

*Cross-border bank-induced spillovers.* The network simulations confirmed the systemic importance of the banking systems of Barbados, Trinidad and Tobago, and the ECCU within the Caribbean financial system. A systemic banking crisis in Trinidad and Tobago triggers a spillover to the ECCU, which, in turn, triggers a spillover to Barbados (Figure 10.9). Systemic banking crises in the ECCU and Barbados trigger spillovers to each other. The high capital ratio of Trinidad and Tobago's banking system leaves it in a relatively strong position and able to buffer shocks and also mitigates its importance as a channel through which indirect spillovers could take place.

The solvency channel dominates as a spillover channel. Both the ECCU's and Barbados' banking systems are susceptible to solvency spillovers because of their large asset exposures to one another (partly in the form of deposits). Liquidity spillovers affect mainly the ECCU because of its large reliance on Barbados for funding. Isolated solvency and liquidity shocks from Trinidad and Tobago to the ECCU appear insufficient to trigger further rounds of spillovers. However, when such a liquidity shock is combined with a simultaneous solvency shock to the Trinidad and Tobago banking system, the impact on the ECCU's banking system is sufficiently large to cause a further spillover to Barbados.

**Figure 10.9. Direct and Indirect Cross-Border Bank Spillovers**

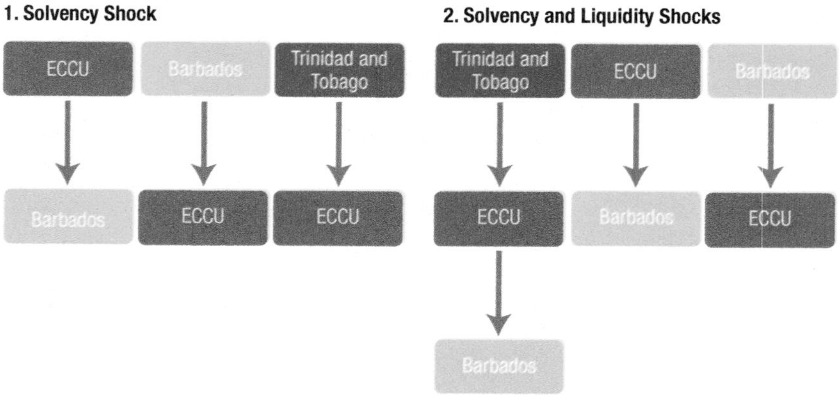

**1. Solvency Shock**

| ECCU | Barbados | Trinidad and Tobago |

↓ ↓ ↓

| Barbados | ECCU | ECCU |

**2. Solvency and Liquidity Shocks**

| Trinidad and Tobago | ECCU | Barbados |

↓ ↓ ↓

| ECCU | Barbados | ECCU |

↓

| Barbados |

Sources: National authorities; and IMF staff estimates.
Note: ECCU = Eastern Caribbean Currency Union.

*Cross-border insurer-induced spillovers.* Network analysis suggested that cross-border vulnerabilities due to balance sheet interconnections among insurers and between banks and insurers were limited, despite the dominance of regional conglomerates in the Caribbean insurance sector, because of the relatively strong reported capital ratios of insurers. For example, although a shock to Jamaica's insurance sector could be expected to propagate to Barbados' insurance sector via Sagicor's presence in both countries, Barbados' insurance sector's reported capital ratio was strong enough to buffer the simulated shock and remain above 8 percent.

*Domestic spillovers between banking and insurance sectors.* As might be expected, given significant connections between banks and insurers within most Caribbean countries, there were several countries in which a systemic banking or insurance crisis would be expected to propagate to the other segment of the domestic financial system. Results of the network analysis suggest that systemic banking crises in Belize and Suriname would cause capital shortfalls of their own insurance sectors. In the other direction, a systemic crisis in Suriname's insurance sector was found to cause a capital shortfall in Suriname's banking system, likely resulting from ownership linkages between a bank and an insurer.

## Economic Shocks

### Methodology

This section simulates a variety of economic shocks to gauge their direct impact on individual Caribbean financial systems as well as the scope for second-round spillovers on other financial sectors through regional financial links. The economic scenarios modeled include shocks to tourism, construction, real estate, households, the energy sector, and sovereigns. The shocks are assumed to be common to all countries in the region since Caribbean economies exhibit co-movement in economic and fiscal performance attributable to, for instance, common exposures to tourism, a narrow set of commodities, or both.

The economic scenarios are modeled in two stages. The first stage simulates the direct impact of each economic sectoral shock (including to sovereigns) on banks, and, given insurance companies' small exposures to other economic sectors, sovereign shocks only to insurers. The economic shocks are mapped into each banking system's loans to that particular sector using varying assumptions for sectoral loan loss rates.[23] The analysis also examines region-wide shocks on banks' total loan portfolios. The second stage assesses potential second-round spillovers to other banking and insurance sectors based on the network analysis methodology described above for direct financial spillovers. Given that the investigation models shocks as common to the whole region, it is, of course, possible for an economic shock to affect more than one sector (for instance, a tourism shock could affect multiple tourism-dependent banking sectors simultaneously), so that all the affected systems then act as a common trigger for the second-round impacts.

This additional element of the analysis provides several advantages. First, it links initial triggers to country-specific sectoral exposures and initial capital buffers. Second, by applying common shocks to the whole region, it can identify Caribbean-wide vulnerabilities. Third, the application of several sectoral shocks simultaneously allows the effects of possible interdependencies among sectors to be captured.

Both single- and multisector economic shocks are modeled. As with the financial shocks modeled above, the modeling of economic shocks implies nothing about the likelihood of such shocks materializing.

*Single-sector shocks.* Shocks to total loans and to the tourism, construction, real estate, household, and energy sectors were considered with loss rates (that is, defaulted loans multiplied by the "loss-given-default" rate) of 2.5 percent and 5 percent of total loans and loss rates of 5, 10, and 15 percent of sectoral loans. The analysis also considers risks from potential sovereign distress, given some Caribbean countries' high public debt and history of debt restructurings. A sharp increase in sovereign distress across the region is assumed, leading to simultaneous and uniform haircuts on Caribbean government debt. Haircuts of various magnitudes (5, 10, 20, and 30 percent of the face value

---

[23]Loss rates were determined based on standard stress-testing practices and expert judgment. For example, losses of 5 percent of total loans would result from defaults on 10 percent of total loans, assuming a loss-given-default of 50 percent. This shock is roughly equivalent to two standard deviations based on the distribution of nonperforming loan ratios across Caribbean banking systems.

of sovereign debt) are applied, and the resulting losses are deducted from banking system capital.[24]

*Multisector shocks.* Some sectors, notably tourism and construction, are strongly correlated. Given Caribbean economies' limited diversification, fiscal performance would also be correlated with key sectors (for example, tourism and commodities). Thus, multi-shock scenarios were modeled to focus on risks from such cross-sectoral correlations. Specifically, simultaneous shocks are applied to (1) tourism and construction, (2) tourism and sovereigns, and (3) a joint shock to tourism, construction, and sovereigns.[25]

## Results

*Domestic impact.* The results of the economic scenario analysis suggest that at moderate levels of stress, the Caribbean banking systems were largely resilient to the economic and sovereign shocks, reflecting their robust capital buffers. Indeed, losses of up to 10 percent of sectoral exposures and 2.5 percent of total credit would not have significantly undermined the capital adequacy of most banking systems in the region (Table 10.1). However, the ECCU was vulnerable to shocks to total loans (loss rates of 2.5 percent and above), sovereign exposures (haircuts of 10 percent and above), real estate lending (loss rate of 5 percent), household lending and joint shocks to tourism and construction (loss rates of 10 percent and above), and tourism, construction and sovereign exposure (loss rate of 5 percent and above) reflecting that its banking system CAR, though higher than the conventional 8 percent threshold, was weaker than that of other Caribbean banking systems (Figures 10.10–10.12).[26]

Broader banking sector fragilities emerged at higher levels of stress. A sovereign haircut of 20 percent would have pushed Barbados, Jamaica, and the ECCU below the 8 percent CAR benchmark. Jamaica's CAR would also have approached 8 percent in the event of a sovereign haircut of 10 percent, if combined with a 10 percent loss on tourism and construction loans. Losses of 15 percent of real estate loans would drive Suriname's CAR slightly below 8 percent.

*Cross-border spillovers.* In the regional economic scenarios, second-round cross-border spillovers occur mainly from the ECCU to Barbados. This spillover pattern prevails because the ECCU emerges as the main trigger of spillovers in

---

[24]The haircuts were determined based on historical experience with debt restructuring in the region.

[25]In the absence of reliable performance data for individual sectors, the cross-sectoral correlation analysis involved judgments about real links across sectors. A better understanding of such economic links in the Caribbean could be a subject for future research.

[26]The analysis used an "adjusted" initial CAR for the ECCU banking system.

## Figure 10.10. Shocks to Total Credit

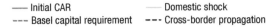

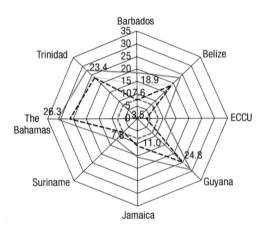

Sources: National authorities; and IMF staff estimates.
Note: Each spoke represents a Caribbean banking system's capital adequacy ratio (CAR), with the CAR increasing as the line moves farther out from the center. The solid blue line indicates initial CAR, the black dotted line is CAR after the domestic shock, and the yellow line represents the cumulative effect of the domestic shock and any inward spillovers. The red dotted line shows the Basel capital threshold. ECCU = Eastern Caribbean Currency Union.

## Figure 10.11. Sovereign Haircuts

—— Initial CAR ——— Domestic shock
--- Basel capital requirement –-– Cross-border propagation

**1. 10 Percent**

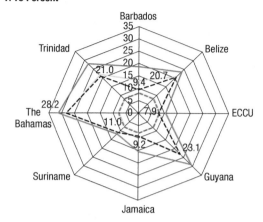

**2. 20 Percent**

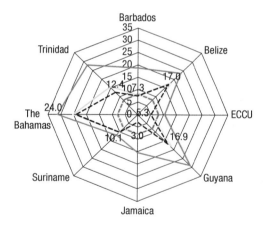

Sources: National authorities; and IMF staff estimates.
Note: Each spoke represents a Caribbean banking system's capital adequacy ratio (CAR), with the CAR increasing as the line moves farther out from the center. The solid blue line indicates initial CAR, the black dotted line is CAR after the domestic shock, and the yellow line represents the cumulative effect of the domestic shock and any inward spillovers. The red dotted line shows the Basel capital threshold. ECCU = Eastern Caribbean Currency Union.

## Figure 10.12. Shocks to Real Estate and Household Loans

—— Initial CAR          —— Domestic shock
--- Basel capital requirement   --- Cross-border propagation

**1. Shock to Real Estate Sector**
**(Loss rate of 10 percent)**

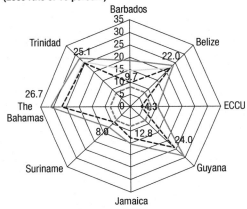

**2. Shock to Household Sector**
**(Loss rate of 10 percent)**

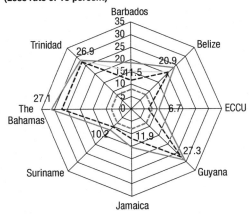

Sources: National authorities; and IMF staff estimates.
Note: Each spoke represents a Caribbean banking system's capital adequacy ratio (CAR), with the CAR increasing as the line moves farther out from the center. The solid blue line indicates initial CAR, the black dotted line is CAR after the domestic shock, and the yellow line represents the cumulative effect of the domestic shock and any inward spillovers. The red dotted line shows the Basel capital threshold.
ECCU = Eastern Caribbean Currency Union.

**Figure 10.13. Single-Sector Shocks: Impact on Insurance Sector CAR**
*(Domestic impact)*

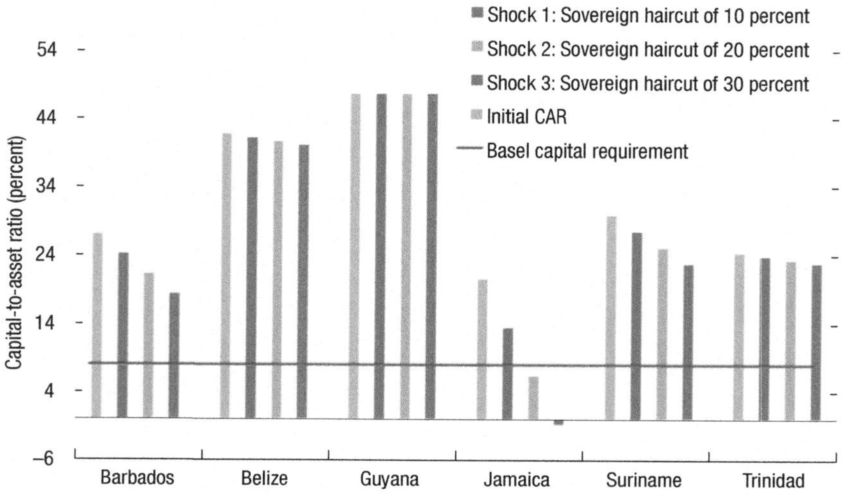

Sources: National authorities; and IMF staff estimates.
Note: CAR = capital adequacy ratio.

most economic scenarios given its relatively lower capital buffers, and because of its large interconnections with Barbados.[27,28]

## Sovereign Risk Scenarios for Insurers

The results of the sovereign scenario analysis for insurers indicate that Caribbean insurance sectors were resilient overall to large sovereign haircuts. Most Caribbean insurance sectors can withstand sovereign haircuts of 20 to 30 percent and remain above the 8 percent CAR threshold (Figure 10.13). Nevertheless, Jamaican insurers would have fallen below this benchmark after a sovereign haircut of 20 percent. A shock to Jamaica's insurance sector could spill over to Barbados' insurance sector through Sagicor's presence in both Barbados and Jamaica.

---

[27]About two-thirds of the cross-border exposures between the ECCU and Barbados were in the form of deposits, which have seniority in bank liquidations and hence a lower risk profile.

[28]It is also worth noting that we abstracted from feedback effects on the trigger country and among trigger countries in multiple-shock scenarios, focusing only on spillovers to target countries. For example, if the initial shock affected Barbados, Jamaica, and the ECCU, we measured only spillovers to other countries.

# PRIORITIES FOR FINANCIAL SECTOR REGULATION AND SUPERVISION IN THE CARIBBEAN

Strong ex ante regulation and supervision of the financial sector, combined with adequate financial safety nets and crisis management frameworks, are needed to safeguard stability of the Caribbean financial system. Against the backdrop of the region's integrated financial system with regionally active financial conglomerates and significant presence of foreign banks, national efforts need to be complemented with regional and global cooperation on financial sector oversight.

The Caribbean has traditionally followed a decentralized institutional structure for financial sector oversight, with different supervisors for each segment of the financial system, but the region is increasingly moving toward an integrated structure to facilitate and strengthen oversight. Most countries have moved to either a single- or dual-supervisory approach, which, in the latter case, means having distinct bank and nonbank supervisors (Table 10.2). Given the importance of financial conglomerates in the regional financial system, centralized financial sector oversight can enhance financial stability by helping limit regulatory arbitrage (by reducing regulatory gaps and the coordination problems among multiple agencies) and helping optimize scarce supervisory resources in the region's resource-constrained economies.

## Cross-Supervisor Cooperation and Coordination

Cross-supervisor coordination, both within and across countries, is at a nascent stage in the region and could be supported through financial stability committees. Although jurisdictions around the world are increasingly creating financial stability committees to assess financial stability risks and coordinate policy responses, such committees are in place in only a limited number of Caribbean countries, and their mandates are largely restricted to information exchange (Table 10.3).[29] Expanding coordination across financial supervisors within countries is particularly important for effective oversight in the Caribbean context, given that oversight remains the responsibility of more than one agency in most countries. Coordination could be expanded to include the measurement of systemic risk and formulation of crisis prevention policies, including the conduct of macroprudential policies. Such coordination could help strengthen national policy responses to systemic risks and, by allocating a crisis resolution role to such committees, help ensure a well-coordinated and timely response to financial risks, particularly those emanating from the region's financial conglomerates (IMF 2011a).[30] Each

---

[29]Exceptions are the Financial Regulatory Council in Jamaica and the newly established Financial Oversight Management Committee in Barbados, which have mandates for crisis prevention and management in addition to information exchange. In Belize and Suriname, the centralization of financial sector supervision within each country's respective central bank obviates the need to put in place formal financial sector oversight committees.

[30]The authorities' intentions in The Bahamas and Trinidad and Tobago to put in place National Crisis Management Groups would be a positive step forward in this regard.

Table 10.2. Financial Sector Supervision in the Caribbean

| Financial Supervisor | Banks | Credit Unions | Insurance Companies | Other Nonbank Financial Institutions |
|---|---|---|---|---|
| Barbados | Central Bank of Barbados | Financial Services Commission (FSC) | FSC | FSC |
| Belize | Central Bank of Belize (CBB) | CBB | CBB | CBB |
| Eastern Caribbean Currency Union[1] | Eastern Caribbean Central Bank (ECCB) | n.a. | n.a. | n.a. |
| Antigua and Barbuda | ECCB | Financial Services Regulatory Commission (FSRC) | FSRC | FSRC |
| Dominica | ECCB | Financial Services Unit (FSU) of Ministry of Finance | FSU | FSU |
| Grenada | ECCB | Grenada Authority for the Regulation of Financial Institutions (GARFIN) | GARFIN | GARFIN |
| St. Kitts and Nevis | ECCB | Financial Services Regulatory Commission (FSRC) | FSRC | FSRC |
| St. Lucia | ECCB | Financial Services Regulatory Authority (FSRA) | FSRA | FSRA |
| St. Vincent and the Grenadines | ECCB | Financial Services Authority (FSA) | FSA | FSA |
| Guyana | Bank of Guyana (BG) | Ministry of Labor | BG | BG |
| Haiti | Central Bank of Haiti (Banque de la Republique d'Haiti - BRH) | BRH | Ministry of Economy and Finance | Unregulated |
| Jamaica | Bank of Jamaica (BOJ) | Department of Cooperatives and Friendly Societies of Ministry of Industry, Investment and Commerce | Financial Services Commission (FSC) | FSC |
| Suriname | Central Bank of Suriname (CBvS) | CBvS | CBvS | CBvS |
| The Bahamas | Central Bank of The Bahamas (CBoB) | CBoB | Insurance Commission of The Bahamas (ICB) | Securities Commission of The Bahamas (SCB) |
| Trinidad and Tobago | Central Bank of Trinidad and Tobago (CBTT) | Cooperative Development Division of Ministry of Labour and Small and Micro Enterprise Development | CBTT | Securities Exchange Commission and CBTT |

Source: National authorities.

Note: n.a. = not applicable.

[1] Offshore and international banks within the Eastern Caribbean Currency Union are managed by their respective national authorities rather than by the Eastern Caribbean Central Bank.

## Table 10.3. Caribbean Domestic Financial Oversight Committees

| Country | Financial Sector Oversight Committee | Mandate | Established | Memorandum of Understanding | Membership |
|---|---|---|---|---|---|
| **Barbados** | Financial Oversight and Management Committee | To manage the production of the annual *Financial Stability Report*, to collaborate in the monitoring of the financial system, and to respond to financial crises | 2013 | Yes | Central Bank of Barbados, FSC |
| **Eastern Caribbean Currency Union** | Regional Oversight Committee | Forum for information exchange, to coordinate harmonization of financial sector regulation and supervision, and to coordinate responses to financial stability risks | 2009 (no longer active) | No | Eastern Caribbean Central Bank, Eastern Caribbean Securities Regulatory Commission, national regulatory agencies of all ECCU members |
| **Jamaica** | Financial Regulatory Council | To develop policies and strategies to facilitate greater coordination and increase information sharing between financial agencies, with a particular focus on crisis management | 2001 | Yes | Bank of Jamaica (BOJ), FSC, Jamaica Deposit Insurance Corporation (JDIC), Ministry of Finance and Public Service (MOFP) |
| | Financial System Stability Committee | To monitor trends in the financial system and in the risk taking of individual institutions and sectors with regard to systemic risk | 2016 | Yes | BOJ, FSC, JDIC, MOFP |
| **The Bahamas** | Group of Financial Services Regulators | To facilitate information sharing and cooperation | 2002 | Yes | Central Bank of The Bahamas (CBoB), Insurance Commission of The Bahamas (ICB), Securities Commission of The Bahamas (SCB), Inspector of Financial and Corporate Services |
| | National Crisis Management Group | | 2014 | No | CBoB, ICB, SCB |
| **Trinidad and Tobago** | National Crisis Management Group (proposed) | | To be determined | No | Central Bank of Trinidad and Tobago, Ministry of Finance, Deposit Insurance Corporation, Trinidad and Tobago Securities and Exchange Commission |

Source: National authorities.
Note: ECCU = Eastern Caribbean Currency Union; FSC = Financial Services Commission.

supervisor's role in crisis resolution should be clearly delineated and agreed to in advance, potentially through national crisis management plans formulated by the financial stability committees. See Box 10.3 for a summary of policy recommendations.

Financial stability committees should be supported with appropriate institutional and legal arrangements. Membership of the few existing such committees in the Caribbean is broadly appropriate, covering all major stakeholders, including central banks, financial supervisors, ministries of finance, and in some instances, deposit insurers.[31] However, it may be helpful to identify a lead institution responsible for financial stability, as Jamaica has done with the Bank of Jamaica. The appropriate lead institution may differ across countries (Nier and others 2011), but in practice, most countries allocate this responsibility to either the central bank, given its typical expertise in risk assessment and incentives to mitigate systemic risk, or the ministry of finance, given its fiscal responsibilities and broader legal powers. With supervision still decentralized in most Caribbean countries, explicitly vesting a lead authority with the mandate and power to conduct macroprudential policy in response to financial stability risks may also facilitate timely and effective responses to emerging risks. Information exchange and coordination among committee members could also be institutionalized through memoranda of understanding (MOUs) as exist in some Caribbean countries. MOU could include mechanisms for cooperation in the event of a crisis, which may help prevent ex ante concerns about the legality of supervisory powers and, in the event of financial distress, facilitate a faster supervisory response (Nier and others 2011).

A regional financial sector oversight committee could complement financial sector oversight committees at the individual-country level. Such cooperation could help strengthen the assessment of financial stability risks at the regional level and, in the event of a systemic risk event such as the CL Financial crisis of 2009, facilitate a coordinated regional response. Such cooperation currently takes place under a Regional Financial Stability Coordination Council (RFSCC), whose role could be transformed into that of a regional financial stability committee. The RFSCC's mandate, currently restricted to information exchange, would need to be clarified, formalized, and broadened to include cooperation on systemic risk oversight and crisis management. To support the transition, the existing multilateral MOU on the exchange of information, cooperation, and consultation could be amended to formally establish the RFSCC's expanded role and principles for supervisory cooperation.[32]

---

[31]Financial sector oversight committees should also be given the power to request and collect information directly from both financial and nonfinancial firms to assess the contribution to systemic risk of firms that may not otherwise be subject to supervision and regulation (IMF 2011a).

[32]The MOU was signed in 2011. Signatories include the Central Bank of Aruba, the Central Bank of The Bahamas, the Central Bank of Barbados, the Bank of Guyana, the Banque de la Republique d'Haiti, the Bank of Jamaica, the Central Bank of Trinidad and Tobago, and the Financial Services Commission of the Turks and Caicos Islands.

## Box 10.3. Summary of Policy Recommendations

### Financial Sector Supervision and Regulation

#### *Cross-Supervisor Cooperation and Coordination*

- Introduce national and regional financial sector oversight committees with broad mandates that include risk assessment, crisis prevention, and crisis resolution
- Institutionalize cross-supervisor information exchange and coordination through formal memoranda of understanding
- Enhance cooperation and collaboration with home supervisors of large foreign banks

### *Financial Institutions*

#### *Microprudential*

- Strengthen supervisory capacity and enhance enforcement
- Finalize adoption of Basel II and harmonize regional prudential standards
- Formalize risk-based supervisory frameworks and harmonize risk assessment frameworks
- Introduce consolidated supervision to mitigate cross-border risks
- Expand supervisory colleges to cover all regional financial institutions

#### *Macroprudential*

- Strengthen macroprudential analysis and systemic risk assessment
- Integrate systemic risk assessment into regulatory and supervisory frameworks
- Identify systemic financial institutions and agree to an enhanced supervisory approach

### *Capital Markets*

- Improve data collection and adopt standard global risk measurements
- Harmonize capital market regulation in line with global standards
- Promote capital market integration
- Identify systemic nonbank non-insurer financial institutions
- Improve understanding of links between nonbank non-insurers and other institutions

### Financial Safety Nets

- Clarify lender of last resort facilities and develop emergency liquidity assistance frameworks
- Introduce deposit insurance in countries where such insurance does not exist and address funding gaps of existing deposit insurers; consider extending deposit insurance to credit unions

### Crisis Management

- Coordinate financial crisis management through national financial sector oversight committees and a regional financial sector oversight committee
- Develop national financial crisis management preparedness and management plans and finalize the regional financial crisis management plan
- Introduce requirement for regionally systemic financial institutions to develop systemic risk management plans
- Develop institution-specific cross-border cooperation agreements and recovery and resolution plans for all regionally systemic financial institutions

Correspondingly, membership of the RFSCC could be expanded to include all lead financial sector supervisors (bank and nonbank) from Caribbean countries, who would then be responsible for coordination with country-level oversight committees.[33] Because some large financial conglomerates in the region operate across segments of the financial sector, broader participation in the MOU and the RFSCC, including by both bank and nonbank supervisors, would help facilitate the assessment of systemic risks originating from these complex institutions and eliminate information asymmetries that could lead to regulatory arbitrage.

Canadian-owned financial institutions have a large presence in the region, making cooperation and collaboration with their home supervisors essential for effective supervision. Caribbean supervisors have made increasing efforts to strengthen cooperation and collaboration with the Office of Superintendent of Financial Institutions, the Canadian banking regulator. The region's host countries for Canadian banks are generally represented on supervisory colleges for the large Canadian banks operating in their jurisdictions, and several countries in the region have signed MOUs with the Office of Superintendent of Financial Institutions. Within the region, a College of Regulators was also established in 2010 for insurers, and supervisory colleges exist for the region's systemic insurers. Nevertheless, scope remains for further improvement, including by strengthening the fluidity of information exchange between the Caribbean host countries and home supervisory agencies, and by establishing a clear legal framework for consolidated supervision of cross-border banking groups and for crisis management and resolution.

## Financial Institutions

Strengthened regulatory and supervisory frameworks for financial institutions and capital markets are also necessary for strengthening financial stability in the region. For banks, a regional effort is underway to strengthen traditional microprudential supervision of individual financial institutions, founded on the expected transition to Basel II by the end of 2017 and the ongoing transition to risk-based supervision.[34] For insurers, progress has been more limited despite the lessons from the collapse of CL Financial in 2009. Critical gaps in the overall legal, regulatory, and supervisory structure for the sector contributed to CL Financial's demise, particularly in Trinidad and Tobago where it was based. The regulatory framework did not formally allow the supervisor to oversee cross-market and cross-border activities and underestimated the risks of

---

[33]Signatories to the MOU are primarily bank regulators, and not all Caribbean countries are signatories. The region is jointly developing common regional supervisory guidelines under Basel II.

[34]The region is jointly developing common regional supervisory guidelines under Basel II. Harmonization of prudential standards, to the extent that it is not accomplished by the ongoing transition to Basel II, could also facilitate supervisory assessments of banks with significant cross-border links.

the insurance business. Specifically, there was no consolidated supervision of insurance entities under common ownership and no powers to exchange information with other regulators. Moreover, investment rules affecting the geographical and sectoral allocation of portfolio assets were not risk based (IMF 2006). These gaps remain largely unaddressed pending finalization of new insurance legislation in Trinidad and Tobago. More generally, throughout the region, the absence of investment limits for statutory funds may lead to concentrations in risky investments and hamper the statutory funds' primary role as cushions against losses in the event of economic or financial downturns. Existing efforts to strengthen regulation and supervision of specific segments of the Caribbean financial system also need to be complemented with a strengthening of consolidated supervision, or group-wide supervision (including of nonbank and nonfinancial subsidiaries), particularly in light of the importance of financial conglomerates.[35] Each country should formalize consolidated supervisory frameworks. A regional framework could then be established under a regional financial stability council to strengthen supervision of financial conglomerates.[36]

Stronger microprudential oversight needs to be complemented by enhanced macroprudential or systemic oversight. As a result of the important macro-financial links revealed by the global financial crisis, the Caribbean has begun to establish macroprudential oversight. Most countries have begun to integrate evaluations of systemic risk into their regulatory and supervisory frameworks, though cross-supervisor collaboration on macroprudential policy remains at the early stages. Several countries in the region have been publishing country-specific financial stability reports, and the region jointly published its first regional financial stability report in 2016. The joint report contains as a significant element an assessment of macroprudential risk (Caribbean Centre for Money and Finance 2016).[37]

Building on these efforts to strengthen systemic risk assessment, the region should start to develop macroprudential policy frameworks. As it stands, the region has yet to explore the potential of macroprudential policy tools to mitigate systemic risks to financial stability.[38] These tools can be useful for targeting

---

[35]Only Barbados has published formalized consolidated supervision guidelines for banks, and Jamaica has developed a framework for nonbank consolidated supervision.

[36]Consolidation frameworks should include national and regional ownership mappings and consolidated balance sheets of significant financial conglomerates (including those that also contain nonfinancial corporations).

[37]See Lim and others (2017) for an assessment of financial stability reports in Latin America and the Caribbean.

[38]For instance, no country in the region has calibrated capital and liquidity requirements according to macroprudential considerations, as recommended by Basel III. Macroprudential objectives can be achieved by recalibrating microprudential requirements, such as targeting higher loan-loss provisioning requirements and risk weights for banks identified as systemically important. These requirements could also be countercyclical to mitigate the buildup of macroprudential risks (IMF 2013).

overall, sectoral, liquidity, or structural (for example, from interconnectedness) risks to financial stability. As part of these efforts, the region should consider identifying regionally systemically important financial institutions and agreeing to an enhanced supervisory approach for these institutions.

## Capital Markets

Significant work also needs to be done to improve the regulatory framework for Caribbean capital markets. Caribbean capital markets remain relatively undeveloped. Nevertheless, it is important to address regulatory weaknesses that persist in data collection and in the adoption of standard risk measurements, in part resulting from a lack of sufficient resources dedicated to effective supervision. If endowed with adequate resources, regulators could improve data coverage and promote information sharing and cooperation with other regional regulators. Moreover, nonbank non-insurance systemic institutions among finance companies, intermediaries (broker-dealers), investment funds, and asset managers need to be identified and regulated, following the principles of investor protection, fairness, efficiency, and transparency of capital markets and the reduction of systemic risk.

## Financial Safety Nets

Financial safety nets are an important complement to strong regulation and supervision for preserving financial stability. In the event of systemic shocks to financial stability, official financial assistance to financial institutions could be necessary for stemming contagion. Emergency liquidity assistance (ELA) is the primary means for providing official financial assistance; however, these facilities remain relatively underdeveloped in the Caribbean, potentially increasing the likelihood of regional spillovers from financial shocks. Although central banks in the region generally have the power to provide liquidity to the banking system through the discount window, explicit ELA facilities, which can play an important complementary role to lending through the discount window in times of financial stress, do not exist in most countries, including, most notably, countries with significant regionally systemic banking sectors such as Barbados and Trinidad and Tobago.[39,40] In part, this hole in the region's financial safety net reflects the limited historical need for such facilities in the region, given that most countries have not faced important liquidity crises or episodes of financial stress

---

[39]Jamaica is a key exception. The Bank of Jamaica implemented an Enhanced Liquidity Management Framework in 2013.

[40]The Central Bank of Trinidad and Tobago and the Central Bank of The Bahamas do have broad authority to extend emergency liquidity for systemically important financial institutions; however, explicit ELA frameworks and associated operational modalities are not in place.

in recent history.[41] Nevertheless, putting in place explicit ELA facilities should be a key priority for the region as it seeks to strengthen crisis preparedness and reform its crisis management framework.[42]

Deposit insurance is also a vital aspect of the financial safety net but is not yet prevalent in the Caribbean. Only four Caribbean countries have formal deposit insurance systems in place: The Bahamas, Barbados, Jamaica, and Trinidad and Tobago. The absence of deposit insurance throughout much of the region is a critical gap in the financial safety net that, if addressed, could strengthen the regional crisis management framework. There is also a need to strengthen the funding of existing deposit insurance schemes, most of which remain underfunded relative to both their target funding levels and international norms, potentially restricting their ability to fulfill their financial stability mandate.[43]

## Crisis Management in the Caribbean

The Caribbean's crisis preparedness depends on putting in place an ex ante crisis management framework. The region's existing framework for crisis management is primarily based on national resolution regimes and associated funding modalities that are specific to the different segments of the financial system and individual countries, rather than an integrated national or regional approach to crisis management. Putting in place an integrated framework could begin at the national level, with the national financial stability committees (once established) coordinating the development of national crisis management plans. At the regional level, efforts to finalize a regional financial crisis management plan, which commenced following the collapse of CL Financial, could be reinvigorated under the auspices of a regional financial stability committee (perhaps a strengthened RFSCC). Finally, to complement the crisis management plans, given the presence of some large financial institutions with significant cross-border operations in the region, Caribbean regulators should require regionally systemic financial institutions to develop systemic risk management plans, and possibly "living wills," that would specify how they would be resolved in a crisis.

---

[41]Important exceptions are the financial crisis experienced in Jamaica in the 1990s and, more recently, the failure of the two regional insurance companies CLICO and BAICO. In the case of CLICO and BAICO, solvency support rather than liquidity support was provided. The Central Bank of Trinidad and Tobago has not provided liquidity support in more than two decades.

[42]Consistent with international best practice, ELA should be provided only to solvent but temporarily illiquid financial institutions, in exchange for sound collateral discounted to take account of counterparty and market risks at penalizing interest rates.

[43]For example, the balance of the funds of Barbados Deposit Insurance Corporation, Jamaica Deposit Insurance Corporation, and The Bahamas Deposit Insurance Corporation as a share of estimated insured deposits stood at 2.6, 4.8, and 0.7 percent as of 2015. Underfunding can be partly attributed to low premiums relative to international norms.

## Annex 10.1. Financial Sector Asset Structure

| | ECU | Haiti | The Bahamas | Barbados | Belize | Trinidad and Tobago | Guyana | Jamaica | Suriname | Caribbean Total |
|---|---|---|---|---|---|---|---|---|---|---|
| | | | | | Millions of U.S. Dollars | | | | | |
| Banks | 10,450.2 | 4,185.3 | 13,220 | 6,610 | 1,613.8 | 20,222 | 2,262.0 | 9,450.0 | 2,363.5 | 70,376.7 |
| Domestic banks | 4,339.4 | 4,002.4 | 6,739 | 0 | 730.3 | 17,088.0 | 1,089.6 | 5,363.0 | 1,976.6 | 41,328.3 |
| Foreign banks | 6,110.7 | 182.9 | 6,481 | 6,610 | 883.5 | 3,134.0 | 1,172.4 | 4,087.0 | 386.8 | 29,048.4 |
| Credit Unions | 1,135.6 | 95.8 | 370.6 | 999.5 | 451.7 | 1,752.7 | 27.7 | 720.2 | 8.4 | 5,562.1 |
| Insurance Companies | 1,153.1 | ... | 1,800 | 1,621.5 | 129.0 | 6,479.0 | 263.0 | 2,900.5 | 298.9 | 14,644.9 |
| Securities Firms | 1,080.5 | ... | ... | 924.5 | 0.0 | 46.2 | 91.9 | 4,052.1 | 0.0 | 6,195.1 |
| Total Financial Sector | 13,819.3 | 4,281.0 | 15,390.6 | 10,155.5 | 2,194.5 | 28,499.9 | 2,644.5 | 17,122.7 | 2,670.8 | 96,778.9 |
| Share of Total (percent) | 14.3 | 4.4 | 15.9 | 10.5 | 2.3 | 29.4 | 2.7 | 17.7 | 2.8 | ... |
| | | | | | Percent of GDP | | | | | |
| Banks | 162.9 | 50.7 | 148 | 144.1 | 92.6 | 96.5 | 65.8 | 67.7 | 66.2 | ... |
| Domestic banks | 67.6 | 48.5 | 75.4 | 0.0 | 41.9 | 81.5 | 31.7 | 38.4 | 55.4 | ... |
| Foreign banks | 95.3 | 2.2 | 72.5 | 144.1 | 50.7 | 14.9 | 34.1 | 29.3 | 10.8 | ... |
| Credit Unions | 17.7 | 1.2 | 4.1 | 21.8 | 25.9 | 8.4 | 0.8 | 5.2 | 0.2 | ... |
| Insurance Companies | 18.0 | ... | 20.1 | 35.3 | 7.4 | 30.9 | 7.7 | 20.8 | 8.4 | ... |
| Securities Firms | 16.8 | ... | ... | 20.2 | 0.0 | 0.2 | 2.7 | 29.0 | 0.0 | ... |
| Total Financial Sector | 215.4 | 51.8 | 172.2 | 221.4 | 125.9 | 135.9 | 76.9 | 122.7 | 74.8 | ... |
| | | | | | Percent of Financial Sector Assets | | | | | |
| Banks | 75.6 | 97.8 | 85.9 | 65.1 | 73.5 | 71.0 | 85.5 | 55.2 | 88.5 | ... |
| Domestic banks | 31.4 | 93.5 | 43.8 | 0.0 | 33.3 | 60.0 | 41.2 | 31.3 | 74.0 | ... |
| Foreign banks | 44.2 | 4.3 | 42.1 | 65.1 | 40.3 | 11.0 | 44.3 | 23.9 | 14.5 | ... |
| Credit Unions | 8.2 | 2.2 | 2.4 | 9.8 | 20.6 | 6.1 | 1.0 | 4.2 | 0.3 | ... |
| Insurance Companies | 8.3 | ... | 11.7 | 16.0 | 5.9 | 22.7 | 9.9 | 16.9 | 11.2 | ... |
| Securities Firms | 7.8 | ... | ... | 9.1 | 0.0 | 0.2 | 3.5 | 23.7 | 0.0 | ... |
| Total Financial Sector | 100.0 | 100.0 | 100.0 | 100.0 | 100.0 | 100.0 | 100.0 | 100.0 | 100.0 | ... |
| | | | | | Number of Institutions | | | | | |
| Banks | 34 | 9 | 8 | 6 | 5 | 8 | 6 | 6 | 9 | 91 |
| Domestic banks | 11 | 7 | 4 | 0 | 3 | 3 | 3 | 2 | 8 | 41 |
| Foreign banks | 23 | 2 | 4 | 6 | 2 | 5 | 3 | 4 | 1 | 50 |
| Credit Unions | 49 | 56 | 8 | 34 | 12 | 126 | 28 | 34 | 24 | 371 |
| Insurance Companies | 121 | 12 | 20 | 21 | 14 | 31 | 16 | 17 | 13 | 265 |
| Securities Firms | 3 | 2 | 15 | 35 | 0 | 45 | 2 | 32 | 0 | 134 |
| Total Financial Sector | 207 | 79 | 51 | 96 | 31 | 210 | 52 | 89 | 46 | 861 |

Sources: Bankscope; Caribbean Confederation of Credit Unions; Caribbean Financial Action Task Force; country authorities; and IMF staff estimates.

Note: ECCU = Eastern Caribbean Currency Union. Table reflects latest available data. Domestic and foreign banks are classified by ownership. Offshore activity is excluded. The Bahamian securities firms' assets were unavailable and were therefore excluded.

# REFERENCES

Caribbean Centre for Money and Finance. 2016. *Caribbean Regional Financial Stability Report 2015*. St. Augustine, Trinidad and Tobago: Caribbean Centre for Money and Finance, University of the West Indies.

Claessens, S., G. Dell'Ariccia, D. Igan, and L. Laeven. 2010. "Lessons and Policy Implications from the Global Financial Crisis." IMF Working Paper 10/44, International Monetary Fund, Washington, DC.

Espinosa-Vega, M., and J. Sole. 2010. "Cross-Border Financial Surveillance: A Network Perspective." IMF Working Paper 10/105, International Monetary Fund, Washington, DC.

Fruchterman, T., and E. Reingold. 1991. "Graph Drawing by Force-Directed Placement." *Software: Practice and Experience* 21 (11): 1129–64.

International Monetary Fund (IMF). 2006. "Trinidad and Tobago: Financial System Stability Assessment, including Reports on the Observance of Standards and Codes on the Following Topics, Banking Supervision, and Payment Systems." IMF Country Report 06/29, Washington, DC.

————. 2011a. "Macroprudential Policy: An Organizing Framework." Washington, DC.

————. 2011b. "Trinidad and Tobago: 2010 Article IV Consultation—Staff Report, Supplement, Staff Statement, Public Information Notice on the Executive Board Discussion, and Statement by the Executive Director for Trinidad and Tobago." IMF Country Report 11/73, Washington, DC.

————. 2013. "Key Aspects of Macroprudential Policy." Washington, DC.

Kaminsky, G., and C. Reinhart. 2000. "On Crises, Contagion and Confusion." *Journal of International Economics* 51 (1): 145–68.

Lim, C. H., A. Klemm, S. Ogawa, M. Pani, and C. Visconti. 2017. "Financial Stability Reports in Latin America and the Caribbean." IMF Working Paper 17/73, International Monetary Fund, Washington, DC.

Nier, E., J. Osiński, L. Jácome, and P. Madrid. 2011. "Institutional Models for Macroprudential Policy." IMF Staff Discussion Note 11/18, International Monetary Fund, Washington, DC.

# CHAPTER 11

# Problem Loans in the Caribbean: Determinants, Impact, and Strategies for Resolution

Kimberly Beaton, Thomas Dowling, Dmitriy Kovtun,
Franz Loyola, Alla Myrvoda, Joel Chiedu Okwuokei,
İnci Ötker, and Jarkko Turunen

## INTRODUCTION

The Caribbean region weathered the global financial crisis relatively well, but the quality of bank assets gradually deteriorated during the subsequent economic recession, leaving many countries with elevated levels of problem loans. Notwithstanding significant heterogeneity across the region, the share of nonperforming loans (NPLs) in total loans, which was relatively low before the global financial crisis, rose to more than 10 percent in 2016 across several Caribbean countries, peaking around 15 percent for many countries over the period 2007–16 (Figures 11.1 and 11.2).[1] The increase in NPLs was more significant in tourism-dependent countries compared with commodity exporters. NPL ratios in many countries have been slow to decline from their elevated levels owing to structural and institutional impediments to resolution, as well

---

This chapter is a condensed version of a forthcoming IMF Working Paper (Beaton and others, forthcoming). It has benefited greatly from the contributions of Shelton Nicholls and from valuable comments and suggestions by Krishna Srinivasan, Dermot Monaghan, Diarmuid Murphy, and the authorities of The Bahamas, the ECCB, and Jamaica. The authors are grateful to the banks and country authorities who participated in this project through responses to the surveys on impediments to NPL resolution, as well as provision of bank-by-bank and country-level data for the empirical analyses.

[1]The analysis in this chapter measures asset quality by the NPL ratio—a commonly used financial soundness indicator in cross-country comparisons, notwithstanding its well-known shortcomings. These shortcomings include (1) lack of uniformity in national definitions, (2) differences in treatment of restructured loans, and (3) its backward-looking nature. These caveats have prompted initiatives for further harmonization of definitions (for example, see Bank for International Settlements 2016).

**Figure 11.1. NPLs by Country**
*(Percent of total loans)*

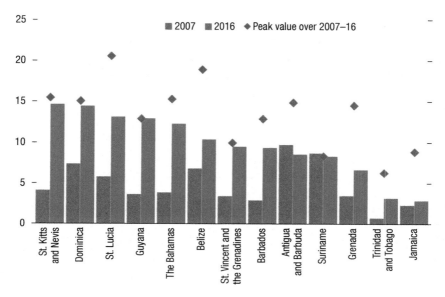

Sources: Country authorities; World Bank, *World Development Indicators*; and IMF staff estimates and calculations.
Note: NPL = nonperforming loan. The latest available data for Suriname are for 2015.

as subdued or declining loan growth and sluggish economic activity, while in a number of countries, NPL ratios have started to fall from their peaks, owing to increased efforts undertaken by country authorities and banks to reduce impaired assets.

The persistently high level of NPLs constrains credit and economic activity in the region and increases banks' vulnerability to shocks. High NPLs have a negative impact on bank profitability, given that they require banks to raise provisioning and do not usually generate income (Aiyar and others 2015). Because Caribbean financial systems are dominated by banks, lack well-developed capital markets, and include a relatively small nonbank financial sector, persistent NPLs constrain the supply of credit to the private sector and hinder economic activity. High NPLs also increase banks' vulnerability to shocks by reducing their profitability, tying up their capital, and raising funding costs. As such, banks with high NPLs present a potential risk to financial stability in the region.

This chapter analyzes the determinants and consequences of NPLs in the Caribbean, explores possible obstacles to their resolution, and suggests a strategy to move forward. It first takes stock of the extent of the NPL problem in the

## Figure 11.2. NPLs and Real GDP Growth

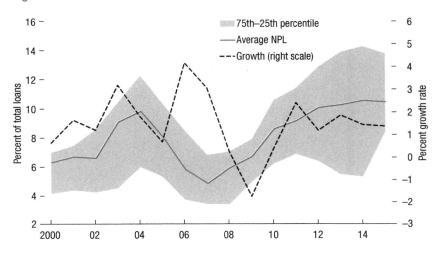

Sources: Country authorities; World Bank, *World Development Indicators*; and IMF staff estimates and calculations.
Note: NPL = nonperforming loan.

region and analyzes its characteristics and evolution. It then examines the determinants of NPLs and their importance as a driver of macro-financial feedback loops. Finally, it explores the main impediments to the resolution of NPLs in the region to draw policy implications for addressing the Caribbean NPL problem. To address these objectives, the paper uses three complementary approaches.

First, a panel vector autoregression (VAR) analysis uses country-level data to examine macro-financial links between NPLs, credit growth, and economic activity in the Caribbean economies. Empirical evidence confirms strong macro-financial links, with deteriorating asset quality lowering private credit growth and spilling over into the broader economy by depressing economic activity and resulting in higher unemployment. An improved macroeconomic environment, however, could enhance borrowers' debt-service capacity and, other things being equal, result in lower NPLs.[2]

Second, dynamic panel regressions analyze the determinants of NPLs using both country data and detailed bank-level data. The results suggest that deteriorating asset quality can be attributed to both macroeconomic and bank-specific

---

[2]These results are broadly consistent with those in Beaton, Myrvoda, and Thompson (2016) for the ECCU, Tintchev (forthcoming) for commodity-exporting Caribbean countries, Jordan and Tucker (2013) for The Bahamas, and similar studies for other regions (see, for example, Espinoza and Prasad 2010; Beck, Jakubík, and Piloiu 2013; Klein 2013; Nkusu 2011).

factors. More specifically, NPLs are affected by the business cycle—low economic growth, including in advanced economies, leads to more problem loans, particularly in tourism-dependent economies. After controlling for endogeneity between NPLs and bank fundamentals, results from similar regressions with a novel bank-level data set also suggest that banks with weaker fundamentals (lower profitability, capital adequacy, and efficiency) also tend to suffer from weaker asset quality.

Third, a survey of regional authorities and commercial banks explores obstacles to NPL resolution in the Caribbean. Consistent with the empirical evidence, survey responses highlight the importance of low growth and high unemployment, as well as weaknesses in regional real estate markets, as determinants of high and persistent NPLs. In addition, the results point to interrelated and mutually reinforcing structural obstacles to NPL resolution. Specifically, the results suggest that the lack of markets for distressed assets, gaps in information systems, and deficiencies in the legal system and insolvency and debt-enforcement regimes are key obstacles to NPL resolution.

The analysis suggests that problem loans should be tackled on multiple fronts. In addition to pursuing policies aimed at securing strong and sustainable growth, as well as micro- and macroprudential policies to limit excessive risk taking during loan origination, the authorities should develop targeted strategies for addressing structural obstacles to the resolution of NPLs. Policies should aim to address information gaps and eliminate impediments to information sharing to facilitate valuation of collateral and development of markets for distressed assets; address deficiencies in insolvency and debt-enforcement frameworks to accelerate and maximize recovery, including through strengthening judicial systems; and establish conditions for nonbanks specialized in servicing problem loans to facilitate collection and disposal of distressed assets. Requiring provisioning independent of collateral values could ensure swift write-off. Consideration could also be given to establishing a pan-Caribbean market for problem loans that would be open to external investors.

## TAKING STOCK: HOW SERIOUS IS THE PROBLEM?

NPLs have risen sharply across the Caribbean following the global financial crisis. Since the crisis, banking systems in many Caribbean countries have been plagued by high ratios of NPLs, which, except in Jamaica and Trinidad and Tobago, are well above prudential guidelines. The average NPL ratio across the Caribbean is also high compared with most other regions in the world. Country-level data for the past 20 years point to a significant deterioration of bank asset quality after the global financial crisis, unlike in Latin America, where the impact was more subdued (Figure 11.3). This outcome could be attributed to stronger macroeconomic fundamentals, on average, in Latin America compared with the Caribbean; greater export diversification; and relatively weaker links to advanced economies, especially the United States. Moreover, subdued bank profitability in the Caribbean has limited the ability of many banks to adequately provision for problem loans, with

## Figure 11.3. Cross-Country NPLs and Provisions

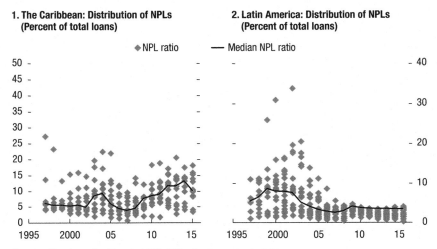

**1. The Caribbean: Distribution of NPLs**
**(Percent of total loans)**

**2. Latin America: Distribution of NPLs**
**(Percent of total loans)**

Sources: Country authorities; and IMF staff estimates and calculations.
Note: NPL = nonperforming loan.

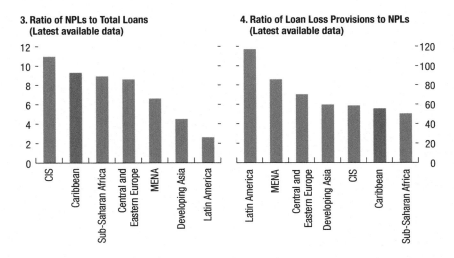

**3. Ratio of NPLs to Total Loans**
**(Latest available data)**

**4. Ratio of Loan Loss Provisions to NPLs**
**(Latest available data)**

Sources: Country authorities; and IMF, Financial Soundness Indicators database.
Note: CIS = Commonwealth of Independent States; MENA = Middle East and North Africa; NPL = nonperforming loan.

provisioning to NPLs low by international comparison—averaging at about 60 percent, though with significant variation within the region.[3]

The high NPLs in the Caribbean are, in large part, a legacy of the global financial crisis, but also reflect some structural problems. Before the crisis, credit growth was strong, spurred by economic activity in the tourism industry and related construction, as well as by favorable global commodity prices for the commodity-exporting Caribbean countries. The credit expansion led to higher private and public sector debt, increasing borrowers' vulnerability to shocks and banks' exposure to credit risk. The crisis was transmitted to the region primarily through lower demand for the region's tourism services. Lower tourism arrivals had a significant negative impact on tourism-dependent industries and related construction, resulting in a sharp increase in unemployment and loss of income for households, which, in turn, impaired their ability to service their loans. As a result, the increase in NPLs was also concentrated in the personal, construction, and tourism sectors (Figure 11.4). In many countries, NPL ratios in these sectors remained elevated subsequent to the crisis, consistent with the slow pace of economic recovery experienced by much of the region. Persistently high NPLs, however, also reflected banks' slow pace of restructuring, sale of NPLs, and write-offs, even after a gradual pickup in economic activity. In most economies, NPL ratios remain above their precrisis levels. In several countries, including Antigua and Barbuda, Belize, and Jamaica, NPL ratios have been falling steadily since 2012 toward their precrisis levels.

Although remaining high, there is considerable heterogeneity in the ratio of NPLs across banks in the region. As of 2015, the NPL ratio varied from about 40 percent of total loans to close to zero. The distribution of NPLs has widened, with more banks experiencing higher NPL ratios after the crisis (Figure 11.5). Domestic (that is, locally owned) banks have higher average NPL ratios than foreign-owned banks, but provisioning ratios, which were much lower in domestic banks before the crisis, are now about the same as foreign-owned banks' provisioning.

## MACRO-FINANCIAL IMPLICATIONS OF HIGH NPLs

High levels of NPLs affect bank lending and may result in adverse macro-financial feedback loops. High NPLs typically reduce the supply of credit, including by reducing bank profitability through higher provisioning, by tying up capital because of higher risk weights on impaired assets, and by raising banks' funding costs because of lower expected revenue streams and investors' heightened risk perceptions (Aiyar and others). Following the global financial crisis, Caribbean banks tightened their lending standards as they focused on cleaning up their balance sheets, reducing extension of credit and downsizing and consolidating their operations to compensate for reduced income flows from NPLs. Reduced

---

[3]In Jamaica, for example, the provisioning ratio rose sharply since 2011, exceeding 100 percent from 2014.

## Figure 11.4. NPLs by Economic Sector

### 1. Caribbean NPLs
**(Percent of loans)**

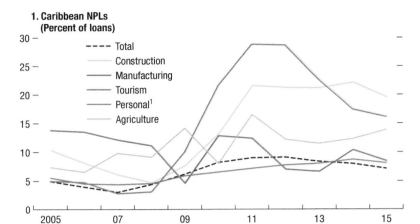

Sources: Country authorities; and IMF staff estimates and calculations.
Note: Calculated as ratio of the sum of nonperforming loans (NPLs) for all countries (in US$) to the sum of loans for all countries (in US$); by sector and total; in percent. Calculations exclude Suriname and The Bahamas due to data unavailability.
[1]Personal loans include real estate and mortgages.

### 2. Distribution of NPLs
**(Percent of total, by sector, end 2015)**

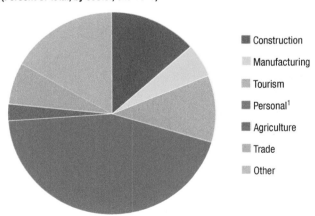

Sources: Country authorities; and IMF staff estimates and calculations.
Note: Calculated as ratio of the sum of nonperforming loans (NPLs) for all countries (in US$) to the sum of loans for all countries (in US$); by sector; in percent. Calculations exclude Suriname and The Bahamas due to data unavailability.
[1]Includes personal, real estate, and mortgage NPLs.

## Figure 11.5. Bank-Level NPLs and Provisioning

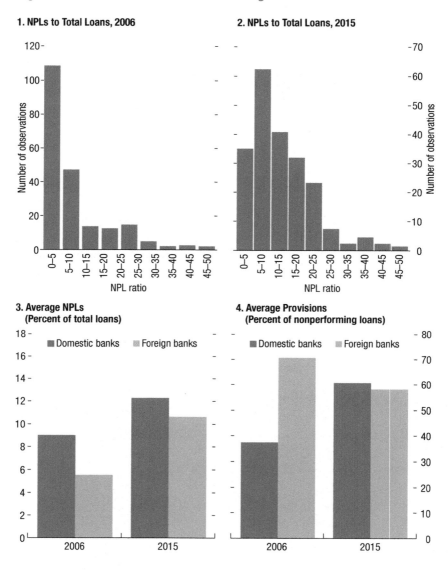

Sources: Country authorities; and IMF staff calculations.
Note: NPL = nonperforming loan.

**Figure 11.6. NPLs and Bank Profitability**
*(Percent)*

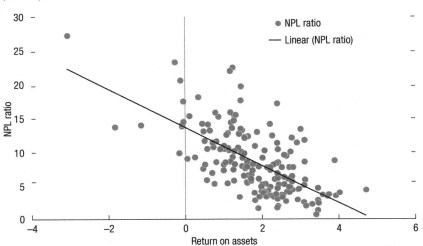

Sources: Country authorities; World Bank, *World Development Indicators*; IMF, *World Economic Outlook*; and IMF staff estimates and calculations.
Note: NPL = nonperforming loan.

credit supply, in turn, contributed to weaker economic activity, with adverse implications for NPLs. Country-level data indicate that NPL ratios have indeed been negatively correlated with bank profitability and private sector credit growth, suggesting that banks with higher NPL ratios have lower profitability and lend less (Figures 11.6 and 11.7), while private credit growth is positively correlated with economic activity, suggesting that high NPLs would be associated with subdued growth.

A panel VAR model is estimated to more formally assess feedback effects between asset quality in the banking sector and the real economy. The approach allows examining the interactions among variables, including the duration and magnitude of the effect. The model includes five endogenous variables (change in the ratio of NPLs to total loans, growth of credit to the private sector, change in the unemployment rate, real GDP growth, and consumer price inflation), a vector of exogenous variables (change in the U.S. unemployment rate and a dummy variable for natural disasters), and country fixed effects.[4] Because the

---

[4]Estimates are produced using lagged regressors as instruments and estimated using generalized method of moments (Klein 2013). Macro-financial feedback effects are assessed using impulse response functions. Orthogonal shocks are identified using the Cholesky decomposition. In the baseline specification, NPLs appear first in the ordering, followed by credit growth, change in unemployment rate, real GDP growth, and CPI inflation.

### Figure 11.7. NPLs, Private Credit, and Economic Activity

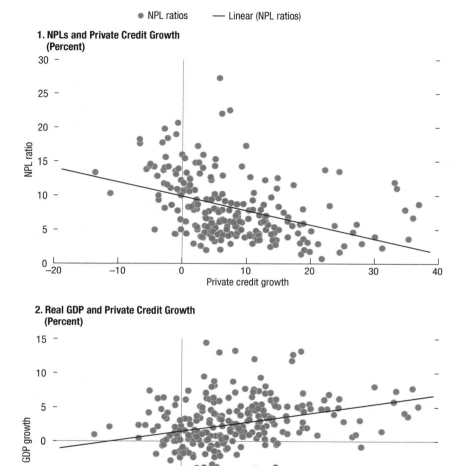

Sources: Country authorities; World Bank, *World Development Indicators*; IMF, *World Economic Outlook*; and IMF staff estimates and calculations.
Note: NPL = nonperforming loan.

## Figure 11.8. PVAR Results: Shock to NPLs

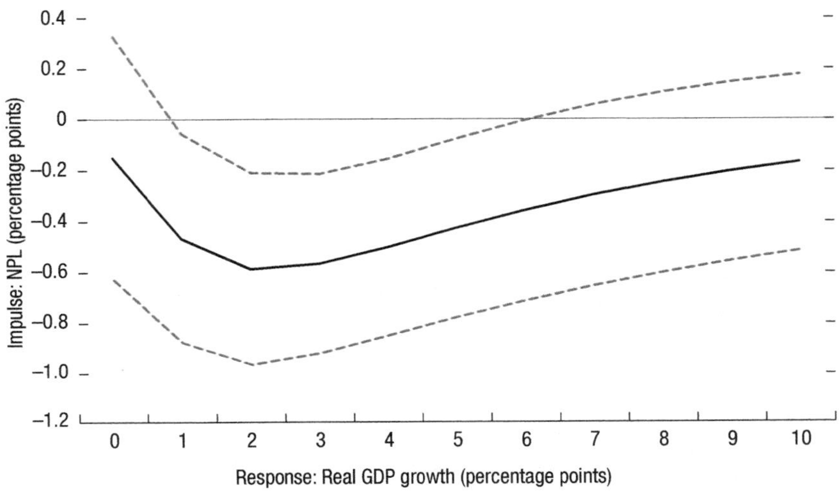

Source: IMF staff estimates and calculations.
Note: Impulse response functions to shocks of one standard deviation. Dashed lines show errors of 10 percent generated by Monte Carlo with 300 simulations. NPL = nonperforming loan; PVAR = panel vector autoregression.

unemployment rate is unavailable for five out of 13 countries in the sample, the baseline model is estimated for eight Caribbean economies, using an unbalanced panel of annual observations for the period 1997–2015, with the major macroeconomic indicators unavailable at a higher frequency.[5] A model excluding unemployment is also estimated for the full sample. Results are broadly robust to alternative specifications.

The results of the analysis point to the presence of strong macro-financial links in Caribbean economies. A shock to the NPL ratio has a statistically significant impact on private sector credit growth, economic activity (Figure 11.8), and the unemployment rate. Specifically, worsening asset quality has persistent negative implications for credit growth, which can last up to five years. The persistent nature of credit cycles also suggests that a shock to credit growth continues for several years. Lower private credit growth, in turn, reduces economic activity and results in an increase in unemployment (Annex 11.1). At the same time,

---

[5]The full sample includes 242 observations from the following countries: Antigua and Barbuda, The Bahamas, Barbados, Belize, Dominica, Grenada, Guyana, Jamaica, St. Kitts and Nevis, St. Lucia, St. Vincent and the Grenadines, Suriname, and Trinidad and Tobago. Time series unemployment data are unavailable for Antigua and Barbuda, Dominica, Grenada, St. Kitts and Nevis, and St. Vincent and the Grenadines.

### Figure 11.9. PVAR Results: Shock to Real GDP Growth

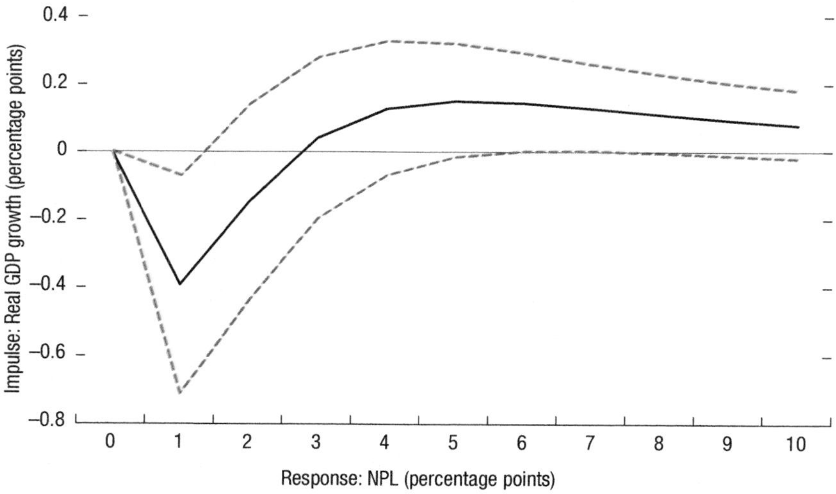

Source: IMF staff estimates and calculations.
Note: Impulse response functions to shocks of one standard deviation. Dashed lines show errors of 10 percent generated by Monte Carlo with 300 simulations. NPL = nonperforming loan; PVAR = panel vector autoregression.

macroeconomic performance also has a significant effect on asset quality: stronger economic performance leads to a statistically significant decline in the NPL ratio (Figure 11.9). Variance decompositions (not shown) indicate that over a five-year horizon, about 22 percent of the variance in the NPL ratios in the productive sectors (including construction, tourism, agriculture, and manufacturing) is driven by shocks to real GDP growth, suggesting that macroeconomic performance is an important determinant of the NPL ratio. Meanwhile, the impact of the NPL

### Table 11.1. Correlation across Macro-Financial Variables
*(Annual frequency)*

|  |  | NPL | Loan | FDI | U | GDP | CPI |
|---|---|---|---|---|---|---|---|
| NPL Ratio Change | NPL | 1 |  |  |  |  |  |
| Loan Growth | Loan | −0.1377* | 1 |  |  |  |  |
| FDI Growth | FDI | −0.0057 | −0.1317* | 1 |  |  |  |
| Change in Unemployment Rate | U | 0.2895* | −0.2525* | −0.1113 | 1 |  |  |
| Real GDP Growth | GDP | −0.1225* | 0.2524* | 0.0159 | −0.3779* | 1 |  |
| Inflation | CPI | −0.0309 | 0.4015* | −0.0152 | 0.0101 | −0.1289* | 1 |

Source: IMF staff estimates and calculations.
Note: CPI = consumer price inflation; FDI = foreign direct investment; NPL = nonperforming loan; U = unemployment.
* $p < 0.1$.

ratio on economic performance is smaller, with shocks to the NPL ratio explaining about 7 percent of the variance in real GDP growth.

The results are consistent with what is suggested by a simple correlation analysis. Simple correlations of key macro-financial variables indicate that the NPL ratio is negatively correlated with inflation, foreign direct investment, real GDP, and credit growth, and positively correlated with the unemployment rate (Table 11.1).

# DETERMINANTS OF NPLs

Country-level and bank-level panel regression analyses are used to more systematically assess the determinants of NPLs in the Caribbean. A dynamic panel regression is estimated, first to analyze the determinants of NPLs at an annual frequency, focusing on macroeconomic determinants of NPLs, and subsequently to analyze the bank-specific determinants of NPLs at a higher frequency. The dynamic panel regression specification for the annual country-level regressions is given by

$$NPLs_{j,t} = \alpha + \beta_1 \sum_k NPLs_{j;t-k} + \beta_2 \sum_k Global_{t-k} + \beta_3 \sum_k Country_{j,t-k} + u_j + \varepsilon_{j,t}, \quad (11.1)$$

where $NPLs_{j,t}$ denotes the logit transformation of the NPL ratio for country $j$ at time $t$. The dependent variable is explained by its lag ($NPLs_{j,t-1}$), global ($Global_t$) and country-specific $\left(Country_{j,t}\right)$ macroeconomic variables, and country fixed effects $(u_j)$. The term $k$ is the number of annual lags. The model is estimated with an unbalanced panel of 13 Caribbean countries.[6] The same baseline model is estimated using bank-level data for bank $i$ in country $j$ at time $t$ with quarterly data. In addition to the variables considered in equation (11.1), the bank-level model includes detailed bank-level $\left(Bank_{i,j,t}\right)$ variables capturing credit risk (including profitability, capital adequacy, measures of efficiency the expense-to-assets ratio, bank size, and credit concentration, as well as bank-level fixed effects.[7] The bank-level model is estimated with an unbalanced panel of 71 banks across 13 Caribbean countries.

---

[6]These include six members of the ECCU, The Bahamas, Barbados, Belize, Guyana, Jamaica, Suriname, and Trinidad and Tobago. For most countries, data are available beginning about 2000.

[7]All models are estimated with dynamic panel regression techniques. To address dynamic panel bias (Nickell 1981) and endogeneity, all models are estimated with the system generalized method of moments (SGMM) developed in Arellano and Bover (1995) and Blundell and Bond (1998). The instrument set is restricted to avoid overfitting bias (see Arellano and Bond 1998). We use as instruments only the first and second appropriate lag of each explanatory variable. To further reduce the number of instruments, the collapsing method of Holtz-Eakin, Newey, and Rosen (1988) was used. In the model specifications, all global and country-specific variables, except for country-specific economic growth, are treated as strictly exogenous. All bank-specific variables and country-specific economic growth are treated as endogenous and instrumented with internal instruments (that is, lagged values of the instrumented variables).

**Table 11.2. Macroeconomic Determinants of NPLs**

| | Full Sample | | | | | Pre-2009 | Post-2009 |
|---|---|---|---|---|---|---|---|
| | (1) | (2) | (3) | (4) | (5) | (6) | (7) |
| NPL ($t-1$) | 1.060*** | 0.891*** | 0.895*** | 0.896*** | 0.894*** | 0.677*** | 0.692*** |
| | (0.0935) | (0.0803) | (0.0665) | (0.0655) | (0.0665) | (0.0727) | (0.188) |
| Real GDP Growth ($t-1$) | −0.0195* | −0.00906 | −0.00961 | −0.00987 | −0.00973 | −0.0111* | −0.00551 |
| | (0.0112) | (0.0122) | (0.00756) | (0.00768) | (0.00775) | (0.00648) | (0.0190) |
| Advanced Economies Real GDP Growth ($t-1$) | −0.0242** | −0.0170** | −0.0236*** | −0.0241*** | −0.0233*** | −0.0355 | −0.0112 |
| | (0.0102) | (0.00813) | (0.00710) | (0.00746) | (0.00711) | (0.0586) | (0.0121) |
| Credit Growth ($t$) | | −0.0128*** | −0.0121*** | −0.0124*** | −0.0122*** | −0.0101*** | −0.00994 |
| | | (0.00327) | (0.00267) | (0.00309) | (0.00285) | (0.00221) | (0.00691) |
| Lending Rate ($t-1$) | | | 0.0225*** | 0.0224*** | 0.0237*** | 0.0133 | −0.0591 |
| | | | (0.00726) | (0.00702) | (0.00704) | (0.0164) | (0.0731) |
| Real Effective Exchange Rate Growth ($t-1$) | | | | −0.00180 | | | |
| | | | | (0.00389) | | | |
| Natural Disaster | | | | | 0.00461 | | |
| | | | | | (0.0528) | | |
| Constant | 0.279 | −0.0992 | −0.398** | −0.387** | −0.416** | −0.905** | 0.0160 |
| | (0.241) | (0.213) | (0.174) | (0.159) | (0.170) | (0.352) | (0.602) |
| Observations | 229 | 223 | 162 | 162 | 162 | 78 | 84 |
| Number of Countries | 13 | 13 | 12 | 12 | 12 | 11 | 12 |
| Number of Instruments | 8 | 11 | 14 | 15 | 15 | 14 | 14 |
| AR(1) | 0.0144 | 0.0149 | 0.0318 | 0.0313 | 0.0313 | 0.158 | 0.108 |
| AR(2) | 0.426 | 0.462 | 0.333 | 0.327 | 0.337 | 0.385 | 0.226 |
| Hansen | 0.329 | 0.257 | 0.289 | 0.546 | 0.571 | 0.615 | 0.510 |

Note: NPL = nonperforming loan; the dependent variable is the logit transformation of the NPL ratio for country $j$ at time $t$.
Robust standard errors in parentheses.
*** $p < 0.01$, ** $p < 0.05$, * $p < 0.1$.

Country-level regressions also suggest that economic activity is an important determinant of banks' asset quality. Asset quality deteriorates as a function of low real GDP growth, both at home and in advanced economies (Table 11.2). Spillovers from global macroeconomic developments are particularly strong, with the coefficient on real GDP growth in advanced economies larger and statistically more significant than that on domestic growth, consistent with the high degree of openness of economies in the region. Asset quality also deteriorates as a function of higher lending rates that reduce borrowers' capacity to service debt. Reduced credit growth also results in a higher NPL ratio, suggesting that NPLs are reduced at a slower rate than the fall in total loans. Estimating the regression separately for the periods before and after 2009 suggests that the global financial crisis explains much of the variation in asset quality, capturing the impact of macroeconomic developments in the postcrisis period.[8]

---

[8]An analysis of the determinants of NPLs across tourism-dependent and commodity-exporting countries suggests that the macroeconomic determinants of NPLs are broadly comparable for both types of Caribbean countries. See Beaton and others (forthcoming) for detailed results.

The bank-level analysis shows that both macroeconomic and bank-specific factors are important determinants of NPLs (Table 11.3). NPLs are persistent (suggested by the coefficient of lagged NPLs), pointing to difficulties in resolving problem loans. Deterioration in advanced economy growth worsens asset quality. Tourism arrivals, included as a proxy for domestic economic conditions, given that real GDP is unavailable for most countries in the region on a quarterly basis, are, by contrast, statistically insignificant. The effect of tourism arrivals is likely captured by advanced economy growth, which is an important determinant of tourism arrivals to the region. Bank-specific factors are also important determinants of credit risk and asset quality. More profitable, more capitalized, and more efficient banks (as measured by expense-to-asset and income-to-expense ratios) tend to have better asset quality. Exposure to credit risk associated with higher lending to the household sector and higher foreign currency lending does not seem to be a significant determinant of NPLs at the bank level. A priori, one would expect the foreign banks—primarily subsidiaries and branches of Canadian banks with global operations—to have stronger risk management practices and greater capacity to dispose of impaired assets. However, the results suggest that asset quality is not affected by whether banks are foreign or domestically owned.[9] The significant dispersion in NPL ratios across banks likely explains this result.[10]

## OBSTACLES TO NPL RESOLUTION

Although the high level of NPLs in the Caribbean has been, in large part, a legacy of the global financial crisis, their persistence owes much to the weak economic recovery in the region, as well as to structural obstacles to resolution. The pace of loan restructuring, NPL sales, and write-offs has been slow, leaving large amounts of impaired assets on bank balance sheets. Results from a survey of country authorities and banks operating in the region highlight some common elements undermining NPL resolution. This section summarizes the results of the survey, which asked banks and authorities to (1) identify the key obstacles to NPL resolution; (2) provide detailed information on structural impediments grouped into five broad areas: supervisory and prudential, insolvency and debt enforcement, informational systems, market for distressed debt, and tax regime; and (3) identify the key measures undertaken by the authorities and banks in recent years toward resolution of NPLs (Annex 11.1).[11] Responses were received from the

---

[9]This is assessed by interacting a foreign bank dummy variable with all other determinants in the benchmark model. Detailed results are available in Beaton and others (forthcoming).

[10]For most ECCU countries, Belize, and Suriname, domestic banks, on average, have higher NPL ratios compared with foreign banks—primarily subsidiaries and branches of international banks that benefit from stronger risk management practices and greater capacity to dispose of or write off impaired assets. On the other hand, in The Bahamas, Grenada, St. Vincent and the Grenadines, and Trinidad and Tobago, the NPL ratio is higher for foreign-owned banks on average.

[11]The survey on the structural obstacles to NPL resolution was adapted from Aiyar and others (2015); questions were customized to fit the Caribbean region.

## Table 11.3. Bank-Level Determinants of NPLs: Bank Performance

| | Baseline | Profitability | | | Capital Adequacy | | Bank Efficiency | | | | Credit Concentration | |
|---|---|---|---|---|---|---|---|---|---|---|---|---|
| | (1) | (2) | (3) | (4) | (5) | (6) | (7) | (8) | (9) | (10) | (11) | (12) |
| NPL (t–1) | 0.631*** | 0.624*** | 0.608*** | 0.614*** | 0.591*** | 0.591*** | 0.789*** | 0.783*** | 0.789*** | 0.579*** | 0.641*** | 0.733*** |
| | (0.0630) | (0.0685) | (0.0723) | (0.0800) | (0.0804) | (0.0772) | (0.0940) | (0.0803) | (0.0873) | (0.0935) | (0.0671) | (0.0894) |
| NPL (t–2) | 0.190*** | 0.151*** | 0.144*** | 0.128** | 0.144*** | 0.124** | 0.0284 | 0.0351 | 0.0329 | 0.146*** | 0.146*** | 0.183*** |
| | (0.0569) | (0.0511) | (0.0525) | (0.0637) | (0.0535) | (0.0559) | (0.0669) | (0.0631) | (0.0649) | (0.0545) | (0.0537) | (0.0537) |
| Advanced Economies Real GDP Growth (t–1) | -0.00704** | -0.00597* | -0.00674** | -0.00480 | -0.00533 | -0.00569 | -0.00285 | -0.00286 | -0.00342 | -0.00783 | -0.00473 | -0.0119*** |
| | (0.00330) | (0.00309) | (0.00337) | (0.00346) | (0.00351) | (0.00380) | (0.00407) | (0.00307) | (0.00344) | (0.00602) | (0.00337) | (0.00415) |
| Credit Growth (t) | -0.00452*** | -0.00429** | -0.00417*** | -0.00405** | -0.00376*** | -0.00496*** | -0.00351** | -0.00353*** | -0.00349*** | -0.00461*** | -0.00478*** | -0.00284*** |
| | (0.00100) | (0.000903) | (0.000933) | (0.00180) | (0.00100) | (0.00117) | (0.00142) | (0.00129) | (0.00136) | (0.00144) | (0.00106) | (0.000961) |
| Return on Assets (t) | | -0.0122* | | | -0.0144* | -0.0150* | -0.00278 | 0.000681 | -0.000286 | -0.0157* | -0.0106 | -0.0119 |
| | | (0.00641) | | | (0.00756) | (0.00785) | (0.00636) | (0.00429) | (0.00457) | (0.00833) | (0.00866) | (0.00749) |
| Return on Equity (t) | | | -0.000291 | | | | | | | | | |
| | | | (0.000219) | | | | | | | | | |
| Net Interest Margin (t) | | | | -0.0810* | | | | | | | | |
| | | | | (0.0428) | | | | | | | | |
| Capital Adequacy Ratio (t) | | | | | -0.00582* | -0.00396 | 0.00779 | 0.00431 | 0.00786 | -0.00530 | | |
| | | | | | (0.00331) | (0.00394) | (0.00874) | (0.00686) | (0.00772) | (0.00359) | | |
| Loan-to-Deposit Ratio (t–1) | | | | | | -0.00618** | | | | | | |
| | | | | | | (0.00307) | | | | | | |
| Expense-to-Assets Ratio (t–1) | | | | | | | 0.0906** | | | | | |
| | | | | | | | (0.0376) | | | | | |
| Income-to-Expenses Ratio (t) | | | | | | | | -0.202*** | -0.181* | | | |
| | | | | | | | | (0.0697) | (0.0925) | | | |
| Total Assets (ln) (t) | | | | | | | | | 0.0263 | 0.0459 | | |
| | | | | | | | | | (0.0512) | (0.105) | | |
| Loans to Households (percent of total) (t) | | | | | | | | | | | -0.00341 | |
| | | | | | | | | | | | (0.00304) | |
| Foreign Currency Loans (percent of total) (t) | | | | | | | | | | | | -2.31e-06 |
| | | | | | | | | | | | | (3.56e-06) |
| Constant | -0.427 | -0.533** | -0.598** | -0.545 | -0.577* | -0.195 | -0.746** | -0.238 | -0.374 | -1.133 | -0.360 | -0.145 |
| | (0.273) | (0.269) | (0.285) | (0.345) | (0.304) | (0.183) | (0.352) | (0.181) | (0.230) | (1.508) | (0.303) | (0.210) |
| Observations | 3,709 | 3,508 | 3,363 | 3,286 | 3,063 | 3,063 | 766 | 766 | 766 | 3,063 | 3,283 | 948 |
| Number of Banks | 71 | 71 | 66 | 62 | 62 | 62 | 22 | 22 | 22 | 62 | 62 | 28 |
| Number of Instruments | 10 | 13 | 13 | 10 | 16 | 19 | 19 | 19 | 22 | 19 | 16 | 16 |
| AR(1) | 3.58e-07 | 5.41e-07 | 7.60e-07 | 2.05e-06 | 2.79e-06 | 2.35e-06 | 0.00985 | 0.00917 | 0.00914 | 2.92e-06 | 1.47e-06 | 0.00105 |
| AR(2) | 0.437 | 0.870 | 0.687 | 0.749 | 0.634 | 0.232 | 0.771 | 0.729 | 0.771 | 0.751 | 0.921 | 0.551 |
| Hansen | 0.485 | 0.446 | 0.756 | 0.520 | 0.624 | 0.484 | 0.836 | 0.564 | 0.460 | 0.650 | 0.282 | 0.913 |

Note: NPL = nonperforming loan; the dependent variable is the logit transformation of the NPL ratio for country $j$ at time $t$.

Robust standard errors in parentheses.

*** $p<0.01$, ** $p<0.05$, * $p<0.1$.

authorities of the Eastern Caribbean Central Bank, The Bahamas, Barbados, Belize, Guyana, Jamaica, Montserrat, St. Kitts and Nevis, Suriname, and Trinidad and Tobago, and 39 banks representing 40 percent of all banks in the region.

Survey responses from the authorities and banks highlight macroeconomic conditions, deficiencies in the legal process, and difficulties with collateral as the key obstacles to NPL resolution (Figure 11.10). Most banks identified macroeconomic conditions, such as slow economic growth, high unemployment, and loss of clients' incomes, as among the most severe obstacles to resolving NPLs. Many banks also pointed to deficiencies in the legal process (including, for example, costly and protracted insolvency procedures, or the absence of specialized courts or judges), difficulties in valuing and realizing collateral, and depressed real estate markets as major obstacles. The authorities, for their part, highlighted deficiencies in the legal process and banks' underwriting and monitoring practices and inability or limited financial capacity in certain banks to recognize loan impairment and provision against it, as well as poor markets for distressed debt and collateral, as top obstacles, followed by macroeconomic factors.

Country-by-country survey responses highlight several key areas of concern in resolving NPLs. Among these, survey respondents ranked the absence of a market for distressed assets as the most challenging area for NPL resolution across the Caribbean (Figure 11.11). As in many European countries with high NPLs (Aiyar and others 2015), the market for trading distressed assets is largely nonexistent in the Caribbean despite the absence of explicit restrictions (Figure 11.12). The survey responses also suggest concerns about gaps in the information framework, deficiencies in insolvency and debt-enforcement regimes (including the legal system, institutional weaknesses, and collateral enforcement related challenges), and weaknesses in prudential and supervisory frameworks. The tax systems in the Caribbean were perceived as posing less concern than other broad areas. Many elements are common across countries; however, detailed responses show significant variation across countries and banks.

## Prudential and Supervisory Framework and NPL Management

Strong supervision and conservative bank practices for loss recognition and provisioning increase incentives to address NPLs in a timely manner. Supervisory authorities in the region generally paid close attention to problem loans, tightening regulations in recent years. In most countries, supervisors have undertaken a thematic review of banks' NPL management capacity, issued formal guidelines to banks on NPL management practices, and issued regulations regarding provisioning (or communicated regulatory expectations with regard to provisions under International Financial Reporting Standards). In some countries, supervisors provided additional incentives for write-offs, such as increased capital charges or time limits for carrying NPLs on balance sheets; performed assessments of collateral valuation practices; and subjected banks to granular asset quality reviews. In some countries, supervisors have strengthened prudential rules for loan classification and provisioning.

## Figure 11.10. Top Obstacles to NPL Resolution in the Caribbean

### 1. Banks' Survey
(Percentage of respondents citing a given factor as one of the top three obstacles for NPL resolution)

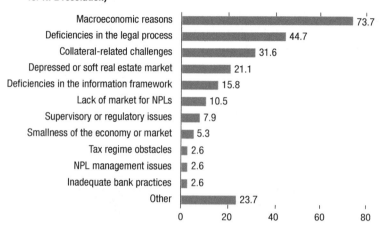

### 2. Authorities' Survey
(Percentage of respondents citing a given factor as one of the top three obstacles for NPL resolution)

Source: IMF staff survey of national authorities and banks.
Note: NPL = nonperforming loan. The figure summarizes responses to a question asking respondents to name top three obstacles to NPL resolution. Panel 2 combines responses from The Bahamas, Barbados, Belize, Guyana, Jamaica, Montserrat, St. Kitts and Nevis, and Trinidad and Tobago.

### Figure 11.11. The Caribbean: Survey-Based Scores on Obstacles to NPL Resolution by Country

| | | Countries | | | | | | | |
|---|---|---|---|---|---|---|---|---|---|
| Institutional Obstacle Scores | | 1 | 2 | 3 | 4 | 5 | 6 | 7 | 8 | Average |
| **1. Market for NPLs** | 3.0 | 3.0 | 2.0 | 2.0 | 3.0 | 2.0 | 3.0 | 1.3 | 2.4 |
| **2. Information obstacles** | 2.4 | 2.1 | 2.2 | 2.3 | 1.9 | 1.9 | 1.5 | 1.4 | 2.0 |
| 2.1 Public registers | 2.0 | 2.2 | 2.2 | 2.2 | 1.9 | 1.9 | 1.6 | 1.5 | 1.9 |
| 2.2 Consumer and data protection | 2.8 | 2.0 | 2.1 | 2.4 | 2.0 | 2.0 | 1.3 | 1.4 | 2.0 |
| **3. Insolvency and debt-enforcement regimes** | 2.8 | 2.0 | 2.7 | 2.0 | 1.3 | 1.7 | 1.1 | 1.5 | 1.9 |
| 3.1 Corporate insolvency and debt-restructuring regime | 2.5 | 1.7 | 2.0 | 1.6 | 1.4 | 1.6 | 1.0 | 1.9 | 1.7 |
| 3.2 Household debt-resolution regime | ... | 1.2 | 3.0 | 1.8 | 1.4 | 1.4 | 1.1 | 1.1 | 1.6 |
| 3.3 Judicial system | 3.0 | 3.0 | 3.0 | 2.4 | 1.1 | 2.0 | 1.3 | 1.4 | 2.2 |
| **4. Prudential and supervisory regime** | 1.7 | 2.0 | 1.6 | 1.5 | 1.8 | 1.9 | 1.8 | 1.5 | 1.7 |
| 4.1 NPL management issues | 1.8 | 2.1 | 1.7 | 1.9 | 1.9 | 2.1 | 2.1 | 1.9 | 1.9 |
| 4.2 Collateral-related issues | 2.0 | 3.0 | 2.0 | 1.5 | 2.6 | 2.0 | 2.0 | 1.0 | 2.0 |
| 4.3 Bank capitalization | 1.0 | 1.2 | 1.0 | 1.0 | 1.3 | 2.0 | 1.0 | 1.4 | 1.2 |
| 4.4 Supervision | 2.0 | 1.9 | 1.8 | 1.7 | 1.6 | 1.6 | 2.1 | 1.9 | 1.8 |
| **5. Taxation** | ... | 1.0 | 1.0 | 1.6 | 1.1 | 1.0 | 1.0 | 1.8 | 1.2 |
| **Overall obstacle level** | 2.5 | 2.0 | 1.9 | 1.9 | 1.8 | 1.7 | 1.7 | 1.5 | 1.9 |

| Coding: | ≤ 1.5 | No (or low) concern | ... Missing response |
|---|---|---|---|
| | > 1.5 | Medium concern | |
| | > 2 | Medium to high concern | |

Source: IMF staff survey of national authorities and banks.
Note: NPL = nonperforming loan. The heat map shows maximum scores from country and bank surveys. The institutional obstacle scores are compiled from individual responses to these surveys. The surveys asked the respondents to indicate their level of concern regarding specific obstacles within five broad areas (such as NPL markets, information obstacles, and so forth), and provide information regarding these areas. Banks' responses within the same jurisdictions were aggregated by averaging. The overall obstacle level is a simple average of obstacle scores in each of the five areas. Values 2.0 appearing a red box are marginally higher than 2.

Notwithstanding these efforts, further work is needed in several areas. In most countries, no licensing and regulatory regime is in place to enable nonbanks to own or manage NPLs, which hampers the development of the NPL market. Many countries have no requirement to apply a real estate valuation standard, which contributes to uncertainty regarding collateral values and therefore poses an obstacle to liquidating collateral during debt enforcement. Difficulties in realizing collateral, in turn, increase banks' reluctance to address NPLs. Requiring banks to have operational targets for NPL reduction or time limits on carrying NPLs on their balance sheets, where these tools are absent, can create incentives for resolving NPLs. Finally, as discussed earlier, provisioning ratios are low in the Caribbean compared with many other regions, suggesting scope for greater provisioning to help recognize losses and write off loans (Figure 11.13).

Banks have the basic tools with which to address NPLs. Most banks have dedicated NPL workout units, and all banks are required to have NPL management strategies and action plans to reduce problem loans. In most countries,

### Figure 11.12. International Comparison
*(Survey-based scores of obstacles to NPL resolution)*

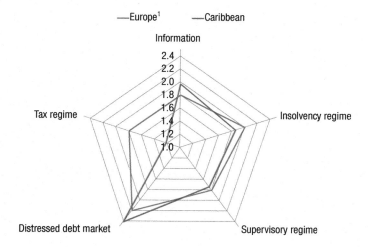

Sources: Aiyar and others (2015); and surveys of banks and the national authorities in the Caribbean.
Note: NPL = nonperforming loan.
[1]Countries with NPL ratio exceeding 10 percent during 2005–14 (Aiyar and others 2015).

### Figure 11.13. Ratio of Loan Loss Provisions to NPLs

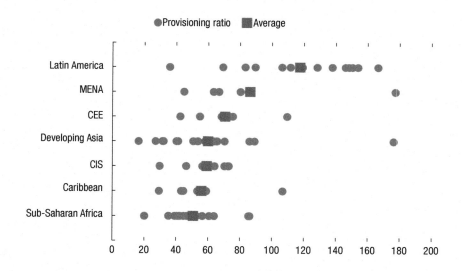

Sources: IMF, *Global Financial Stability Report*; and national authorities.
Note: Latest available data. CEE = Central and Eastern Europe; CIS = Commonwealth of Independent States; MENA = Middle East and North Africa; NPL = nonperforming loan.

banks can also outsource NPL management. Survey responses suggest that banks use a variety of tools to restructure NPLs, including interest-only loans, reduced repayments, and performance-based write-offs (Figure 11.14). Restructured loans averaged about 10 percent of NPL portfolios in the sample, although they reached as high as 40 percent in a few banks. However, lack of coordination mechanisms among creditors and the absence of a market for problem loans constrain NPL resolution. Banks disposed of about 16 percent of their NPL portfolios (on average in 2013–15), mostly through write-offs. Difficulties liquidating collateral and uncertainties regarding collateral valuations create incentives to keep distressed assets on bank balance sheets much longer than warranted, despite the availability of resolution tools. NPL management is also constrained by the lack of interbank or public-private creditor coordination.

## Debt-Enforcement and Insolvency Framework

Effective insolvency regimes and debt enforcement are essential for NPL resolution. An effective insolvency regime should provide mechanisms for creditors to realize their claims in a predictable, speedy, and transparent manner, while at the same time protecting and maximizing value for all parties (Aiyar and others 2015). An effective debt-enforcement and insolvency framework has, in turn, two pillars: first, an adequate resolution toolkit that provides for rehabilitation for viable firms and liquidation for non-viable firms (and in the case of personal insolvency, a second chance for good faith entrepreneurs while preserving credit discipline), and second, an effective institutional framework that operates in a predictable, efficient, and transparent manner. Strengthening insolvency regimes by enhancing insolvency laws, creating incentives for out-of-court settlement, and institutional reforms such as creating specialized courts were key elements of strategies for reducing NPLs in a number of countries.[12]

The surveys highlighted several gaps in the resolution toolkit and its implementation. Even though all countries have corporate insolvency regimes in place, many do not have fast-track pre-pack insolvency procedures (where the court expeditiously approves a debt restructuring plan negotiated between the debtor and its creditors in a consensual manner before the initiation of an insolvency proceeding) or rehabilitation procedures, and only a few have out-of-court settlement mechanisms or actively promote such techniques (e.g., through guidance issued by the central bank or informal arrangements between banks). These gaps, in turn, impede business rescue, slow down realization of claims, and reduce expected recovery of value. Several countries reported that creditors do not have adequate control or influence over the process of business restructuring. Personal insolvency regimes exist in only half of the surveyed countries, and this regime is applicable to individual entrepreneurs in only two cases. Weak institutions are even a more significant concern—half of the surveyed banks consider implementation of insolvency and debt-enforcement

---

[12]For example, in Indonesia and Thailand (1999), Turkey (2002), Japan (1999, 2008), and Korea (1998, 2006) (Aiyar and others 2015).

## Figure 11.14. Use of Debt-Restructuring and NPL Disposal Tools

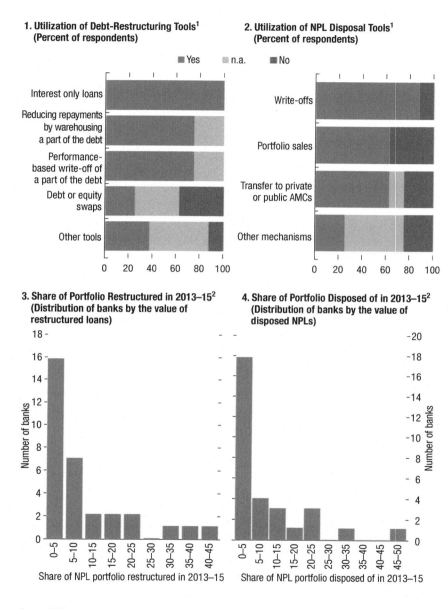

**1. Utilization of Debt-Restructuring Tools[1]**
**(Percent of respondents)**

**2. Utilization of NPL Disposal Tools[1]**
**(Percent of respondents)**

**3. Share of Portfolio Restructured in 2013–15[2]**
**(Distribution of banks by the value of restructured loans)**

**4. Share of Portfolio Disposed of in 2013–15[2]**
**(Distribution of banks by the value of disposed NPLs)**

Source: IMF surveys of national authorities and banks.
Note: AMC = asset management company; ECCU = Eastern Caribbean Currency Union; n.a. = not available; NPL = nonperforming loan.
[1]Compiled from supervisory authority responses in eight jurisdictions: ECCU, The Bahamas, Barbados, Belize, Guyana, Jamaica, Suriname, and Trinidad and Tobago.
[2]Compiled from responses of 35 banks from the following jurisdictions: ECCU, The Bahamas, Belize, Barbados, Guyana, Jamaica, Suriname, and Trinidad and Tobago.

**Figure 11.15. Dealing with Insolvency: Time to Complete and the Cost of Insolvency**

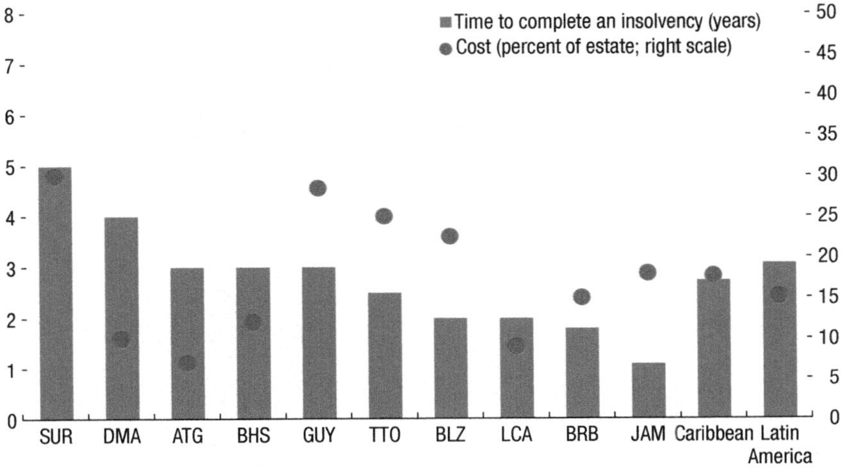

Source: World Bank, Doing Business Database.
Note: Data labels in figure use International Organization for Standardization (ISO) country codes.

regimes to be important obstacles to NPL resolution. Courts or judges that specialize in insolvency cases do not exist, and in the absence of time-bound procedures in many cases, resolving insolvency takes a long time, on average 2.7 years for the region—a high- or medium-level concern for about 60 percent of the bank respondents (Figure 11.15). In the ECCU region, for example, foreclosure laws are typically debtor-friendly, which lengthens considerably the foreclosure process and delays recovery by banks. These obstacles reduce recovery rates, with subsequent adverse effects on credit provision and lending rates.

## Data Gaps and Impediments to Information Sharing

Access to adequate information is essential for borrowers and creditors to price risk, value collateral, and narrow pricing gaps by reducing uncertainty. Public registries are important for maintaining complete information about credit and transaction histories and asset characteristics. The ability to share information for debt-workout purposes among creditors is also important. Reducing information asymmetries was a key pillar in strategies to reduce NPLs in many European economies.[13]

The surveys identified significant gaps in the information framework in the Caribbean (Figure 11.16). For example, 80 percent of banks consider that lack of

---

[13]For example, Cyprus has set up a centralized credit registry, allowing banks to make more informed credit decisions. Serbia set up a database on real estate collateral valuations and loans secured by such collateral. Italy improved transparency and availability of NPL-specific data, fostering the development of a market for distressed assets.

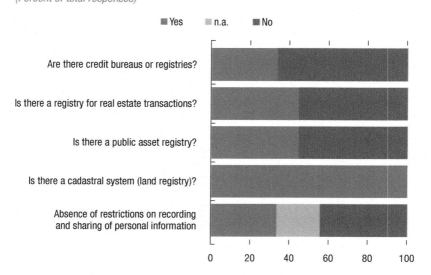

**Figure 11.16. Information Obstacles**
*(Percent of total responses)*

Source: Survey of national authorities.
Note: Based on responses from nine countries. n.a. = not available.

credit registries significantly raises the cost of due diligence. Most countries do not have credit bureaus. Although most countries have land registries accessible to creditors, only four out of nine have registries of assets and real estate transactions, and access to the existing asset registries is more restricted. Even where registries exist, there are concerns about the quality of the data and access. For example, existing credit bureaus lack basic elements such as scoring for borrowers and information on connected borrowers. Four countries reported restrictions on recording and sharing of personal information for debt-workout purposes. These restrictions hinder the resolution of NPLs by undermining the debt-workout process in the absence of a full assessment of debtors' liabilities and wealth. The importance of addressing these information gaps is highlighted by the experience of Jamaica, where the operationalization and increased use of credit bureaus since 2014 have helped incentivize borrowers to preserve good credit ratings and improve credit underwriting and management by deposit-taking institutions, and played a role in reducing new NPLs and recoveries.

## Market for NPLs

An active, liquid market for distressed debt can facilitate disposal of NPLs and reduce uncertainty about collateral valuations, thereby helping strengthen recovery values. Allowing banks to move problem loans off their balance sheets would reduce the burden on banks and can boost recovery values by providing a more

**Figure 11.17. Restrictions in the Market for Distressed Assets**
*(Percent of total responses)*

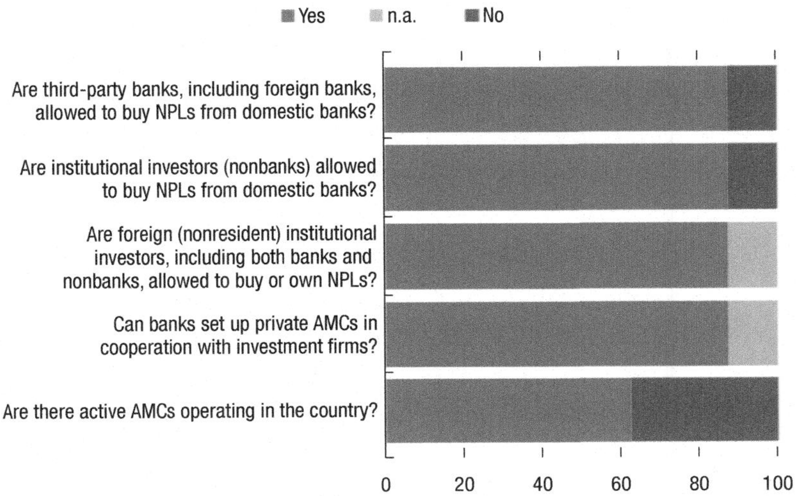

Source: Survey of national authorities.
Note: AMC = asset management company; n.a. = not available; NPL = nonperforming loan. Based on responses from eight jurisdictions.

cost-effective alternative to internal NPL management, especially for smaller banks that lack expertise and economies of scale in managing NPLs. Market approaches to dispose of NPLs may include direct sales, as well as securitization of NPLs. The latter has been used in a number of countries as a strategy for dealing with NPL overhang (e.g., Ireland and Spain) and as a useful approach to expanding the universe of distressed debt investors and to offering a way through which governments could jump-start the NPL market (e.g., by co-investing, together with private investors, in junior or mezzanine tranches) (see, for example, Aiyar and others 2015).

Survey responses show that markets for NPLs in the Caribbean are largely nonexistent, including in countries that do not have specific restrictions on trading NPLs. Half of the banks consider the lack of markets to be a medium- or high-level concern and, hence, an obstacle to resolution. Most countries reported no prohibitions on sales of NPLs to domestic or foreign buyers (Figure 11.17).[14] Yet NPL sales are either sporadic or nonexistent. Many banks point out that the lack of a market for NPLs stems from large pricing gaps: values offered by potential buyers are much lower than the prices at which banks would be willing to sell

---

[14]One potential obstacle to market development and sale of NPLs is the Alien Land Holding License requirement in several Caribbean countries (for example, some ECCU countries). Regional efforts to remove these obstacles are in process, but countries must agree to waive the legislation to allow for cross-border land and property purchases, and there is some resistance to doing so.

their distressed assets. This may be a particularly important concern for banks with low levels of provisioning and capital to absorb the losses that could arise from selling bad assets. These considerations are similar to those highlighted by the surveys of European authorities and banks in Aiyar and others (2015).

### Tax Regime Obstacles

Unfavorable tax treatment can create disincentives for adequate provisioning and loan write-offs. The survey responses suggest that tax treatment of provisioning and write-offs are not a major concern for NPL resolution in the Caribbean (Figures 11.11 and 11.12). Only a small share of banks, most of which operate in two countries, flagged tax treatment as posing a medium or high concern for NPL resolution. This result stands in contrast with the actual rules, which suggest that tax treatment is not favorable in many countries. Half of the countries do not grant tax deductions for loan write-offs and loan loss provisioning, and two countries do not have a loss-carrying mechanism such as a deferred tax asset, thereby providing limited incentives for provisioning for or writing off impaired loans.

## WAY FORWARD: STRATEGY FOR NPL RESOLUTION

The Caribbean NPL problem is a legacy of the global financial crisis, but its persistence at high levels owes much to continued weaknesses in economic growth in the region, as well as to structural impediments to their resolution. To address the problem, a multifaceted approach is needed involving macroeconomic policies to support growth and employment, prudential policies to ensure macro-financial stability, and a comprehensive strategy to reduce the structural bottlenecks for resolution of problem loans—including through tighter bank supervisory regimes; stronger insolvency; debt-enforcement; and legal frameworks; closing of information gaps; and development of markets for distressed debt (Figure 11.18) (see Liu and Rosenberg 2013; Bergthaler and others 2015; and Aiyar and others 2015).

*Strong macroeconomic policies.* With macroeconomic conditions identified as a key determinant of NPLs and as one of the main obstacles to their resolution, by banks and authorities in many countries, priority should be given to implementing macroeconomic policies and structural reforms that promote strong and sustainable growth. Evidence suggests that growth recoveries associated with lower unemployment, higher household incomes, and higher corporate profits help resolve problem loans by improving the ability of firms and households to service their loans.

*Strengthening prudential and supervisory frameworks.* Strengthening supervisory and prudential frameworks, where needed, would help prevent a buildup of problem loans in the future. While the region is still at a low growth stage of the credit cycle, authorities could preemptively set up a toolkit of well-targeted micro- and macroprudential policies to reduce excessive risk taking during loan origination and to mitigate emerging risks subsequently identified. Strong supervisory regimes are also key to addressing existing problem loans. Banks must follow prudent loss-recognition and provisioning practices and apply appropriate real estate

**Figure 11.18. Strategy to Address the Obstacles to NPL Resolution**

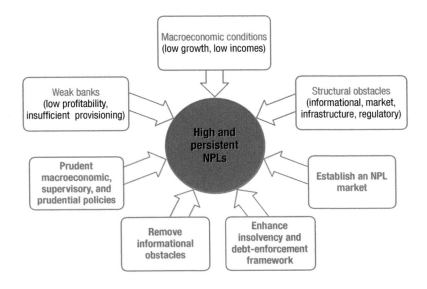

Source: Authors' illustration.
Note: NPL = nonperforming loan.

valuation standards to improve collateral valuation and liquidation during debt enforcement. Incentives should be in place to write off bad loans and increase provisioning to facilitate recognition of losses.[15] Policies should also focus on facilitating outsourcing of NPL management, including establishing a regulatory framework for nonbanks to manage NPLs and fostering bilateral NPL sales, undertaking independent asset quality reviews, as well as ensuring high quality of governance and senior management oversight in banks. Effective coordination mechanisms between banks and between public and private creditors should be in place.

*Addressing informational obstacles.* Policies should focus on removing information gaps that hinder the pricing of risk, collateral valuation, and the narrowing of large pricing gaps between buyers and sellers of properties that hamper development of NPL markets. Where missing, efforts could focus on establishing well-functioning public registries and credit bureaus to reduce information asymmetries and improve management of credit risk, and on setting up public records on assets or real estate transactions to improve the functioning and revival of real estate markets. The quality of data also needs improvement even when registries exist. Improving data quality and closing data gaps are crucial not only to facilitate

---

[15]Such incentives could include additional capital charges and time limits for carrying NPLs on balance sheets, tighter provisioning requirements, or tax incentives for write-offs and loan-loss provisioning.

NPL resolution and foster market development, but also to address other regional challenges, such as de-risking and assessing emerging risks in the financial sector.

*Improving insolvency and debt-enforcement frameworks* is essential for a predictable and transparent system that enables business rescue (for firms) or a second chance (for individuals) and helps creditors to realize claims promptly and protect recovery value. All countries have corporate bankruptcy regimes, but some countries could expand the toolkit by establishing fast-track and rehabilitation procedures and promoting out-of-court mechanisms for debt restructuring. Several countries could consider introducing personal bankruptcy mechanisms. Policies should focus on strengthening the institutions that support/implement the legal frameworks, for instance by improving judicial systems (a key obstacle noted in the surveys) to reduce the time required for resolution. Specialized courts and judges and experienced resolution professionals could strengthen the expertise necessary to facilitate timely and effective resolution.

*Introducing a pan-Caribbean market for NPLs.* The small size of the Caribbean economies, as well as structural obstacles such as gaps in the information framework and cultural and social factors, prevent development of a well-functioning domestic market for distressed assets to facilitate the disposal of NPLs. Access to timely information on distressed borrowers, collateral valuations, and recent NPL sales are critical for developing an active NPL market for distressed assets (Aiyar and others 2015). Policies should focus on building a market based on a common pan-Caribbean platform open to external investors to create economies of scale and address some of the cultural and social obstacles, while also ensuring adequate capital and provisioning levels. Introducing asset management companies (AMCs) can help initiate markets; the experience with AMCs in the region is limited but promising (Box 11.1).[16] While NPL securitization may not be a viable solution for the Caribbean at this juncture, given the small and underdeveloped financial markets and weaknesses in legal and regulatory frameworks, efforts to develop the necessary ingredients for securitizing NPLs, including regulatory and legislative changes, could pave the way to using this tool as a means of pooling risk and facilitating the market for NPLs in the future.

While priority should be given to implementing the strategies outlined above, implementation may face challenges. Some of the strategy's measures, such as enhanced supervision to ensure loss recognition and provision, can be introduced quickly. However, others, such as legal reforms, measures to address informational obstacles, and establishing a market for problem loans, require time to implement. The strategy needs to recognize that each country would require a separate diagnostic that could help in prioritizing and sequencing the reforms, given the differences within the region. The institutional capacity constraints in small Caribbean states

---

[16]AMCs (both private and public) have been used in some countries, particularly Asia, to facilitate NPL disposal (for example, in Indonesia, Korea, Malaysia, Sweden, and Thailand) by separating good assets from bad, allowing the ceding banks and AMCs to focus on their respective objectives, and by helping close the gap between the price at which banks were willing to sell and investors were willing to buy, and in so doing helping to nurture a market for distressed assets (Aiyar and others 2015).

## Box 11.1. Asset Management Companies (AMCs) in the Caribbean

AMCs can enable more efficient collection and disposal of distressed assets and help maximize the value of impaired assets in the banking system, while at the same time preventing credit discipline from deteriorating. International evidence (see, for example, Klingebiel 2000) points to mixed experience in the use of AMCs and suggests that there is no single recipe for establishing a successful AMC. However, common factors for successful AMCs include a supporting legal and regulatory environment, strong leadership, operational independence, appropriate incentives, and a commercial orientation (Ingves, Seelig, and He 2004).

A large majority of Caribbean banks that responded to the IMF survey argue that banks can set up private AMCs and that indeed there are active AMCs operating in their countries. At the same time, there are few examples of operational public AMCs.

- *Eastern Caribbean Currency Union (ECCU).* In the context of bank restructuring within the ECCU, the Eastern Caribbean Central Bank has created an AMC to resolve problem loans. A regional asset management company (ECAMC) has been granted extraordinary powers to acquire collateral and to resolve problem loans. ECAMC will acquire the problem loans from three now-defunct ECCU banks and will be able to purchase NPLs from other banks in the region. A new banking act was passed by all ECCU jurisdictions providing the legislation for the establishment of the ECAMC. It is anticipated that ECAMC will operate for three years.
- *The Bahamas.* Both public and private AMCs have made some progress in removing bad loans from bank balance sheets. First, in 2014, the government established a special purpose vehicle (Bahamas Resolve) to manage $100 million of nonperforming commercial loan assets from the largely state-owned Bank of The Bahamas. There has reportedly been little to no progress in sale of the underlying real estate assets. Second, one commercial bank operating in The Bahamas sold a portfolio of NPLs (about $75 million) to a newly established specialized mortgage servicing company (Gateway). Anecdotal evidence suggests that the experience has been positive thus far, with no major consumer protection complaints related to loan restructuring and potential for other banks to follow suit.

call for coordination of reforms within the region. Some of the ongoing regional initiatives, such as establishing a regional AMC and credit bureaus, enhancing insolvency and debt-enforcement regimes, and establishing guidelines for collateral valuation in the Eastern Caribbean region, are positive steps in this regard.[17] Reforms should also be fine-tuned based on the detailed institutional framework and coordinated across stakeholders, such as the central bank and ministries of finance. National and regional efforts could be supported by well-targeted capacity-building assistance from international financial organizations.

---

[17]These steps indeed form part of a broader comprehensive strategy by the ECCB to address the negative protracted impacts of the global financial crisis on the economies of the ECCU, strengthen the supervisory frameworks to ensure macro-financial stability, and create incentives for problem loan resolution and developing markets for distressed loans. Toward this goal, the ECCB is facilitating the implementation of an Eight-Point Programme approved by the Monetary Council in 2009, working with regional and international partners to build institutional capacity to bolster the resilience of the ECCU banking system (for example, by moving toward implementation of the Basel II framework, which is expected to help banks identify, measure, mitigate, and monitor their risks in a more proactive manner).

# ANNEX 11.1

Annex Table 11.1. Key Measures Implemented in the Past Three Years to Resolve NPLs

| Measures taken by country authorities | Measures taken by banks |
|---|---|
| • Mortgage relief program (The Bahamas)<br>• Tighter prudential requirements and enforcement of changes to prudential regulations (loan classification and provisioning); restriction of banks from declaring, paying dividends, and repatriating profits until all prior losses are written off, all impaired assets are adequately provisioned, and central bank directives are complied with (Belize)<br>• Establishing/operationalization of credit bureaus (ECCU, Jamaica)<br>• Introduction of a new insolvency regime (Jamaica)<br>• Establishment of an Asset Management Cooperation and new Banking and AMC Laws (ECCU)<br>• Establishment of a collections unit and hiring of delinquency officers and issuance of loan policy and procedures manual, recommendation of minimum annual write-offs (St. Kitts and Nevis, for credit unions)<br>• Enactment of bankruptcy laws regarding receivership and development of procedures for the receivership (Trinidad and Tobago [TTO]) | • **Prevention/prudential:** Stricter lending criteria (The Bahamas, Suriname, TTO); continuous review of credit analysis and close monitoring of credit portfolio to limit development of NPL (Guyana, Jamaica, Monserrat, Suriname); implementation of quality control unit and use of reporting mechanisms for proactive portfolio management (Guyana); close monitoring/ follow-up of delinquency for early detection of deterioration and corrective measures (The Bahamas, ECCU, Guyana, TTO); tighter loan delinquency/ adjudication management to mitigate migration to NPLs (Jamaica, TTO); tighter loan provisioning (Suriname, TTO)<br>• **Restructuring and relief:** Refinancing/restructuring/repayment plans to foster remediation/reinstatements/repayments (The Bahamas, Belize, ECCU, Guyana, Jamaica, Suriname, TTO); accepting reduced payment arrangements (Barbados); restructuring to forgive/discount interest payments (Jamaica, Suriname); proactive approach in collection and restructuring of loans (Belize); participating in mortgage relief plans by the government; forbearance agreements (The Bahamas)<br>• **Loss recognition:** Aggressive approach to loan-loss provisioning and write-offs (Belize, Jamaica); encouragement of settlement offers for long outstanding non-accruals (Guyana)<br>• **Recovery:** Establishment of a specialized recovery unit (Belize, Guyana, Suriname); disposal of collateral to reduce debts (Suriname, TTO); follow up with the borrower rigorously for recovery of dues (Guyana); strengthened arrears management unit with required skills and resources (Jamaica); timely legal measures for recovery (TTO)<br>• **Collection:** Strengthened collection activity/methodology/ tools, more focused attention on NPLs by specialized teams to work on resolution, taking legal action against delinquent customers to facilitate access to property by potential buyers (The Bahamas, Guyana, Jamaica); undertake intensive collections (Suriname); enhanced focus on specific borrower categories and early collection action (Guyana, TTO); seek shorter legal processes (Barbados); various forms of litigation (foreclosure proceedings, seizures/repossession of movable assets, appointment of receivers/receiver-managers, selected cases of settlement of indebtedness based on individual merits) (Guyana)<br>• **Sales:** Repricing/aggressive marketing of properties for sale (Belize, ECCU, Jamaica); financing to eligible customers to purchase banks' distressed properties (The Bahamas); encouraging voluntary sales by owners and proactive selling approach for repossessed properties (Barbados); prepare legal processes for sale and foreclosure (Suriname, TTO); early sales of property when possible (Monserrat); sales of NPLs to SPVs (Jamaica)<br>• **Other:** Reviewing alternative measures for asset realization – e.g. wholesale, assigning more assets to realtors, etc. (The Bahamas); training and updating policies/procedures (Belize); educating customers, including on negative effects of NPLs on financial profile (Jamaica) and on early-warning signs (Suriname) |

**Annex Figure 11.1. Panel VAR: Main Model (Impulse response functions, annual frequency)**

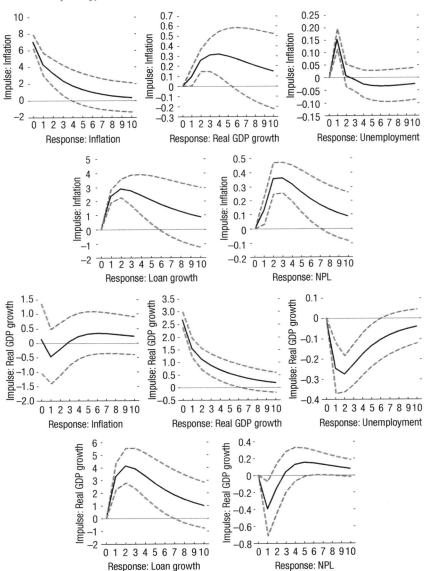

**Annex Figure 11.1. Panel VAR: Main Model (Impulse response functions, annual frequency)** *(continued)*

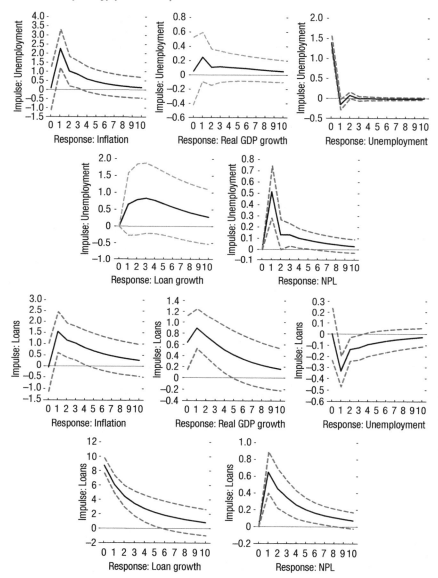

**Annex Figure 11.1. Panel VAR: Main Model (Impulse response functions, annual frequency) *(continued)***

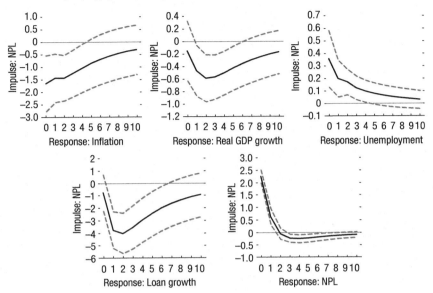

Source: IMF staff estimates and calculations.
Note: CPI = consumer price index; NPL = nonperforming loan; VAR = vector autoregression. Panel VAR includes change in NPL ratio, credit growth, change in unemployment rate, real GDP growth, CPI inflation. Shocks are of one standard deviation. Errors are 10 percent generated by Monte Carlo with 300 simulations. Red signifies the presence of a statistically significant effect.

# REFERENCES

Aiyar, S., W. Bergthaler, J. M. Garrido, A. Ilyina, A. Jobst, K. Kang, D. Kovtun, Y. Liu, D. Monaghan, and M. Moretti. 2015. "A Strategy for Resolving Europe's Problem Loans." IMF Staff Discussion Note 15/19, International Monetary Fund, Washington, DC.

Arellano, M., and S. Bond. 1991. "Some Tests of Specification for Panel Data: Monte Carlo Evidence and an Application to Employment Equations." *Review of Economic Studies* 58 (2): 277–97.

Arellano, M., and O. Bover. 1995. "Another Look at the Instrumental Variable Estimation of Error-Components Models." *Journal of Econometrics* 68 (1): 29–51.

Bank for International Settlements. 2016. *Guidelines on Prudential Treatment of Problem Assets–Definitions of Nonperforming Exposures and Forbearance.* Basel: Bank for International Settlements.

Beaton, K., T. Dowling, D. Kovtun, F. Loyola, A. Myrvoda, J. Okwuokei, I. Ötker, and J. Turunen. Forthcoming. "Problem Loans in the Caribbean: Determinants, Impact, and Strategies for Resolution." IMF Working Paper, International Monetary Fund, Washington, DC.

Beaton, K., A. Myrvoda, and S. Thompson. 2016. "Non-Performing Loans in the ECCU: Determinants and Macroeconomic Impact." IMF Working Paper 16/229, International Monetary Fund, Washington, DC.

Beck, R., P. Jakubík, and A. Piloiu. 2013. "Non-Performing Loans: What Matters in Addition to the Economic Cycle?" European Central Bank Working Paper 1515, European Central Bank, Frankfurt.

Bergthaler, W., K. Kang, Y. Liu, and D. Monaghan. 2015. "Tackling Small and Medium Sized Enterprise Problem Loans in Europe." IMF Staff Discussion Note 15/04, International Monetary Fund, Washington, DC.

Blundell, R., and S. Bond. 1998. "Initial Conditions and Moment Restrictions in Dynamic Panel Data Model." *Journal of Econometrics* 87 (1): 115–43.

Constâncio, V. 2017. "Resolving Europe's NPL Burden: Challenges and Benefits." Keynote Speech "Tackling Europe's Non-performing Loans Crisis: Restructuring Debt, Reviving Growth" organized by Bruegel, Brussels. February 2.

Espinoza, R., and A. Prasad. 2010. "Nonperforming Loans in the GCC Banking System and their Macroeconomic Effects." IMF Working Paper 10/224, International Monetary Fund, Washington, DC.

Holtz-Eakin, D., W. Newey, and H. S. Rosen. 1988. "Estimating Vector Autoregressions with Panel Data." *Econometrica* 56 (6): 1371–95.

Ingves, S., S. Seelig, and D. He. 2004. "Issues in the Establishment of Asset Management Companies." IMF Policy Discussion Paper 04/3, International Monetary Fund, Washington, DC.

Jordan, A., and C. Tucker. 2013. "Assessing the Impact of Nonperforming Loans on Economic Growth in The Bahamas." *Monetaria* I (2): 371–400.

Klein, N. 2013. "Non-Performing Loans in CESEE: Determinants and Impact on Macroeconomic Performance." IMF Working Paper 13/72, International Monetary Fund, Washington, DC.

Klingebiel, D. 2000. "The Use of Asset Management Companies in the Resolution of Banking Crises: Cross-Country Experiences." Policy Research Working Paper 2284, World Bank, Washington, DC.

Lexology. 2016. "Non-Performing Loans and Securitization in Europe." https://www.lexology .com/library/detail.aspx?g=5907bb19-7e3e-4060-84c1-d73bcfaccc28.

Liu, Y., and R. Rosenberg. 2013. "Dealing with Private Debt Distress in the Wake of the European Financial Crisis: A Review of the Economics and Legal Toolbox." IMF Working Paper 13/44, International Monetary Fund, Washington, DC.

Nickell, S. J. 1981. "Biases in Dynamic Models with Fixed Effects." *Econometrica* 49 (6): 1417–1426.

Nkusu, M. 2011. "Nonperforming Loans and Macrofinancial Vulnerabilities in Advanced Economies." IMF Working Paper 11/161, International Monetary Fund, Washington, DC.

Tintchev, K. Forthcoming. "Commodity Price Shocks and Bank Credit Quality in the Caribbean." IMF Working Paper, International Monetary Fund, Washington, DC.

# CHAPTER 12

# Loss of Correspondent Banking Relationships in the Caribbean: Trends, Impact, and Policy Options

Trevor Alleyne, Jacques Bouhga-Hagbe, Thomas Dowling, Dmitriy Kovtun, Alla Myrvoda, Joel Chiedu Okwuokei, and Jarkko Turunen

## INTRODUCTION

A correspondent banking relationship (CBR) is a bilateral arrangement between banks, often involving a cross-border relationship in multiple currencies. According to Erbenová and others (2016), a correspondent banking arrangement involves one bank (the correspondent, for example, a major international bank) providing a deposit account or other liability accounts and related services to another bank (the respondent, for example, a bank located and doing business in the Caribbean). The arrangement requires the exchange of messages to settle transactions by crediting and debiting those accounts. Correspondent banking relationships are a key component of a well-functioning international financial system. They enable a range of crucial transactions and services, including the execution of third-party payments such as wire transfers and credit card transactions, trade finance, and transactions related to the banks' own cash-clearing, liquidity management, and short-term borrowing or investment needs.

Following the global financial crisis, banks reduced their involvement in less profitable and riskier activities worldwide, including correspondent banking. Large global banks have recently come under increasing pressure to increase their capital, streamline their business models, and reevaluate their risk exposures (Lagarde 2016). As a result, these banks have been reducing activities in areas that they perceive to be either less profitable or, more generally, detrimental to their

---

This chapter is based on an IMF Working Paper (Alleyne and others, forthcoming) by the same authors.

risk tolerance—a process that is sometimes referred to as "de-risking."[1] The underlying drivers of this global de-risking trend are multidimensional. They include advanced economy regulators' attempts to strengthen prudential regulations and enhance economic and financial stability; their concerns about tax avoidance, money laundering, and terrorist financing; and business decisions by correspondent banks in a new macroeconomic environment characterized by low interest rates and increased costs of regulatory compliance. This global trend has been most evident in the reduction of CBRs.

Banks across the Caribbean have lost CBRs, with negative impacts on some services and sectors. Surveys show that the extent of CBR loss varies across Caribbean countries (Table 12.1).[2] Existing studies of the withdrawal of CBRs in the Caribbean draw from diverse and sometimes anecdotal sources to document the loss of CBRs and the resulting impact on financial institutions and the economy more broadly. Further analysis is hampered by a lack of timely data on the number of CBRs, the value and volume of related financial flows, and the nature of the factors driving the loss of CBRs. This chapter brings together existing evidence on the loss of CBRs in the Caribbean, drawing from global surveys (such as World Bank 2015b); regional surveys by Caribbean authorities (CARICOM 2016), the Caribbean Association of Banks (CAB 2016), and IMF staff (IMF 2016b; Alleyne and others, forthcoming); and discussions with both authorities and banks in the context of the IMF's engagement with member countries. The chapter also examines the key drivers of the loss of CBRs and the potential economic effect of a substantial loss of CBRs. Finally, it reviews policy responses thus far and discusses available policy solutions for the Caribbean.

## WHY DO CBRs MATTER?

Caribbean economies, characterized by their extensive interconnections with the global economy, depend on the reliable functioning of CBRs. Additional potential links arise from the presence of offshore sectors in several countries. The loss of CBRs can affect the economy through reduced international trade, remittances, or investment flows (Figure 12.1):

- *International trade and commerce.* All countries in the Caribbean rely heavily on international trade, including tourism and other services, requiring CBRs to carry out cross-border transactions. The average openness ratio (the sum of exports and imports of goods and services divided by GDP) in

---

[1]IMF (2017) has argued that that the indiscriminate use of the term "de-risking" has confused the dialogue on the trends and drivers of the withdrawal or termination of CBRs.

[2]Data show the number of banks that have been affected as a share of banks that were surveyed. Differences across the two surveys can be explained by different samples and time periods. The IMF Survey from Alleyne and others (forthcoming) covers all commercial banks in many countries, while CAB (2016) represents a sample of members of the Caribbean Association of Banks.

**Table 12.1. Banks that Have Lost Correspondent Banking Relationships**
*(share)*

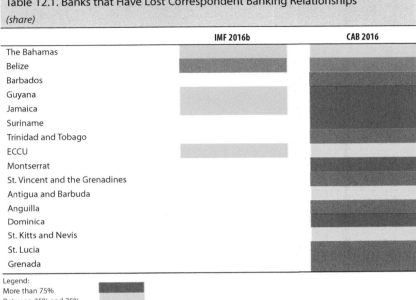

| | IMF 2016b | CAB 2016 |
|---|---|---|
| The Bahamas | | |
| Belize | | |
| Barbados | | |
| Guyana | | |
| Jamaica | | |
| Suriname | | |
| Trinidad and Tobago | | |
| ECCU | | |
| Montserrat | | |
| St. Vincent and the Grenadines | | |
| Antigua and Barbuda | | |
| Anguilla | | |
| Dominica | | |
| St. Kitts and Nevis | | |
| St. Lucia | | |
| Grenada | | |

Legend:
More than 75%
Between 25% and 75%
Fewer than 25%
Sources: IMF 2016b; and Caribbean Association of Banks 2016.
Note: ECCU = Eastern Caribbean Currency Union.

the Caribbean amounted to 95 percent during 2011–15, which is slightly higher than the world average of 91 percent. An increase in the cost of making payments or a disruption in the ability to make or receive international payments would seriously undermine economic activity.

- *Remittances.* The degree to which Caribbean countries rely on remittances varies significantly. Remittances amounted to 6.3 percent of GDP, on average, in 2011–15, which was higher than the world's average (4.8 percent of GDP), with Guyana (13 percent of GDP), Haiti (22 percent of GDP), and Jamaica (15 percent of GDP) exhibiting high dependence on these flows. Thus, a reduced ability to receive remittances inflows would pose a significant risk in these economies. In addition, reduced access to money transfer services or an increase in transfer costs could push remittances to informal channels, making them more difficult to monitor.

- *Financial account flows.* Financial account flows contribute a major part to financing investment. The average of financial account balances in the region was close to 9 percent of GDP over 2011–15. Foreign direct investment (FDI) is especially important for the Caribbean, with total inflows averaging nearly 8 percent of GDP in 2011–15. A disruption in CBRs could constrain these investment flows, including through difficulties in repatriating reinvested earnings.

### Figure 12.1. The Caribbean: Balance of Payments Linkages

*The Caribbean's openness to trade is slightly higher than the world average ...*

**1. Trade Openness—Goods and Services**
**(Percent of GDP, 2011–15 average)**

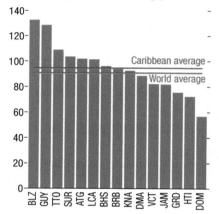

*... because of large tourism sectors in many of the countries.*

**2. Tourism Receipts**
**(Percent of GDP, 2015 or latest available)**

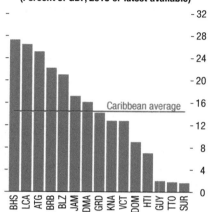

*Several countries critically depend on the inflows of remittances.*

**3. Remittances**
**(Percent of GDP, inflows, 2011–15 average)**

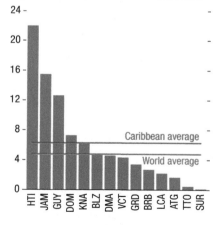

*The FDI inflows are an important source for investment.*

**4. Net FDI Inflows**
**(Percent of GDP, 2011–15 average)**

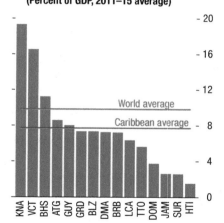

Sources: World Bank, Remittances Database; IMF, World Economic Outlook Database; and IMF staff estimates and calculations.
Note: FDI = foreign direct investment. Data labels in figure use International Organization for Standardization (ISO) country codes.

- *Offshore banks.* Risks to offshore banks and subsequently to the economy depend on the size of offshore sectors and their links with domestic economies. Some countries in the region have large offshore sectors consisting of offshore banks, other financial institutions, and international business companies that provide various services. In principle, the "firewall" between the domestic and offshore sectors should limit the risks to domestic economies, but large offshore sectors can nevertheless be an important source of employment and government revenue. For example, the offshore sector contributed 0.7 percent (2015) and 4.1 percent (2013) of fiscal revenues in The Bahamas and Barbados, respectively. There are also examples of more direct links between these sectors; for instance, Belize's offshore banks are an important source of financing for the domestic economy and have direct ties with the domestic banking system.

## THE WITHDRAWAL OF CBRs—HOW SEVERE HAS IT BEEN?

### Global Trends

Recent surveys have highlighted key features of the global pressure on CBRs. Global evidence on loss of CBRs is largely based on surveys of banks (such as World Bank 2015a, 2015b; IMF and Union of Arab Banks 2015; ASBA 2015), complemented by other evidence collected in the context of the IMF's engagement with member countries. Erbenová and others (2016) summarize this survey evidence as well as regional implications based on a few specific country case studies. Finally, BIS (2015) and IMF (2017) analyze global trends in cross-border transactions using SWIFT data.[3] Although the information and data are far from comprehensive, they point to the following stylized facts:

- *Globally, no clear trends in CBRs are apparent.* The BIS (2015) indicates that while CBR trends vary widely across countries, the aggregate data on volumes and values of transactions show no clear trend in correspondent banking activity. However, based on median statistics, the number of correspondent banks and the value of transactions fell during 2012–15, even as the volume of transactions increased.

- *Loss of CBRs has affected different types of countries.* The largest declines in CBRs as measured by transaction values were observed in advanced economies under economic stress (for example, Cyprus and Greece), fragile states under sanctions or involved in social and political conflict (for example, Chad, Syria, Ukraine, and Yemen), and small island states (for example, Dominica, Timor-Leste, and Seychelles).

---

[3]SWIFT, an electronic financial messaging system, is used to transact payments between financial institutions worldwide. Metadata attached to each transaction provide information about the sender and receiver and the type and purpose of the transaction.

- *The economic impact has been limited thus far.* There is critical pressure on CBRs in some countries, especially in smaller countries in the Caribbean and the Pacific, the Middle East and North Africa (MENA) region, Central Asia, Africa, and Europe, but the economic and financial stability impact has been limited thus far. Financial institutions have typically found other arrangements to compensate for the loss of CBRs.

- *Financial fragilities have been accentuated in some affected countries.* The pressure on CBRs exacerbates financial fragilities in some affected countries because of the concentration of cross-border flows through fewer CBRs or CBR maintenance through alternative arrangements.

## Caribbean Developments

Respondent banks have largely avoided serious disruption to correspondent banking services. In most cases, Caribbean banks have found alternative cross-border means of payment, including relying on remaining CBRs or finding replacement CBRs. World Bank (2015b) suggests that Latin America and the Caribbean has experienced a greater loss of CBRs than many other parts of the world, and that within the region, the incidence of withdrawals of CBRs was greater in the Caribbean. A survey by the Caribbean Association of Banks (2016) indicates that 58 percent of banks had lost at least one CBR, directly affecting 12 countries.

Results from a 2016 IMF survey confirm that banks in several Caribbean countries have lost CBRs.[4] However, only five out of 14 countries that responded to the survey experienced a decline in the aggregate number of CBRs in the five years up to September 2016. Belize saw the largest decline by far, losing more than two-thirds of its CBRs, with most of the decline taking place from April 2015 to February 2016 (Box 12.1). Loss of CBRs has been less dramatic in other Caribbean countries. Among commercial banks, the smaller indigenous banks have tended to be the most affected. These banks generate a relatively small volume of cross-border business for correspondent banks and are less likely to have sophisticated transaction monitoring mechanisms to satisfy correspondent bank's own anti-money laundering/combating the financing of terrorism (AML/CFT) protocols. In contrast, foreign-owned branches and subsidiaries, which often have the backing of a larger parent institution and can rely on its network of CBRs, do not seem to have been affected at all. In many Caribbean countries, these establishments include subsidiaries of large Canadian banks that play an important role in the domestic banking system. Banks in several countries have found replacement CBRs (also in line with CAB 2016), although some banks have had difficulties. Available SWIFT data also point to a decline in

---

[4]The IMF survey, which is detailed in Alleyne and others (forthcoming), was undertaken in September 2016 in 14 Caribbean countries and covers commercial banks operating in the domestic banking system. The survey does not cover international (offshore) banks, which primarily focus on providing services to nonresident customers. In some countries, the responses cover only a part of the onshore domestic banking sector.

## Box 12.1. Potential Macroeconomic Impact of Loss of CBRs: An Illustrative Case for Belize

Following the taxonomy of channels through which correspondent banking relationships (CBRs) can affect an economy as described in the main text, bank-level data are used to illustrate the potential impact of the withdrawal of CBRs in Belize, which has experienced the largest loss of CBRs of all countries in the Caribbean. The analysis examines the effect on exports and imports, foreign direct investment (FDI), remittances, bank deposits, disposable income, and bank balance sheets from the inability of economic agents to send or receive cross-border payments. The exercise simulates two scenarios, a "low-stress" scenario that assumes that loss of CBRs reduces the value of cross-border transactions by 10 percent, and a "high-stress" scenario in which 70 percent of transactions are eliminated.

### Key Findings

The loss of CBRs could have a sizable impact on economic activity and financial stability. Fewer CBRs, the different business models of the local banks, and stricter due diligence requirements could remove many economic agents from formal trade and finance channels. Under the high-stress scenario, real GDP could drop by as much as 5.3 percentage points annually relative to the baseline during 2017–21. Trade (that is, the value of exports and imports of goods and services) would fall by 23–26 percentage points of GDP during the same period, and FDI would decline by about 1.9–2.5 percentage points of GDP. The banking system's capital adequacy ratio would fall by close to 7.5 percentage points but would remain above the prudential minimum of 9 percent, although some banks could become insolvent.

### Table 12.1.1 Impact of the Loss of CBRs: Stress Scenarios Relative to the Baseline

|  | 2017 | 2018 | 2019 | 2020 | 2021 |
|---|---|---|---|---|---|
| Low-Stress Scenario | | | | | |
| Changes in Real GDP (US$ million) | −14.2 | −13.9 | −14.4 | −14.2 | −14.4 |
| Changes in Real GDP Growth (percent) | −1.0 | −1.0 | −1.0 | −0.9 | −0.9 |
| Changes in Exports (percent of GDP) | −3.3 | −3.3 | −3.3 | −3.3 | −3.3 |
| Changes in Imports (percent of GDP) | −3.7 | −3.6 | −3.5 | −3.5 | −3.5 |
| Changes in FDI (percent of GDP) | −0.3 | −0.4 | −0.4 | −0.4 | −0.4 |
| Changes in Banks' NFA (US$ million) | −3.2 | −6.9 | −6.8 | −6.0 | −5.3 |
| In months of imports | −0.03 | −0.07 | −0.07 | −0.06 | −0.05 |
| Changes in Banks' CARs (percent) | −3.6 | −3.5 | −3.4 | −3.2 | −3.1 |
| High-Stress Scenario | | | | | |
| Changes in Real GDP (US$ million) | −75.6 | −76.2 | −76.4 | −77.1 | −78.9 |
| Changes in Real GDP Growth (percent) | −5.3 | −5.2 | −5.1 | −5.1 | −5.1 |
| Changes in Exports (percent of GDP) | −23.3 | −23.1 | −22.8 | −22.8 | −22.8 |
| Changes in Imports (percent of GDP) | −25.7 | −24.9 | −24.6 | −24.6 | −24.6 |
| Changes in FDI (percent of GDP) | −1.9 | −2.6 | −2.5 | −2.5 | −2.5 |
| Changes in Banks' NFA (US$ million) | −22.2 | −48.2 | −47.6 | −41.7 | −36.9 |
| In months of imports | −0.2 | −0.5 | −0.5 | −0.4 | −0.3 |
| Changes in Banks' CARs (percent) | −7.4 | −7.3 | −7.1 | −7.0 | −6.9 |

Sources: Central Bank of Belize; and IMF staff calculations.
Note: CAR = capital adequacy ratio; CBR = correspondent banking relationship; FDI = foreign direct investment; NFA = net foreign assets. For details, see IMF 2016a.

active correspondent banks over the 2011–15 period, accompanied by declining value of cross-border transactions.[5]

Even in cases in which respondent banks have maintained CBRs, certain types of services have been adversely affected. The services most affected include operations that are cash intensive or that involve large numbers of relatively small transactions. Thus, all countries that responded to the IMF survey reported that money transfer services have been affected, including *cambios* in Jamaica, where a leading bank no longer accepts foreign instruments and remittances from some money services businesses. A bank in The Bahamas has lost its cash-intensive Western Union money transfer business. Other bank services that have been negatively affected include foreign currency check clearing, cash letter deposits, bank draft settlement, trade finance, and routing of funds for charities and foundations (CAB 2016; CARICOM 2016).

The costs of maintaining correspondent banking services have risen substantially in some cases. Such costs can be both explicit (charges by correspondent banks for accessing CBRs) and implicit, such as those arising from more robust due diligence efforts, expenses dedicated to improvements in AML/CFT compliance, and training of employees. The IMF survey found that correspondent banking fees have increased for some of the banks in each Caribbean jurisdiction (Figure 12.2). In the Eastern Caribbean Currency Union (ECCU), for example, correspondent banking fees doubled or tripled for some banks. In Belize, costs of cross-border transactions, particularly wire transfers, have also increased significantly (CARICOM 2016). The IMF survey found that some of the costs, both explicit and implicit, may be transmitted to consumers: jurisdictions that noted an increase in explicit correspondent banking fees generally reported significant increases in fees charged to bank customers for wire transfers and foreign currency drafts. However, available data do not definitively point to an increase in the cost of inbound remittances.

To safeguard their CBRs, some respondent banks have terminated relationships with clients from certain sectors, notably those undertaking seemingly riskier businesses. In Belize, for example, banks have discontinued processing international wire transfers for credit unions because this process represents "nesting," that is, a situation in which a financial institution uses the CBR of another bank to carry out cross-border transactions. Nesting is strongly discouraged, and in many cases prohibited by the correspondent bank because of concerns about the inability of the respondent bank to carry out appropriate due diligence on the customer of the financial institution that is generating the transaction. For similar reasons, foreign-owned banks in St. Vincent and the Grenadines discontinued deposit services to local credit unions in mid-2016, resulting in a consolidation of credit unions' deposits in an indigenous bank. Termination of banking services to online gaming companies in some ECCU jurisdictions has forced these companies to search for banking services providers in Asia. According to the IMF

---

[5]Based on SWIFT data published in BIS (2015).

## Figure 12.2. Cost of CBRs and Remittances

*In many jurisdictions, correspondent banks have increased their CBR fees ...*

*... and the respondent banks have increased fees for CBR-related transactions to their customers.*

**1. Increases in CBR Fees by Correspondent Banks**
**(Percent)**

**2. Increases in Fees to Customers for Transactions Involving CBRs**
**(Percent)**

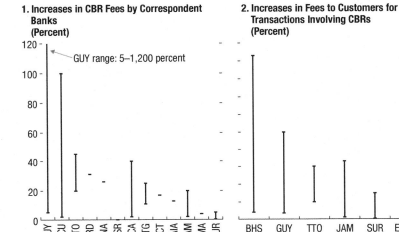

*However, there is little evidence that the cost of remittances has increased.*

**3. Cost of Remittances**
**(Percent)**

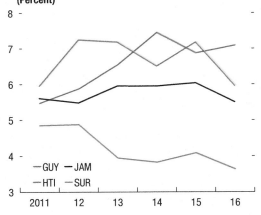

Sources: Panels 1 and 2, country authorities and banks; panel 3, World Bank, Remittances Prices Worldwide (http://remittanceprices.worldbank.org).
Note: In panels 1 and 2, the bars represent ranges of increases in fees over past five years as reported in IMF 2016b. In panel 3, the lines represent an average cost of sending an equivalent of US$500 to a particular destination from sources covered by the database. CBR = correspondent banking relationship; ECCU = Eastern Caribbean Currency Union. Data labels in figure use International Organization for Standardization (ISO) country codes.

survey results, services to customers in gambling and gaming sectors have also been negatively affected in The Bahamas, Suriname, and Trinidad and Tobago. Although statistics are unavailable at this stage, anecdotal evidence suggests that some banks have increased the level of scrutiny for deposits associated with citizenship programs in some ECCU jurisdictions, refusing to accept such deposits in some cases.

As respondent banks have replaced lost CBRs, there has been a change in the type of correspondent banks serving the region. Historically, banks in the Caribbean had CBRs with major international banks, mainly of U.S. origin, given the importance of U.S. dollar transactions. Because these banks have withdrawn from the region, some Caribbean banks report establishing replacement relationships with smaller, less well known ("second tier") banks (IMF 2016b). In Belize, some banks managed to establish relationships, often with a restricted menu of services, with banks in Europe and Asia, or with smaller banks in the United States.

The withdrawal of CBRs has had a more serious impact on the offshore financial sector. CBRs are particularly important for offshore banks, which rely on international transactions for their core business. Regulations in several jurisdictions also require an offshore bank to have an active CBR before a license is granted or renewed. Declines of CBRs in this sector and the resulting decline in the number of license applications have put the future growth of the offshore sector at risk in many Caribbean economies.

- In St. Lucia, for instance, several offshore banks have had their CBR relationships terminated; some of these banks have been unable to find replacements. Some newly licensed offshore banks have been unable to commence operations, while others have had to surrender their licenses, largely because of the inability to establish CBRs.[6]

- In Belize, whose five offshore banks were the most affected, 13 out of 16 CBR accounts were lost from April 2015 to February 2016. Thus, offshore banks have scaled down operations, and domestic banks now play a greater role in the banking system.

- In The Bahamas, responses to a 2016 central bank survey revealed that 10 offshore banks had CBRs terminated or restricted, up from just three banks the previous year.[7]

- Meanwhile, the provision of banking services to international business companies (IBCs) has declined consistently across the Caribbean, largely affecting Barbados and the ECCU.

- In Barbados, banks have terminated relationships with some corporate vehicles established in the international business and financial services sector,

---

[6]St. Lucia Financial Services Regulatory Authority, Annual Report, 2016.

[7]However, the central bank warned that the apparent increase in affected banks could be explained partly by the difference in coverage between the 2015 and 2016 surveys.

which is depressing that sector's growth prospects.[8] This phenomenon has been largely reflected in the closing of entire business lines, termination of services, or placement of arduous restrictions on IBC accounts. Some IBCs reportedly have also had to search for alternative financial partners in other jurisdictions. Along with greater due diligence and scrutiny, account terminations and waiting periods for new accounts have increased significantly, jeopardizing future development of the IBC sector.

## Potential Factors behind the Withdrawal of CBRs

Withdrawal of CBRs reflects business decisions by global banks. They have reassessed their individual business models, adopting different strategies in response to changes in the macroeconomic and regulatory environment. In general, macroeconomic conditions, such as persistently low interest rates since the global financial crisis, together with changes in regulatory frameworks have reduced the attractiveness of high-volume, low-return business lines like correspondent banking.

Four main groups of factors have contributed to global banks' decisions to end their CBRs. First, compliance issues related to AML/CFT regulations are the most often cited reasons for termination of CBRs, in the context of more aggressive enforcement by regulators, especially in the United States. Second, tax transparency agreements impose an additional regulatory burden that carry their own set of compliance costs. Third, trade and economic sanction violations have very large fines and require another layer of due diligence. Fourth, additional profit- and risk-related reasons for withdrawing CBRs, not directly related to AML/CFT compliance, reflect shifts in the banking landscape since the global financial crisis. These factors are not mutually exclusive and any one of them can be a sufficient reason for a bank to decide to terminate a CBR. Examining these factors can help explain the extent to which Caribbean countries have been affected by the withdrawal of CBRs.

### More Intense AML/CFT Efforts

AML/CFT compliance–related issues are the most widely referenced reason for withdrawal of CBRs. The international standard for AML/CFT efforts was updated by the Financial Action Task Force (FATF) in 2012 with a view toward broadening the assessment to include effective implementation and with a greater emphasis on a risk-based approach. The compliance costs associated with the due diligence required to meet these standards, combined with low expected profits and the large fines and reputational damage for violations, are primary reasons given for withdrawing CBRs (World Bank 2015). Banks have identified potential

---

[8]See Worrell and others (2016) for a discussion of how more stringent regulations by advanced economy regulators have driven IBCs away from offshore financial centers in the Caribbean to those in advanced economies, despite equal or sometimes stronger institutional frameworks in the Caribbean.

channels of exposure to AML/CFT risks associated with shortfalls in the supervisory or legal frameworks in the countries of the respondent banks; uncertainty about the quality of respondent bank's customer due diligence processes; and the presence of relatively higher-risk businesses such as money or value transfer services, payment settlement services, offshore sectors, or gaming, especially those businesses lacking physical presence (IMF 2017).

Various characteristics of the Caribbean economies make them more vulnerable to perceptions of potential AML/CFT risks. For example, many Caribbean countries tend to transact a higher-than-average volume of remittances per capita (see Figure 12.1). Money or value transfer services can be a channel through which banks face exposure to AML/CFT violations owing to the large number of cash transactions (often in relatively small amounts per transaction), which makes due diligence more challenging. Another common feature of several Caribbean economies is the presence of cash-intensive casino operations or online gambling. In some cases, regulation and supervision of both money or value transfer services and gaming operations are less established than for the banking system and, as a result, may elicit concerns from correspondent banks. Several Caribbean jurisdictions also offer offshore services, which are sometimes perceived to be higher-risk businesses.

Available evidence reveals no clear relationship between the loss of CBRs and compliance with the 2002 FATF standard in the Caribbean (Figure 12.3). This is consistent with results in Collin, Cook, and Soramaki (2016), who examine the impact of AML/CFT regulation on cross-border transactions using detailed SWIFT payment data. They find that while inclusion of a country in a list of high-risk countries reduces the number of payments received from other jurisdictions, there is no impact on outgoing payments. This finding is also aligned with the results presented by IMF (2017), indicating that correspondent banks are more focused on the quality of an individual relationship with a respondent bank than on the country's AML/CFT framework.

Caribbean countries have made significant progress since their initial AML/CFT assessments.[9] To address new and emerging issues, and to clarify and strengthen many of the existing obligations, FATF released a set of revised standards in 2012 that seek to assess the effectiveness of the AML/CFT institutional framework, with a focus on a risk-based approach. However, at this stage, only two Caribbean countries, Jamaica and Trinidad and Tobago, have completed the initial evaluation based on the 2012 FATF recommendations. Both countries were assessed with at least a "moderate" level of effectiveness in about half of the categories and a "low" rating in the other half.

---

[9]Initial Caribbean Financial Action Task Force (CFATF) 3rd mutual evaluation of compliance with the 2002 FATF standards was conducted between 2007 and 2010 for most Caribbean countries. Most countries were found to be noncompliant or partially compliant in the majority of categories. Follow-up assessments were conducted to evaluate ongoing improvements in compliance.

## Figure 12.3. CFATF Ratings and Changes in Cross-Border Transactions

**CFATF Ratings from the Latest Follow-up Report of the *Third Mutual Evaluation Report***

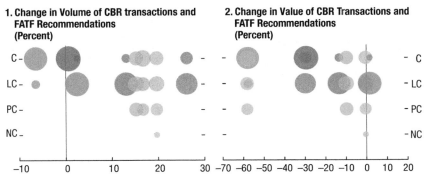

1. **Change in Volume of CBR transactions and FATF Recommendations (Percent)**

2. **Change in Value of CBR Transactions and FATF Recommendations (Percent)**

Sources: Bank for International Settlements; Caribbean Financial Action Task Force (CFATF); and IMF staff estimates and calculations.
Note: The charts plot percent change in volume or value of CBR transactions during 2012–15 against the ratings (authors' assessment) based on the latest follow-up reports of the *Third Mutual Evaluation Report*. C = compliant; LC = largely compliant; NC = noncompliant; PC = partially compliant. Higher values on the vertical axis represent better anti-money laundering/combating the financing of terrorism compliance. Each color represents a country. Bubble size represents the number of categories corresponding to a particular rating (for each color-coded country). For example, looking at the light-blue color-coded country, although the CFATF ratings are high (that is, all categories compliant or largely compliant), the country still experienced a large decline in the volume of CBR transactions. Follow-up reviews of the *Third Mutual Evaluation Reports* based on the 2002 FATF standard are used except for Jamaica and Trinidad and Tobago, where the latest CFATF ratings refer to the *Fourth Mutual Evaluation Report* (based on the 2012 FATF standard).

## *Increased Focus on Tax Transparency*

Increased global pressure in recent years to enhance tax transparency may have contributed to the loss of CBRs. This issue is particularly relevant for jurisdictions that have offshore financial services centers, including several Caribbean countries, and that have traditionally relied on zero or low tax rates to attract business. Offshore financial services are a major industry in many Caribbean countries. As a result, several jurisdictions that in the past have been identified as destinations for tax avoidance have come under increasing international pressure to share more information in a timelier fashion. For example, failing to comply with the U.S. Foreign Account Tax Compliance Act (FATCA) can have serious consequences for countries doing business with U.S. firms. Compliance with tax information agreements, such as FATCA and the Organisation for Economic Co-operation and Development's (OECD's) tax information exchange agreement and Common Reporting Standard (CRS), imposes an additional regulatory burden that increases compliance and transaction costs (Erbenová and others 2016). This increase in costs, as well as the cost of potential fines and associated reputational risks, is

**Table 12.2. Tax Information Compliance[1]**

| Jurisdiction | United States<br>FATCA | OECD<br>Convention on Mutual Administrative Assistance in Tax Matters | Committed to First Exchange under CRS[1] | Multilateral (MCAA) or Bilateral Exchange Agreement | Compliance with EOIR |
|---|---|---|---|---|---|
| Anguilla | ✓ | ✓ | 2017 | MCAA | PC |
| Antigua and Barbuda | ✓ | ✗ | 2018 | MCAA | PC |
| Aruba | ✗ | ✓ | 2018 | MCAA | LC |
| The Bahamas | ✓ | ✗ | 2018 | Bilateral | LC |
| Barbados | ✓ | ✓ | 2017 | MCAA | LC |
| Belize | ✓ | ✓ | 2018 | MCAA | LC |
| Curaçao | ✓ | ✓ | 2017 | MCAA | PC |
| Dominica | ✓ | ✗ | 2018 | Bilateral | PC |
| Grenada | ✓ | ✗ | 2018 | MCAA | LC |
| Guyana | ✓ | ✗ | – | | |
| Jamaica | ✓ | ✓ | – | | LC |
| Montserrat | ✓ | ✓ | 2017 | MCAA | LC |
| St. Kitts and Nevis | ✓ | ✓ | 2018 | MCAA | LC |
| St. Lucia | ✓ | ✓ | 2018 | MCAA | LC |
| St. Vincent and the Grenadines | ✓ | ✓ | 2018 | MCAA | LC |
| Suriname | ✗ | ✗ | – | | |
| Trinidad and Tobago | ✗ | ✗ | 2017 | Bilateral | NC |

Sources: U.S. Treasury; and OECD.
Note: CRS = Common Reporting Standard; EOIR = Exchange of Information on Request; FATCA = Foreign Account Tax Compliance Act; LC = largely compliant; MCAA = Multilateral Competent Authority Agreement; NC = noncompliant; OECD = Organisation for Economic Co-operation and Development; PC = partially compliant.
[1]As of September 19, 2016. In Trinidad and Tobago, FATCA legislation was passed by the House of Representatives and the Senate in early 2017, and is currently awaiting proclamation by the president.
http://www.oecd.org/tax/automatic-exchange/international-framework-for-the-crs/MCAA-Signatories.pdf.

likely to reduce global banks' appetite for dealing with offshore financial institutions (Worrell and others 2016).

Several Caribbean jurisdictions have or are in the process of entering into agreements to share tax information. Most Caribbean countries are already implementing FATCA or are moving toward FATCA compliance (Table 12.2). The OECD Global Forum on Transparency and Exchange of Information for Tax Purposes assesses jurisdictions according to three key criteria for tax transparency: (1) compliance with the standard for exchange of information on request, (2) commitment to implement the CRS on automatic exchange of information, and (3) participation in the Multilateral Convention on Mutual Administrative Assistance in Tax Matters. Many Caribbean countries comply with at least two of the three criteria. Many countries have agreed to a multilateral agreement on tax information sharing and are committed to the CRS, which standardizes the financial account information to be shared and implements an automatic exchange of information (Table 12.2).[10] However, implementation of the CRS is at an early stage, requires significant effort toward both domestic legislation and international negotiations, and is not expected to be completed before 2018.

## International Sanctions

Economic and trade sanctions require banks to implement another layer of compliance and due diligence. Like AML/CFT violations, sanctions can result in expensive fines and increase the cost of maintaining CBRs. Evidence indicates that countries that face U.S. economic and trade sanctions have seen a larger decline in CBRs as well as in the volume and value of CBR transactions. For Caribbean countries and their domestic banking systems, this is unlikely to be an important driver of CBR withdrawals in the region. However, even though Caribbean countries have not been directly affected by those sanctions, they are indirectly affected (and therefore subject to increased scrutiny for customer due diligence) because offshore banks in the region facilitate international transactions from all over the world and citizenship-by-investment programs receive applicants from around the world, including from countries subject to sanctions.

## Lower Profitability and Risk Aversion by Global Banks

Global banks have also decided to withdraw CBRs because of the macroeconomic environment and the enhanced prudential regulations they face. Since the global financial crisis, banks have been reexamining their business practices for exposure to risk. Vulnerabilities in banking systems as well as in individual banks during the crisis have led to consolidation of the banking sector, particularly in the United States and Europe. Regulators have also sought to increase buffers, requiring banks to hold more capital and more liquid assets, thus increasing the cost of holding risk in their balance sheets. In addition, the low growth, low interest rate environment has prompted banks to become leaner and more risk averse while concentrating on higher profits and core businesses, leading them to withdraw their CBRs, particularly from jurisdictions with low volumes or regulatory shortfalls (Erbenová and others 2016).

As small states, the Caribbean countries are likely to generate a relatively low level of CBR transactions, making it more difficult for correspondent banks to generate economies of scale and therefore higher profits from CBR activity. Countries with smaller or less developed financial systems may also present fewer opportunities for "bundling" less profitable CBR activities with other financial services activities that can generate profits. However, there is no statistical evidence that the size of the country or the domestic banking sector matters for CBR

---

[10]Worrell and others (2016) compare several Caribbean international financial centers with those outside the region, including advanced economies, and argue that Caribbean compliance is comparable or superior.

**Table 12.3. Regression Results**

| Variables | (1) Change in CBRs | (2) Change in Volumes | (3) Change in Value |
|---|---|---|---|
| Caribbean | −0.439 | −5.982 | −18.23* |
| | (0.865) | (0.367) | (0.0732) |
| Offshore Financial Center | 1.013 | −6.320 | −3.193 |
| | (0.607) | (0.213) | (0.680) |
| Real GDP Growth, 2011–15 Average | 0.498*** | 1.169*** | 0.998* |
| | (0.000840) | (0.00225) | (0.0847) |
| Log (Nominal GDP in US$) | 0.0935 | −1.816** | 0.812 |
| | (0.751) | (0.0176) | (0.484) |
| U.S. Sanctions | −7.336*** | −6.605 | −24.13** |
| | (0.00872) | (0.355) | (0.0278) |
| European Union Crisis | −20.10*** | −33.29*** | −47.60*** |
| | (2.42e−07) | (0.000676) | (0.00143) |
| Constant | −3.151** | 20.31*** | 1.341 |
| | (0.0277) | (1.03e−07) | (0.810) |
| Observations | 176 | 176 | 176 |
| $R^2$ | 0.231 | 0.168 | 0.129 |

Source: IMF staff estimates and calculations.
Note: CBR = correspondent banking relationships.
p-value in parentheses.
*** $p < 0.01$, ** $p < 0.05$, * $p < 0.1$

loss.[11] Many Caribbean countries have, however, experienced relatively low real GDP growth since the global financial crisis, and some evidence suggests that stronger economic activity is associated with an increase in the number of CBRs and in the value of CBR transactions.

Our analysis suggests that some of the drivers mentioned above may have played a role in the withdrawal of CBRs.[12] The results point to statistically significant correlations between CBR loss and a set of explanatory variables that serve as proxies for potential drivers at the country level, although these drivers explain a relatively small portion of the change in CBR activity (Table 12.3):

- *Size and growth.* The proxy for size—log of nominal GDP—has the expected positive (but not statistically significant) sign for the change in active CBRs and change in the value of transactions. Somewhat counterintuitively, the size proxy is significant and negatively correlated with the change in volume of transactions. The regressions indicate that an increase in economic activity is perhaps the most important determinant of changes in CBR

---

[11]The opportunity to generate profits from a higher volume of transactions is likely to depend more on the size of the financial institution than on the size of the country or the financial system. However, data on CBRs and correspondent banking transactions are not available at the bank level.

[12]Based on SWIFT data reported in BIS (2015) for a sample of 204 economies, which includes estimates of changes between 2012 and 2015 (in percentage terms) in the number of active correspondents, volume, and value of SWIFT transactions.

activity, suggesting that banks remain profit driven and will increase CBRs in a country experiencing growth.

- *Other.* As expected, U.S. economic and trade sanctions are an important determinant of changes in CBR activity. The European Union crisis indicator variable is also highly significant, with large negative estimates for all three dependent variables. This outcome is in line with the notion that banking crises have negative effects on foreign transactions and on CBRs. The significant negative estimate for the constant term in the regression that models changes in active CBRs suggests that, to some extent, the decline in CBRs may be a general phenomenon that is due to reasons not captured in the econometric model.

- *Caribbean.* Controlling for several possible determinants of CBR activity, the regressions point to the expected negative (albeit not always statistically significant) estimates of the regression coefficients on the Caribbean dummy variable, suggesting that the decline in CBR activity may be more pronounced in the Caribbean for reasons not captured in the other explanatory variables. In addition, a negative sign is observed for changes in CBR values and volumes for offshore financial centers, as expected.

# POLICY OPTIONS TO ADDRESS THE LOSS OF CBRs

The loss of CBRs has generated great concern throughout the Caribbean. At the regional level, via CARICOM, Caribbean policymakers have established a task force to study the de-risking phenomenon, and have made it a key aspect of their engagement and dialogue with international financial institutions and advanced economy financial regulators and political leaders.[13]

Given the various drivers, there is no "silver bullet" that can solve the problem of withdrawal of CBRs. Coordinated efforts by various stakeholders are called for to mitigate the risk of financial exclusion and the potential negative impact on financial stability (IMF 2017). Policy initiatives must address drivers related to risk or risk perceptions as well as those related to profitability.

## Initiatives to Address Drivers Related to Risk or Risk Perceptions

- *Ensure compliance with international standards.* Caribbean countries need to continue to prioritize efforts to meet international AML/CFT and tax transparency standards. For example, national programs to ensure compliance with the 2012 FATF standards should move ahead expeditiously, as should those aimed at complying with the OECD's CRS on tax transparency and exchange of information. One notable example has been the

---

[13]The CARICOM Task Force on De-Risking is led by the prime minister of Antigua and Barbuda, with technical work coordinated by the Central Bank of Barbados.

ECCU's move to consolidate national AML/CFT supervision into one regional operation at the Eastern Caribbean Central Bank to maintain consistent standards of supervision across the region and mitigate concerns about AML/CFT risks. Technical assistance by international financial institutions and the U.S. Treasury has been provided to aid capacity building. The efficacy of a regional information repository that could share information on suspicious transaction flows among regional financial intelligence units could enhance the effectiveness of countries' AML/CFT frameworks and should be explored.

- *Clarify regulators' expectations of global banks.* Although regulators and international standards-setting agencies (such as FATF) have recently issued clarifications, correspondent banks still remain concerned about the clarity and consistency of regulatory expectations. Thus, more outreach by regulators would be beneficial. Authorities in some home countries of global banks are already taking steps to clarify regulatory expectations. For example, the U.S. Department of the Treasury has put considerable resources into educating financial institutions on the precise nature of transactions and behaviors that are subject to sanctions. In a recently issued fact sheet, it noted that 95 percent of AML/CFT-related violations are corrected without penalties, and the very few instances in which large fines have been imposed were a result of repeated failure to correct practices that had been ongoing for more than five years (Board of Governors of the U.S. Federal Reserve and others 2016). In addition, regulators should provide more guidance and oversight to banks regarding their voluntary remedial actions undertaken in lieu of formal enforcement actions by regulators. These voluntary actions, which in some cases go beyond what might have been required by regulators, have also influenced bank behavior in ways not necessarily intended by regulators. It is within this context that the FATF issued revised guidance on correspondent banking, clarifying, among other things, that "know your customer's customer," which correspondent banks had come to view as an obligatory part of their customer due diligence process, was not required.

- *Improve information sharing and communication between respondent and correspondent banks.* Respondent banks in the Caribbean have at times been taken aback by the withdrawal of CBRs by correspondent banks after many years of a business relationship without any reason provided for the decision nor an opportunity to correct the unknown problem. Enhanced communication could allow global banks to express to respondent banks their own risk tolerance policies or their reasons for terminating a specific CBR. It would also allow respondent banks to better convey the steps that they have taken to address drivers of CBR withdrawal. Some global correspondent banks that maintain a strong presence in the region have highlighted their close engagement with their respondent banks as key to sustaining the relationship because it allows them to understand their clients' customer due diligence protocols and provide guidance on what changes they require. Similarly, some respondent banks have indicated that their success in maintaining CBRs has been attributable to the close lines of communication they maintain with their correspondent bank. The Caribbean Development Bank is launching a program to assist commercial banks with raising their capacity to address the growing requirements associated with customer due diligence and transaction monitoring. Some respondent banks have noted that an important factor in maintaining CBRs has been their investment in automated transactions monitoring systems, which can quickly transmit information to correspondent banks when requested. To facilitate enhanced communication, countries may need to ensure that no legal barriers prevent cross-border information sharing.

- *Improve the quality of payment messages.* The quality of information contained in payment messages can be improved to enhance information available to banks, helping reduce compliance costs and reduce concerns about the legitimacy of cross-border payments. To this end, all commercial banks regulated by the ECCB have complied with its instruction to adopt the SWIFT system. Establishing guidelines that would increase the amount of mandatory information contained in SWIFT messages would also be useful. In the longer term, the development of know-your-customer utilities that allow respondent banks to store and update their customer information, which could easily be accessed by correspondent banks, should continue to be pursued. Similarly, the wider adoption of standardized legal entity identifiers—to identify and trace distinct legal entities as they engage in financial transactions—should be promoted.

- *Special protocols for higher-risk activities by respondent banks.* Terminating relationships with clients in high-risk sectors (such as gaming, offshore business, money transfer services, charities, and citizenship-by-investment) may indeed lower the overall risk level of CBRs and assuage concerns by global banks. However, such actions may exclude legitimate but risky business and hamper financial inclusion. An example is remittances, which are generally considered to be a high-risk activity but have an overall positive social and economic impact. Thus, respondent banks should develop special protocols, in consultation with their correspondent banks, for customer due diligence with respect to higher-risk but legitimate activities. A longer-term solution, which has been proposed by some regulators in the Caribbean, would be to replace the use of cash with digitized payments for commercial transactions to facilitate tracking the trail of the funds underlying the transactions.

- *Use central bank CBRs on behalf of a commercial bank's clients.* This approach could be a short-term or emergency measure in the event of a complete loss of CBRs in a country and has already been used in Belize. However, assessing the legal and operational feasibility of this solution, and the central bank's ability to mitigate potential risk exposures so as not to jeopardize its own CBRs, would be important.

## Initiatives to Address Drivers Related to Profitability

- *Consolidate transactional traffic to exploit economies of scale.*
  - The Caribbean's small size and the high-volume, low-return nature of correspondent banking may suggest that region could be "overbanked" from the standpoint of the number of correspondent banks serving the region. Coordination among respondent banks to maintain or establish CBRs with fewer specific correspondent banks could provide economies of scale and increase the volume of transactions and income for those correspondent banks and reduce their average costs associated with providing correspondent banking services. Such consolidation is already taking place because of the exit of some correspondent banks. The consolidation of transactional traffic through "downstreaming" is also gaining traction in the region. Downstreaming refers to a situation in which the correspondent bank has a relationship with an intermediary bank, which has relationships with other respondent banks and provides for a transparent flow of customer and transaction information to the correspondent bank.
  - An alternative way to consolidate transactional traffic would be for respondent banks to bundle correspondent banking services with other products. Thus, a respondent bank can offer its correspondent bank additional business lines (for example, credit card clearing, letters of credit, and wealth-management operations). This bundling would generate economies of scale by allowing the correspondent bank to use the same robust compliance system to spread the cost of compliance over a wider set of banking services.
  - The consolidation and merger of small respondent banks is another potential solution that could produce sufficient volume and profitable traffic to large foreign correspondent banks, as well as provide economies of scale to reduce average due diligence costs for both correspondent and respondent banks. For the respondent banks, the investment in more sophisticated information technology systems and implementation of better risk management protocols for higher-risk activity becomes more feasible, thereby also addressing risk concerns of the correspondent bank. The ECCU is promoting this solution for the subregion, but it will take some time. However, some banks are already exploring possible mergers.
- *Increase fees charged by correspondent banks.* Charges have already increased across the Caribbean, and respondent banks have passed some of these costs on to customers. There may also be scope for risk-based pricing by correspondent banks to allow them to factor compliance costs into their fee structure and make the risk-return profile more favorable. However, higher prices for cross-border transactions, although allowing CBRs to be maintained in some cases, will have a negative effect on both competitiveness—by raising the cost of doing business—and financial inclusion. The extent

to which a respondent bank might pass on costs to its customers is, of course, limited, making this solution one of restricted scope and short-term effectiveness.

- *Explore technological innovations to reduce costs and improve risk management.* Emerging Fintech solutions could provide a more efficient alternative to CBRs for carrying out cross-border transactions. For example, blockchain providers have suggested that their technology could alleviate some correspondent banking issues by reducing costs of transfers, improving risk management and transparency, and shortening the time required to settle transactions. However, these technologies, which correspondent banks are already exploring, seem to be longer-term solutions. Moreover, effective oversight frameworks for new payment methods would still need to be developed to safeguard public confidence and financial stability.

- *Subsidize compliance costs.* Where compliance costs exceed the benefits from maintaining the business relationship and prevent financial inclusion, the public sector may need to consider subsidizing part of the compliance costs of respondent banks or the fees charged to their customers (or both). This approach may be required to sustain remittances or to safeguard access to finance for charitable organizations or trade finance for small and medium enterprises. However, such a solution may create market distortions and run into budgetary constraints and would face the practical challenge of defining the scope of categories at risk of being financially excluded.

- *Establish CBRs with smaller second- or third-tier U.S. banks.* The provision of correspondent banking services to small Caribbean banks could provide a more significant income stream for smaller banks than for the major international banks and hence may fit better into their business models. Given the smaller scale, the costs and fees would likely be higher than those charged by large banks, but (1) respondent banks would avoid withdrawal of CBRs and (2) given the importance of the relationship to both sides, the correspondent bank would have an incentive to understand the respondent bank's business model, customer due diligence processes, and the like, and potential cost savings could be explored. Caribbean banks have been reasonably successful in establishing new CBRs with smaller correspondent banks to replace lost CBRs with major international banks. However, moving toward second- or third-tier providers may also carry reputational costs for respondent banks, including because these lower-tier banks may process transactions less efficiently than their first-tier counterparts.

## CONCLUSION

Global banks have reassessed their individual business models, adopting different strategies in response to changes in the macroeconomic and regulatory environment that have lowered the expected profitability of correspondent banking. Depending on specific country characteristics and those of the correspondent and respondent banks, we see a full spectrum of outcomes: some global banks have broadly withdrawn from CBRs worldwide, others have withdrawn from the Caribbean region or a particular country (Belize, for instance), others have targeted individual banks, and others have maintained services only to a restricted set of clients of respondent banks and charged higher fees.

Available evidence confirms that the number of CBRs and the value of CBR transactions have indeed fallen in several Caribbean countries over the past few years. Some services, such as international wire transfers, and sectors, such as offshore financial services and gaming, have been particularly affected. However, the loss of CBRs has so far not resulted in major disruptions to financial intermediation. Most Caribbean banks have found replacements or are coping with a reduced number of CBRs. Although a confluence of factors potentially drive this phenomenon, evidence for the Caribbean points to specific perceived risk factors related to respondent-bank business models. For example, banks in various countries are involved in activities that global banks consider riskier, such as offshore financial services and banking services to the gaming industry. Indeed, there is some evidence that the reduction in CBR activity has been more pronounced in countries that are offshore financial centers. In contrast, the available data provide little support to the suggestion that the size of the economy or the banking system is an important driver. The size of the bank could be important, however.

Further loss of CBRs remains a significant risk to the region and could have large economic costs. Caribbean countries are small open economies with extensive links to the global economy, making them vulnerable to a loss of CBRs. A disruption in CBRs could adversely affect the economy through several links, including (1) reduced international trade, remittances, and investment flows; (2) higher costs of doing business; and (3) direct negative impacts on key sectors or activities (such as gaming and offshore financial sector and citizenship-by-investment programs). Stress scenarios that attempt to model these links using bank-level data in Belize suggest that the loss of CBRs could result in a sizable reduction in real economic activity, ranging from 1 percent of GDP in a low-stress scenario to up to 6 percent in a high stress-scenario.

Caribbean authorities have taken several steps to address risks. Caribbean authorities are strengthening the region's voice in global forums and are improving communication across stakeholders. Country-specific efforts are also underway to improve compliance with international standards and enhance risk-based supervision, even though challenges remain in ensuring effective implementation of national AML/CFT frameworks.

Nonetheless, enhanced international coordination and action by all stakeholders are still required to address the CBR challenge. Home authorities of global banks should continue to proactively communicate their regulatory expectations to correspondent banks. International standards-setters need to be more mindful of the unintended consequences to developing countries of efforts to improve the resilience of the international financial system. At the same time, the affected countries should continue to strengthen their regulatory and supervisory frameworks, including for AML/CFT, to meet relevant international standards, with technical assistance where needed. Respondent banks need to proactively engage with correspondent banks to reassure them of the adequacy of their own customer due diligence, transaction monitoring, and AML/CFT frameworks. Similarly, correspondent banks need to be more forthcoming with respondent banks about their expectations with respect to these issues. Industry initiatives will be crucial to facilitating enhanced customer due diligence expectations and to helping reduce compliance costs. Small respondent banks in the region should actively explore options, including through mergers or other forms of collaboration, to bundle transactions to generate more business volume for correspondent banks and improve their own risk management processes. In countries facing a severe loss of CBRs and diminishing access to the global financial system, the public sector may need to consider the feasibility of temporary emergency mechanisms, such as the use of the central bank's CBRs, to avoid a disruption of crucial cross-border transactions. The IMF has launched a Caribbean CBR initiative to help the region find solutions in line with these recommendations. The initiative includes technical assistance in the area of AML/CFT as well as forums involving correspondent and respondent banks aimed at coming up with actionable policies, including related those related to improving communication and information sharing, consolidating transactions to exploit economies of scale, and addressing gaps in risk management.[14]

## REFERENCES

Alleyne, T., J. Bouhga-Hagbe, T. Dowling, D. Kovtun, A. Myrvoda, J. Okwuokei, and J. Turunen. Forthcoming. "Loss of Correspondent Banking Relationships in the Caribbean: Trends, Impact, and Policy Options" IMF Working Paper, International Monetary Fund, Washington, DC.

ASBA (Asociación de Supervisores Bancarios de las Américas). 2015. "Informe de Resultados de: Encuesta sobre el Impacto del riego de Cumplimiento/Regulatario en la Actividad Financiera." Asociación de Supervisores Bancarios de las Américas, September.

BIS (Bank for International Settlements). 2015. "Consultative Report: Correspondent Banking." Committee on Payments and Market Infrastructures, Bank for International Settlements, Geneva. http://www.bis.org/cpmi/publ/d136.htm.

Board of Governors of the Federal Reserve System, Federal Deposit Insurance Corporation, National Credit Union Administration, Office of the Comptroller of the Currency, and US Department of the Treasury. 2016. "U.S. Department of the Treasury and Federal Banking Agencies Joint Fact Sheet on Foreign Correspondent Banking: Approach to BSA/AML and OFAC Sanctions Supervision and Enforcement." Washington, DC. https://www.treasury.gov/press-center/press-releases/Documents/Foreign%20Correspondent%20Banking%20Fact%20Sheet.pdf.

CAB (Caribbean Association of Banks). 2016. "Summary of Findings: Correspondent Banking Survey." St. Lucia.

CARICOM (Caribbean Community). 2016. "De-Risking and Its Impact: The Caribbean Perspective." CCMF Working Paper 01/2016, Caribbean Center for Money and Finance, Republic of Trinidad and Tobago.

---

[14]IMF (2017) provides some detail on the results of the first roundtable held in Barbados in February 2017.

Collin, M., Samantha Cook, and K. Soramaki. 2016. "The Impact of Anti-Money Laundering Regulation on Payment Flows: Evidence from Swift Data." CGD Working Paper 445.

Erbenová, Michaela, Yan Liu, Nadim Kyriakos-Saad, Alejandro López-Mejía, Giancarlo Gasha, Emmanuel Mathias, Mohamed Norat, Francisca Fernando, and Yasmin Almeida. 2016. "The Withdrawal of Correspondent Banking Relationships: A Case for Policy Action." IMF Staff Discussion Note, International Monetary Fund, Washington, DC.

International Monetary Fund. 2016a. "Belize: Selected Issues." IMF Country Report 16/335, Washington, DC.

―――. 2016b. "Impact of the Withdrawal of Correspondent Banking Relationships in the ECCU." Annex to the ECCU Staff Report "Eastern Caribbean Currency Union. 2016 Discussion on Common Policies of Member Countries." IMF Country Report 16/333.

―――. 2017. "Recent Trends in Correspondent Banking Relationships—Further Considerations." IMF 17/57, Washington, DC.

―――, and Union of Arab Banks. 2015. "The Impact of De-Risking on MENA Banks." Joint Survey by the Union of Arab Banks and International Monetary Fund, Washington, DC.

Lagarde, C. 2016. "Relations in Banking—Making It Work for Everyone." Speech at the Federal Reserve Bank of New York, July 18.

World Bank. 2015a. *Report on the G20 Survey on De-Risking Activities in the Remittance Market.* Washington, DC: World Bank.

―――. 2015b. "Withdrawal from Correspondent Banking: Where, Why and What to Do about It." Finance and Markets Global Practice of the World Bank Group, Washington, DC.

Worrell, Delisle, Michael Brei, Lauren Cato, Sadie Dixon, Bradley Kellman, and Shamika Wahlrond. 2016. "De-Risking in the Caribbean: The Unintended Consequences of International Financial Reform." Central Bank of Barbados Working Paper, Central Bank of Barbados, Bridgetown, Barbados.

# CHAPTER 13

# Energy Diversification: Macro-Related Challenges

MEREDITH A. McINTYRE AND AHMED EL ASHRAM

## INTRODUCTION

The cost of electricity in the Caribbean has been persistently high over the past two decades, and has eroded competitiveness. This situation is largely due to serious inefficiencies in the power sector and dependence on expensive imported petroleum products, reflecting limited energy diversification. In turn, these problems have contributed to the region's high cost of doing business and increased external sector vulnerabilities, and have undercut growth in many Caribbean economies.

The substantial decline in oil prices since mid-2014 does not obviate the need for energy sector reform. The impact of the oil price decline is global, so it has not improved relative prices for the Caribbean compared with its trading partners. Moreover, competitiveness challenges are escalating, particularly with the appreciation of the U.S. dollar, to which many Caribbean countries are pegged. Hence, any gains from oil price declines only provide a temporary respite; solutions for sustained cost reductions are still needed for the region to be competitive.

The chapter focuses on answering some fundamental macro-level questions related to moving energy reform forward in the region. First, how important is energy sector reform to boosting growth and competitiveness? Second, are existing energy sector strategies adequate for addressing current challenges? Third, what gains could be expected from the implementation of these energy strategies? Fourth, what investment costs would be associated with achieving the announced energy targets? And fifth, could countries afford it—in other words, would the envisaged energy reform be consistent with preserving fiscal space and debt sustainability?

### State of the Caribbean Energy Sector

Caribbean countries (other than Haiti) have very high access to electricity,[1] but use expensive off-grid supply to compensate for deficiencies in the utilities

---

This chapter draws on McIntyre and others (2016).

[1] Per World Bank indicators, Caribbean countries have, on average, electrification rates that exceed 90 percent.

**Figure 13.1. Caribbean Residential Electricity Tariffs (2002–12)**
*(US ¢/kWh)*

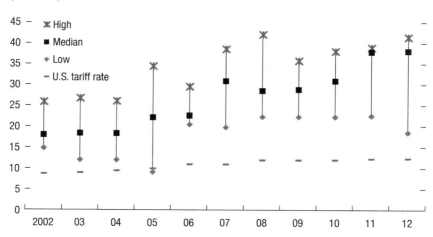

Sources: CARILEC Tariff Survey 2012; and U.S. Energy Information Administration database.
Note: Includes data for The Bahamas, Barbados, Belize, Dominica, Grenada, Jamaica, St. Lucia, and St. Vincent and the Grenadines; limited data available for Antigua and Barbuda and Nevis; excludes Trinidad and Tobago and Suriname.

generation and transmission of power. Although each country has unique energy sector conditions, most face the same supply constraints, including limited generation capacity, outdated power systems, isolated grids, and lack of technical expertise, which, combined with episodes of high and volatile oil prices, have resulted in high average electricity costs. Electricity tariffs increased by almost 80 percent from 2002 to 2012 (Figure 13.1), exceeding US$0.30 per kilowatt-hour for most of the region in 2012 (Figure 13.2).

The single most important cost problem is the region's heavy dependence on expensive imported fossil fuels. As in the United States, the cost of using petroleum to produce electricity is several times higher than the cost of alternative fuels. Except for Trinidad and Tobago—the only net exporter of oil and natural gas—all Caribbean countries are net oil importers.

For importers, other than Suriname,[2] about 87 percent of primary energy consumed is in the form of imported petroleum products (Figures 13.3 and 13.4).[3] Imports are mostly diesel fuel for electricity generation, gasoline for transportation, and liquefied petroleum gas for cooking use in households. Of

---

[2]Suriname is the second-largest oil producer in the region after Trinidad and Tobago but remains a net importer of petroleum products. Limited (though growing) refinery capacity explains Suriname's significant imports of refined petroleum products.

[3]Primary energy refers to energy from all sources in its crude form before any transformation.

**Figure 13.2. Domestic Electricity Tariffs, 2012**
*(U.S. ¢/kWh)*

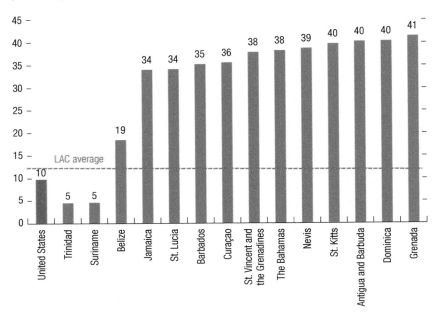

Sources: CARILEC 2012; and World Bank staff estimates.
Note: LAC = Latin America and the Caribbean.

the net oil importers, only Barbados and, more recently, Jamaica have installed capacity that uses natural gas[4] for electricity generation (Figure 13.3.), which has partly contributed to its higher efficiency rates.[5] Hydroelectric power, harnessed through facilities in Belize, Dominica, St. Vincent and the Grenadines, and Suriname, supplies about 6 percent of regional electric energy consumption. Excluding Haiti, biomass accounts for about 11 percent of Caribbean energy supply, mostly concentrated in Jamaica.

An important characteristic of the power sector in the Caribbean is that the market structure is not diversified and is underregulated, resulting in inefficient, high-cost supply. Regulatory deficiencies impede greater involvement of the

---

[4]Jamaica has recently increased its natural gas capacity, thereby reducing its dependence on imported oil from 97 percent to about 80 percent; additional capacity planned to come on stream by 2019 is expected to reduce dependence on oil further, to 60 percent. The text chart reflects data for the region to 2013.

[5]After Trinidad and Tobago, in the Caribbean the Dominican Republic has the second-largest share of natural gas–fired power plants, representing about 20 percent of installed generation capacity.

### Figure 13.3. Installed Generation Capacity in Caribbean Countries
*(Percent of total capacity)*

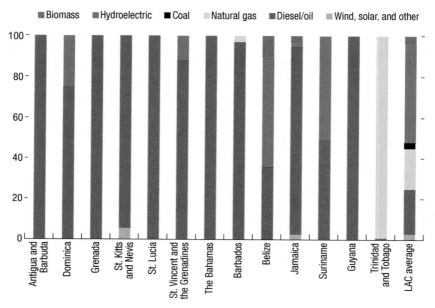

Sources: Inter-American Development Bank; World Bank; and IMF staff calculations.
Note: LAC = Latin America and the Caribbean.

private sector in the industry. The Caribbean electricity market is served by a mix of state-owned and private utility companies (Table 13.1). For the most part, electric utilities are vertically integrated monopolies that hold exclusive licenses for generation, transmission, distribution, and sale of electricity. Some of these monopolies are unable to finance necessary investments in generation capacity and the national grid, leaving consumers with unreliable and unaffordable energy access. As discussed later in the chapter, if weaknesses in regulation related to independent power producers (IPPs)[6] were to be addressed, private sector participation in the electricity sector could be enhanced.

Despite high prices, Caribbean energy consumption has been growing, putting further pressure on total energy bills. Consumption has grown fastest in energy-rich Trinidad and Tobago because of the abundance of natural gas, cheap electricity, and significant expansion of its hydrocarbon industries. Consumption in the smaller Eastern Caribbean countries that import oil also grew—almost tripling to 28.7 trillion British thermal units in 2012. The transformation of

---

[6]This issue is dealt with in the discussion on regulatory reforms.

## Figure 13.4. Primary Energy Consumption by Source and Use
(Percent of total)

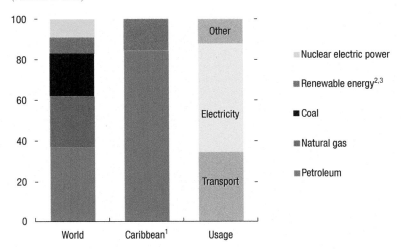

Sources: Inter-American Development Bank; U.S. Energy Information Administration database; and IMF staff calculations.
[1]Excludes Haiti and Trinidad and Tobago.
[2]Includes hydroelectric power, geothermal, solar/photovoltaic, wind, and biomass.
[3]For the Caribbean, renewables include hydropower and biomass.

many Caribbean economies from reliance on agriculture to reliance on tourism has been accompanied by significant capital accumulation and expansion of energy consumption as energy needs of the tourism industry have increased. On a per capita basis, tourism-dependent Caribbean economies appear to be more energy intensive than commodity-exporting countries like Belize, Guyana, and Suriname (Figure 13.5).

## The Macroeconomic Impact of Energy Costs

The region's dependence on imported fossil fuels exposes the countries to adverse oil market developments, terms-of-trade shocks, fiscal costs, and resulting macroeconomic imbalances (Figure 13.7). In the net oil-importing countries, the average value of net oil imports doubled between 2005 and 2014. This increase widened the trade deficit by an average of 3.7 percent of GDP annually compared with the previous decade, and put pressure on foreign exchange reserves.

The domestic economy has also suffered from high oil prices.

- About 40 percent of Caribbean firms identify electricity costs as a major constraint to doing business, compared with the average of about 30 percent in the LA6 group and other developing countries (Figure 13.6).[7] This

[7]The LA6 comprise Brazil, Chile, Colombia, Mexico, Peru, and Uruguay.

## Table 13.1. Electric Utility Companies in the Caribbean

| Country | Main Utilities | Ownership |
|---|---|---|
| Antigua and Barbuda | Antigua Public Utilities Authority (APUA) | State owned |
| The Bahamas | Bahamas Electricity Corporation (BEC) | State owned |
| | Grand Bahama Power Company (GBPC) | Privately owned |
| Barbados | Barbados Light and Power Ltd. | Privately owned |
| Belize | Belize Electricity Limited | State owned |
| Dominica | Dominica Electricity Services Ltd. (DOMLEC) | Privately owned |
| Grenada | Grenada Electricity Services Ltd. (GRENLEC) | Privately owned |
| Guyana | Guyana Power and Light Inc. (GPL) | State owned |
| Jamaica | Jamaica Public Service Company (JPSCo) | Privately owned |
| St. Kitts and Nevis | St. Kitts Electricity Co. Ltd. (SKELEC) | State owned |
| | Nevis Electricity Company Ltd. (NEVLEC) | State owned |
| St. Lucia | St. Lucia Electricity Services Ltd. (LUCELEC) | Private-public entity |
| St. Vincent and the Grenadines | St. Vincent Electricity Services Ltd. (VINLEC) | State owned |
| Suriname | Energy Companies of Suriname (EBS) | State owned |
| Trinidad and Tobago | Trinidad and Tobago Electricity Commission | State owned |
| | Power Generation Company of Trinidad and Tobago Ltd. (PowerGen) | Private-public enterprise |

Sources: National Renewable Energy Laboratory; and Organization of American States.

## Figure 13.5. Energy Consumption per Capita, 2012
*(Million BTU per capita )*

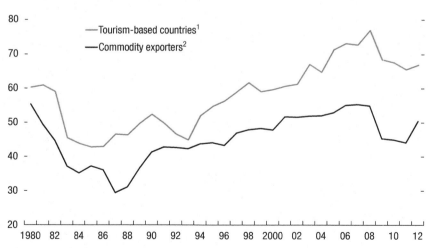

Sources: U.S. Energy Information Administration database; and IMF staff calculations.
Note: BTU = British thermal unit.
[1]Includes Eastern Caribbean Currency Union countries, Barbados, and The Bahamas.
[2]Includes Jamaica, Belize, Guyana, and Suriname; excludes Trinidad and Tobago.

**Figure 13.6. Average Current Account Deficit in the Caribbean**
(Percent of GDP)

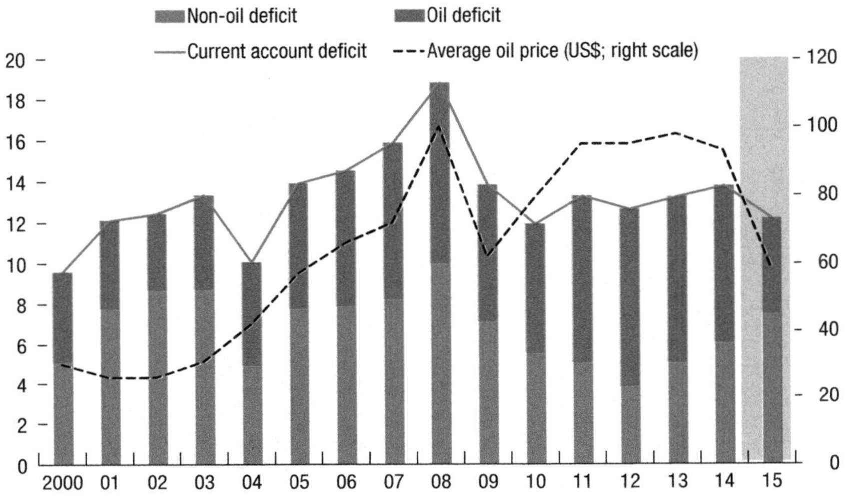

Sources: Country authorities; and IMF staff calculations.
Note: Excludes Haiti and Trinidad and Tobago.

creates increased uncertainty for domestic and foreign investment, with unfavorable repercussions for capital formation, the inflow of foreign direct investment, and long-term growth.

- The high pass-through of oil price shocks has also contributed significantly to inflation dynamics through the higher cost of electricity (a fuel surcharge) and higher transportation costs. Some of the energy price movement filters into core inflation and further affects competitiveness (Figures 13.8 and 13.9).[8]

## Impact of Energy Costs on Growth: How Important?

To analyze the macroeconomic effects of energy costs in the Caribbean, the impact of oil price shocks on near-term growth and the real exchange rate was

[8]In the Eastern Caribbean Currency Union (with a fixed exchange rate), core inflation peaked at 4.7 percent year over year in November 2008, after oil prices surged to a record high of US$145 per barrel in July 2008. In Jamaica, headline and core inflation also reached all-time highs of 25.6 percent year over year and 15.8 percent year over year, respectively, in July 2008. In Suriname, core inflation largely traced oil price swings, partly reflecting the automatic pass-through system of retail fuel prices in place since 2005; also, the authorities raised the fuel tax by about 70 percent in January 2011, which, along with a 20 percent devaluation of the official exchange rate, led to an increase of about 40 percent in fuel prices at the pump.

## Figure 13.7. Electricity as a Major Constraint to Firms

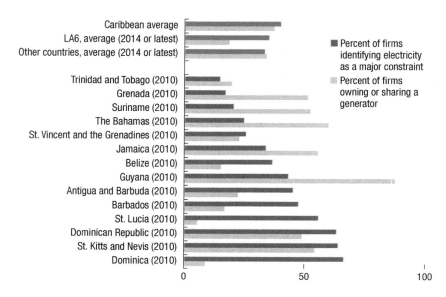

Sources: World Bank Enterprise Survey 2015; and IMF staff calculations.
Note: LA6 = Latin American 6 (Brazil, Chile, Colombia, Mexico, Peru, Uruguay).

## Figure 13.8. ECCU: Energy Price Volatility vs. Core Inflation
*(Year-over-year percent change)*

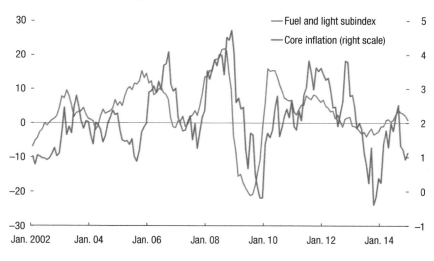

Sources: Eastern Caribbean Central Bank; and IMF staff calculations.
Note: Core inflation excludes food and fuel; weights are based on St. Lucia consumption basket. ECCU = Eastern Caribbean Currency Union.

**Figure 13.9. Core Inflation Indices and Oil Price Volatility**
*(Year-over-year percent change)*

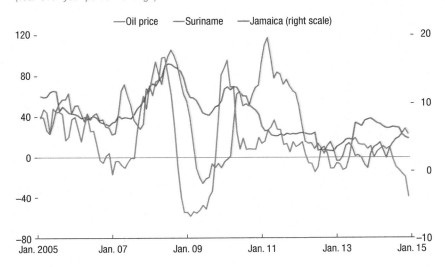

Sources: Country authorities; and IMF staff calculations.
Note: Core inflation excludes food and fuel. In Suriname, fuel tax increased by 70 percent in January 2011.

modeled.[9] McIntyre and others (2016) also examined the potential for improvements in the power sector's efficiency to deliver higher long-term sustainable growth. Overall, the investigation found that changes in real oil prices have an important short-term impact on growth, although other factors dominate. Estimates suggest that movements in real oil prices explain, on average, 7 percent of real GDP growth variation in the Caribbean (Figure 13.10)—with variability across countries ranging from 15 percent in Dominica to less than 1 percent in Guyana.[10] These results suggest that a reduction in countries' dependence on oil would materially alleviate the cost of adverse oil price movements. However, the exercise also showed that a greater share of real growth variation (30 percent) is explained by external demand shocks—meaning that energy sector reform alone is not a panacea for solving Caribbean growth problems.[11] Estimates also suggest that a 10 percent increase in oil prices could lead to an appreciation of the real effective exchange rate (that is, reduce competitiveness) by 2.8 percentage points

---

[10]In the short and medium terms, the impact of higher oil prices on real GDP growth and the real exchange rate of Caribbean economies is estimated with a vector autoregression model with block exogeneity restrictions in line with the spillover effects literature. See Cashin and Sosa (2013) and Osterholm and Zettelmeyer (2008).

[11]The results are comparable with those for other Latin American countries, such as Chile and Guatemala.

**Figure 13.10. Impact of External Factors on Real GDP Movements**
*(Percent, average over three years)*

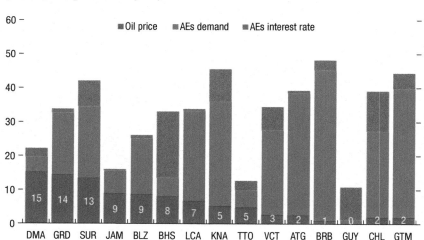

Source: McIntyre and others (2016).
Note: AEs = advanced economies. Data labels in figure use International Organization for Standardization (ISO) country codes.

over five years in tourism-intensive economies and by 3.8 percentage points for commodity producers.[12]

The negative impact of oil prices on growth and external competitiveness can be mitigated through efforts to reduce oil dependency and lower the energy bill. Although countries have no control over oil price movements, they can save over the longer term by diversifying their energy mix and improving the efficiency of energy consumption to reduce fuel imports and thereby limit the impact of price shocks. To assess the potential effectiveness of such savings, McIntyre and others (2016) estimate the impact of energy consumption and efficiency on long-term output.[13] Their analysis indicates that an improvement of 1 percent in energy efficiency[14] would be accompanied by a 0.2 percent increase in GDP per capita in the long term. An increase of 1 percent of gross capital formation per capita is associated with a 0.15 percent increase in long-term GDP per capita.[15] In sum,

---

[12]These results are based on elasticities derived from impulse response functions.

[13]The role of energy consumption and efficiency in determining long-term output is estimated using the augmented mean group estimator (McIntyre and others 2016).

[14]Energy efficiency is defined as energy consumption per unit of GDP. This follows a large body of analytical studies focusing on the link between energy and growth that has led to the energy consumption–GDP nexus (McIntyre and others 2016).

[15]This estimate is based on capital formation in all sectors, not only in the energy sector.

the analysis indicates that improving energy efficiency, including through diversification of the generation mix by incorporating cheaper and more efficient alternative energy sources and by adopting energy efficient technologies, will have a significant impact on GDP in the long term.

## Caribbean Energy Sector Strategies

Caribbean authorities have recognized energy sector challenges and the negative implications for their economies since the mid-2000s. Most countries have formulated draft energy policies that spell out key objectives and a general framework that focuses on shifting to cheaper energy sources and improving energy efficiency. In some countries, action plans have been developed with specific targets, although progress on implementation remains slow. In 2013, a Caribbean-wide initiative[16] was undertaken to harmonize these policies, and an overall regional strategy was developed. Figure 13.11 summarizes existing and proposed reforms in Caribbean Community (CARICOM) states.

McIntyre and others (2016) survey countries' existing energy strategies and find that most of them reflect international best practices advice on policies to achieve energy sector transformation—regulatory reform, energy efficiency improvements, and diversification of the generation mix. Regional targets[17] for energy efficiency, renewable power generation, and carbon dioxide emissions are well aligned with national targets for energy efficiency and renewable energy. Hence, the Caribbean already has in place most of the key building blocks needed to achieve substantial energy reform, albeit with some important exceptions on the regulatory side.

## Regulatory Reforms

Reform of the legal and regulatory framework for the Caribbean power sector is the first important prerequisite for sustainable and affordable energy solutions. Reforms that address regulatory deficiencies relating to IPPs are key. Although independent generation is permitted in many Caribbean economies, no clear framework governs the licensing of utility-scale IPPs and their ability to sell to the grid. Facilitating licensing procedures and introducing feed-in tariffs and net billing schemes are likely to be critical to the development of private sector–led projects that supply electricity to the grid at competitive cost. IPPs are particularly instrumental for exploiting the renewable energy potential in the region, and because these projects involve large upfront capital costs and no fuel cost, feed-in tariffs and net-billing schemes should aim to establish adequate cost recovery

---

[16]The CARICOM Energy Policy (CEP), complemented by an action plan in the Caribbean Sustainable Energy Roadmap and Strategy (C-SERMS) Phase 10.

[17]The targets comprise a 33 percent reduction in energy intensity by 2027; 20 percent renewable power capacity by 2017 (currently at about 15 percent); and carbon dioxide emissions reductions of 18 percent by 2017, 32 percent by 2022, and 46 percent by 2027 (see CARICOM Energy Policy 2013).

**Figure 13.11. Summary of Existing and Proposed Energy Policies in CARICOM States**

| | Renewable Energy | | | | | | | |
|---|---|---|---|---|---|---|---|---|
| | Regulatory Policies | | | | Fiscal Incentives and Public Financing | | | |
| | Feed-in Tariff | Net Metering/ Billing | Renewable Portfolio/ Standard Quota | IPPs Permitted | Tax Credits | Tax Reduction/ Exemption | Public Loans/ Grants | Green Public Procurement |
| Antigua and Barbuda | Suggested | X | Suggested | X | X | X | Suggested | |
| The Bahamas | In development | In development | | In development | | X | | Suggested |
| Barbados | In development | X | In development | X | X | X | X | |
| Belize | Suggested | Suggested | Suggested | | Suggested | | | |
| Dominica | | X | | X | | X | | |
| Grenada | Suggested | X | In development | X | In development | X | In development | |
| Guyana | | Suggested | | X | | X | | |
| Haiti | Suggested | Suggested | Suggested | X | Suggested | Suggested | In development | |
| Jamaica | | X | | X | X | X | X | X |
| Montserrat | | | | | Suggested | Suggested | | |
| St. Kitts and Nevis | | | | X | | X | X | |
| St. Lucia | Suggested | X | | X | Suggested | X | | |
| St. Vincent and the Grenadines | Suggested | X | | X | Suggested | Suggested | | |
| Suriname | In development | Suggested | | X | | Suggested | | |
| Trinidad and Tobago | In development | | | Suggested | X | X | | Suggested |

| | Energy Efficiency | | | | | |
|---|---|---|---|---|---|---|
| | National Energy Efficiency Standards | Tax Credits | Tax Reduction/ Exemption | Public Demonstration | Prohibited Use/ Import of Incandescent Bulbs | Appliance Labeling Standards |
| Antigua and Barbuda | Suggested | | | | | Suggested |
| The Bahamas | Suggested | Suggested | | Suggested | X | Suggested |
| Barbados | | X | X | | | |
| Belize | | | Suggested | | | |
| Dominica | Suggested | Suggested | X | Suggested | | Suggested |
| Grenada | | | Suggested | Suggested | | Suggested |
| Guyana | Suggested | | X | X | | Suggested |
| Haiti | Suggested | Suggested | X | | | |
| Jamaica | In development | | X | X | | X |
| Montserrat | | | | | | |
| St. Kitts and Nevis | | | | | | |
| St. Lucia | | In development | X | | | |
| St. Vincent and the Grenadines | | | Suggested | | X | Suggested |
| Suriname | Suggested | | | | Suggested | |
| Trinidad and Tobago | Suggested | | X | Suggested | Suggested | Suggested |

X denotes implemented.
Source: McIntyre and others 2016.
Note: IPP = independent power producer.

mechanisms to ensure viability while reducing the overall cost of energy. So far, net metering[18] has been introduced in Barbados, Grenada, Jamaica, and St. Lucia.

Creation of independent national and regional regulators would help promote a predictable and transparent regulatory environment for energy investors. The lack of an independent regulator in many Caribbean countries is an impediment to new market entrants, given the need to assure them of a level playing field. Establishing an independent power sector regulator requires building sufficient institutional capacity to competently perform the key functions of tariff setting, license issuance, and effective market oversight. The office of the pilot launch of the Eastern Caribbean Energy Regulatory Authority project in Grenada and St. Lucia supports these objectives in the Eastern Caribbean Currency Union (ECCU), as does the Office of Utility Regulation in Jamaica.

## Energy Efficiency

Energy efficiency measures—for both generation and consumption—are a focus in most country strategies, and are likely to be the most feasible short- and medium-term way to reduce energy costs.

- On the generation side, gains could be achieved by replacing old and inefficient power plants and transmission and distribution lines, which cause major technical losses for the grid.

- On the consumption side, improving the energy consumption patterns of heavy energy users is key. For example, in small tourism-dependent countries, improving the energy efficiency of hotels through the adoption of energy-efficient technologies could significantly reduce the national energy bill and improve tourism competitiveness.[19]

- Despite potential gains from energy efficiency, the region has not taken decisive action to implement rules-based policies. Generally, policies to promote efficiency improvements should focus on (1) encouraging households and businesses to buy energy-efficient appliances; (2) promulgating energy-efficient building codes, particularly for hotels; and (3) requiring energy labeling for consumer goods and appliance efficiency standards to encourage the use of energy-efficient items. However, such policies have not been adopted in the region because of constraints on financing, weaknesses in institutional capacity, and insufficient expertise regarding labels and standards.

- Some CARICOM states have set energy efficiency targets that, if achieved, would have a positive macroeconomic impact. For instance, if Antigua and

---

[18]Net metering is a billing mechanism that credits renewable energy owners for the electricity they add to the grid. For example, if a residential customer has a solar system on the home's rooftop, it may generate more electricity than the home uses during daylight hours.

[19]Based on the CHENACT (2012) study based on data from Barbados, air-conditioning alone accounts for 48 percent of total electric consumption by hotels (Figure 13.2).

**Table 13.2. Summary of Viable Renewable Energy Sources by Country**

| Country | Solar | Wind | Geothermal | Hydro | Biomass |
|---|:---:|:---:|:---:|:---:|:---:|
| Antigua and Barbuda | ✓ | ✓ | | | |
| Dominica | ✓ | ✓ | ✓ | ✓ | |
| Grenada | ✓ | ✓ | ✓ | ✓ | |
| St. Kitts and Nevis | ✓ | ✓ | ✓ | | ✓ |
| St. Lucia | ✓ | ✓ | ✓ | ✓ | ✓ |
| St. Vincent and the Grenadines | ✓ | ✓ | ✓ | ✓ | ✓ |
| The Bahamas | ✓ | ✓ | | | ✓ |
| Barbados | ✓ | ✓ | | | ✓ |
| Guyana | | | | ✓ | |
| Haiti | ✓ | ✓ | | ✓ | ✓ |
| Jamaica | ✓ | ✓ | | ✓ | ✓ |
| Suriname | | | | ✓ | ✓ |

Source: McIntyre and others 2016.

Barbuda meets its target of improving overall energy efficiency in the economy (including the transport sector) by 20 percent, estimated impacts include an equivalent 20 percent drop in oil imports, a 13 percent decline in the national energy bill, and a long-term cumulative increase of 4 percent in the level of GDP.[20]

## Energy Diversification

The other focus of most reform strategies is diversification of energy sources, especially toward cost-effective renewables. Some Caribbean countries already have existing renewable energy capacity in their generation mix. Although Belize and Suriname have considerable renewable power capacity, more than half of the countries in the region still have a very low share of renewables in their energy mix.

The region possesses significant potential for the use of renewable energy. Some CARICOM states have conducted assessments that provide an overview of available renewable energy resources (Table 13.2). Except for Antigua and Barbuda, ECCU countries have significant geothermal potential that could cover their likely base load, potentially allowing for self-sufficiency in electric power generation. Geothermal development is advanced in Dominica, Nevis, and Montserrat, with progress in St. Vincent and the Grenadines. St. Kitts and Nevis has launched several solar power initiatives, including two solar farms, while in Jamaica, three renewable energy projects have recently been developed—two wind plants and a solar farm.

Quantitative estimates indicate significant positive macroeconomic impacts from meeting the renewable energy targets in the CARICOM roadmap.[21]

---

[20]McIntyre and others (2016, Figure 4) present estimates that show similar positive impacts for other CARICOM countries achieving energy-efficiency targets—lower oil imports, decline in the national energy bill, and a positive long-term impact on the level of GDP.

[21]McIntyre and others (2016) show that achieving individual country renewable energy targets would lower the national electricity bill and fuel imports.

## Table 13.3. Implied Effects of Energy Efficiency Targets

| | | Implied Effects | | |
|---|---|---|---|---|
| Country | Effective Efficiency Target[1] (%) | Implied reduction in oil imports (%) | Implied reduction in national electricity bill[2] (%) | Implied impact on long-term GDP level (%) |
| Dominica | 1 | 1 | 1 | 0 |
| St. Lucia | 1 | 1 | 1 | 0 |
| Barbados | 12 | 11 | 9 | 2 |
| St. Kitts and Nevis | 12 | 11 | 8 | 2 |
| St. Vincent and the Grenadines | 12 | 10 | 5 | 2 |
| Antigua and Barbuda | 20 | 20 | 13 | 4 |
| Belize[3] | 30 | 20 | 1 | 6 |
| Jamaica | 71 | 69 | 31 | 14 |

Sources: McIntyre and others 2016; Castalia Strategic Advisors 2010, 2013; Inter-American Development Bank; IMF, *World Economic Outlook*; and IMF staff estimates.
[1]Announced efficiency targets presented in the Caribbean Sustainable Energy Roadmap are normalized to the same base to reflect targeted improvement in energy consumption in the entire economy, including the transport sector.
[2]Reflects savings in the energy bill of end users from introducing energy-efficient technologies at an average cost of US$0.13/kWh.
[3]The impact on the national electricity bill from achieving the target reflects the smaller savings from energy efficiency technologies in Belize, where the electricity tariff rate is relatively low.

## POTENTIAL GAINS FROM REFORM

Taken together, the quantitative estimates indicate that substantial potential gains could be obtained from pursuing already-specified energy strategies. Tables 13.3 and 13.4 present summary estimates of what could be achieved by meeting country targets for efficiency improvements and renewables. Although some national targets are quite ambitious (such as 100 percent renewables in Dominica and Grenada), and the estimates of gains from meeting the targets are necessarily broad-brush, they illustrate the scope for eventual savings with energy transformation.

## ENERGY SECTOR TRANSFORMATION: COSTS AND FEASIBILITY

Implementation of the national and regional energy strategies requires substantial upfront investments to achieve the targets, but these costs are not quantified nor is the financing sourced. Significant investment is also needed to upgrade existing power infrastructure, reduce technical losses, and ensure system integrity as electricity demand grows. With the support of the Inter-American Development Bank (IDB), McIntyre and others (2016) estimate the investment envelope needed to implement the energy strategies already specified by Caribbean countries.

### Energy Investment Needs

Based on the IDB's estimates, total energy sector investment requirements are about 7 percent of regional GDP (Table 13.5). These include investments to (1)

**Table 13.4. Implied Effects of Renewable Energy Targets**

| Country | Renewable Energy Target for Electricity (%) | Implied Effects[1] | | |
|---|---|---|---|---|
| | | Implied reduction in oil imports (%) | Implied reduction in the national electricity bill[2] (%) | Implied impact on long-term GDP level (%) |
| Antigua and Barbuda | 20 | 10 | 6 | 1 |
| Jamaica | 20 | 5 | 4 | 0 |
| Barbados | 29 | 13 | 6 | 1 |
| The Bahamas | 30 | 17 | 11 | 1 |
| St. Lucia | 35 | 22 | 11 | 1 |
| St. Kitts and Nevis[3] | 40 | 24 | 9 | 1 |
| Belize | 89 | 25 | 10 | 1 |
| Guyana | 90 | 28 | 21 | 2 |
| Dominica | 100 | 45 | 16 | 2 |
| Grenada | 100 | 49 | 31 | 3 |

Sources: McIntyre and others 2016; Castalia Strategic Advisors 2010, 2013; Inter-American Development Bank; and IMF staff estimates.
[1]Reflects the impact of achieving the target using viable renewable power technologies, up from the existing renewable penetration rate in each country.
[2]Assumes a 100 percent pass-through of cost savings from renewable energy technologies to end users.
[3]Target is the average of a 20 percent renewable target for St. Kitts and 100 percent target for Nevis, weighted by size of electricity generation on each island.

expand and upgrade existing power plants to meet growing electricity demand, improve generation efficiency, and reduce system losses; (2) introduce renewable energy sources (geothermal, solar, wind, and hydro) where the associated technologies are viable; and (3) implement energy efficiency initiatives (for example, solar water heating systems and smart street lighting).[22] In addition, the IDB also estimated the size of the investment envelope for introducing natural gas in Western Caribbean countries.

## Effects of Energy Investment on Public Debt Sustainability[23]

The feasibility of public financing of energy investments depends on the magnitude of the investment, the cost of financing, the current level of public debt, and the availability of fiscal space. For countries with solid public finances, the envelope proposed above could be financed by the public sector without undermining debt sustainability. However, in several Caribbean countries, public finances remain under strain, limiting large energy infrastructure investments.

---

[22]Investments for new plant and equipment cover projected needs through 2023.

[23]See McIntyre and others (2016) for the technical details of Scenario 1 and Scenario 2, efficiency gains under different price scenarios, and the translation of efficiency gains to growth benefits. The key findings are presented in this chapter.

## Table 13.5: Energy Sector Investment Needs in the Caribbean (2018–23)
(Millions of U.S. dollars)

| | Building or Upgrading Power Plants[1] | Introducing Natural Gas Facilities[2] | Renewable Energy Investments[3,4] | Energy Efficiency and Conservation Initiatives[5] | Total Investment | Total Investment (% of GDP)[6] | Average GDP Growth (2006–15) | Gross Public Debt (% of GDP)[6] |
|---|---|---|---|---|---|---|---|---|
| The Bahamas | 150 | 251 | 70 | 40 | 511 | 5.8 | 0.4 | 60.8 |
| Barbados | 190 | 129 | 80 | 40 | 439 | 9.9 | 0.6 | 103.8 |
| Belize | | 59 | – | – | 59 | 3.3 | 2.6 | 78.1 |
| Guyana | 135 | 110 | 5 | 20 | 270 | 8.4 | 4.4 | 70.2 |
| Jamaica | 400 | 280 | 60 | 120 | 860 | 6.2 | 0.1 | 127.7 |
| Suriname | 100 | 223 | 45 | 10 | 378 | 7.5 | 3.8 | 36.9 |
| ECCU | | | 421 | 30 | 451 | 9.8 | 1.2 | 82.9 |
| Antigua and Barbuda | | | 42 | 5 | 47 | 3.7 | 1.2 | 101.9 |
| Dominica | | | 52 | 5 | 57 | 10.6 | 2.4 | 79.4 |
| Grenada | | | 88 | 5 | 93 | 9.7 | 0.7 | 90.3 |
| St. Kitts and Nevis | | | 87 | 5 | 92 | 10.3 | 2.0 | 66.3 |
| St. Lucia | | | 66 | 5 | 71 | 4.9 | 1.1 | 82.6 |
| St. Vincent and the Grenadines | | | 87 | 5 | 92 | 12.0 | 1.0 | 77.0 |
| **Region Total** | **975** | **1,052** | **681** | **260** | **2,968** | **6.9** | **1.9** | **80.0** |

Sources: Inter-American Development Bank (IDB); and IMF staff estimates.

Note: ECCU = Eastern Caribbean Currency Union.

[1]Includes cost of building new capacity of natural gas-fired power plants. IDB estimates do not include expansions for generation capacity in Belize, which imports a significant share of its electric power from Mexico. For Guyana and Suriname, includes costs for rural electrification.

[2]Includes estimated costs of converting existing plants to natural gas and the construction of regasification facilities.

[3]Includes solar, hydro, wind, and waste-to-energy projects. For the ECCU, reflects cost for geothermal power development.

[4]For Antigua and Barbuda, reflects cost estimates for solar and wind power penetration of 20 percent by 2020.

[5]Includes cost for solar water heaters, grid loss reduction, street lighting retrofit, and smart fund for EE projects.

[6]Based on 2015 estimates.

## Public versus private financing[24]

The impact of the investment cost on public debt sustainability can be alleviated through higher private participation. To assess the impact of individual countries estimated investment needs on their public debt trajectories, two financing scenarios are compared with a baseline scenario based on IMF staff's macro-framework assumptions made in 2016.

- *Scenario 1: The public sector fully finances the investment in energy infrastructure.* This scenario assumes that major infrastructure investments shown in Table 13.5 are financed by the public sector through a 20-year commercial loan, disbursed over three years (2016–18).[25]

- *Scenario 2: The private sector undertakes 80 percent of the investment.* This scenario assumes that a private sector partner will finance the bulk of the infrastructure projects, particularly those that lend themselves to a public-private partnership type setup, like the development of renewable or natural gas–fired power plants.

To the extent that energy investments improve growth, pressures on debt sustainability from financing them will wane. The model results for the elasticity of GDP to energy efficiency reviewed earlier in this chapter show that a 10 percent improvement in energy efficiency across the entire economy could increase the level of GDP by 2 percent in the long term.[26] In addition, spending on energy investment has a short-term impact on growth through the direct expansion of aggregate demand. Earlier work by IMF staff on a sample of Caribbean countries estimates the cumulative public investment multiplier to be about 0.37 after four quarters (IMF 2013). Collectively, the impact of energy investments on growth is expected to improve the public debt ratio over the long term.

## Planned investments and the size of the efficiency gains

The analysis in this chapter finds that net of debt service, estimated average cost savings from planned energy investments (Table 13.5) could improve operational efficiency in the region by more than 25 percent over a 20-year period (2019–38). The key findings include the following:

- The largest cost savings accrue to countries where the introduction of natural gas is viable. The savings average about 35 percent of recent utility oper-

---

[24]This assessment considers only the cost of large infrastructure investments for natural gas and renewable power and excludes the cost of energy efficiency and conservation initiatives identified in Table 13.5.

[25]Projects are assumed to be self-financing over the 20-year period 2019–38.

[26]Based on our model that a 1 percent increase in energy efficiency would be accompanied by an increase in GDP per capita of 0.2 percent in the long term.

ating costs under the U.S. Energy Information Administration's baseline projections for the prices of natural gas and distillate fuel oil.[27]

- Countries where hydroelectric power capacity is significant, such as Belize and Suriname, will enjoy overall lower energy costs.
- Under baseline energy price projections (2019–38), efficiency gains in ECCU countries average 19 percent.[28] Moreover, future scaling-up of geothermal power development in countries with higher geothermal potential could result in lower generation costs, implying higher efficiency gains.

As stated earlier, the efficiency gains are expected to translate into long-term growth benefits. It was pointed out earlier that energy investments would increase efficiency, and the impact on growth is estimated using the model results of the elasticity of GDP to energy efficiency. The growth rate assumed for the long-term debt dynamics of Scenarios 1 and 2 presented in the next section has been augmented to reflect the improved power sector efficiency from the investments and the resulting improvements in energy efficiency (cost savings). The ultimate impact on growth will likely depend on how the efficiency gains are spread across the economy. This exercise assumes a pass-through of energy efficiency or cost savings to end users of about 50–60 percent to accommodate potential required return on capital to the investor (whether private or public). Hence, in ECCU countries, where efficiency gains under baseline assumptions averaged 19 percent, growth was enhanced to reflect a 10 percent efficiency gain passed on to end users. Higher pass-through of cost savings could possibly result in higher growth dividends in the long term.[29]

## Results of the Debt Sustainability Analysis

Although results differ by country, there are important general conclusions:

- *The magnitude of proposed energy investments does not materially alter the trajectory of public debt in most countries (Scenario 1).* Although undertaking the investment through the public sector increased the public debt ratio for all countries over the medium term, the modeled cost recovery for debt service and the positive impact on growth (from both the investment impact and the lower energy costs) offset this increase in the long term.
- *Private sector financing of energy projects moderately improves the debt-to-GDP ratio compared with the baseline (Scenario 2).* This result, however, is likely to be contingent on the private sector developer passing a measurable share of the cost savings to end users. Retaining the bulk of the cost savings as

---

[27]Cost savings are calculated as a percentage of historical average operating expense over the period 2012–15. Cost reductions may be lower if shown as a percentage of projected operating expenses that reflect a higher oil price.

[28]Under lower oil prices than in the baseline, geothermal power provides negligible cost savings.

[29]McIntyre and others (2016) show more formally that the trajectory of public debt would be governed by a debt dynamics equation augmented by the impact of energy investments on debt-service costs, growth, and the public sector primary balance.

returns on investment could limit the transmission of benefits to the wider economy and reduce projected growth dividends from the lower cost of energy. In this regard, power purchase agreements that provide for limited reductions in consumer tariff rates are unlikely to generate the anticipated improvements in cost competitiveness in Caribbean economies.[30]

- *The impact of the investment on the debt trajectory will be less favorable than modeled if the efficiency of public sector investment is low or the overall cost of capital for the private sector is high.* The exercise assumes that the return on investment is the same whether it is undertaken by the public or private sector. If, however, public investment efficiency is low, resulting in lower rates of return than in the private sector, then debt accumulation would be higher. Alternatively, a higher cost of financing for the private sector than the public sector could raise the required rate of return for the project and lower the potential share of cost savings passed on to the end consumer, resulting in lower growth dividends.

- *Fiscal risks would be higher if the income stream of the power utility cannot be safeguarded.* For example, administrative practices that dictate a specific tariff rate or limit its adjustment to allow for full cost recovery would pose significant risks to the financial position of the power utility and, ultimately, the budget, for state-owned power companies.[31]

Countries fall into three categories with respect to capacity to undertake these large-scale energy investments. See Figure 13.12 (ECCU countries) and Figure 13.13 (rest of the Caribbean).

- Countries with a lower initial debt load and sustainable debt dynamics can reap the benefit of reducing energy costs without weakening fiscal or debt sustainability.

- Countries with a high public debt load and unsustainable debt dynamics are not well-positioned to undertake such investments using public sector financing.

- Countries undertaking significant adjustment to bring debt back to sustainable levels could elect to finance high-yielding investments under certain conditions.

## A SUSTAINABLE PRIVATE INVESTMENT FRAMEWORK IN THE ENERGY SECTOR

Given public financing constraints, private investment may be pivotal for successful energy sector reform. However, public-private partnerships (PPPs) have been

---

[30]However, under this scenario the country may still realize some benefits to the balance of payments by reducing the cost of imports of expensive fuel oil.

[31]Also, a low collection rate on utility bills would negatively affect cash flow and debt-servicing capacity.

## Figure 13.12. Impact of Energy Investments on Debt Sustainability[1]

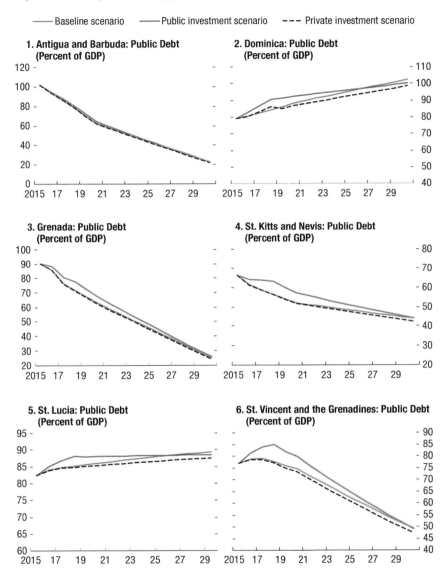

——— Baseline scenario      ——— Public investment scenario      – – – Private investment scenario

**1. Antigua and Barbuda: Public Debt (Percent of GDP)**

**2. Dominica: Public Debt (Percent of GDP)**

**3. Grenada: Public Debt (Percent of GDP)**

**4. St. Kitts and Nevis: Public Debt (Percent of GDP)**

**5. St. Lucia: Public Debt (Percent of GDP)**

**6. St. Vincent and the Grenadines: Public Debt (Percent of GDP)**

Source: McIntyre and others (2016).
[1]Reflects IMF staff macroeconomic assumptions as of the end of October 2015.

### Figure 13.13. Impact of Energy Investments on Debt Sustainability[1, 2]

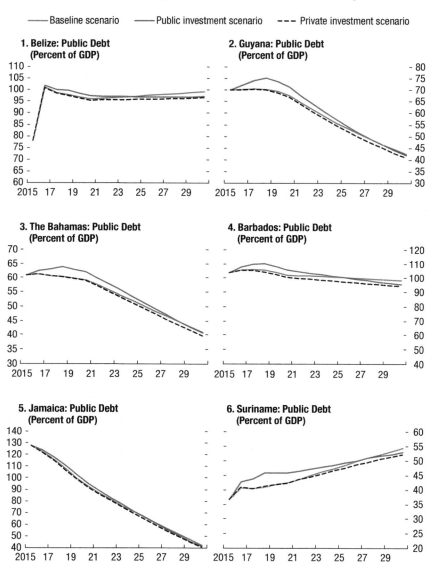

——— Baseline scenario    ——— Public investment scenario    – – – Private investment scenario

**1. Belize: Public Debt**
(Percent of GDP)

**2. Guyana: Public Debt**
(Percent of GDP)

**3. The Bahamas: Public Debt**
(Percent of GDP)

**4. Barbados: Public Debt**
(Percent of GDP)

**5. Jamaica: Public Debt**
(Percent of GDP)

**6. Suriname: Public Debt**
(Percent of GDP)

Source: McIntyre and others (2016).
[1]Reflects IMF staff macroeconomic assumptions as of the end of October 2015.
[2]Does not fully reflect debt of state-owned enterprises for The Bahamas, Barbados, and Jamaica.

**Figure 13.14. PPP investments in the Energy Sector**
*(Average percent of GDP, 1990–2013)*

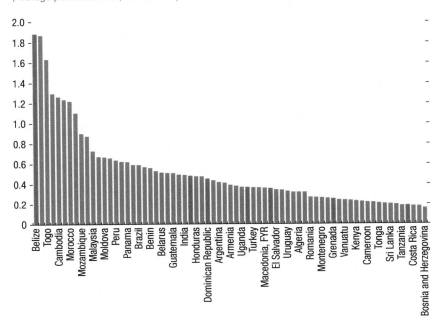

Source: World Bank Public-Private Partnership Database.
Note: Lao P.D.R., a large outlier at 7.9, was excluded to show scale. PPP = public-private partnership.

slow to take off in the Caribbean, and an important contributing factor has been the absence of appropriate PPP institutional arrangements and legislation. The status of energy PPP development is uneven. In some countries, such as Belize (Figure 13.14), the private sector is actively involved in electricity infrastructure investments. In others, such as Guyana and Grenada, the size of energy sector PPPs is quite limited.

**Despite their prospective benefits, PPPs often carry significant risks**. Compared with traditional procurement, the involvement of private partners increases the complexity of PPP contracts. This complexity calls for a strong institutional framework with appropriate supervision and safeguards, including to protect against risks from a power purchase agreement. These risks could arise from potentially lax selection standards, lack of transparency or sufficient competition in the bidding process, and inadequate risk sharing and risk transfer in the project design.

Successful institutional frameworks for PPPs include the following key elements:

- *A predictable, low-risk policy and regulatory environment.* A strong policy and regulatory environment would ensure a level playing field across all energy sector investors and participants, including state-owned utilities, and would provide long-term clarity about the future of power sector regulation, without providing undue concessions to the private sector players.[32]

- *A clearly defined energy sector strategy.* A long-term vision for the direction of the power sector, including targets for energy source diversification and the scope and process for private sector participation, backed up by specific policies such as the announcement of standard guidelines on power purchase agreements, will serve to assure the private sector of the government's commitment to a transparent process and will make it easier to secure project financing.

- *An accommodating legal framework.* Where a legislative framework is absent or deficient, governments should consider drafting a dedicated energy sector law—with possible technical assistance from international financial institutions—that recognizes the country's renewable energy resource, if any, as a national resource and defines the terms and restrictions of permits, licenses, and concessions to private sector developers.

- *Sufficient institutional capacity and human resources within the government.* PPP projects tend to be larger and more complex than traditional procurement, and thus require significant resources and expertise from the government in establishing PPP policies, identifying and evaluating projects, negotiating with private partners, and monitoring project execution.[33]

## CONCLUSION

Estimates in this chapter support the view that cutting Caribbean energy costs could materially improve the region's macroeconomic performance. Empirical analysis suggests that oil price movements influence real growth and the real exchange rate. Strategies to reduce exposure to oil price movements can help improve growth and competitiveness over the short and medium term, and alleviate pressures on the region's external accounts. In the long term, improvements in energy efficiency are shown to support higher sustainable growth. Hence, measures to conserve energy and to diversify the energy mix toward cheaper sources should be a high priority for regional reform efforts.

Most of the building blocks for substantial energy reform are present in the region, but important deficiencies still exist in regulation. Establishing clear licensing and operational procedures for independent power producers, including the introduction of feed-in tariffs and net billing schemes, are key reforms. Establishing independent energy regulators in the region with the appropriate

---

[32]The UN-Energy report (2011) showed that the main contribution of government is creating a low-risk, predictable, and enabling political, legal, and regulatory environment with established electricity sector development goals.

[33]Whatever the institutional arrangement created—an agency or unit—strong capacity will be critical to success, and this is an area in which Caribbean countries will require significant technical assistance.

institutional capacity is also crucial to providing a low-risk, predictable environment for private energy sector investors.

Achieving targets already set in national and regional energy sector strategies would generate valuable savings but require strong commitments by national authorities and substantial investments in the power sector. Implementing these targets for renewable energy penetration and boosting energy efficiency could generate significant cost savings by lowering electricity tariffs and fuel import costs. However, announced targets are ambitious, and strategies have yet to specify the magnitude of investments and identify the potential sources of financing required for their implementation.

Augmenting the IMF staffs Debt Sustainability Analysis of individual Caribbean economies with IDB-based estimates of energy investment needs would not materially alter the public debt trajectory of most countries. However, countries with unsustainable baseline debt paths or acute fiscal vulnerabilities are not well-positioned to finance significant investments using public resources. In addition, countries where structural conditions are weak, characterized by low returns on public capital, low public investment efficiency, and low user-fee collection rates, are likely to face higher risks to fiscal and debt sustainability from large-scale public sector energy investments. The analysis also suggests that private sector financing of investments can significantly improve the public debt path over the long term through their potential growth-enhancing impact, if a measurable share of the cost savings is passed on to the rest of the economy.

Finally, Caribbean authorities are encouraged to pursue private financing of energy investments, particularly in projects that involve significant upfront capital injection. PPPs are one modality for private sector participation; however, strong institutional arrangements and an appropriate legislative framework are crucial to ensuring successful implementation in line with best practices and to limit contingent liability risks to the fiscal sector, including those related to the specific terms of the power purchase agreement.

## REFERENCES

Auth, K., M. Konold, E. Musolino, and A. Ochs. 2013. "Caribbean Sustainable Energy Roadmap (C-SERMS)-Phase 1." Working Draft as of June 2013, CARICOM.

Caribbean Electric Utility Services Corporation (CARILEC). 2012. "Tariff Survey of Member Electric Utilities."

Caribbean Hotel Energy Efficiency Action Programme (CHENACT). 2012. "Energy Efficiency and Micro-Generation in Caribbean Hotels." Tetra-Tech, Arlington, VA.

Caribbean Community. 2013. *Energy Policy 2013.* http://cms2.caricom.org/documents/10862 -caricom_energy_policy.pdf.

Cashin, P., and S. Sosa. 2013. "Macroeconomic Fluctuations in the Eastern Caribbean: The Role of Climatic and External Shocks." *Journal of International Trade and Economic Development: An International and Comparative Review* 22: 729–48.

Castalia Strategic Advisors. 2010. "Sustainable Energy Framework for Barbados Final Report." Washington, DC. https://bajan.files.wordpress.com/2011/07/barbados-sustainable-energy -framework-vol-i.pdf.

———. 2013. "Energy Monograph (Various Countries)." Draft to the World Bank. Washington, DC.

International Monetary Fund (IMF). 2007. "Issues Paper on Public-Private Partnerships and Fiscal Risks." IMF Issues Paper 07/138, Washington, DC.

———. 2013. "Fiscal Multipliers in the ECCU." IMF Working Paper 13/117, Washington, DC.

McIntyre, A., A. El-Ashram, M. Ronci, J. Reynaud, N. Che, S. Acevedo, M. Lutz, F. Strodel, A. Osueke, and H. Yun. 2016. "Caribbean Energy: Macro-Related Challenges." IMF Working Paper 16/53, International Monetary Fund, Washington, DC.

Osterholm, P., and J. Zettelmeyer. 2008. "The Effect of External Conditions on Growth in Latin America," *IMF Staff Papers* 55 (4).

Petersen, S. 2002. "Micro Econometric Modeling of Household Energy Use: Testing for Dependence between Demand for Electricity and Natural Gas." *Energy Journal* 23 (4): 57–83.

UN-Energy. 2011. "Strengthening Public-Private Partnerships to Accelerate Global Electricity Technology Development: Recommendations for the Global Sustainable Electricity Partnership Survey," United Nations.

U.S. Energy Information Administration Database. 2015. Washington, DC.

World Bank Group. 2014. *Caribbean Infrastructure PPP Roadmap*. Washington, DC: World Bank.

# CHAPTER 14

# Emigration and Remittances in the Caribbean

JOYCE WONG

## INTRODUCTION

Outward migration has been an important phenomenon for countries in the Caribbean, where emigrants account for more than 20 percent of the region's population, compared with about 2 percent, on average, for emerging market and developing economies and 5 percent for Latin America and the Caribbean (LAC) overall. Caribbean emigrants typically emerge from the younger and more productive segment of the population—an average emigrant is between 20 and 25 years old with a higher education level. Emigrants remit substantial funds, averaging about 7 percent of the region's GDP, to support family members back home. Remittances are now the most important external flow for the region, dwarfing foreign direct investment and official aid (Figure 14.1).

Against this background, this chapter examines recent trends for, as well as the costs and benefits of, emigration and remittances to the Caribbean. Does the loss in population from emigration hurt economic growth? Do remittances compensate for this loss and function as engines of growth? Are remittances macroeconomic stabilizers? The analysis in this chapter, which is largely based on the work of Beaton and others (2017), offers three key messages for the Caribbean:

- Caribbean emigrants are quite different from other Latin American emigrants in that they have more diversified migrant destinations (not only to the United States, but also to Canada and the United Kingdom) and are more educated, and, consequently, are more likely to be employed in higher-skilled occupations.

- Emigration and remittances, taken jointly, are not drivers of growth in the Caribbean. The negative impact of emigration on real per capita growth (through brain drain) outweighs gains from remittances (through investment, education, and other commercial links).

This chapter is based on work by K. Beaton, S. Cerovic, M. Galdamez, M. Hadzi-Vaskov, F. Loyola, Z. Koczan, B. Lissovolik, J. K. Martijn, Y. Ustyuogova, and J. Wong. For further details, see Beaton and others (2017).

### Figure 14.1. Caribbean: Remittances and Other Inflows
*(Percent of GDP)*

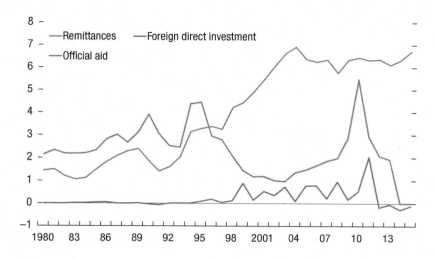

Sources: IMF, *Balance of Payment Statistics*; World Bank, *World Development Indicators*; and IMF *World Economic Outlook*.

- Remittances, however, are an important macroeconomic stabilizer in the Caribbean. As one of the most important sources of external financing, remittances facilitate private consumption smoothing (for example, in the face of shocks such as natural disasters), while boosting financial sector soundness and fiscal space.

## STYLIZED FACTS ABOUT CARIBBEAN MIGRATION AND REMITTANCES

### Migration

Emigration has been very important for Caribbean countries over the past decades. While the stock of emigrants is estimated to be about 5 percent of the population in the LAC region, it is more than 20 percent for the Caribbean alone, with significant differences across countries (Figure 14.2). Caribbean emigration has historically been driven by economic reasons and natural disasters, and has been less centered on the United States than emigration from Mexico or from Central America, Panama, and the Dominican Republic (CAPDR). About half of Caribbean emigrants settle in the United States (versus nearly all Mexican and four-fifths of CAPDR emigrants); Canada and the United Kingdom also figure prominently as key destinations (with about 15 percent of Caribbean emigrants settling in each).

## Figure 14.2. Emigrants

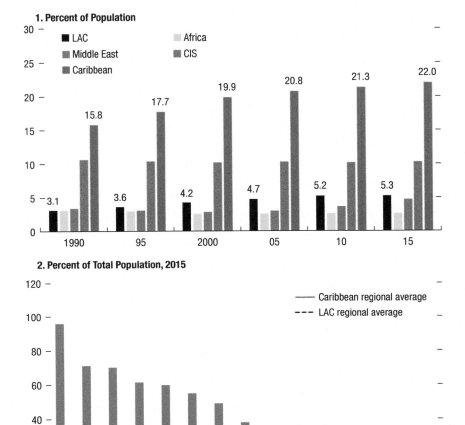

### 1. Percent of Population

### 2. Percent of Total Population, 2015

Sources: United Nations Population Division; and IMF staff calculations.
Note: CIS = Commonwealth of Independent States; LAC = Latin America and the Caribbean. Data labels in figure use International Organization for Standardization (ISO) country codes.

Caribbean emigrants tend to be well educated. Nearly half of Caribbean emigrants to the United States have at least a college education, a ratio comparable to the U.S. native-born population (Figure 14.3). In contrast, only one-quarter of other LAC emigrants in the United States have at least a college education. These educational differences are reflected in the types of occupations of Caribbean emigrants. Whereas emigrants from Mexico and CAPDR tend to work in lower-skilled occupations (construction, maintenance, transportation, production, and food preparation), Caribbean emigrants tend to be employed in office and administration, sales, management, and health-related occupations. Caribbean emigrants also earn more: their hourly wages average about 60 percent more than those of immigrants from Mexico and CAPDR.

To truly examine brain drain from the home country, however, educational levels of immigrants in the host country are not sufficient—attainment levels in the home country are also needed. For instance, evidence for Jamaica—for which comparable educational attainment data are available—indicates significant brain drain, especially among women. Among Jamaican-born women living in the United States (who emigrated after age 22), 50 percent have at least a college education; this is double the attainment rate in the home country, where only one-quarter of women have a college education. A simple calculation implies that nearly one-third of all women with at least a college education in Jamaica have emigrated, compared with about 13 percent of those with high school or less. These patterns are reflected in the significant numbers of Jamaican nurses and health care practitioners—65 percent of Jamaican immigrants are in these sectors versus 7 percent of the U.S.-born population. For men, the statistics are less striking, albeit evidencing brain drain: whereas 21 percent of men in Jamaica are college educated, 37 percent of those who migrated to the United States have at least a college education.

## Remittances

Caribbean emigrants maintain strong connections with their home countries, transferring sizable remittances (Figure 14.4), which reached 6.7 percent of regional output in 2015. As a share of GDP, remittances flows to Caribbean countries dwarf those received by most other world regions except for CAPDR (7.7 percent of GDP). In Haiti and Jamaica, remittances exceed 15 percent of GDP.

Remittances to the Caribbean grew rapidly from the mid-1990s and peaked at nearly 7 percent of regional output before the global financial crisis. Because of the Caribbean's more diversified emigration destinations and employment in more-skilled occupations, the region was more sheltered from the financial crisis's impact on the United States. For example, the fall in remittances observed for CAPDR countries, where the majority of emigrants reside in the United States and work in occupations hit hard by the crisis (such as construction and building maintenance), was not observed for the Caribbean. Thus, while remittances to the Caribbean remain somewhat below their precrisis peak, they have been broadly constant for the past decade.

Transferring remittances to the Caribbean is costly. Although the cost of sending remittances to the LAC region is lower than the global average of 7.4 percent of the remittance amount, it remains substantial at about 6 percent (Figure 14.5). Banks

## Figure 14.3. Educational Attainment and Wages

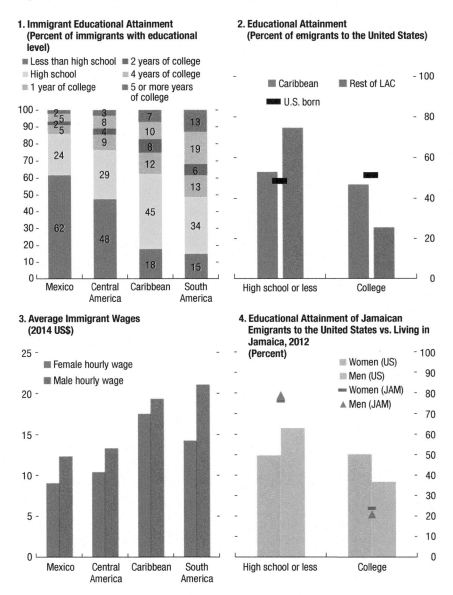

**1. Immigrant Educational Attainment**
**(Percent of immigrants with educational level)**

■ Less than high school  ■ 2 years of college
■ High school  ■ 4 years of college
■ 1 year of college  ■ 5 or more years of college

**2. Educational Attainment**
**(Percent of emigrants to the United States)**

■ Caribbean  ■ Rest of LAC
■ U.S. born

**3. Average Immigrant Wages (2014 US$)**

■ Female hourly wage
■ Male hourly wage

**4. Educational Attainment of Jamaican Emigrants to the United States vs. Living in Jamaica, 2012 (Percent)**

■ Women (US)
■ Men (US)
━ Women (JAM)
▲ Men (JAM)

Sources: American Community Survey; and World Bank.
Note: JAM = Jamaica; LAC = Latin America and the Caribbean.

**Figure 14.4. Remittances**

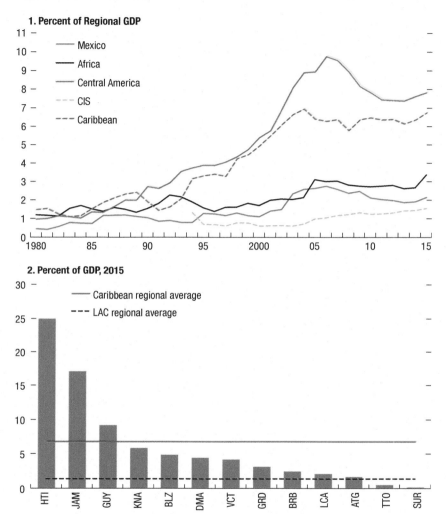

**1. Percent of Regional GDP**

- Mexico
- Africa
- Central America
- CIS
- Caribbean

**2. Percent of GDP, 2015**

- Caribbean regional average
- LAC regional average

Sources: World Bank; and IMF, *World Economic Outlook.*
Note: CIS = Commonwealth of Independent States; LAC = Latin America and the Caribbean. Data labels in figure use International Organization for Standardization (ISO) country codes.

## Figure 14.5. Cost of Sending US$200 in Remittances

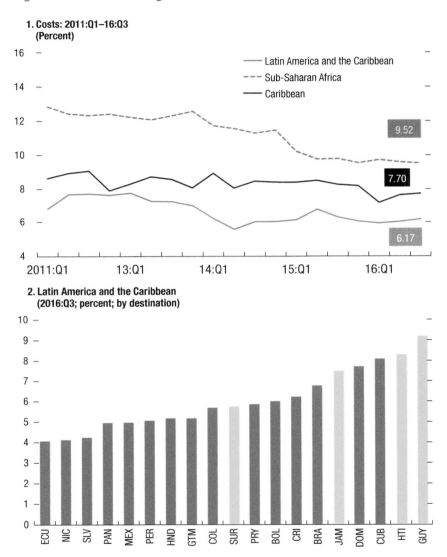

**1. Costs: 2011:Q1–16:Q3**
**(Percent)**

**2. Latin America and the Caribbean**
**(2016:Q3; percent; by destination)**

Source: World Bank, Remittances Prices Worldwide.
Note: Data labels in figure use International Organization for Standardization (ISO) country codes.

are the most expensive channel through which to send remittances, at 11 percent, followed by money transfer operators (MTO) at 8 percent; mobile remittances service providers are a low-cost option, at about 3 percent. Whereas costs have declined significantly for remittances to sub-Saharan Africa, partly because of the entry of mobile money, costs in LAC have remained broadly flat. Costs in some Caribbean countries, for example, Jamaica, have declined significantly—nearly 15 percent over the period 2001–15 (Orozco, Porras, and Yansura 2016), but remitting nevertheless remains costly. These higher transfer costs to the Caribbean partly reflect the region's more diversified host countries (Canada and the United Kingdom), since remitting costs are generally lowest from the United States.

The cost of remitting has also come under upward pressure from the global withdrawal of correspondent banking relationships, even though some of these effects have been dampened by new technologies in regions such as Africa. The withdrawal of global banks from correspondent banking has disproportionately affected MTOs, given the greater challenges they face in meeting the stringent know-your-customer anti-money laundering/combating the financing of terrorism standards. According to a survey carried out by the World Bank (2015), global banks have closed the correspondent bank accounts of MTOs, particularly smaller MTOs, on a widespread basis, curtailing their ability to transmit remittances. Coming under similar pressure, local banks in some countries and regions have also faced challenges in maintaining their correspondent banking relationships, with 60 percent of the *Asociación de Supervisores Bancarios de las Américas* reporting that remittances to LAC have been affected.

Caribbean immigrants in the United States tend to remit less than other Latin American immigrants. Only one-quarter of Caribbean households remit, compared with more than 40 percent for immigrants from Mexico and CAPDR. In addition, Caribbean immigrants also remit less as a proportion of their income—on average, 2 percent—compared with about 30 percent of income for lower-income Mexican and CAPDR immigrants (Figure 14.6). A potential driver for these differences is the fact that Caribbean immigrants have fewer family members left in the home countries, often the case when families immigrate together or single women (particularly in teaching and health care professions) pursue opportunities in the United States.

## HOW DO MIGRATION AND REMITTANCES AFFECT GROWTH?

Given the significant levels of emigration and remittances flows for the Caribbean, a key question is whether the net effect is beneficial for the home country. In theory, emigration and remittances can have opposite effects on growth. On the one hand, emigration can negatively affect growth because the departure of working-age people reduces the labor force and, especially in the Caribbean, human capital. Remittances could then further aggravate the decline in labor supply as recipients substitute remittances income for labor income, generating higher reservation wages. On the other hand, remittances could have a positive impact on growth by providing financial resources for investment and education.

## Figure 14.6. Remittance Senders in the United States

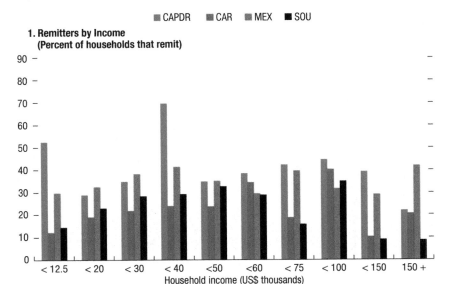

1. Remitters by Income
(Percent of households that remit)

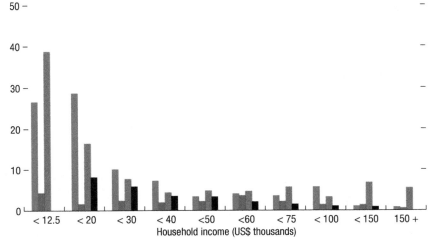

2. Amounts Remitted, Conditional on Remitting
(Percent of income)

Sources: 2008 American Community Survey; and IMF staff estimates.
Note: CAPDR = Central America, Panama, and the Dominican Republic; CAR = Caribbean; MEX = Mexico;
SOU = South America.

**Figure 14.7. Net Effect of Migration and Remittances on GDP Growth, 2003–13**
*(Percent of GDP)*

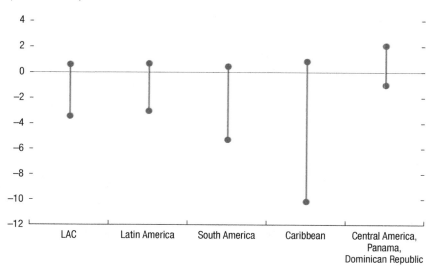

Source: Beaton and others (2017).
Note: LAC = Latin America and the Caribbean.

Empirical analysis confirms the mixed results. Figure 14.7 shows the potential range of the estimated cumulative joint impact on growth of actual emigration and remittances for 2003–13. The net effect points to a potential negative impact on growth, which is most pronounced in the Caribbean because of the high levels of brain drain. Remittances, however, have positive (though not always statistically significant) growth effects, which are largest in the high-remittances-receiving subregions such as the Caribbean and CAPDR. On balance, the Caribbean could have lost as much as 10 percent of GDP in cumulative growth as a result of the joint negative effect. Isolating the effects of only migration or remittances is difficult because of their high correlation (remittances cannot occur without migration). However, given the significant negative impact from emigration and brain drain, remittances are an unlikely driver of durable growth for the Caribbean.

## ARE REMITTANCES MACROECONOMIC STABILIZERS?

Even if emigration and remittances have negative net implications for growth, remittances could still play a significant role as a macroeconomic stabilizer. Empirical analysis suggests that remittances support consumption smoothing and generate fiscal revenues with little evidence of possible adverse "Dutch disease" effects. In a region vulnerable to natural disasters, remittances also appear to respond to them.

## Figure 14.8. Remittances and Natural Disasters

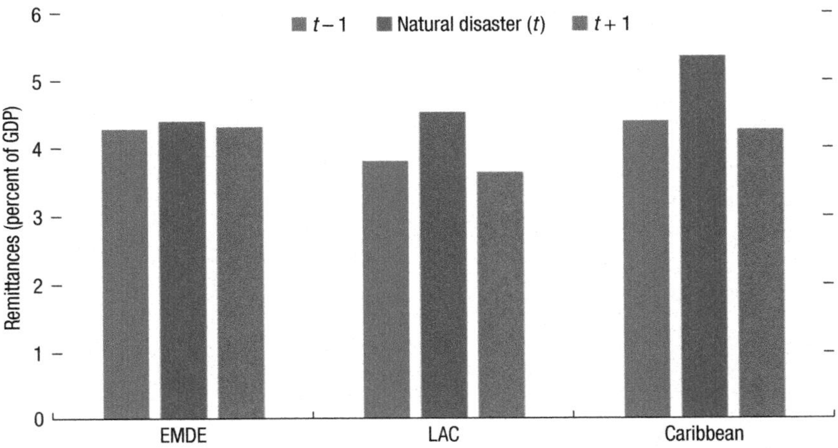

Sources: EM-DAT database; and IMF staff calculations.
Note: EMDE = emerging market and developing economies; LAC = Latin America and the Caribbean.

Remittances can help smooth consumption in the home country as emigrants send additional funds to cushion economic shocks. For example, remittances (as a share of GDP) jump when a natural disaster hits the remittances-recipient country (Figure 14.8). This effect appears to be especially important for the Caribbean, likely driven by its higher susceptibility to large natural disasters. Using an event analysis, the average remittances-to-GDP ratio increases from 4.4 percent in the year before a natural disaster to 5.4 percent in the year of the disaster.

Remittances also reduce income volatility in the home country (Figure 14.9). For most LAC countries, overall income including remittances is less volatile than domestic income. This effect is more important for LAC countries than for emerging market and developing economies as a whole, and even stronger for the Caribbean.

Remittances can also support stabilization through the fiscal accounts (Table 14.1). Remittances help raise fiscal revenues, although they typically are not directly taxed.[1] Instead, remittances-supported consumption is part of the base for indirect taxation. For large remittances-receiving countries, empirical analysis finds that a higher remittances-to-GDP ratio is positively associated with a higher revenue-to-GDP ratio. In the Caribbean, a 1 percentage point increase in the remittances-to-GDP ratio is associated with an increase in the revenue-to-GDP ratio of 1.2 percentage points;[2] this is significantly higher than the 0.4 percentage

---

[1]The few countries that tried to tax remittances directly later repealed these taxes. Examples include the Philippines, Tajikistan, and Vietnam (see Ratha 2017).

[2]The high elasticity of revenues to remittances is driven by a combination of (1) high elasticity of revenues to consumption (usually more than 1) and (2) positive elasticity of consumption to remittances.

### Figure 14.9. Remittances and Income Volatility

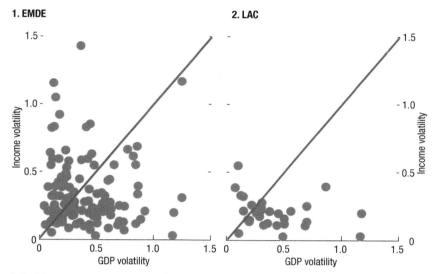

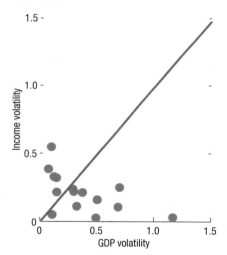

Sources: IMF staff calculations.
Note: EMDE = emerging market and developing economies; LAC = Latin America and the Caribbean.
Standard deviations of income (domestic income plus remittances) are plotted on the vertical axis and
GDP standard deviations are plotted on the horizontal axis. Dots below the 45-degree line indicate that
remittances lower income volatility.

**Table 14.1. Macro-Stabilizing Effect of Remittances**

| Effect on | Priors | Results |
|---|---|---|
| Fiscal Revenues | + | Yes. Significant for CAPDR and Caribbean. |
| Real Exchange Rate | + (appreciation) | Results generally insignificant and not strong. |
| Inflation | + | Yes. Significant for Caribbean and CAPDR. |

Source: IMF staff calculations.
Note: CAPDR = Central America, Panama, and the Dominican Republic.

point effect for CAPDR, the other high remittances-receiving region in LAC. Furthermore, higher remittances in the Caribbean are also associated with improved fiscal balances, in contrast to CAPDR where they are instead associated with higher public expenditures.

Although remittances support stabilization, these benefits may be counteracted by risks to competitiveness and inflation through pressure on nontradables prices and interest rates. The empirical analysis of Beaton and others (2017), however, does not point to a significant impact of remittances on the real effective exchange rate, likely reflecting leakage of remittances through imports given the small size and openness of many Caribbean countries. This theory is in line with the findings of Izquierdo and Montiel (2006), who find no impact of remittances on the equilibrium exchange rate in Jamaica. With regard to inflation, empirical results indeed confirm that the level of remittances is positively related to some inflationary pressure in the Caribbean. These results are consistent with the literature (for example, Ball, Lopez, and Reyes 2013), which has found that inflation effects from remittances are more pronounced in fixed exchange rate regimes because of the absence of a shock absorber that would help relative prices adjust quickly between the tradables and nontradables sectors.

## CONCLUSIONS AND POLICY IMPLICATIONS

For the Caribbean, remittances and emigration, on net, adversely affect growth. Although remittances are beneficial for the home country, the negative impact on labor resources and productivity outweighs growth gains from remittances. Given the Caribbean countries' highly educated emigrants, the negative effect from the loss of labor resources and human capital is large.

Nevertheless, accepting the existing stock of emigrants as a "sunk cost," remittances flows can still play key financing and stabilizing roles. They are the most important external flow to the region and facilitate private consumption smoothing and fiscal revenues, without strong evidence of harmful competitiveness effects through shifts in the real exchange rate.

Thus, policy measures to support remittances should focus on reducing the cost of remitting while facilitating formal intermediation. Given the recent challenges associated with correspondent banking relationships and the strengthening of anti-money laundering/combating the financing of terrorism frameworks, exploring regional solutions for cooperation can help improve Caribbean countries' regulatory environment and keep formal financial channels open.

Development of and enhancements to payments systems (including through new solutions like mobile money) and ensuring remittances-service providers' access to them would help foster competition and reduce prices. Educating consumers about the costs of remittances can also help users make informed decisions. Improving transparency on the cost of remittances, as the World Bank has done with its Remittance Prices Worldwide database, can help in this regard.

Steps to curb brain drain from the Caribbean are especially important. Because emigrants linked to brain drain typically remit less per person, the net effect for the Caribbean can be especially negative. A case can be made for development of measures to retain potential emigrants, either through structural reforms that foster job opportunities for the highly educated (for example, development of a medical tourism industry) or actions to limit the subsidizing of brain drain with public funds (for example, through bonding schemes whereby people who have benefited from public funding for education must remain in the home country for some years).

More generally, improvements in the business environment and strong institutions can help raise productivity and thereby limit incentives for outward migration. Productivity can also benefit from steps to promote return migration by skilled workers, for example, through the recognition of foreign qualifications and experience in professional regulations and public sector hiring, or the provision of portable social security benefits. Effective policies to improve the security situation in some Caribbean countries may also relieve key bottlenecks to productive use of remittances, including their greater use for investment. Countries could also seek to leverage economic ties with diasporas, which could bolster foreign direct investment and tourism receipts. The adverse impact of a real appreciation on competitiveness, if there were to be a spike in remittances inflows, can be cushioned using steps to reduce labor and product market rigidities and to support the provision of credit to firms.

## REFERENCES

Ball C., C. Lopez, and J. Reyes. 2013. "Remittances, Inflation and Exchange Rate Regimes in Small Open Economies." *World Economy* 36 (4): 487–507.

Beaton, K., S. Cerovic, M. Galdamez, M. Hadzi-Vaskov, F. Loyola, Z. Koczan, B. Lissovolik, J. K. Martijn, Y. Ustyuogova, and J. Wong. 2017. "Migration and Remittances in Latin America and the Caribbean: Engines of Growth and Macroeconomic Stabilizers?" In *Western Hemisphere Regional Economic Outlook*, April, International Monetary Fund, Washington, DC.

Izquierdo, A., and P. Montiel. 2006. "Remittances and Real Effective Exchange Rate in Six Central American Countries." Unpublished, Inter-American Development Bank, Washington, DC.

Orozco, M., L. Porras, and J. Yansura. 2016. "The Costs of Sending Money to Latin America and the Caribbean." Inter-American Dialogue, Washington, DC.

Ratha, D. 2017. "Why Taxing Remittances Is a Bad Idea." https://blogs.worldbank.org/peoplemove/why-taxing-remittances-bad-idea.

World Bank. 2015. *Report on the G20 Survey on De-Risking in the Remittance Market.* Washington, DC: World Bank.

# CHAPTER 15

# Violence in the Caribbean: Cost and Impact

HEATHER SUTTON, LAURA JAITMAN, AND JEETENDRA KHADAN

## INTRODUCTION

Crime—particularly violent crime—is pervasive in the Caribbean and imposes a serious economic and social burden on the countries in the region. An average of 40 percent of the Caribbean population identifies crime and security-related issues as the overarching problem facing their countries, even more so than poverty or inequality.[1] In several Caribbean countries, crime has risen sharply since 2007, with homicide rates more than doubling (UNODC/World Bank 2007; UNDP 2012).

Studies of crime and its impact on economic prospects and social outcomes in the Caribbean are few and, more important, narrow in scope, owing notably to the limitations of data. In particular, data on crime in Caribbean countries are generally from either national police or citizen security opinion surveys. Although such data are an important source of information, many crimes go unreported to the police, meaning that both the "real" prevalence of crime and its impact on society at large are invariably understated. Because of the data shortcomings, existing studies have not been able to generate comparable cross-country estimates of the impact of crime between Caribbean countries and between the Caribbean and the rest of the world. More important, there has been little analysis of the impact of crime on the private sector and on investment prospects.

To help improve understanding of crime and violence and possible solutions in the Caribbean, the Inter-American Development Bank (IDB) undertook two initiatives between 2013 and 2015 to generate comparable primary data on crime in the Caribbean. First, a Caribbean Crime Victimization Survey module was attached to the Latin American Public Opinion Project Survey in five Caribbean countries (The Bahamas, Barbados, Jamaica, Suriname, and Trinidad and Tobago). Second, a business victimization survey module was attached to the

---

The chapter authors are from the Inter-American Development Bank.

[1]Latin American Public Opinion Project 2014/2015 Caribbean data sets.

Productivity, Technology, and Innovation Survey of 2014 to canvass the views of a representative sample of private sector firms in 13 Caribbean countries.[2] Simultaneously, the collection of administrative and survey data, combined with development of a new standardized methodological approach, allowed the first comparable estimates to be made of the cost of crime among 17 Latin American and Caribbean countries and six other advanced economies.[3]

The findings of these initiatives are detailed in three recent IDB publications (Ruprah and Sierra 2016; Sutton and Ruprah 2017; Jaitman 2017). This chapter summarizes some of the main findings of these publications, with a preliminary assessment of their possible implications.

## STYLIZED FACTS ON CRIME IN LATIN AMERICA AND THE CARIBBEAN

Homicides are the most widely recognized and comparable indicators of the levels of violence within a society.[4] Globally, the Latin America and the Caribbean (LAC) region has the highest homicide rates.[5] Within LAC, Caribbean homicide rates are generally higher than those of countries in the Southern Cone of Latin America, but well below those of Central America (Figure 15.1).

A common trend among the five Caribbean countries surveyed is the dominance of violent crimes (Figure 15.2). The number of victims of assault and threat as a share of the population[6] (6.8 percent) is markedly higher than in any other region. New Providence (The Bahamas) and Kingston (Jamaica) stand out with the highest levels of assault and threat in the Caribbean, at nearly twice the world average. By comparison, property crimes (theft and burglary) in the Caribbean are relatively low compared with the international scale. More worryingly, the victims of violent crime are predominantly young, which can have a significant bearing on economic and social outcomes both in the near term and in the long term. Homicide victims are disproportionately youth between the ages of 18 and 35 (Table 15.1).

Victimization rates for assault and threat also differ significantly by sex, age, and income (Figure 15.3). For instance, the rates are significantly higher for men

---

[2]Countries include Antigua and Barbuda, The Bahamas, Barbados, Belize, Dominica, Grenada, Guyana, Jamaica, St. Lucia, St. Kitts and Nevis, St. Vincent and the Grenadines, Suriname, and Trinidad and Tobago.

[3]LAC countries include: Argentina, The Bahamas, Barbados, Brazil, Chile, Colombia, Costa Rica, Ecuador, Guatemala, Honduras, Jamaica, Mexico, Paraguay, Peru, El Salvador, Trinidad and Tobago, and Uruguay. Advanced economies include Australia, Canada, France, Germany, United Kingdom, and United States.

[4]Homicide is the most visible and reliably reported form of violent crime. Given that most countries have a legal requirement that all deaths be registered, homicide data are generally captured fairly accurately by police or public health systems.

[5]At 23 per 100,000, the LAC average homicide rate was four times the international average (UNODC 2015).

[6]Assault and threat refer to physical attack or threat of physical attack with the use of violence, but do not include incidents of a sexual nature or incidents of domestic violence.

**Figure 15.1. Homicide Rates per 100,000 Population in Latin America and Caribbean Countries, 2015 or Latest Available Year**

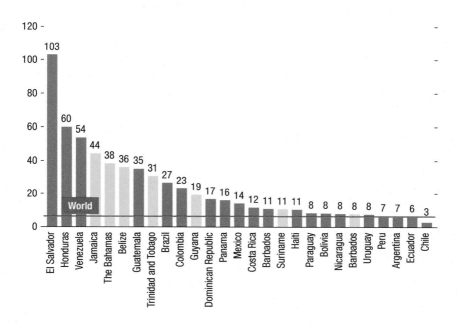

Source: Official national sources in each country.

than for women[7] and for youth ages 18–30 than for the overall population. Rates of assault and threat among the poorest 25 percent of the population are twice as high as for the richest 25 percent.

Additional stylized facts emerge from the survey data. First, violent crime happens close to home and is concentrated in neighborhoods that report having higher physical disorder (for example, graffiti, trash, abandoned buildings) and lower social cohesion (such as trust among neighbors). Second, neighborhoods with a gang presence are associated with higher odds of victimization by violent crime. Indeed, gang presence in a neighborhood is a significant predictor of victimization even after controlling for other individual and neighborhood characteristics. Third, firearms are used more frequently in crime in the Caribbean than elsewhere in the world. For instance, guns are used about twice as often in robbery and three times as often in assault in the Caribbean compared with the global average.

---

[7]Note the "assault" category specifically excludes domestic violence and sexual violence. These types of violence require specific dedicated surveys for reliable estimates to be obtained.

**Figure 15.2. Percent of the Population Victimized in a 12-Month Period, Capital Cities of Seven World Regions, by Type of Crime**

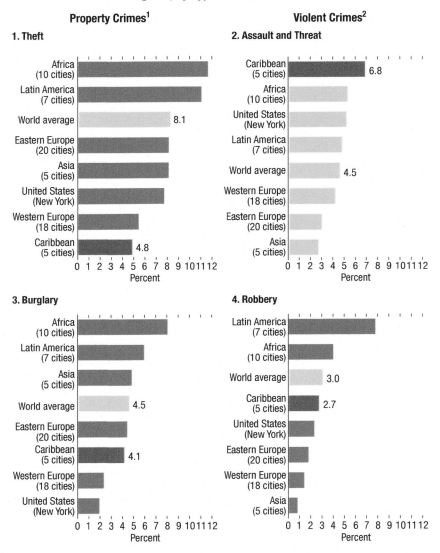

Property Crimes[1]

1. Theft

Violent Crimes[2]

2. Assault and Threat

3. Burglary

4. Robbery

Source: Sutton, van Dijk, and van Kesteren (2017) using data from the Inter-American Development Bank Caribbean Crime Victimization Survey module attached to the 2014/2015 Latin American Public Opinion Project Survey and the International Crime Victimization Surveys (latest available year).
Note: Theft is stealing without violence. Burglary is break-in and stealing, or attempted stealing, without use of violence. Assault and threat refers to physical attack or threat of physical attack with the use of violence.
[1]Without the use of threat or force.
[2]With the use of force or threat.

Table 15.1. Homicide Rates by Age Group, Four Caribbean Countries
*(Per 100,000)*

| Country | Under 18 | 18–25 Years Old | 25–35 Years Old | Total Population |
|---|---|---|---|---|
| The Bahamas | 5.3 | 84.8 | 64.7 | 33.3 |
| Barbados | 1.9 | 24.6 | 22.6 | 10.6 |
| Jamaica | 6.3 | 64.0 | 90.8 | 47.3 |
| Trinidad and Tobago | 8.6 | 52.8 | 69.6 | 34.8 |

Source: Sutton and Ruprah 2017.

Figure 15.3. Percent of the Population Victimized by Assault and Threat in a 12-Month Period, by Sex, Age, and Income, for Five Caribbean Capital Metropolitan Areas

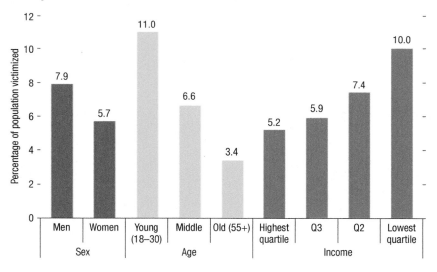

Source: Inter-American Development Bank Caribbean Crime Victimization Survey module attached to the 2014/2015 Latin American Public Opinion Project Survey.
Note: The "assault" category specifically excludes domestic violence and sexual violence. These types of violence require specific dedicated surveys for reliable estimates to be obtained.

# THE COST OF CRIME

Crime and violence adversely affect economic prospects and social outcomes. At the same time, efforts to combat crime lead to costly behavioral responses (e.g. loss of privacy) and distortions in the allocation of private and public resources (Jaitman 2015). Because the public and private sectors often have to spend large amounts of resources, both to prevent crime and to deal with its negative consequences, it can have a significant impact on economic prospects, particularly in the Caribbean where many economies are stuck in a low growth–high debt trap.

A variety of direct and indirect costs are associated with crime. In particular, direct costs are associated with injury, damage, and loss; public and private expenditures on security; and response to crime, such as the cost of the criminal justice system. In addition, indirect or intangible costs arise from changes in behavior caused by the fear of crime or the costs to families of victims.

How can the costs associated with crime be estimated? The most common approach is the accounting methodology, which values and sums up damages and losses in monetary terms. Although this methodology considers only part of the costs of crime, and the estimates are therefore conservative, it allows for cross-country comparison if done systematically. Jaitman and Torre (2017) apply this methodology for 17 LAC countries, and the results for the Caribbean are highlighted below. This is believed to be the first attempt to systematically study the costs of crime for a group of Caribbean countries.

Three types of costs are included in these estimates (detailed further in Jaitman and Torre 2017):

- *Public spending* on security, including policing services, criminal justice, and prison administration. Upper bound estimates assume that all of the police budget is allocated to crime-fighting activities (that is, it includes costs of activities not directly linked to crime fighting, such as traffic violations).

- *Spending* on security by private firms. Private costs are measured in the World Bank's Business Environment and Enterprise Performance Survey. The lower bound excludes costs borne by sectors such as agriculture, mining, utilities, and financial services, while the upper bound includes imputed costs.

- *Social costs* of crime, defined as victims' and prisoners' forgone income. For the prison population and homicide victims, the social cost is equal to the full loss of income while for victims of rape, robberies, and assault, it is equivalent to a fraction of the imputed income.

The aim is not to establish exact amounts, but rather to identify orders of magnitude of the cost of crime and violence across a range of countries.

## International Comparisons

Figure 15.4 presents the estimates of the overall costs of crime for selected countries in the Caribbean (The Bahamas, Barbados, Jamaica, and Trinidad and Tobago), compared with the 17-country LAC average and six other advanced economies. The estimated cost of crime in the Caribbean is 3.7 percent of GDP, slightly higher than the regional Latin American average of 3.5 percent of GDP. The cost in the Caribbean far surpasses the average of costs in Australia, Canada, France, Germany, the United Kingdom, and the United States. To put the magnitude of the cost in context, it is comparable to the income share of the poorest 30 percent of the Caribbean population.

Within LAC, the Caribbean has the highest overall costs after Central America (Figure 15.5), but the Caribbean economies top the list in public spending

## Figure 15.4. Crime-Related Costs, International Comparison

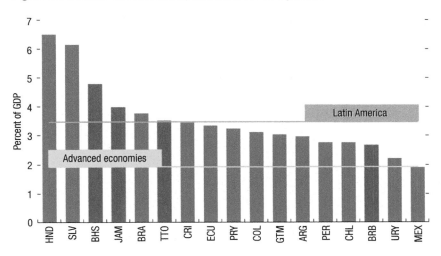

Source: Jaitman 2017.
Note: Data labels in figure use International Organization for Standardization (ISO) country codes.

## Figure 15.5. Overall Crime-Related Costs, 2014
*(Percent of GDP)*

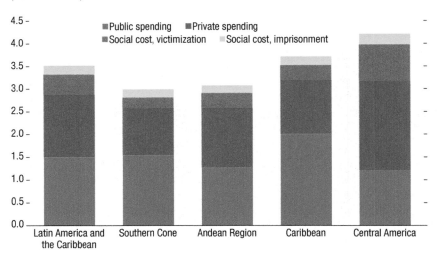

Source: Jaitman 2017.

associated with crime by a significant margin. The Caribbean spends more than 2 percent of GDP on public security (including expenditure on police, administration of justice, and prisons), which is about 0.5 percentage point of GDP higher than the LAC average. Other crime-related costs include 1.2 percent of GDP in private spending and about 0.5 percent of GDP in social costs.

## Regional Comparisons

Within the Caribbean, The Bahamas incurs the highest crime-related costs (Figure 15.6). At a cost of 4.7 percent of GDP, it ranks third among 17 countries (Jaitman 2017), after Honduras and El Salvador, where crime is recognizably widespread. This cost is mostly driven by spending on security by private firms, potentially indicative of tourism sector–related security costs in the all-inclusive resorts. Barbados ranks the lowest in the Caribbean, with an estimated cost of crime of about 2.7 percent of GDP. Jamaica and Trinidad and Tobago fall in between.

Delving deeper into the regional cost estimates, the following results emerge:

- Public expenditure ranged between 1.5 percent of GDP (Trinidad and Tobago) and 2.5 percent of GDP (in Jamaica, the highest of the 17 LAC countries). However, The Bahamas, Barbados, and Jamaica spend the least on justice administration among LAC countries—well under 0.1 percent of GDP—contributing to low capacity and potential bottlenecks in courts.

**Figure 15.6. Crime-Related Costs**
*(Percent of GDP)*

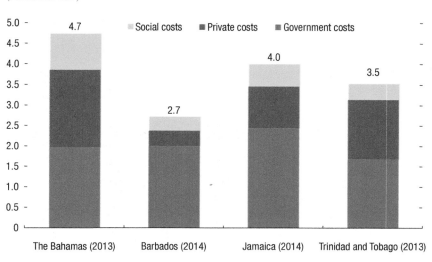

Source: Jaitman and Torre 2017.

- Private sector and social costs of crime are also highly variable, ranging from 0.2 percent of GDP to 1.9 percent in Trinidad and Tobago and 0.3 percent of GDP to 0.9 percent of GDP in Jamaica. The Bahamas incurs the most of both costs while Barbados incurs the least.

- Homicides are the largest contributor to social costs in all countries except Barbados. For example, in The Bahamas, the income forgone because of homicides is equivalent to almost 0.5 percent of GDP, while forgone income of the imprisoned population is the second largest, at 0.35 percent of GDP.

These estimates provide a first look at the costs of crime. The differences across these estimates likely reflect, among other factors, differences across each country's social, demographic, and income profiles, which require further analysis to disentangle.

## IMPACT OF CRIME ON THE PRIVATE SECTOR

The literature on crime and private sector performance suggests a negative relationship between crime and key performance indicators such as revenue, employment, and hours worked (Montoya 2012; Fiestas and Sinha 2011). These effects vary based on type of firm, with small firms being affected the most (Montoya 2012). In addition, crime is also a major deterrent to firm entry (Mahofa, Sundaram, and Edwards 2015), while it also raises the cost of doing business. For example, firms experience losses from theft and vandalism, financial resources forgone on security expenditure, and reduced working hours, which can limit firms' ability to grow (Detotto and Otranto 2010). Crime and insecurity also diminish the quality of the workforce and undermine innovation (Lacoe 2013).

Based on the Productivity, Technology, and Innovation Survey of firms in 13 Caribbean countries, 22 percent of firms, on average, report crime as either a major or a severe obstacle to their performance. There is, however, substantial differentiation across countries in the region (Figure 15.7), which could potentially be explained by differences in the sampling of firms or in other underlying firm and country characteristics. For instance, in The Bahamas, large private and public sector spending on preventing crime and addressing its negative impact could possibly explain why few firms identify crime as an obstacle. About 23 percent of Caribbean firms reported losses due to crime. This share is higher than the world average from the World Bank Enterprise Survey (19 percent), but lower than for the LAC region (27 percent).[8] The percentage of businesses victimized ranged from 8 percent in Belize to 33 percent in Guyana, with firms most likely to be victims of theft, vandalism, and attempted robbery (Figure 15.8).

---

[8]World Bank Enterprise Survey average for all countries and LAC using the latest available year.

**Figure 15.7. Crime as a Major or Severe Obstacle to the Private Sector**
*(Percent of firms)*

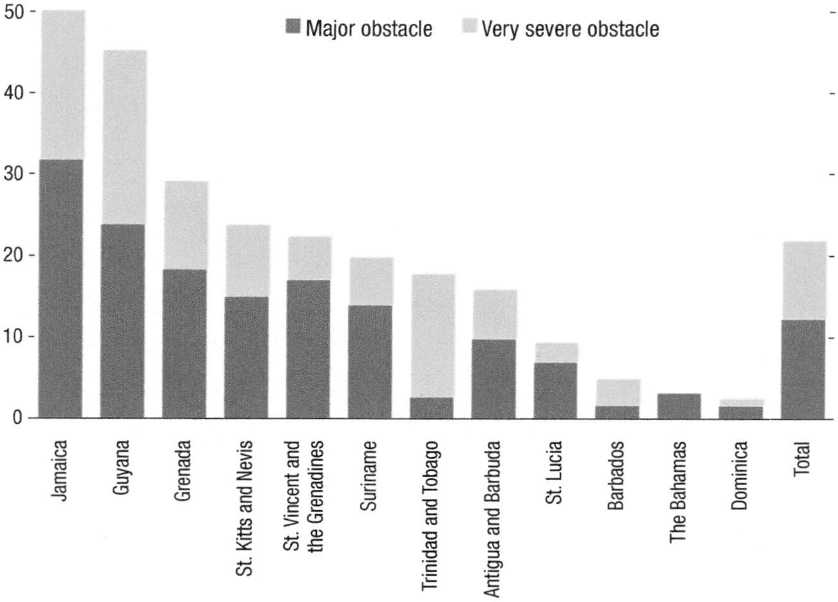

Source: Productivity, Technology, and Innovation Survey, 2014.

Among the affected firms, 47 percent of small and medium enterprises report that they experienced a loss due to crime, compared with 25 percent of large firms (Figure 15.9).

## Cost of Crime for Firms

Caribbean firms report that, on average, 2.4 percent of annual sales are lost due to crime (Figure 15.10); the losses range from 1.3 percent for Barbados to more than 4 percent for Jamaica. Almost 70 percent of Caribbean firms also use private security to mitigate potential losses from crime, compared with the world average on the World Bank Enterprise Survey of 56 percent (latest available year for each country). Private security costs for Caribbean firms were, on average, about 2.6 percent of their annual sales, ranging from 1.5 percent for Guyana to about 6 percent for St. Kitts and Nevis. It is noteworthy that businesses that engage in self-protection enjoy better sales performance, although the costs of self-protection reduce profitability and private investment (Kimou 2015). Taking again the example of The Bahamas to illustrate how these constraints work together, although private costs from crime were high as a percentage of GDP (Figure 15.6), they are not as significant when examined against annual sales and thus not a sizable concern to most firms (Figure 15.7).

**Figure 15.8. Type of Crime in the Previous Fiscal Year among Businesses that Reported Crime-Related Losses, Average of 13 Caribbean Countries**

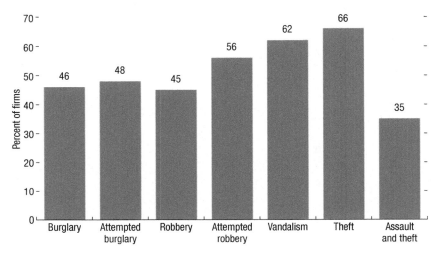

Source: Sutton and Ruprah 2017 using data from Productivity, Technology, and Innovation Survey, 2014.

**Figure 15.9. Percentage of Firms Affected by Crime, by Firm Characteristic, 2014**

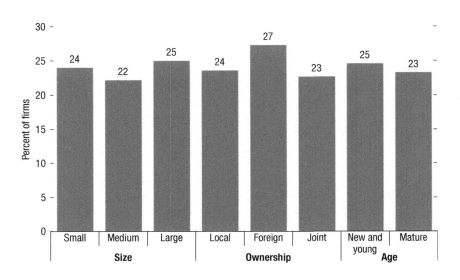

Source: Productivity, Technology, and Innovation Survey, 2014.

**Figure 15.10. Crime and Security–Related Costs for Firms**
*(Percent of annual sales)*

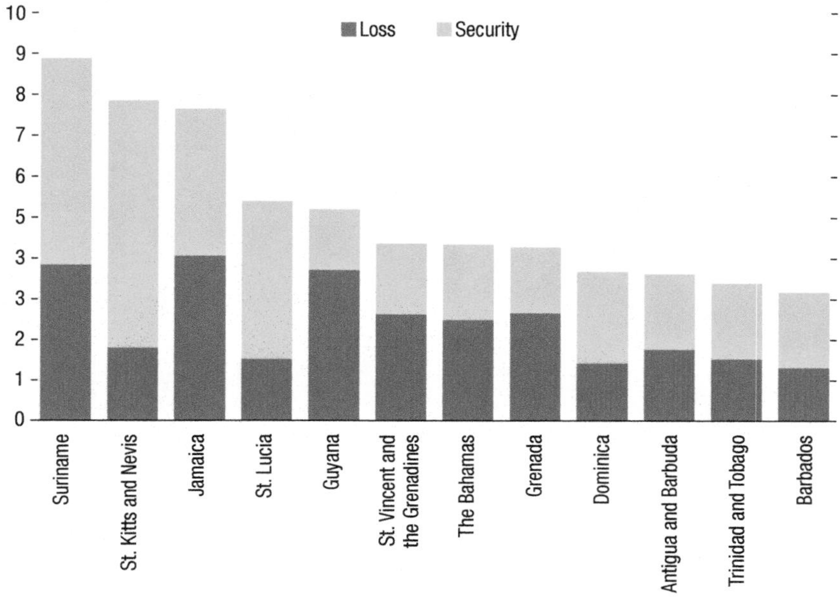

Source: Productivity, Technology, and Innovation Survey, 2014.

## The Economic Impact of a Reduction in Crime

To quantify the relative impact of several constraints on firm performance in the Caribbean, the regression equation specified in Annex 15.1 was applied.[9] The estimated coefficients and the mean value of each constraint on firm performance were then used to simulate the effect on firm performance of a 10 percent reduction in each constraint (Figure 15.11). Sales growth is used as the performance indicator and Caribbean countries are separated into two groups: tourism-dependent (The Bahamas, Barbados, and Jamaica) and commodity-dependent (Guyana, Suriname, and Trinidad and Tobago) countries.

The simulation exercise indicates that tackling crime yields the second-largest improvement in sales growth compared with other constraints. A 10 percent reduction in crime is associated with an 8 percent increase in sales growth for firms that are tourism dependent and a 4 percent increase in sales growth in commodity-dependent countries. Thus, the tourism-dependent economies

---

[9]See Ruprah and Sierra (2016) for further details.

**Figure 15.11. Potential Increase in Sales Growth with 10 Percent Reduction in Each Constraint**
*(Percent)*

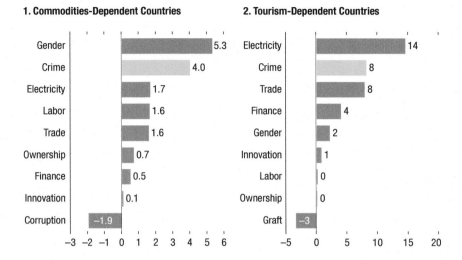

Source: Ruprah and Sierra 2016.

(Jamaica and The Bahamas, both of which have high crime rates) stand to make the greatest return for the private sector by investing resources in preventing and combating crime.

The effects on tourism are similar. The same reduction in homicide rates would yield an increase of 2.1 percent in annual tourism arrival growth. On an individual level, crime has also been shown to affect emigration decisions (and thus labor supply in the country)—victims of crimes are more likely to report being dissatisfied with life and considering emigration. Intentions to emigrate in the next three years increase by more than 30 percent for victims or witnesses of violence.

## CONCLUSIONS AND POLICY RECOMMENDATIONS

Although crime has been identified as a key deterrent to growth in the Caribbean, very little research exists on the types and incidence of crime, its drivers, and especially on quantifying the consequences of crime. The reasons are many, including data limitations, capacity and resource constraints in conducting analysis in this area, a bias toward punitive rather than preventive measures, and political and cultural sensitivities around the topic. The data presented in this chapter are a significant step forward, but much analysis on the drivers and impact of crime remains to be done.

From an economic perspective, as articulated in the seminal paper by Becker (1968), criminals are rational individuals who compare the expected cost and benefit of committing crimes with those of legal activities. Thus, taking the profit out of crime is an important policy goal that requires raising the expected return to education, increasing formality, and raising the cost of committing crimes or violence.

Thus, crime prevention and deterrence are equally important. Prevention interventions help increase the expected net benefit of legal and nonviolent activities. For example, targeting at-risk youth for vocational programs and social programs increases the possibility that they will gain legal earnings and obtain respect through nonviolent means, while concurrently potentially reducing youth unemployment. Likewise, improved policing and a more effective criminal justice system would increase the expected cost of committing crimes, increasing deterrence.

Within this framework, and considering international evidence of what works to reduce crime, Sutton and Ruprah (2017) provide some recommendations for addressing crime:

- *Prevention and control:* A balanced approach is required that includes both smart prevention and smart crime control. Current prevention programs in the Caribbean (for example, parenting and mentoring programs, urban renewal programs, victims' support) are understaffed and underresourced, while law enforcement continues to dominate national budgets for public safety. Achieving a balance means recognizing that crime prevention is a proven means for effectively reducing violence and therefore bolstering crime-prevention programs politically, administratively, and financially.

- *Targeted and evidence-based intervention:* Scarce resources should be invested where they may make the most difference—in high-crime areas and with those who are most at risk. In addition, crime-reduction initiatives should consider what has been proven to work, and should be subjected to rigorous evaluation to establish effectiveness. This effort will require better data collection and widespread sharing of data, provision of funding support for evaluations, and integration of research with policy.

- *Monitoring:* A dashboard of key metrics is needed for high-frequency monitoring to inform policymakers of the current issues and their status so policies could be adapted accordingly. For example, number of arrests, types of crime (violent, property, drug offenses), cases that proceed to trial and conviction, prison population, and participants in rehabilitation programs and prevention and social programs could all be informative indicators for policymaking.

In addition, given the high costs to the private sector of crime in the Caribbean, the private sector could potentially partner with the government to prevent and fight crime, including through urban renewal programs and crime-prevention projects to help train at-risk youth. The private sector could also become directly involved in funding project evaluation and research programs, including conducting field experiments to evaluate "out-of-the-box" measures. Examples of such initiatives in Latin America include corporate volunteerism (SulAmerica Peace Parks in Brazil), corporate funding of victimization surveys (Peru), and organizing forums in which to discuss public safety policies (Colombia). Building corporate social responsibility by sponsoring roads, neighborhoods, or communities could potentially help prevent crime.

## ANNEX 1.1.

Equation (15.1.1)

$$
\begin{aligned}
O_r = {} & \beta_0 + \beta_1 Age_r + \beta_2 Age2_r + \beta_3 Size_r + \beta_4 Size2_r + \beta_5 Own\_foreign_r \\
& + \beta_6 Own\_joint_r + \beta_7 Privatelyheld_r + \beta_8 SoleProprietorship_r \\
& + \beta_9 Partnership_r + \beta_{10} LimitedPartnership_r + \beta_{11} Own\_female_r \\
& + \beta_{12} Manager\_female_r + \beta_{13} Exporter_r + \beta_{14} Importer_r + \beta_{15} Corruption_r \\
& + \beta_{16} Corruption2 + \beta_{17} Outages_r + \beta_{18} Outages\_generator_r \\
& + \beta_{19} New\_product_r + \beta_{20} New\_process_r + \beta_{21} Crime\_loss_r \\
& + \beta_{22} Labor\_constraint_r + \beta_{23} Credit\_denied_r + \theta_s + \mu_c + \epsilon_r
\end{aligned}
$$

A description of the variables is provided below.

- $O_{ri}$: Firm-level outcome (sales growth, purchasing-power-parity adjusted)
- $Age_{ri}$: Firm age in years
- $Age2_{ri}$: Firm age in years squared
- $Size_{ri}$: Number of employees
- $Size2_{ri}$: Number of employees squared
- $Own\_foreign_{ri}$: Dummy equal to one if firm is predominately foreign owned
- $Own\_joint_{ri}$: Dummy equal to one if firm is owned jointly by local and foreign entities
- $Privatelyheld_{ri}$: Dummy equal to one if firm is a private limited liability company
- $SoleProprietorship_r$: Dummy equal to one if firm is a sole proprietorship
- $Partnership_r$: Dummy equal to one if firm is a partnership
- $LimitedPartnership_r$: Dummy equal to one if firm is a limited partnership
- $Own\_female_r$: Dummy equal to one if firm is owned by a female
- $Manager\_female_r$: Dummy equal to one if firm is managed by a female
- $Exporter_r$: Dummy equal to one if firm is an exporter
- $Importer_r$: Dummy equal to one if firm is an importer
- $Corruption_r$: Index constructed in Jaitman and Torre (2017)
- $Corruption2$: $Corruption_r$ squared
- $Outages_r$: Dummy equal to one if firm reported outages

- ***Outages_generator$_r$***: Interaction term, which accounts for firms that experienced outages and owned or shared a generator
- ***New_product$_i$***: Dummy equal to one if firm introduced significantly improved products
- ***New_process$_r$***: Dummy equal to one if firm introduced a significantly improved process for producing or supplying products
- ***Crime_loss$_r$***: Dummy equal to one if firm reported losses (percent of sales) due to crime
- ***Labor_constraint$_i$***: Dummy equal to one if firm identified labor as a major problem and provided training to its employees
- ***Credit_denied$_r$***: Dummy equal to one if firm application for credit was rejected
- $\theta_s$: Sector-specific fixed effects
- $\mu_c$: Country-specific fixed effects

and $r \in$ {Caribbean-Commodities, Caribbean-Tourism} and $i$ {Sales growth, purchasing-power-parity adjusted}.

## REFERENCES

Becker, G. S. 1968. "Crime and Punishment: An Economic Approach." *Journal of Political Economy* 76 (2): 169–217.

Detotto, C., and E. Otranto. 2010. "Does Crime Affect Economic Growth?" *Kyklos* 63 (3): 330–45.

Fiestas, I., and S. Sinha. 2011. "Constraints to Private Investment in the Poorest Developing Countries–A Review of the Literature." Nathan Associates London, Ltd.

Jaitman, L. 2015. "The Welfare Costs of Crime and Violence in Latin America and the Caribbean." IDB Monograph 354, Inter-American Development Bank, Washington, DC.

———. 2017. "The Cost of Crime and Violence: New Evidence and Insights in Latin America and the Caribbean." Inter-American Development Bank, Washington, DC.

———, and I. Torre. 2017. "The Cost of Crime in the Caribbean: The Accounting Method." In *Restoring Paradise in the Caribbean: Combatting Violence with Numbers*, edited by H. Sutton and I. Ruprah. Washington, DC: Inter-American Development Bank.

Kimou, A. J. C. 2015. "Crime, Self-Protection and Business Growth in Côte d'Ivoire." *Modern Economy* 6: 1101–14

Lacoe, J. R. 2013. "Too Scared to Learn? The Academic Consequences of Feeling Unsafe at School." Institute for Education Sciences Working Paper 02–13, New York University, New York, NY.

Mahofa, G., A. Sundaram, and L. Edwards. "Impact of Crime on Firm Entry: Evidence from South Africa." Paper presented at the Conference of the European Social Simulation Association in Groningen, Netherlands 2015, School of Economics, University of Cape Town.

Montoya, E. 2012. "Violence and Economic Disruption: Firm-Level Evidence from Mexico." Working Paper. https://goo.gl/dIwE28.

Ruprah, I., and R. Sierra. 2016. *Engine of Growth? The Caribbean Private Sector Needs More Than an Oil Change*. Washington, DC: Inter-American Development Bank.

Sutton, H., and I. Ruprah, eds. 2017. *Restoring Paradise in the Caribbean: Combatting Violence with Numbers*. Washington, DC: Inter-American Development Bank.

Sutton, H., J. van Dijk, and J. van Kesteren. 2017. "The Size and Dimensions of Victimization in the Caribbean." In *Restoring Paradise in the Caribbean: Combatting Violence with Numbers*, edited by H. Sutton and I. Ruprah. Washington, DC: Inter-American Development Bank.

UNDP (United Nations Development Programme). *Caribbean Human Development Report 2012: Human Development and the Shift to Better Citizen Security*. New York: United Nations Development Programme. http://www.undp.org/content/dam/undp/library/corporate/HDR/ Latin %20America %20and %20Caribbean %20HDR/ C _bean _HDR _Jan25_2012_3MB.pdf.

UNODC and World Bank. 2007. "Crime, Violence, and Development: Trends, Costs, and Policy Options in the Caribbean." Report 37820, World Bank and UNODC, Washington, DC. https://www.unodc.org/documents/data-and-analysis/Caribbean-study-en.pdf.

# Index